EXPLORING DATA

An Introduction to Data Analysis for
Social Scientists

Catherine Marsh

Polity Press

First published 1988 by Polity Press in association with Basil Blackwell

Editorial Office:
Polity Press, Dales Brewery, Gwydir Street,
Cambridge CB1 2LJ, UK

Basil Blackwell Ltd
108 Cowley Road, Oxford OX4 1JF, UK

Basil Blackwell Inc., 432 Park Avenue
South, Suite 1503, New York 10016, USA

British Library Cataloguing in Publication Data

Marsh, Catherine
   Exploring data: an introduction to data analysis for social scientists.
   1. Statistical analysis. For social sciences
   I. Title
   519.5'024301

   ISBN 0–7456–0171–5
   ISBN 0–7456–0172–3 Pbk

Library of Congress Cataloging in Publication Data

Marsh, Catherine
   Exploring data: an introduction to data analysis for social scientists/Catherine Marsh.
     p. cm.
   Bibliography: p.
   Includes index.
   ISBN 0–7456–0171–5 (B. Blackwell)
   ISBN 0–7456–0172–3 (B. Blackwell: pbk.)
   1. Social sciences–Statistical methods. I. Title.
   HA29.M26126 1988
   300'.1'5195–dc19
   87–37514
   CIP

Typeset in 11 on 12½ pt Times by Opus
Printed in Great Britain by Page Bros (Norwich) Ltd

This book is dedicated to Jamie and Geoffrey, who were born between chapters 2 and 3 and 14 and 15 respectively

Contents

Foreword

Sir Claus Moser

It is a pleasure to welcome a book on statistics which focuses, as its title rightly indicates, on the problems of exploring data.

The literature of statistical textbooks is vast. There is something for every taste and level of mathematical sophistication. But, though many of the texts are good at illustrating how specific techniques can illuminate real-life problems, there still often remains a certain 'separateness' between the technique and the substantive problem. This is the gap Catherine Marsh seeks to close in her approach, and she does so most successfully.

That approach, chapter by chapter, is to get immersed in the substance of a problem, and then to see how – by skilful exploration of data – one can throw light on it. So substance and analysis become totally intertwined, which is as it should be.

Having spent many years teaching statistics, I know how difficult it is to achieve this combination. Teaching techniques is one thing and so is teaching about real-life social and economic problems. But to integrate the two in an exciting manner is invariably tough for teachers and students, and this book will be a great help.

It, in fact, covers a wide range of techniques. We start with the simplest univariate measures and diagrammatic presentations and gradually move to bivariate and multivariate techniques, with interesting illustrations of index numbers, time series, standardization, contingency tables, causal analyses and much else. Various unconventional approaches to data analysis are introduced.

All this is done, almost imperceptibly, within discussion of some of the major issues of our time; these include national income and welfare, education policies, distribution of incomes and inequality, health care, morbidity and mortality, unemployment and so forth. In each case, specific problems are displayed and then we learn how to illuminate them by an appropriate and often ingenious use of data.

It is this continuing quest for data insights that makes this book exciting. Moreover, Catherine Marsh has achieved her avowed ambition of not writing a boring book on statistics. Her style throughout is lively and unfrightening, even when the more complex approaches are being discussed. The treatment is also enriched by remarks on sources, and by the exercises with which each chapter ends.

In short, this is a novel and valuable approach to the study of statistics, which undoubtedly fills a gap in the literature. It will be invaluable for students in the social sciences, and indeed for anyone who is interested in the power of data when suitably displayed.

Acknowledgements

This book has had a long gestation period, and I have accumulated debts to many people *en route*. It was John Bibby who originally suggested collecting material for a data analysis course with a strong exploratory flavour for British students. He and I, together with Tony Weekes from York University and Allan Seheult from Durham University, and with the generous assistance of the Nuffield Foundation, met over a two year period to exchange views on how data analysis should be taught, to swop ideas for examples and to argue about methods of presentation. This book is a product of those interactions, and my debt to the other three is great. At one point we planned to write the book together; Allan drafted the first version of a chapter on smoothing and Tony produced materials on price indices and SMRs. But four-way collaboration on something as detailed as a textbook proved impossible, and we agreed that I should smooth the materials for publication. Allan, John and Tony now stand in the enviable position of being able to take credit for any of the ways in which this book succeeds, and to blame me for its shortcomings.

There are many others who have helped enormously. Eddie Shoesmith, Diego Gambetta and Archie Levey helped me teach a course based on these materials in earlier years, and provided very stimulating feedback. Tony Wojciechowski, David Calderbank and Christopher Castleton provided essential research assistance, particularly in preparing small datasets. Don Manning and Geoff Mason helped with reproduction of materials.

Many people helped me by answering my queries, or by providing detail for individual chapters: Pat Altham, Sara Arber, R. J. Bennett, Martin Bulmer, Brendan Burchell, Roy Carr-Hill, Jennifer Church, Frank Cowell, Angela Dale, Chris Denham, Dave Drew, Roderick Floud, Don Forster, John Fox, Peter Goldblatt, Brian Gooddale, Anne E. Green, Mary Gregory, Ted Harding, Martin Hargreaves, Geoffrey Hawthorn, Sophie Houston, Mark Kleinman, Ian Knight, Peter Laslett, Alistair McCauley, Alison Macfarlane, Ian Miles, Panos Pashardes,

David Raffe, Irene Rauta, Bob Redpath, David Rhind, Jan Siltanen, Peter Shepherd, Nigel Walker, Norman Webb, Julie Wells, and Jane White.

Others took the task of colleagueship one stage further and read either parts of or all of the manuscript and gave me a multitude of useful comments: John Bibby, Bob Blackburn, Angela Dale, Jim Davis, Tony Giddens, Nigel Gilbert, and the man himself, John Tukey.

I owe three special debts of gratitude. The first is to Dave Marsh, with whom I have argued extensively over the years about most things, the philosophy and practice of data analysis not least among them, and upon whose judgement I have come to depend. The second is to Claire Young, who, as well as providing detailed assistance in many different ways, coordinated the final production of the text, ensuring that the chapters on the disk, the datasets on the computer and the hard copy all corresponded: an amazing achievement. Finally, I want to thank the students studying Social and Political Sciences at the University of Cambridge. They proved pretty scathing critics, but in the most charming and constructive of manners; they helped make the whole enterprise enjoyable.

Preface

Data analysis is fun. Most students, however, start a data analysis course with two firm convictions: it is going to be dreary, and they are not going to be very good at it. This seems to be as true of students studying the natural and biological sciences as of those studying the social sciences. Different teachers try different tactics to deal with these near universal fears. I know of one who spends the whole of the first term of his data analysis course on group psychotherapy, trying to expunge the collective mythology about what it takes to be good with figures; his students, when asked to describe 'the person at my school who was best at maths', write him essays of frightening uniformity about the same spotty, inadequate, bespectacled male.

Counselling not being among my strong points, I am forced to take a different approach to justify my claim that data analysis can be fun. I have therefore tried to select a range of real examples that show how different techniques can illuminate interesting substantive debates in the social sciences. The data is as up to date as possible, within the limits of producing a text that has been submitted to a moderate amount of piloting.

Bright students, who otherwise have insightful and interesting things to say about their subject, often believe that their substantive knowledge has no part to play in data analysis: the practice of statistics appears to be the rote following of a set of recipes according to rules which have been designed specifically to avoid individual judgement. It is vital that they are disabused of these misconceptions. Understanding a little of the history of data analysis can help do this.

The subject matter of statistics has, since the Second World War in particular, come to be seen and taught as a branch of applied mathematics. But it was not always like this. The word 'statistics' comes from German, and originally referred to pieces of information about the *state*, particularly its military strength. With the birth of industrialism came an interest in social data; for the early Victorians, 'statisticians' were those who collected social information about the citizens of the new bourgeois republics. The first volumes of the *Journal of the Royal Statistical Society* were full of articles describing the social conditions of the time. Gradually the word 'statistics' was restricted to quantitative information of that kind, and came to be synonymous with what we would now call 'data', spreading its meaning beyond social data to biological and other types of data. Finally, as theoretical advances were made, particularly in the theory of sampling and of the regularities which random subsets of data display, it swopped disciplinary camps and came under the provenance of mathematics.

Mathematical statisticians have solved some very important problems in the area of sampling theory; they can tell us in great detail how likely it is that a property of a small sample drawn at random from a larger population holds true for that larger population. In general, they have elaborated the process of *inference*, generalizing from small samples. And because people who teach mathematical statistics are justly proud of these achievements, inferential statistics tends to occupy a large place in their courses.

Unfortunately, these subjects do not occupy such a large place in the set of problems faced by those who are trying to analyse features of the social world, particularly when experimentation is not available to them as a method. What is the point of having very elaborate rules of proof, governing what evidence is required before conclusions can be drawn about a population, if we have no developed techniques for discovering the evidence in the first place? The subject seems to have bred too many lawyers and too few detectives.

This book therefore does not set out to be a course in statistical theory, or even in applied statistics as it is usually understood. It seeks to restore the emphasis to data analysis. The techniques which are presented here are designed to help the researcher look at batches of numbers and make sense of them. Some of the best of these techniques have been put forward in recent years by John Tukey, whose hero is Sherlock Holmes, and whose maxim is 'Seeing is believing'. The techniques of exploratory data analysis (EDA), which he has systematized and popularized, are based on a different philosophy from the deductive logic of the inferential approach. Instead of testing the data, to see if it can be peppered with one or more asterisks and grandly called 'significant', the researcher interrogates it, often interactively, and has to listen to the response before proceeding.

In fact, Tukey has probably done little more than formalize the kind of logic in use by practising statisticians the world over. Data is usually pretty expensive stuff, and few of us can afford to be so high-minded that we restrict our attention to those hypotheses which we thought of before we collected it. EDA provides the data analyst with a set of techniques with which to explore numerical data and to force attention on its most salient features through emphasizing graphical display. The main sourcebooks are Tukey's *Exploratory Data Analysis* (1977) and Mosteller and Tukey's *Data Analysis and Regression* (1977); more introductory accounts of EDA are given by Velleman and Hoaglin (1981) and Hartwig and Dearing (1979), and the Open University (1983) course *Statistics in Society* draws heavily on these techniques.

Anyone who is eventually going to make a career analysing data must be able to answer the question 'Is your sample size big enough for you to be fairly sure of that?' This is, however, a second-order question in comparison with 'What does this data say?' or 'Might that result be spurious?' Second-order questions are best kept for the second year; this book aims to form a first-year course. There is more than enough interesting material to be covered in a course designed to answer the first question without worrying that more should have been put in.

How to use this book

The book is divided into three parts. The first covers various techniques for examining variables one at a time. The second covers relationships between two variables. And – you guessed it – the third covers situations in which a third variable is brought into the picture. Three does duty for many; once you understand how to manipulate three variables together, you are ready to understand in principle how to extend the techniques to many variables. The chapters have been arranged in an order that I have found works well, but others may prefer to tackle topics in a different order; I have therefore suggested at or near the beginning of each chapter which others are required reading.

Data analysis is not a spectator sport; no amount of reading about it substitutes for doing it. The exercises at the end of each chapter are therefore an integral part of the chapter, and should not be skipped. Sometimes they allow illustration of a point which the example used in the chapter did not show. Read my suggested answers, but don't be put off if you did something different, or came to rather different conclusions. One of the most important rules of data analysis is that there is no one model that best or uniquely fits a set of data.

Most of the chapters also contain an appendix introducing a major data source. They have been put at the end of the chapters so that they can be referred to quickly and easily from other parts of the book, not as a judgement on their centrality to the course. It is more important for social scientists to know the major sources of income information available than it is for them to know how to calculate a Gini coefficient.

While the book places great stress on simple pencil and paper techniques for understanding data, the computer has now become an important part of the data analyst's armoury. At the time of writing, a statistical computer package called Minitab offers users of both large college mainframes and individual micros a fast, efficient and well-documented interactive package for data analysis (Ryan et al. 1985). The package also has the advantage of incorporating Velleman and Hoaglin's (1981) algorithms for EDA. I have therefore shown how the various techniques can be done with Minitab (version 5.1) in at least one exercise in most chapters; these can be ignored if Minitab is not available, or if something better replaces it.

There are a series of small datasets which are used for the computer exercises and which can be used for further exploratory work of your own devising. They are listed and documented at the end of the book, and usually explained more fully in the text. The datasets have all been deposited at the ESRC Data Archive at the University of Essex, and machine-readable copies can be obtained for a nominal handling charge.

Key terms are put in bold type in the text when they first appear or where they are given a clear definition. The index entry will have a bold page number to direct the reader to such definitions; in this way the index can be used as a glossary of terms.

Part I   Single Variables

In this first part, methods are introduced to display the essential features of one variable at a time; we defer until the next part the consideration of relationships between variables. This first part is therefore concerned primarily with the accurate and elegant *description* of features of the social world, rather than with their *explanation*.

Description, classification and summary are the cornerstones of the scientific method. In the words of the great nineteenth century statistician, William Farr: 'Classification is another name for generalisation, and successive generalisations constitute the laws of the natural sciences' (quoted in Cullen 1975:34). If the world, natural or social, revealed its key features easily, then people would not have had to struggle over the centuries to develop better methods to describe it; indeed, some of the techniques which we shall present in the forthcoming chapters have only been in use for the past decade or so.

The part contains five chapters. In the first, we learn how to look at the whole of a distribution, while in the second we concentrate on summarizing key features. Sometimes we need to rework the original numbers to make them more easy to summarize, to combine information into complex measures or to purify them of contaminating influences; this is discussed in chapters 3 and 4. Finally, the special techniques which have been developed for looking at inequality in the distribution of income are treated in chapter 5.

1 Distributions and Variables

1.1 Preliminaries

Some stylization of the social world is necessary if we are to describe it systematically and provide explanations for why it is as it is. Two organizing concepts have become the basis of the language of data analysis: cases and variables.

The **cases** are the basic **units of analysis**, the things about which information is collected. There can be a wide variety of such things. Researchers interested in the consequences of long-term unemployment may treat unemployed individuals as their units of analysis, and collect information directly from them. Those who wish to demonstrate the consensus that exists in industrial societies about the relative prestige of various occupations may take the occupation as their unit of analysis, and then show that the average amount of pay or status associated with each is similar in all industrial societies. Historians may collect information on a series of years, and look for similar patterns in such things as the unemployment rate and the incidence of suicide or depression; here years are the units of analysis.

Sometimes it is possible to do research on all the cases one is interested in. The Census of Population, for example, aims to cover all people resident in the country on a particular night; in fact it still misses some people (see appendix to chapter 14), but in principle everyone is covered. Most research, however, is done on subsets of the total population of interest, and some selection of cases has to be made.

The problem of **sampling** is the problem of ensuring that the cases selected look like the population from which they were drawn in as many respects as possible. One of the greatest intellectual discoveries of the last hundred years has been that **randomly selected** samples differ from the parent population on average in a predictable way. This book will not teach you how to calculate the likely margin of error in any particular sample. Nevertheless, it is important to recognize that sample data is only worthy of attention if there is reason to believe that it resembles the population from which it was drawn in important respects. The smaller a sample is, the less likely it is to resemble its parent population. Many of the examples in this book make use of small samples for purely pedagogic reasons; large numbers make hand calculations tedious.

Researchers usually proceed by collecting information on certain features of all of the cases in their sample; these features are the variables. In a survey of individuals, their age, income, sex and satisfaction with life are some of the variables that might be recorded. The word **variable** expresses the fact that this feature varies across the different cases. We mean that the individual cases do not all have the same income, and are not all the same sex. We do not mean that income or sex are things that vary for any one person: at any point in time, when the survey is conducted for example, they are fixed.

In this chapter, we shall look at some useful techniques for displaying information about the values of single variables, and then shall introduce the important notion of fitting a model to data.

1.2 Variables on a household survey

Household surveys have a long tradition in Britain. Almost as soon as capitalism spawned the first industrial slums, pioneers were out with their notepads and pencils, investigating what they called Britain's 'black continents', observing details of lifestyle from the type of dress to the existence of religious pictures on the walls. These early Victorian statisticians were more interested in people's morals than in their means of existence. Later in the nineteenth century, income information began to be sought; these details were usually collected from employers, rather than from the 'untrustworthy' testimony of the poor themselves. Charles Booth's study of *The Life and Labour of the People of London* in the lean years of the 1890s, for example, documented the widespread nature of poverty, not only among the feckless poor but even among families Booth considered to be 'deserving'; Booth, however, relied mainly on the testimony of School Board visitors to reach his conclusions.

Nowadays the state has taken over many of the functions of data collection that were performed by volunteer, charitable organizations in the nineteenth century. Much of the data collection is required for the administration of an increasingly complex society. Some of the information is required for purposes of social control. But some modern data collection exercises are still motivated by a similar kind of benevolent paternalism, stressing the need for information to gauge whether society is doing a good job in meeting the needs of its citizens.

One official survey which is a modern inheritor of the nineteenth century survey tradition is the General Household Survey (GHS), which has been conducted continuously in Britain since 1971. It is a large survey, with a sample size of nearly 12,000 households, and is a major source for social scientists; there is an appendix at the end of this chapter with more information about it. The sample is designed so that all households in the country have an equal probability of being selected. Problems of bias in sample coverage and non-response are dealt with in the appendix.

Interviews are sought with all adults in the household; the data therefore lends itself immediately to treating either the individual or the household as the unit of analysis. A third unit can also be constructed. Researchers interested in poverty and the distribution of income and wealth have viewed the family as the important social group; the assumption is made by researchers – but also and more importantly by the Department of Health and Social Security when they assess the benefit to which individuals are entitled – that income is shared within the family. (This assumption, inadequately researched in the past, may be somewhat inaccurate; see Pahl 1983.)

The dataset we shall use in this chapter summarizes information from the GHS about a sample of family units, defined in such as way as to correspond to the definition used to calculate entitlement to welfare benefits. A family unit is taken to consist of single people or married couples living with dependent children. A dependent child is one who is either under 16 or between 16 and 18 and still at school or in full-time further education; a child of 17 who lives at home and who is employed counts as a separate family unit.

When analysing this data, you should bear in mind that this is not the conventional definition of a family used by other social scientists, or even by the Office of Population Censuses and Surveys (OPCS) which is responsible for the GHS. It does not readily correspond with the popular stereotype of a standard family, namely married couples with dependent children; such families only account for a quarter of all family units as defined above, and 45 per cent of family units are single persons. It does, however, enable us to compare the incomes that such units actually receive with those to which they would be entitled if they were claiming state benefits.

Figure 1.1 shows a specimen case by variable **data matrix**. It contains the first few cases in a subset of the 1979 GHS. Information about the first family unit is contained in the first row, and so on.

The combined gross income of the adult members of each family unit is shown in column 1; this represents income from all sources, whether from state benefits, employment, capital invested or whatever, as reported to a government interviewer. The problems of income definition and the reliability of income data will be discussed further in chapter 5.

The social class of the family unit is shown in column 2. Most British schemes for placing people in social classes rely on grouping them on the basis of occupation. When the unit is the family, whose members may not

Figure 1.1 Specimen data from the 1979 GHSc

1 Weekly family income (£)	2 Social class	3 Income relative to supplementary benefit (× 100)	4 Region
20	3	67	2
65	3	275	4
79	4	123	5
47	3	193	3
28	5	119	1
75	4	277	6
23	4	72	2
98	5	232	5
255	1	530	4
31	2	85	5
21	−1	117	5
36	5	95	2
139	5	302	2
24	6	113	5
73	4	109	4
140	2	327	1
20	6	50	4
111	4	248	3
79	4	335	1
112	4	162	1
35	5	81	6

The cases are family units as defined in the text; for an explanation of the columns, see the text
Source: first 21 cases of POVERTY dataset

all have jobs or may be in different jobs, the occupation of one person (here the person with the highest income) is used to index other family members. This is a rough procedure, which may involve significant information loss about the status of other family members. Indeed, there is controversy about whether it is ever worth trying to identify a 'chief wage earner' or a 'head of household'; we shall discuss the issue again in the answer to exercise 7.1. The GHS uses a social class scheme which is formed by combining the Registrar-General's socio-economic groups. It has six ranked categories:

1 professional
2 managers and employers
3 intermediate and junior non-manual

4 skilled manual
5 semi-skilled manual
6 unskilled manual

Column 3 indicates how much the family unit is getting in income relative to what they would be entitled to, if they had no income, from the state welfare scheme of supplementary benefit. The total *net* income of the family, less housing costs, has been divided by the amount that a family of that size would be entitled to if they were to claim supplementary benefit at long-term rates, and the result multiplied by 100. Figures under 100 therefore represent families whose income fell below the subsistence supplementary benefit level.

The region in which the family lives is shown in column 4; each code refers to a region and will be abbreviated as follows in section 1.6:

1 North (NO)
2 Midlands and East Anglia (MI)
3 London (LO)
4 South East (SE)
5 South West and Wales (SW)
6 Scotland (SC)

In any survey there will be instances of **missing values** for particular variables; it is quite common, for example, to find 10 per cent of respondents failing to provide income information. Some arbitrary numbers are usually chosen to mean 'missing'; any case for which a valid code has not been obtained is then given this value. The number −1 is used in all the datasets in this book to represent a missing value.

There are no missing values on income in this particular dataset because the subset of cases chosen was designed to exclude such families. There is, however, a −1 in column 2. This might be a family where no adult member has ever worked, for example. It is important to check whether there are any such arbitrary numbers in any dataset before you analyse it, particularly when the information is held on a machine-readable file rather than on paper; computers, which know no better, will treat all the numbers the same unless they are explicitly told to do otherwise.

The numbers in the different columns of figure 1.1 do not all have the same properties; some of them merely differentiate categories (as in region) whereas some of them actually refer to a precise amount of something (like pounds in the case of income). They represent different **levels of measurement**. When numbers are used to represent categories which have no inherent order, this is called a **nominal scale**. When numbers are used to convey full arithmetic properties, this is called an **interval scale**. The techniques of analysis appropriate for the former differ from those appropriate for the latter; important mathematical

operations can be performed on variables measured on interval scales –
we can say that one family has twice the income of another – but they
cannot be performed on nominal scale variables.

There is a difficult grey area between the two, represented by variables
such as social class. The numbers contain information about the
supposed rank order of the classes, but we cannot say that managers
(code 2) have half of anything that skilled manual workers (code 4) have.
Measures such as these are known as **ordinal scales**. Twenty years ago,
statistics texts for social scientists were full of special techniques of
analysis to handle variables measured on ordinal scales. These techniques have fallen out of fashion recently, partly because it proved so hard
to adapt them to summarize relationships between more than two
variables, and partly because ways could often be found to promote them
to interval scales. In this book, we shall present techniques that are
designed specifically for nominal or interval scale measures. We can get a
long way with them.

1.3 Reducing the number of digits

One final point should be made before we start considering techniques
for actually getting our eyes and hands on these variables. The human
brain is easily confused by an excess of detail. Numbers with many digits
are hard to read, and important features, such as their order of
magnitude, may be obscured.

Some of the digits in a dataset vary, while others do not. In the
following case:

$$134$$
$$121$$
$$167$$

there are two **varying digits** (the first is always 1). In the following, there
are also two varying digits:

$$0.034$$
$$0.045$$
$$0.062$$

whereas in the following case:

$$0.67$$
$$1.31$$
$$0.92$$

there are three varying digits. Two varying digits are almost always all
that is necessary to get across the important features of a variable. If,
however, we wish to perform calculations on the numbers, it is usually
best to keep three varying digits until the end, and then display only two.
(This rule of thumb produces generally sensible results but there can be
exceptions; if, for instance, the values were in the range 199.0 to 200.0, it

would probably be necessary to work to four and display three varying digits.) Of course, if a computer is doing the calculation, there is no point in reducing the precision at all until the display stage.

There are two techniques for reducing the number of digits. The first is known as **rounding**. Values from 0 to 4 are rounded down, and 6 to 10 are rounded up. The digit 5 causes a problem; it can be arbitrarily rounded up or down according to a fixed rule, or it could be rounded up after an odd digit and down after an even digit. The trouble with such fussy rules is that people tend to make mistakes, and often they are not trivial: it is easy to round 899.6 to 890. A second method of losing digits is simply **cutting** off the ones that we do not want. Thus, when cutting, all the numbers from 899.0 to 899.9 become 899. This procedure is much quicker and does not run the extra risk of large mistakes.

1.4 Bar charts and histograms

Blocks or lines of data are very hard to make sense of; prolonged gazing at them is more likely to lead to watery eyes than profound insight. We need an easier way of visualizing how any variable is **distributed** across our cases. How can nominal scale variables, such as region in figure 1.1, be represented pictorially? One simple device is the **bar chart**, a visual display in which bars are drawn to represent each category of a variable such that the length of the bar is proportional to the number of cases in the category. For instance, a bar chart of the regions in figure 1.1 is shown in figure 1.2.

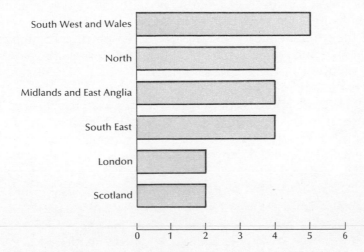

Figure 1.2 Bar chart showing the population of regions in GHS specimen data
Source: column 4 of figure 1.1

Bar charts can be an effective medium of communication if they are well drawn; for example, since there is no inherent ordering in the categories, thought has to be given to the order in which to display them. Some guidelines about their construction are given in the appendix on effective plotting at the end of chapter 10.

Similar charts may be used to display interval scale variables grouped into categories; these are properly called **histograms**. They are constructed in exactly the same way as bar charts except, of course, that the ordering of the categories is fixed, and care has to be taken to show exactly how the data was grouped. There is, however, a much better alternative available for displaying interval scale variables.

1.5 Stem and leaf plots

The **stem and leaf display** allows a fine grain visual inspection of a distribution. It also conveniently orders the data points and makes it easy to count them. The technique is simple, and can be done with a pencil on the back of an envelope. It is so called because it works on the principle of splitting the data values up into two components, a stem and a leaf: the display is constructed by placing one leaf for every data point at the appropriate level of the schematic plant's stem.

Consider the family income variable in figure 1.1. To construct the display, each value is first split into two components: the tens form the stem and each unit forms a leaf. The first data point of 20, for example, is split into a stem of 2 and a leaf of 0. A vertical stem is drawn, as in figure 1.3, with a place for every possible value, even if it did not appear in the dataset; there is a stem value of 5, for example, even though there are no incomes between £50 and £59. Finally the units are drawn on at the level labelled with the appropriate stem value; 20 is depicted by putting a 0 alongside the stem labelled 2, 65 is depicted by putting a 5 alongside the stem labelled 6, and so on. (Some people prefer to draw the plot with the high stem numbers at the top so that the values ascend the page; this is a matter of taste.)

Ideally the stem should have been drawn right up to 25, since there is one family unit in this dataset with an unusually high income of £255 per week. Instead of trying to accommodate this unusual value, the stem has been trimmed at 14, and 255 has been listed as a 'HI' value, to stop the plot looking long and straggly. HI (and LO) values are not split into a stem and leaf, as they are not part of the main display.

Features visible in stem and leaf displays

Stem and leaf plots allow inspection of four important aspects of any distribution:

Figure 1.3 Constructing a stem and leaf display of weekly family income

2 0			
6 5			
7 9		leaf unit = £1	
4 7		2 0 represents £20	
2 8			
7 5		2	083140
2 3		3	165
9 8		4	7
25 5		5	
3 1		6	5
2 1	becomes	7	9539
3 6		8	
13 9		9	8
2 4		10	
7 3		11	12
14 0		12	
2 0		13	9
11 1		14	0
7 9			
11 2			
3 5		HI 255	

Source: data in column 1 of figure 1.1

level What are typical values in the distribution?
spread How widely dispersed are the values? Do they differ very much from one another?
shape Is the distribution flat or peaked? Symmetrical or skew?
outliers Are there any particularly unusual values?

We shall operationalize each of these important terms formally in subsequent chapters. In this chapter, they will be used fairly loosely.

Inspecting figure 1.3 we might consider an income of around £70 per week, a popular value near the middle of the distribution, typical of the values represented here. (We might, however, want to argue that there was another typical value at around £20 per week.) Most incomes are in the range £20 to £140, and the highest value is over ten times the lowest.

The distribution has two humps or peaks; this is why it was hard to find an obvious typical value. Distributions with one peak are called **unimodal**, and those with two peaks as here are called **bimodal**. Bimodal distributions should always make us wonder if there are not two rather different groups being depicted in combination, which would be better analysed separately.

There are other things to notice about the shape of the display. Some gaps in the distribution are visible; there appear to be no families with incomes between £50 and £59 per week, despite there being plenty of cases above and below. The gap might just be a fluke of the small sample size, but, in the absence of other information, we must take note of it. Again, distributions with pronounced gaps in the middle are best split into two and analysed separately. The lower-income **tail** (end) of the income distribution ends abruptly, but the upper-income tail **straggles** up a long way, even without drawing the stem right up to £255: there are a few families whose income is very much higher than the incomes of the majority. This bunched up lower tail and straggling upper tail, evidence that the distribution is **skewed**, is a common feature of almost all income distributions.

The family with an income of £255 per week is seen to be a substantial distance from the body of the data; perhaps it deserves to be called an 'outlier'.

Changing the scale of the stem

The display in figure 1.3 is rather long and thin. If there had been more cases, there would have been more leaves and the plot would have been more revealing; we would have been able to tell if the absence of family units with incomes of around £50 per week was real or just a fluke because of the small sample size. We are free to choose any stem subdivisions we wish; we will always try to make the height of the stem appropriate for the number of cases.

Figure 1.4 Weekly family income: shrinking the scale of the stem by the t-f-s method

```
0 2
0 6
0 7
0 4
0 2                        leaf unit = £10
0 7                        0 2 represents £20–£29
0 2
0 9                               0.
2 5                               0t   222323223
0 3                               0f   4
0 2        becomes                0s   67777
0 3                               0*   9
1 3                               1.   11
0 2                               1t   3
0 7                               1f   4
1 4
0 2
1 1                               HI 255
0 7
1 1
0 3
```

Source: as in figure 1.3

How could the stem in figure 1.3 be reduced to make it shorter? Figure 1.4 shows one way of doing this – the **t-f-s** method. To shrink the stem to half the size by this method, the numbers in the final column of weekly incomes in figure 1.3 (the digits which formed the leaves for the first plot) are dropped. A new stem is now formed; the Twos and Threes are put together beside the label 't', the Fours and Fives beside the label 'f', and so on. The leaf unit is now ten times as large as it was, and the stem is split into five sections instead of ten. The 0t stem, for example, represents incomes between £20 and £39 per week.

We could go further. The original stem values in figure 1.3 could be grouped together in fives. This is done by the **five-ten** method: leaves from 0 to 4 go on a stem marked '*', and those from 5 to 9 go on a stem marked '.', as in figure 1.5. We have probably gone too far in this particular instance; the plot is very cramped, and the bimodal nature of the distribution is now impossible to see.

Figure 1.5 Weekly family income: shrinking the scale still further by the five-ten method

leaf unit = £10
0 2 represents £20–£29

```
0*  | 2422323223
0.  | 677977
1*  | 3411
```

HI 255

Source: as in figure 1.3

So, to stretch or shrink the stem, we multiply or divide it by two, five or ten. No other subdivisions are worth trying, or very odd categories ensue and the stem and leaf displays are hard to read. The choice of scale is a matter of judgement; choosing either too long or too short a stem has the same effect: important features of the distribution cannot be seen. How long the stem needs to be depends on how many cases there are. You should experiment, varying the stem until you feel you have produced a plot that allows the important features of the data to be seen clearly.

Ordering and counting in

The leaves are usually rearranged at each level, and sorted into ascending order. Get into the habit of working in pencil: the display can then easily be reordered by rubbing the leaf values out and restoring them in order one stem at a time.

An important characteristic of any case is its **depth** – how far into the distribution it falls. Once the stem and leaf display has been sorted into order, cases at different depths in the distribution – half-way through, one-tenth from the top, or whatever – can quickly be identified. The procedure is as follows.

The number of leaves at each level is tallied, and a note kept of the **count** – the number of cases which lie either on this line or on any of the lines nearer to the end of the stem and leaf display. The counts represent running cumulative totals; to obtain them you start at both ends and count towards the centre. The column of counts is put on the left of the stem and leaf display (figure 1.6). It is useful to differentiate the counts from the stem and leaf values in some way, perhaps by using a coloured pen; the counts are in bold print in this text.

Figure 1.6 Weekly family income: sorting and counting the display

leaf unit = £1
2 0 represents £20

6	2	001348
9	3	156
10	4	7
	5	
(1)	6	5
10	7	3599
	8	
6	9	8
	10	
5	11	12
	12	
3	13	9
2	14	0

1 HI 255

Source: as in figure 1.3

Counting up from the lowest incomes (at the top of the stem and leaf display), there are six family units with incomes of less than £30, there are nine family units with incomes less than £40, and so on. Counting down from the highest incomes (at the bottom of the plot), there is one family unit with a weekly income of £255, two with incomes of £140 or over, and so on. The count proceeds from both ends towards the centre.

At the centre of the plot, a different procedure is adopted. The count of the line containing the middle value is put in brackets without being cumulated with the line above or below. If the count is even and the hypothetical middle value falls between the two lines, the two equal cumulated totals are left with no separate count in brackets.

The total count is obtained by adding together the cumulated total from the bottom, the cumulated total from the top, and the count on the middle line in brackets. This total is conventionally referred to as N, the number of cases. Thus, from figure 1.6, we can quickly see that $N = (10 + 1 + 10) = 21$.

It is straightforward to find values at any depth in the distribution from displays such as figure 1.6. If we want to find the family unit which is one-third of the way from the bottom in a dataset of 21 cases, we read off the case at depth 7: the family unit has an income of £31 per week.

1.6 Refinements of stem and leaf plots

Stem and letter leaves

It is sometimes illuminating to use letters for leaves. The number of letters chosen should be the same in each case or the shape will not be maintained.

Sometimes letter leaves are used to keep a track of which case is which. If our cases had been countries, and we had been looking at the variation in gross national product, it might have been useful to remember which country was which; letters to represent each country would have helped achieve this. The cases in a survey are often individuals or families whose exact identity is rarely of interest to the researcher; in this case, therefore, letter mnemonics for the name of each family would be pointless.

Sometimes letter leaves are used to remind us into which category of a second variable the individual cases fall. We might, for example, find it

Figure 1.7 Weekly family income by region: stem and letter leaves

```
        leaves represent regions
        2 MI represents an income of £20–29 in the Midlands

    6    2 | MI, SE, SW, MI, SW, NO
    9    3 | SW, MI, SC
   10    4 | LO
         5 |
   (1)   6 | SE
   10    7 | SE, SC, SW, NO
         8 |
    6    9 | SW
        10 |
    5   11 | LO, NO
        12 |
    3   13 | MI
    2   14 | NO
           >

    1  HI   255 SE
```

Source: as in figure 1.3: regions shown in column 4 of figure 1.1

illuminating to display which region each of the families came from, as shown in figure 1.7. The family with exceptionally high income comes from the South East, but there is no general pattern in this data to suggest that there is a clear North/South split in incomes.

Back to back stem and leaf displays

One effective way of comparing two distributions is to hang the two sets of leaves off the same stem in a **back to back display**. A comparison between the incomes of middle and working class family units is shown in this way in figure 1.8; middle class family units are those whose chief wage earner had a job coded as 1, 2 or 3 in column 2 of figure 1.1, and working class family units had codes 4, 5 or 6.

Figure 1.8 Weekly family income by class: back to back stem and leaf display

<pre>
            leaf unit = £10
            0 2 represents £20–£29

            working   middle
             class   class
                          │ 0. │
            322322   │ 0t │ 23
                          │ 0f │ 4
              7777   │ 0s │ 6
                 9   │ 0* │
                11   │ 1. │
                 3   │ 1t │
                          │ 1f │ 4

                   HI 255
</pre>

Source: as in figure 1.3: class information derived from column 2 of figure 1.1

There still seem to be two peaks in the distribution of working class incomes; this suggests that the two peaks noticed in the whole distribution are not explained by two different underlying distributions, one for the middle and one for the working class. It is also clear that there is a great deal of variation within each class: social class and income are not the same thing. One very important feature missing from the information in figure 1.8 is how many earners there are in the families.

Negative numbers

When the dataset contains negative numbers, both +0 and −0 must be included on the stem, otherwise the zero stem will cover twice the range of all the others and its size will be artificially inflated. A value of exactly zero causes a problem. When there are a very large number of exact zeros for some reason, it may be necessary to put them on a separate stem of their own; this will be discussed further in chapter 9. Otherwise, the solution is to place them alternately on the +0 and on the −0 lines. When sorting the values for a stem and leaf display, the order of the digits at the negative end of the stem will be opposite to the order of the digits at the positive end (figure 1.9 illustrates this).

1.7 Data = fit + residual

The term **model** has many different meanings; all suggest attempts to summarize, formalize and generalize some aspect of the world. The notion of fitting a model – some kind of provisional description – to a set of data values is fundamental. The process of data analysis can be thought of as a set of interactions with the data, slowly refining the researcher's understanding and improving the model being fitted. The notion of fitting a model to the distribution of one single variable is a little forced (models are much more interesting when they are called upon to explain the relationships between variables), but we can illustrate the idea.

We have been looking closely at a sample of incomes. It might be interesting to relate these incomes to typical earnings. The GHS in 1979 collected information about how much each member of the household earned from employment before tax. A typical amount being earned by a male in the survey was £84; fifty per cent of men had incomes higher than this and fifty per cent had lower. When one hears statistics being quoted about average wages, it is easy to think that this means that most *families* have access to this sort of amount as income. To emphasize how far from the truth this is, the incomes can be recast in terms of distances from typical male earnings.

We are therefore going to fit the value £84. Any data value can always be thought of as being composed of two components: a **fitted** part and a **residual** part which was not fitted. This is expressed as an equation, the **DFR equation**, which we shall often return to:

$$Data = Fit + Residual$$

For example, the income of the first family unit in figure 1.1, £20, can be recast as having a fitted component of £84 and a residual of −£64; the residual is just the number required to make the total come to the right answer. The entire column of data values can be recast in this way:

$$20 = 84 + (-64)$$
$$65 = 84 + (-19)$$
$$79 = 84 + (- 5)$$
$$47 = 84 + (-37)$$
$$\downarrow \qquad \downarrow \qquad \downarrow$$

Figure 1.9 Displaying weekly family income as residuals from £84

leaf unit = £10
−6 0 represents −£60

```
     5  −6 | 44310
     7  −5 | 63
     9  −4 | 98
    10  −3 | 7
        −2 |
   (2)  −1 | 91
     9  −0 | 955
         0 |
     6   1 | 4
     5   2 | 78
         3 |
         4 |
     3   5 | 56
         6 |
```

1 HI 171

Source: as in figure 1.3

Having subtracted the fitted component, we can display the residuals as before, in a stem and leaf; this is shown in figure 1.9. Notice the order of the leaves on the negative part of the stem.

The change that has been made to the original dataset is fairly trivial. The display emphasizes with a negative symbol that two-thirds of these family units do not have access to an income equivalent to that typically earned by a male worker; a high proportion of these units will be retired individuals or couples, with no-one in the family in paid work. The result is a sobering reminder of the effect that an unequal distribution of work in society has on the distribution of incomes.

We have illustrated the important DFR equation by starting with a single, arbitrary value, chosen to represent a typical male wage, and by looking at the residuals from that. It is up to the researcher what value to select: nothing in the data forces a specific value. In the next chapter, we shall look at single number summaries of features of the distribution which it may prove useful to fit. But the notion is more general than that, and fits do not have to be single numbers. A model could be fitted which described family income as a function of the number of wage earners in the family, for example.

You will hear the phrase 'good fit' or 'better fit' quite often if you spend your time in the company of people whose addiction is data analysis; while the value to be fitted is arbitrary, it can be more or less thoughtful, and better or worse at illuminating interesting aspects of a dataset. When you hear the phrase 'best fit', however, the time has come to change your spare-time associates. There is no such thing as one fit which is always best for the data; it all depends on what you are trying to achieve.

This is not to say that you can read what you like into data, that there are 'lies, damned lies and statistics' or other such hackneyed phrases. When we are clear about what we are trying to achieve, there are standard ways to compare models. They crucially depend upon the residuals from the fit. We shall learn that the residuals are essential tools in data analysis, and there is often much to be gained from inspecting them carefully.

In general, researchers strive to elaborate models which produce residuals with the following ideal properties, listed in increasing order of importance:

1 They form a smooth, bell-shaped distribution.
2 A typical value is zero.
3 They are small.
4 They are patternless.

If the residuals are large, this suggests that the model has not provided a very powerful or complete summary of the data. If they contain some patterned element (if at least the centre of the residual distribution is not zero), this suggests that the model can be further refined to incorporate that element into the fit. If their distribution is smooth and bell-shaped in appearance, this may help the analyst calculate error margins in the model. By and large, however, residuals are more helpful as diagnostics about what to do next than as aids to summarizing what is at hand.

Good data analysis is an **iterative** procedure: it may need to be repeated, perhaps several times, before a satisfactory solution is reached. A common cycle in the process is to fit a model, subtract the fit and obtain residuals; to inspect these and use them to assess how well the model fits, or to suggest new lines of enquiry; to fit an extra component, find new residuals and inspect these; and so on. The end of the process is not a perfect model or a complete explanation, but greater understanding than previously.

1.8 Conclusion

We shall come back to the DFR equation again and again. Model fitting is a vital part of scientific activity. Data analysis can be thought of as a process of fitting a model, looking at a display of the residual values which were not fitted by the model, forming a hypothesis about these, fitting a new model, and so on. In this chapter, some ground rules were established for desirable properties in the residual distribution.

The technical emphasis so far has been on pictorial displays of numerical data. Bar charts were introduced as a technique for displaying nominal scale variables, and stem and leaf displays were introduced as an effective way of displaying interval scale variables. The latter allow inspection of the full distribution, while eyes and hands are kept on each of the data values.

What should we look for in a stem and leaf display? Inspecting the whole of a distribution can give unexpected insights about how the data was originally recorded, or about the dynamic of the variable in question. A stem and leaf display of the sizes of British towns straggles up a very long way, but the cut-off at the bottom is as flat as a pavement. Why? The researcher who defined a 'town' in this case restricted it to something with a population of over 50,000. A stem and leaf display of the ages of individuals in a survey reveals that there are more people at 20, 30, 40 and 50 than at any other ages. Why? The respondents were not sure of their exact age and rounded to the nearest ten years.

In general, there are four features of any distribution that are worth systematic attention: level, spread, shape and any unusual data values. At the moment these concepts are still rather fuzzy; we use statements like 'family incomes cluster at £70.' After looking at these four features in the stem and leaf display, it is often helpful to find numbers to summarize them. That will be the subject of the next chapter.

We should, however, not rush too fast to reach succinct summaries, especially if this means by-passing the stage of display. Brevity may be the soul of wit, but, as Aldous Huxley (1958: vii) reminds us:

> The soul of wit may become the very body of untruth. However elegant and memorable, brevity can never, in the nature of things, do justice to all the facts of a complex situation. On such a scheme, one can be brief only by omission and simplification. Omission and simplification help us to understand – but help us, in many cases, to understand the wrong thing.

Exercises

1.1 Construct a stem and leaf display of the third column in figure 1.1, which shows income relative to what the family unit would have been entitled to on supplementary benefit. Comment on the standard four features of the distribution: level, spread, shape and outliers.

1.2 Recall that the value of 100 is the value at which the family unit's income is equal to its entitlement under supplementary benefit. Fit the value 100 to each of the individual data values and display the batch of residuals. In what way does the stem and leaf display of the residuals differ from that of the original data?

1.3 Collect a dataset for yourself. You might like to ask some of your friends and acquaintances what they think is the typical wage that a full-time male worker receives nowadays. Construct a stem and leaf display of their answers. Consult the *Employment Gazette* to discover the most recent estimate given on the basis of data from the New Earnings Survey (as described in the appendix to chapter 2). What lessons do you learn about armchair 'guesstimation' from this?

1.4 The dataset called POVERTY contains fifty cases, the first twenty one of which were shown in figure 1.1. Use Minitab to:

(a) Select a different twenty-one cases and construct a stem and leaf display of column 1. Are there any differences between this display and that in figure 1.6? If so, why?

(b) Construct a stem and leaf display of the third column, income relative to supplementary benefit.

You will need to use three Minitab commands, READ, SAMPLE and STEM.

Appendix: the General Household Survey

The General Household Survey is a continuous survey of the general population resident in private households in Great Britain. It is conducted by the Office of Population Censuses and Surveys (OPCS) for government departments, to provide information needed to formulate policy. It always includes some standard questions about population, housing, employment, education, health, the family and income; other topics are covered less regularly. It has been running since 1971, and its large sample size and comprehensive contents make it a valuable source of data on social change for both policy-makers and social scientists. A report is published yearly showing tabulations for one year's aggregated data (e.g. General Household Survey 1985). The data is also lodged in machine-readable form at the ESRC Data Archive at the University of Essex.

Data collection

Interviews to collect information for the GHS are conducted throughout the year by interviewers working for OPCS. They try to get all the adult members of a sample of private households to respond. This is inevitably very hard; rather than waste the data about the rest of the household when an interview with one member proves impossible, limited proxy data is collected from another household member.

The sample

The sample size was over 15,000 households until 1982, when it was reduced to nearly 12,000. The sample design has changed over the years in which the GHS has been running. The following description refers to the practice between 1975 and 1981, as the data used in this chapter was collected in 1979.

The sample was drawn in two stages. Instead of trying to cover every square mile of the country, the researchers first picked a random sample of areas in which to work. Selecting a sample of smaller geographical **clusters** reduces costs and eases the interviewers' task. However, since any two households within the same cluster are likely to be more similar than two from the country at large, care must be taken to avoid underestimating the full variation of different features in the country as a whole.

The small areas used as the first-stage sampling unit here were wards (administrative subdivisions of parliamentary constituencies, usually containing around five thousand adults). All the wards in the country were first ordered into regions, then subdivided into metropolitan and non-metropolitan, then, within that, arranged in descending order of the proportion of households whose heads were in professional and managerial jobs.

The list was then divided into 168 equally sized groups (strata) and, within these groups, wards were further ordered in descending proportion of households in owner-occupation. Selecting wards systematically from this carefully ordered list ensured a sample which covered the full regional and socio-economic variation of wards very well. Categorizing a list in some logical way before sampling from it is known as **stratification**. Sampling from a stratified list is preferable to sampling from a list which is in a haphazard order whenever the variables used to stratify the list are related to the subject matter of the survey; the units selected are bound to represent the stratification variable accurately at least.

The plan was to select four wards from each stratum, and to give interviewers a fixed number of interviews per ward. However, it would have been wrong to give all wards equal probability of being picked, since some wards are almost twice as large as others. The probability of selection was therefore made proportional to the population of the ward. Every year one-third of the wards were replaced by new wards selected at random from the same stratum.

The second stage involved deciding who should be interviewed within each ward. For this a list, or **sampling frame**, was required. Until 1984, the GHS used the Electoral Register of people entitled to vote as its sampling frame. It is not a complete list of the adult population; migrants, young people and ethnic minorities in particular are underrepresented (Todd and Butcher 1982). However, although individuals may be missing from the list, 96 per cent of addresses are on it. In each selected ward, therefore, 20 or 25 addresses were picked at random from the Electoral Roll.

Since 1984, the Postcode Address File has replaced the Electoral Roll as the frame used at the second stage of sampling. It is a list of all known addresses, drawn up by the Post Office, and is constantly updated on the basis of information supplied by postmen. Its coverage is excellent, and it is compute-rized, which greatly facilitates the drawing of samples (Wilson and Elliot 1987). It is now commonly used for most government household surveys; its use for the Family Expenditure Survey is described in the appendix to chapter 4.

Response

However well designed a sample, there is always a group of people who either cannot be contacted or who, when contacted, refuse to take part in the survey.

Such **non-respondents** generally differ from those who respond to surveys in several respects (Goyder 1987). It is therefore always important to note what proportion of any original sample contacted actually end up being interviewed; this critical figure is called the **response rate**. It is worrying that response rates have been declining all over the industrialized world in recent years.

There are different ways in which a response rate can be calculated in a survey which attempts to interview every individual in a household. If one makes a strict definition and includes as responding households only those from which every piece of information is collected, the response rate to the GHS is usually somewhat over 70 per cent. In fact, however, most of the information is regularly collected for well over 80 per cent of households contacted. The overwhelming majority of the non-respondents are those who refuse to be interviewed, rather than people who cannot be contacted.

The response rate is very high for a survey of this kind, but the non-respondents inevitably pose a potential threat to the representativeness of the data. What kind of people could not be interviewed? Characteristics of non-responders to the GHS in 1981 were compared against their returns on the census to answer this question (Rauta 1985). Older people tended to have substantially lower response rates, as did households without dependent children. But many other possible differences were investigated and found to be unimportant.

2 Numerical Summaries of Level and Spread

This chapter leads on very directly from the previous one, and presents summary measures which will be used repeatedly throughout the book.

2.1 Tall is beautiful

Both nature and society seem to favour the tall. The higher status or income groups in most societies are taller. Babies born to tall women in most European societies suffer lower perinatal risk. Moreover, people of higher stature are of higher than average intelligence; Galton, a founding father of statistics and a cousin of Charles Darwin, noted that many of the reputed geniuses in British society that he studied were not only related to one another but also taller than average.

The time when public opinion becomes most concerned about these differences between groups is when it wishes to propel some of the lower status groups into battle in pursuit of national glory, but doubts their fighting capabilities. During the Boer War, for example, when conscription was being discussed, an influential piece appeared in the *Contemporary Review*, entitled 'Where to get men?' The author complained that there would be no need for conscription if something could be done about the fact that only two in five of the recruits who applied to the army proved to have the necessary physique to soldier.

The author, Sir Frederick Maurice, had his own breathtakingly simple analysis of where the root of the problem lay: 'An immense proportion of the stunted, anaemic specimens of humanity who never could develop into men fit for any vigorous exercise are so because they are the children of children.' While acknowledging that poverty and bad nutrition played a part, he placed great emphasis on genetics; if healthy breeding to replenish the virile stock was to be encouraged, he thought that something would have to be done about 'the hot-pressed life of our times

. . . and . . . the small accommodation in the houses' (Maurice 1902: 81–2).

In response to these and similar worries, the government set up an official enquiry into the 'physical deterioration of the working classes', which reported in 1904. The Committee considered the hypothesis that the average height of the nation was actually declining; on the basis of the available data it thought this was unlikely, but called upon the government to provide regular monitoring of the stature of the population (Fitzroy 1904).

However, although matters may have been worse during the nineteenth century, the signatories to the report agreed that the poor physique of many working class people was cause for concern. Its recommendations concentrated less on the excitements of city life which Sir Frederick Maurice believed led to the excessive multiplication of degenerate working class genes, and more on tangible steps to improve health and nutrition such as school meals, provision of a school medical service and so on.

In fact, in the light of more evidence today, it seems that there has in fact been a very gradual increase in average adult heights for about the last hundred years in most Western countries, of about a centimetre a decade; this secular trend is, however, coming to an end in many places. (Some more evidence about the long-term trends in height is given in exercise 9.2.)

It should not be concluded from this, however, that tallness is an indicator of general genetic advantage, despite the popularity of this view amongst many early social scientists. A species that has been evolving for at least a million years cannot have sustained a growth rate in height like this for long. There are some non-industrial societies today where height is not synonymous with success: babies born to tall women in the Peruvian Andes fare worse than those born to mothers whose form is better physically adapted to their surroundings.

2.2 Getting good data on height

Despite the call for data in the 1904 report, until comparatively recently no data existed on the heights of a complete cross-section of British people; the only evidence was on highly studied occupational groups such as miners, on the elderly and the young, and on those who apply for such expensive life insurance policies that the companies insist on a medical report. The Department of Health and Social Security commissioned OPCS to undertake a survey of the heights and weights of a random sample of the population aged 16–64 in August and September 1980 to rectify this gap (Knight 1984).

Before we consider how well height was measured, two key terms which social scientists use to evaluate the success of measurement procedures must be introduced. The first way in which researchers assess the adequacy of their measures is to look at their **reliability**: if exactly the same measurement procedures are repeated, then a perfectly reliable measure will produce exactly the same answer. The other important concept in measurement is **validity**: a valid measure will tap precisely the underlying construct intended.

People often make unfavourable comparisons between the soft variables that are the stock in trade of the social scientist (social class, religious identification and so on) and supposedly more reliable and valid objective factors. One only has to look at the history of the natural sciences, however, to realize what a struggle it was in many disciplines to get agreement between laboratories on the measurement of some really basic objective properties, such that two instruments would give nearly identical readings when measuring an identical object.

It is hard to measure people's height reliably. Ideally, individuals would be invited to come to a laboratory where sophisticated equipment was available. However, the problems of non-response of conducting a survey in this way would prove very large, and it was decided to accept some inaccuracy rather than risk weighty response bias in the OPCS study. Interviewers were therefore trained in the use of portable height measures which they took to people's homes; these stadiometers were reliable to within 4 mm. Human height is greatly affected by stance; moreover, the response of many people to being asked to stand up straight is to raise their eye level by tilting their chin upwards, which in fact reduces their height. Interviewers underwent special training to get respondents to stand in the correct position, and were issued with display cards to explain about the chin problem.

Five thousand addresses were selected at random from the Electoral Roll. Then the interviewers attempted to interview, measure and weigh every adult aged between 16 and 64 in each household. The data is therefore particularly rich, because it allows investigation of some interesting hypotheses about how the height of individuals might be an important factor in selection of marriage partner, for example, as we shall discuss later.

The original data contains information on over ten thousand individuals. The material used in this chapter and in the exercises at the end is based on the dataset HEIGHT; this is a random sample of husband and wife pairs drawn from this dataset. Husbands and wives may not be representative of all men and women: it is, for example, possible that the very shortest or the tallest may be excluded.

2.3 Heights of husbands and wives

Figure 2.1 shows the heights of fifteen husband and wife pairs; running an eye over the numbers reveals that men tend to be taller than women.

Figure 2.1 Heights in centimetres of husbands and wives

1 Husbands	2 Wives
180	159
184	156
165	162
177	154
161	142
169	166
173	161
175	163
174	158
168	161
173	159
171	161
173	170
171	152
179	168

Source: columns 3 and 6 of HEIGHT dataset

The stem and leaf display of the height distributions of men and women (ignoring which husband is linked to which wife) are shown in figure 2.2.

In the third plot in figure 2.2, in which the heights of men and women are displayed together, there is a hint of a bimodal distribution; bimodality often acts as an important indicator of the existence of two rather different underlying populations. It is therefore better to

Figure 2.2 Stem and leaf display of heights

leaf unit = 1 centimetre
14 2 denotes 142 centimetres

Husbands			Wives			Both together		
			1	14*	2	1	14*	.2
				14.			14.	
			3	15*	24	3	15*	24
			7	15.	6899	7	15.	6899
1	16*	1	(5)	16*	11123	13	16*	111123
4	16.	589	3	16.	68	(5)	16.	56889
(6)	17*	113334	1	17*	0	12	17*	0113334
5	17.	579				5	17.	579
2	18*	04				2	18*	04
	18.						18.	

Source: as in figure 2.1

concentrate on the first two plots which show men and women separately.

We can compare these in terms of the four features introduced in the previous chapter, namely level, spread, shape and outliers. The male batch is at a higher level than the female batch; the two distributions are somewhat similarly spread out; both distributions seem relatively symmetrical and bell-shaped; and there are no particularly high or low data values (although the wife of height 142 centimetres is quite a bit shorter than the other wives).

These verbal descriptions of the differences between the male and female height distributions are rather vague. Perhaps the features could be summarized numerically, so that we could give a typical numerical value for male height, a single number summary for how spread out the two distributions were, a cut-off point to allow us to count unusual values, or (perhaps more ambitiously) a numerical description of the shape of the distribution.

Summarizing always involves loss of information; as the quote from Huxley at the end of the previous chapter reminded us, summaries cannot be expected to contain the richness of information that existed in the original picture. They do, however, have important advantages. They focus the attention of the data analyst on one thing at a time, and prevent the eye from wandering aimlessly over a display of the data. They help focus the process of comparison from one dataset to another, and make it more rigorous. And, once calculated, the summaries can be fitted to the data and residuals calculated; the data analyst can then concentrate on these residuals.

In this chapter, we shall look at different ways of finding a number to summarize the level and spread of a distribution. It is not so easy to suggest numerical summaries for shape, but the problem will be discussed at the end of the next chapter. A more rigorous definition of what are to be considered as unusual data points will be given in chapter 6.

2.4 Summaries of level

The **level** expresses where on the scale of numbers found in the dataset the distribution is concentrated; in the above example, it expresses where on a scale running from 142 cm to 184 cm is the distribution's centre point. To summarize these values, one number must be found to express a typical height of a man, for example. The problem is: how do we define 'typical'?

There are many possible answers. The value half-way between the extremes might be chosen, or the single most common height, or a summary of the middle portion of the distribution: with a little imagination we could produce many candidates. It is important therefore to agree on what basis the choice should be made. As we shall see below, if the numerical summaries are fitted to some data and residuals are calculated, one way of evaluating different summaries is by looking for certain desirable properties in the residual distribution.

The median

The value of the case at the middle of an ordered distribution would seem to have an intuitive claim to typicality. Finding such a number is easy on a stem and leaf display. In the example of male heights (figure 2.2), the value of 173 cm fits the bill; there are six individuals taller than this, six smaller, and three cases of exactly 173 cm. Similarly, in the female heights, the value of the middle case is 161 cm; the median height for women in this sample is 12 cm less than the median for men.

The data value which meets this criterion is called the **median**: the value of the case which has equal numbers of data points above and below it. The median is easy to find when, as here, there is an odd number of data points. When the number of data points is even, it is an interval, not one case, which splits the distribution into two; the value of the median is conventionally taken to be half-way between the two middle cases. Thus the median in a dataset with fifty data points would be half-way between the values of the 25th and 26th data points.

Put formally, with N data points, the median M is the value at depth $(N+1)/2$. (Refer back to chapter 1 if you are not familiar with the concept of depth.) It is not the value at depth $N/2$; with twenty data points, for example, the tenth case has nine points which lie below it and eleven above.

Why choose the median as the typical value? It is a point at which the sum of absolute residuals from that point is at a minimum. (An **absolute value** denotes the magnitude of a number, regardless of its sign.) In other words, if we fit the median, calculate the residuals for every data point and then add them up ignoring the sign, the answer we get will be the same or smaller than it would have been if we had picked the value of any other point. This is illustrated in exercise 2.1, which you could do now.

In short, the median defines 'typical' in a particular way: making the size of the residuals as small as possible. It's not the only definition, but it yields one fixed answer, and it has intuitive appeal. Galton called it the 'democratic value': any higher or lower, and there would be a majority against. It is determined by information from the whole of the dataset (albeit only the rank order information in most of the dataset).

The arithmetic mean

Another commonly used measure of the centre of a distribution is the **arithmetic mean**. Indeed, it is so commonly used that it has even become known as *the* average. It is conventionally written as $\overline{Y}$ (pronounced 'Y bar'). To calculate it, first all the values are summed, and then the total is divided by the number of data points. In more mathematical terms:

$$\frac{\Sigma\ Y_i}{N}$$

We have come across N before. The symbol Y is conventionally used to refer to an actual variable. The subscript i is an index to tell us which case is being referred to. So, in this case, Y_i refers to all the values of the height variable. The Greek letter Σ, pronounced 'sigma', is the mathematician's way of saying 'the sum of'.

When we defined 'typical' to mean a point at which half the cases were higher and half lower, thus minimizing the size of deviations from that point, the median fitted the bill. What definition of 'typical' leads us to the mean? It turns out to be the number which makes the sum of the *squared* distances from that point as small as they can be. This is not the most obvious definition of 'typical', but, as we shall discuss later, it has important mathematical properties. In any dataset, the absolute magnitudes of deviations are smallest from the median, the squared deviations are smallest from the mean.

So what? Well, one important consequence is that the mean is more affected by unusual data values than the median. The mean of the male heights in the above dataset is 172.9 cm, almost exactly the same as the median in this case. The mean and the median will tend to be the same in symmetrical datasets. However, if one very tall individual had been included in the sample, the mean would have been seriously affected, but the median would only be slightly altered, if at all. Whether this is a good or a bad thing is discussed below.

2.5 Summaries of spread

The second feature of a distribution visible in a stem and leaf display is the degree of variation or spread in the variable. The stem and leaf display allows visual inspection of the extent to which the data values are *relatively* spread out or clustered together. The word 'relatively' is important: a single distribution can look very tightly clustered simply because the stem values have not been carefully chosen.

Once again, there are many candidates we could think of to summarize the spread. One might be the distance between the two extreme values (the **range**). Or we might work out what was the most likely difference between any two cases drawn at random from the dataset. There are also two very commonly used measures which follow on from the logic of using the median or mean as the summary of the level.

The midspread

The range of the middle 50 per cent of the distribution is a commonly used measure of spread; because it concentrates on the middle cases, it is quite stable from sample to sample. The points which divide the distribution into quarters are called the **quartiles** (or sometimes 'hinges'). The lower quartile is usually denoted Q_L and the upper quartile Q_U. (The middle quartile is of course the median.) The distance between Q_L and Q_U is called the **midspread**, (sometimes the 'interquartile range'), or the **dQ** for short.

Just as the median cut the whole distribution in two, the upper and lower quartiles cut each half of the distribution in two. So, to find the depth at which they fall, we take the depth of the median (cutting the fractional half off if there is one), add one and divide by two. There are 15 cases in the height dataset; the median is at depth 8, so the quartiles are at depth 4.5. Counting in from either end of the male distribution, we see that Q_L is 170 cm and Q_U is 176 cm. The distance between them, the dQ, is therefore 6 cm.

The midspread is a rather inexact measure. In datasets with 15 and 16 cases, for example, the quartile is defined as the value of the 4.5th data point in both cases. A more fussy rule could be given which would be more precise, and could be implemented on a computer, but it would in practice run more risk of calculating error if done by hand; this formula is easily remembered and applied.

The standard deviation

The arithmetic mean, you will recall, minimizes squared residuals. There is a measure of spread which can be calculated from these squared distances from the mean. The **standard deviation** essentially calculates a typical value of these squared distances from the mean. It is conventionally denoted s, and defined as:

$$s = \sqrt{\left[\frac{\Sigma (Y_i - \overline{Y})^2}{(N - 1)} \right]}$$

The deviations from the mean squared, summed and divided by the sample size (well, $N - 1$ actually, for technical reasons), and then the square root is taken to return to the original units. The order in which the calculations are performed is very important; as always, calculations within brackets are performed first, then multiplication and division, then addition (including summation) and subtraction. Without the square root, the measure is called the **variance**, s^2.

The layout for a worksheet to calculate the standard deviation of the heights of husbands is shown in figure 2.3. The original data values are written in the first column, and the sum and mean calculated at the

Figure 2.3 Worksheet for standard deviation of husbands' heights

1 Y_i	2 $Y_i - \bar{Y}$	3 $(Y_i - \bar{Y})^2$
180	7	49
184	11	121
165	−8	64
177	4	16
161	−12	144
169	−4	16
173	0	0
175	2	4
174	1	1
168	−5	25
173	0	0
171	−2	4
173	0	0
171	−2	4
179	6	36
2593		484

$\bar{Y} \approx 173$

Source: as figure 2.1, column 1

bottom. The residuals are calculated and displayed in column 2, and their squared values are placed in column 3. The sum of these squared values is shown at the foot of column 3, and from it the standard deviation is calculated.

$$s = \sqrt{\left[\frac{\Sigma (Y_i - \bar{Y})^2}{(N - 1)} \right]}$$

$$= \sqrt{[484/14]}$$

$$= 5.88$$

In most distributions, the standard deviation is smaller than the midspread; in this case, it is only very slightly smaller.

When working by hand, it takes much longer to calculate the standard deviation than does to find the dQ. Quicker 'computational formulae' exist which make the task somewhat less burdensome; you may come across them in older textbooks. However, in the day of the computer and calculator, compuational speed is better obtained by programmed instructions; your calculator may have a function key to obtain the standard deviation directly. Minitab responds smartly to the instruction STDEV.

The point of working through the above example using the definitional formula is to obtain insight into the composition of the standard deviation, and to show that, like the mean, it is more influenced by more extreme numbers. The fifth husband in the dataset, whose height is 161 cm, is 12 cm below the mean, which becomes 144 cm when squared; that individual alone is contributing a substantial part of the standard deviation.

You will sometimes come across a formula for the standard deviation with N rather than $N - 1$ in the denominator. You may even have a calculator which offers you the choice between a standard deviation using N and one using $N - 1$. (It may not offer you the choice; you should then experiment to find out which formula it uses.) The formula given above using $N - 1$ is preferable when using sample data to estimate variation in a population. The difference made by the adjustment, however, is trivial unless N is very small.

2.6 Other locational statistics

The information about the value of the median and the quartiles tells us quite a lot about a distribution. For some applications, we may want more detail, and wish to calculate summaries for points at other depths of the distribution. This is easily done from the stem and leaf display.

The **extremes** – the values of the top and bottom data point – are easy to find. It is also possible to define **eighths**, the seven values which divide the distribution into eight equal portions. (In practice the distribution may not divide equally into eight, of course). The outer eighths are the points which divide the upper and lower quartiles into two, and can be found in an analogous way: the depth of an eighth is the depth of the quartile (ignoring any halves) plus one divided by two.

Other commonly calculated points are **deciles**, which divide the distribution into ten, and **percentiles**, which divide the distribution into one hundred; these measures are regularly used by those studying the distribution of income and wealth, as we shall see in chapter 5. In fact, the distribution can be divided into equal parts at any number of depths. The general word given to such dividing points is **quantiles**; deciles are the quantiles at depth $N/10$, the percentiles are the quantiles at depth $N/100$, and so on.

The tails of a distribution contain important diagnostic information, and often reward careful attention. Tukey suggests that we focus this attention by looking first at the quartiles, then at the eighths, then at the sixteenths, and so on, dividing the depths of the distribution in two each time until we run out of cases and reach the extremes.

Displaying locational summaries

It is good to get into the habit of displaying locational summaries in standardized form. The following display format of the most common numerical summaries is used in this book:

Depths	Median		
	Q_L	Q_U	dQ
	Min.	Max.	

Two further summaries of level can be calculated easily from this summary and added to it: the **midquartile** (the point half-way between the two quartiles) and the **midextreme** (the point half-way between the two extreme values). The point half-way between the quartiles on the male distribution, for example, is (170 + 176)/2 or 173.0. Figure 2.4 displays the numerical summaries of the male and female height distributions.

Figure 2.4 Numerical summaries of heights

Husbands				Wives			
M 8.0		173		*M* 8.0		161	
Q 4.5	170	(173.0) 176	6	*Q* 4.5	157	(160.0) 162.5	5.5
X 1.0	161	(172.5) 184		*X* 1.0	142	(156.0) 170	

Source: as figure 2.1

To the left of the summaries, the appropriate **letter values** and their depths are written: *M* for median, *Q* for quartile, and *X* for extreme. Given enough cases, we could have added the value of the eighths (*E*), the sixteenths (*D*), the thirty-seconds (*C*) and so on, as Tukey suggests.

In general, if the distribution has a straggly upper tail, the midpoint summaries of the level of the distribution – the median, the midquartile and the midextreme – will systematically increase in value. If they decrease systematically, as the female heights do to a limited extent in figure 2.4, this indicates that the lower tail is somewhat longer.

The numerical summaries allow us to compare all husbands and all wives quite succinctly. In this small dataset, the men are typically 12 cm taller than the women, and both distributions are similarly spread out: the d*Q* among men is 6 cm and among women is 5.5 cm.

2.7 Choosing between measures

How is one to decide between the median and mean to summarize a typical value, or between the range, the midspread and the standard deviation to summarize spread?

One important consideration is the intuitive intelligibility of the measure. On this count, locational statistics such as the range, median and midspread generally fare better than the more abstract means and standard deviations. If someone asks how much variation there is in men's heights, a reply that the standard deviation is 6 cm might not convey much. On the other hand, the answer that the middle 50 per cent of the population span 6 cm in height might be more intelligible, and almost everyone would understand the statement that the range was between 161 cm and 184 cm. However, intelligibility is partly a product of familiarity. It is therefore not a good sole criterion. What other grounds might there be for choice?

We have already noted that means and standard deviations are more influenced by unusual data values than medians and midspreads. In fact, the former measures are usually more influenced by a change in *any* individual data point than the latter. Should we therefore prefer them for this reason? Should we be happy that a measure gives greater weight to particularly unusual data values?

If we were entirely confident that the numbers collected were accurate, we might prefer measures that used more information. We might even think that a data point that was really out of line with the rest of the distribution *deserved* more attention than the similar points around the centre. But the time has come to introduce Twyman's law, perhaps the most important single law in the whole of data analysis:

Twyman's law   The more unusual or interesting the data, the more likely it is to have been the result of an error of one kind or another.

We must recognize that errors of all sorts creep into the very best data sources; the values found at the extremes of a distribution (which contribute disproportionately to the mean and standard deviation) are more likely to have suffered error than the values at the centre.

John Tukey has introduced an important general principle in comparing different measures. We say that one measure is more **resistant** than another if it tends to be less influenced by a change in any small part of the data. The mean and the standard deviation are less resistant as measures than the median and midspread. For this reason, they are often preferable for much descriptive and exploratory work, especially in situations where we are worried about measurement error; we shall concentrate on them in this book.

There are, however, advantages which the mean and standard deviation are sometimes felt to have over the more resistant measures. The fact that they sometimes use more of the information available is viewed by some as an advantage. They also have an important relationship to one particular shape of distribution which will be discussed in the next chapter. The sampling theory of the mean and standard deviation is more developed than that of the median and midspread, which makes the former measures more popular among those who want to try to make very precise statements about the likely degree of sampling error in their data.

Finally, you should notice that the range has all of the disadvantages discussed above and none of the advantages. It only uses information from two data points, and these are drawn from the most unreliable part of the data. Despite its intuitive appeal, therefore, it cannot be recommended as a summary measure of spread.

2.8 Height as a predictor of marriage partner

So far the information about which husband is linked to which wife has been ignored. How might we use this to find out if there is any tendency for tall men to marry tall women? In chapter 10, we shall look at ways of displaying and summarizing paired data of this kind more fully. We can, however, get some idea by calculating a new variable, the difference in height in each pair of husbands and wives; in the first couple, the husband is 21 cm taller than the wife, in the second he is 28 cm taller, and so on. The distribution of this derived variable can then be examined as usual. Figure 2.5 shows the stem and leaf display of differences between the heights of the husband and wife pairs.

Figure 2.5 Differences in height between husbands and wives: stem and leaf
           display

leaf unit = 1 centimetre
0 3 denotes 3 centimetres

3	0*	333
4	0.	7
(5)	1*	01224
6	1.	699
3	2*	13
1	2.	8

Source: differences between columns 1 and 2 of figure 2.1

Figure 2.2 showed that the bottom quarter of the distribution of male heights overlapped with the top quarter of the female one. However, in the small sample in figure 2.5 there are no cases where the wife is taller than her husband; wives, it seems, have to be able to look up to their husbands.

The typical difference between husbands and wives is 12 cm, the same as the difference between the medians of the two distributions. A little thought will reveal that this was a likely finding; if the difference between the height of husband and the height of wife was typically much smaller, a substantial pool of short men and tall women would be left over at the end of the marriage competition without partners.

2.9 Conclusion

In this chapter we have seen how aspects of a whole distribution may be reduced to single number summaries. Unless the distribution has a very simple shape, such summaries are bound to involve information loss. But the compensation is greatly enhanced power to describe important features succinctly.

Two summaries of the level of a distribution, the mean and the median, were discussed in detail. The median was seen to minimize the absolute size of residuals, whereas the mean minimized squared residuals. Two summaries of spread, the standard deviation and the midspread, were also presented. The concept of resistance was introduced as a way of comparing different summary measures; the median and midspread are more resistant than the mean and standard deviation.

To conclude, the value of numerical summaries will be illustrated by a further example from the heights of the ten thousand individuals in the OPCS study.

We have not yet considered whether different social classes are on average different in height. The arithmetic means of male and female heights within each of the Registrar-General's class categories (class of head of household) are shown in figure 2.6. Class differences in height do indeed exist among British adults, both among men in different occupational groups and among wives of men in those groups; among men, for example, professional and managerial workers are over three centimetres taller on averge than semi-skilled and unskilled manual workers.

Figure 2.6 Mean height in centimetres by social class and sex

	Professional + managerial	Routine non-manual	Skilled manual	Semi- and unskilled manual
Men	175.5	174.9	173.4	172.3
Women	162.5	161.6	160.2	159.6

Source: Knight (1984: table 2.2)

There are many possible explanations of such differentials. Sir Frederick Maurice, quoted above, would have viewed them as evidence of the inbred genetic inferiority of the lower social classes. Some early students of social mobility (e.g. Sorokin 1927 and Illsley 1955) noted that the tallest members of the lower social classes were the most likely to be upwardly mobile out of that class. Alternatively, different patterns of nutritional or other environmental factors could provide an explanation.

If genetic or social mobility arguments were the sole explanation, it is unlikely that they would be eradicated by social policy. However, Sweden, a country with one of the lowest degrees of income inequality in the world, no longer has differentials in height between its social classes (Tanner 1978). It is left for the reader to discover if class differentials in height are lessening or increasing in Britain; this question could be pursued in Knight (1984).

Further questions suggest themselves. Does height influence the choice of marriage partner? Does social class influence the choice? Is height a direct influence on the choice of marriage partner independently of class? We shall learn more direct ways of investigating this idea of an association between variables later, but we can gain some insight by looking at figure 2.7, which shows the typical differences in husbands' and wives' heights in the full sample of ten thousand individuals.

Figure 2.7 Mean difference in centimetres between husband's and wife's height by social class and height of husband

| Height of husband (cm) | Social class of husband | | | |
	Professional + managerial	Routine non-manual	Skilled manual	Semi- and unskilled manual
Up to 165	3.0	3.8	5.5	5.2
165.1–167.5	6.5	6.9	8.3	6.6
167.6–170.0	9.7	9.7	9.9	10.7
170.1–172.5	10.2	11.3	12.1	13.5
172.6–175.0	12.0	11.7	13.5	14.3
175.1–177.5	14.7	14.4	15.0	15.4
177.6–180.0	15.9	16.6	17.8	19.1
180.1–182.5	17.1	18.7	19.9	18.6
Over 182.5	21.8	27.4	23.0	21.4
All husbands	13.4	13.3	13.4	12.6

Source: Knight (1984: table 6.3)

Figure 2.6 suggested that people from higher social classes tended to be taller than people from lower classes. If neither class nor height influences the choice of marriage partner, then men from each class group would tend to marry women of average height, and so the typical difference between the height of husband and wife would decrease as one descended the social scale. We can see from the bottom row of figure 2.7, however, that this is not the case; the differences in height between husband and wife in the first three occupational groups are virtually identical.

Reading down the columns of the table, it is clear that the difference in height increases as the husband's height increases; this is hardly surprising. But closer inspection reveals that the differences in height between husband and wife do not just increase by the same amount as the average husband's height increases. For example, men in the eighth row of the table (average height 181.3 cm) are 15 cm taller than men in the second row of the table (average height 166.3 cm), but men in the eighth row are 17.1 cm taller than their wives whereas men in the second row are 6.5 cm taller, a discrepancy of only 10.6 cm. This suggests that within each class the taller men marry the taller women.

Furthermore, inspection of the rows of figure 2.7 reveals that the differences between husband and wife tend to be greater in the lower social classes for husbands of the same height; the rule holds fairly well amongst all height groups except the very tallest men. In other words, for any given height group, the higher class men marry taller women.

Figure 2.7 turns out to contain a very rich summary of social patterns which would have been impossible to discern from the raw data. It is left as an exercise for the reader to hypothesize the social processes that could be responsible for such marriage selection rules!

Exercises

2.1 Pick any three numbers and calculate their mean and median. Calculate the residuals and squared residuals from each, and sum them. Confirm that the median produces smaller absolute residuals and the mean produces smaller squared residuals. (You are not expected to prove that this is bound to be the case.)

2.2 The dataset below shows the gross earnings in pounds per week of twenty men and twenty women drawn randomly from the 1979 New Earnings Survey (see appendix to this chapter). The respondents are all full-time adult workers; men are deemed to be adult when they reach age 21, women when they reach age 18.

Men		*Women*	
150	58	90	39
55	122	76	47
82	120	87	80
107	83	58	42
102	115	50	40
78	69	46	99
154	99	63	77
85	94	68	67
123	144	116	49
66	55	60	54

Calculate the median and dQ of both male and female earnings, and compare the two distributions.

2.3 Calculate the mean and standard deviation of the male earnings of the data in exercise 2.2. Compare them with the median and midspread you calculated. Why do they differ?

2.4 Calculate the median income of family units in the GHS sample from figure 1.6. The median gross weekly pay of men in the GHS sample was £84 per week. Compare both of these with the median you obtained in exercise 2.2, and try to explain why they differ.

2.5 The first column of the dataset POVERTY contains information about the incomes of family units. Use Minitab to compute the mean, median, standard deviation and midspread of this variable. (Experiment with the Minitab commands AVERAGE, STDEV, DESCRIBE, MEDIAN and LVALS.)

2.6 The HEIGHT dataset contains information on the height of 200 husbands and wives, sampled from all husbands and wives in Britain in 1980. Use Minitab to get an idea of how different sample means and medians may be from the means and medians of the population from which they were drawn:

(a) Treat the 200 cases in the HEIGHT dataset as the parent population, draw ten samples of size 50 and ten of size 5, and calculate the mean and median height of the wives in each case. Display and discuss your results. (The STORE . . . EXECUTE facility on Minitab is useful for repeated commands.)

(b) Treat the 200 cases as a sample once more, and estimate how stable means and medians based on such a sample will be by dropping a random 10 per cent of the sample ten times and calculating the mean and median each time.

Appendix: the New Earnings Survey

The New Earnings Survey has, in its current form, been conducted yearly since 1970 under the auspices of the Department of Employment. It is a continuous survey of employees in Britain.

A 1 per cent sample of employees is drawn at random from the list of people in employment paying National Insurance contributions; a pair of terminating digits in the NI number identify those to be sampled, and, since these remain constant each year, the changes over time documented in the survey are very stable. The employers of those sampled are asked to complete a form from their own records, giving details of each employee's hours, earnings and overtime in a particular week in April every year. Earnings are defined as 'the employee's total gross earnings for the particular pay period, before statutory and other deductions'. Turning these into annual earnings by simply multiplying this figure up is not a safe procedure.

Because it is a sample of people in employment, it excludes the self-employed, those not currently in the labour force, the unemployed, people working abroad, and any employees who do not pay National Insurance contributions – those working few hours and those evading tax, for instance. Apart from a minority of cases where both the employers of people with two jobs pay contributions, it keeps no records of second jobs. In general, it collects no other information on the employees – their household situation, their receipt of other forms of income and so on. It is therefore not a source of *income* information.

However its sheer size makes it possible to examine the earnings of employees in quite small occupational, industrial or regional subdivisions. Furthermore, information on earnings is published within six months of being collected, which makes it the most up to date source of information on pay. And it is the longest-running series providing data on earnings. For these reasons it is regularly used by labour economists.

Non-response is not a major problem, since employers are required, under the Statistics of Trade Act, to respond. In the 1980s, fewer than 5 per cent of the employers of individuals sampled failed to complete a return, but the information relating to at least a further 7 per cent of individuals could not be processed for various reasons.

The results are published annually by the Department of Employment in six parts, in the form of tables giving earnings details broken down into categories based on age, sex, industry, hours worked, occupational groupings and so on. The main published analyses exclude information on part-time employees, juveniles and those whose pay was affected by absence. A minimum group size of 100 is usually imposed before information is reported, to ensure that estimates are reasonably reliable; this can restrict the disaggregation possible from the published tables. Access to the raw data is subject to restriction because of the legal requirement of employers to participate in the survey. Researchers can, however, gain access to the data for secondary analysis in a form where the individual records are not retrievable; such secondary analysis forms the basis of a study of earnings changes over time (Thomson and Gregory 1988), for example. The ESRC Data Archive at the University of Essex holds data tapes for the years 1970–82; in order to ensure that no-one can be identified, individuals are aggregated into groups of at least three on the archived dataset.

3   Scaling and Standardizing

3.1 Data is produced not given

The word 'data' must be treated with caution. Literally translated, it means 'things that are given'. Classical scholarship must, however, be rejected: the numbers that present themselves to us are not given naturally in that form. Any particular batch of numbers has been fashioned by human hand; it did not drop from the sky ready made. The numbers usually reflect aspects of the social process which created them. Data, in short, is produced, not given. (The English idiom, incidentally, seems gradually to be rejecting classical scholarship in a second way, by converting the word 'data' into a singular noun.)

There are often problems with using official statistics, for example, especially those which are the by-products of some administrative process like reporting deaths to the Registrar-General or licensing immigration. Data analysts have to learn to be critical of the measures available to them, but in a constructive manner. As well as asking 'Are there any errors in this measure?' we have to ask 'Is there anything better available?' and, if not, 'How can I improve what I've got?'

Improvements can often be made to the material at hand without resorting to the expense of collecting new data. We must feel entirely free to rework the numbers in a variety of ways to achieve the following goals:

- to make them more amenable to analysis
- to promote comparability
- to focus attention on differences.

The first improvement that can often be made is to change some aspect of the scale of measurement on which the data has been recorded. There is nothing sacrosanct about the particular way in which the numbers are given; the question is not which is the *right* way to express them, but rather which is the *most appropriate* way to express them for the purpose at hand.

No measurement system is perfect and manages completely to represent our theoretical concepts. The numbers we work with are only indicators of the thing we are really interested in. The measures can therefore also often be improved by combining several indicators of the same underlying concept into a composite score, on the assumption that the errors in each indicator will tend to cancel each other out and leave a purer measure of the thing we are really driving at.

This chapter considers various manipulations that can be applied to the data to achieve the above goals. We start by recalling how a constant may be added to or subtracted from each data point, and then look at the effect of multiplying or dividing by a constant, sneaking a preview at logarithms *en route*. Then we consider a powerful standardizing technique which makes the level and spread of any distribution identical. This allows us to return to an issue left uncovered at the end of chapter 2, namely how to summarize the shape of a distribution. It also allows us to consider the construction of composite measures. Finally, we look at the standardization of a batch of numbers using some external frame of reference.

The discussion of the shape of distributions in this chapter follows on from the discussion of their level and spread in chapter 2. Some may, however, like to read it in conjunction with chapter 11, which develops many of the ideas presented here.

3.2 Adding or subtracting a constant

One way of focusing attention on a particular feature of a dataset is to add or subtract a constant from every data value. We saw an example of this in chapter 1; weekly family incomes were re-expressed as deviations from £84 per week to focus attention on the distance between many family incomes and a typical male wage. Another similar re-expression might have been to subtract the median from each of the data values, thus drawing attention to which families had incomes below or above a hypothetical typical family.

The change made to the data by adding or subtracting a constant is fairly trivial. As you will have discovered from exercise 1.2, only the level is affected; spread, shape and outliers remain unaltered. The reason for doing it is usually to force the eye to make a division above and below a particular point: a negative sign was attached to all those incomes which were below a typical male wage in the example in section 1.7. However, we sometimes add or subtract a constant to bring the data within a particular range; we shall mention a use for this in section 10.4.

3.3 Multiplying or dividing by a constant

Instead of adding a constant, we could change each data point by multiplying or dividing it by a constant. A common example of this is the re-expression of one currency in terms of another: in order to convert pounds to lire, for example, the pounds are multiplied by the current exchange rate. When dividing values by a constant, we often say that each value is expressed **relative** to that constant. As we shall see in chapter 4, a common use of relatives is to examine change over time, using the value of a variable in one particular year as the base, and expressing subsequent years relative to this.

Multiplying or dividing each of the values has a more powerful effect than adding or subtracting. The result of multiplying or dividing by a constant is to **scale** the entire variable by a factor, evenly stretching or shrinking the axis like a piece of elastic. To illustrate this, let us see what happens if the family incomes in figure 1.1 are divided by the median family income, £65. The first five values of £20, £65, £79, £47 and £28 become 0.3, 1.0, 1.2, 0.7 and 0.4 respectively. Figure 3.1 shows the distribution of all twenty-one values (the raw data are shown below in column 3 of figure 3.2).

Figure 3.1 Weekly income relative to the median of £65: stem and leaf display

leaf unit = 0.1
0 3 represents 0.3 of £65

```
0. |
0t | 3333
0f | 44555
0s | 7
0* |
1. | 011
1t | 22
1f | 5
1s | 77
1* |
2. | 11
```

HI 3.92

Source: column 1 of figure 1.1 divided by £65

The overall shape of this distribution is approximately the same as that shown in figure 1.3. The data points are all in the same order, and the relative distances between them have not been altered apart from the effects of rounding. The whole distribution has simply been **scaled** by a constant factor, so neither the level nor the spread takes the same numeric value as previously. The original scale has been lost temporarily, but it could always be retrieved by rescaling.

The value of multiplying or dividing by a constant is to promote comparability between datasets where the absolute scale values are different; one way to compare the cost of a loaf of bread in Britain and Italy, for example, is to express the British price in lire. Percentages are the result of dividing frequencies by one particular constant – the total number of cases. Their use to promote comparability between rows and columns of a table will be discussed in chapter 7. The principle of scaling variables will be an essential ingredient in the technique of variable standardization to be discussed below.

3.4 A quick look at logarithms

First, however, we shall consider another re-expression of the scale of measurement – taking logs. This keeps all the data points in the same order, but stretches or shrinks the scale by varying amounts at different points. To press the hosiery analogy, the scale of measurement is treated as a piece of elastic which is stretched to a different extent at different places along the elastic.

There is, in fact, a whole set of re-expressions which will achieve this effect to varying degrees. Many of them involve raising each of the data values to a particular power. They are very important in data analysis, and chapter 11 is devoted to them. But logs are so useful that some mention of them here will be helpful.

Without for the moment considering why this might be an appropriate thing to do, let us just see what happens to both original income as shown in figure 1.1 and income relative to the median (figure 3.1) if we take logs of each of the numbers. (Don't worry if you can't remember exactly what a log is; you can always find the log of a number by entering it on your calculator and pressing the button marked 'log'.) The results are shown in figure 3.2.

A remarkably useful feature emerges from column 5 of figure 3.2. Logging a set of numbers that have been scaled by a multiplicative constant has the same effect as adding or subtracting a constant to the log of those numbers; the level of the distribution changes (here by about 1.81), but nothing else changes. If two distributions differ only by a multiplicative constant, their essential similarity can often be portrayed more forcefully if the numbers are first logged. We shall come back to logs. Don't worry if you don't understand what they *are*; just notice carefully what they *do* to a set of numbers, how they convert a multiplicative situation into an additive one.

Figure 3.2 Logging two income distributions which differ by a scaling factor

1 Original income	2 Log of column1	3 Income divided by 65	4 Log of column 3	5 Difference between cols 2 and 4
20	1.30	0.31	−0.51	1.81
65	1.81	1.00	0.00	1.81
79	1.90	1.22	0.09	1.81
47	1.67	0.72	−0.14	1.81
28	1.45	0.43	−0.37	1.82
75	1.88	1.15	0.06	1.82
23	1.36	0.35	−0.46	1.82
98	1.99	1.51	0.18	1.81
255	2.41	3.92	0.59	1.82
31	1.49	0.48	−0.32	1.81
21	1.32	0.32	−0.49	1.81
36	1.56	0.55	−0.26	1.82
139	2.14	2.14	0.33	1.81
24	1.38	0.37	−0.43	1.81
73	1.86	1.12	0.05	1.81
140	2.15	2.15	0.33	1.82
20	1.30	0.31	−0.51	1.81
111	2.05	1.71	0.23	1.82
79	1.90	1.22	0.09	1.81
112	2.05	1.72	0.24	1.81
35	1.54	0.54	−0.27	1.81

Source: column 1 is taken from column 1 of figure 1.1

3.5 Standardized variables

In sections 3.2 and 3.3, we saw that subtracting a constant from every data value altered the level of the distribution, and dividing by a constant scaled the values by a factor. In this section we shall look at how these two ideas may be combined to produce a very powerful tool which can render any variable into a form where it can be compared with any other. The result is called a **standardized variable**.

To standardize a variable, a typical value is first subtracted from each data point, and then each point is divided by a measure of spread. It is not crucial which numerical summaries of level and spread are picked. The mean and standard deviation could be used, or the median and midspread:

$$\frac{Y_i - \overline{Y}}{s} \quad \text{or} \quad \frac{Y_i - M(Y)}{\mathrm{d}Q}$$

A variable which has been standardized in this way is forced to have a mean or median of 0 and a standard deviation or midspread of 1.

Two different uses of variable standardization are found in the social science literature. The first is in building causal models, where it is convenient to be able to compare the effect that two different variables have on a third on the same scale. But there is a second use which is more immediately intelligible: standardized variables are useful in the process of building complex measures based on more than one indicator. If, as we argued, the things we actually measure are often only indicators of the underlying theoretical concept which really interests us, it stands to reason that several such indicators, if added together, could tap a theoretical concept more fully.

In order to illustrate this, we shall use some data drawn from the National Child Development Study (NCDS), a subset of which is in the dataset EDUCATE. This is a longitudinal survey of all children born between 3 and 9 March 1958; fuller details about the survey are to be found in the appendix to this chapter. There is a great deal of information about children's education in this survey; information was sought from the children's schools about their performance at state examinations, but the researchers also decided to administer their own tests of attainment.

Rather than attempt to assess knowledge and abilities across the whole range of school subjects, the researchers narrowed their concern down to verbal and mathematical abilities. Each child was given a reading comprehension test which was constructed by the National Foundation for Educational Research for use in the study, and a test of mathematics devised at the University of Manchester; the tests were administered at the child's school. The two tests had very different methods of scoring, and as a result they differed in both level and spread.

The first two columns of figure 3.3 show the scores obtained on the reading and mathematics test by fifteen respondents in this study. There is nothing inherently interesting or intelligible about the raw numbers; the first score of 22 for the reading test can only be assessed in comparison with what other children obtained. Both tests can be thought of as indicators of the child's general attainment at school; it might be useful to try to turn them into a single measure of that construct.

In order to create such a summary measure of attainment at age 16, we want to add the two scores together. But this cannot be done as they stand, because the scales of measurement of these two tests are so different: in these fifteen cases, the reading test median is 23 and midspread is 8, whereas the maths median is 14 and the midspread is 12 (to the nearest integer). If the two tests can be forced to take the same scale, then they can be summed.

This is achieved by standardizing each score. The median is first subtracted from each data value, and the result is divided by the midspread. The first value of 22 in the reading test, for example, becomes $(22 - 23)/8$, or -0.12, and the value of 18 on the maths test

Figure 3.3 Scores of reading and mathematics tests at age 16

1 Raw reading score	2 Raw maths score	3 Standardized reading score	4 Standardized maths score	5 Composite score of attainment
22	18	−0.12	0.33	0.21
20	4	−0.37	−0.83	−1.20
26	18	0.37	0.33	0.70
18	5	−0.62	−0.75	−1.37
23	10	0.00	−0.33	−0.33
29	27	0.75	1.08	1.83
34	14	1.37	0.00	1.37
17	7	−0.75	−0.58	−1.33
34	29	1.37	1.25	2.62
20	9	−0.37	−0.42	−0.79
26	14	0.37	0.00	0.37
11	7	−1.50	−0.58	−2.08
23	23	0.00	0.75	0.75
33	23	1.25	0.75	2.00
12	13	−1.37	−0.08	−1.45

Source: National Child Development Study respondents at age 16; these are the first fifteen cases from dataset EDUCATE

becomes $(18 - 14)/12$, or 0.33; this first respondent is slightly below average in reading and somewhat above average at maths. To summarize, we can add these two together and arrive at a score of 0.21 for attainment in general. Similar calculations for the whole batch are shown in columns 3 and 4 of figure 3.3. It is left as an exercise to confirm that the median and midspreads of both columns 3 and 4 are now 0 and 1 respectively.

The final column of figure 3.3 now gives a set of summary scores of school attainment, created by standardizing two component scores and summing them; attainment in reading and maths have effectively been given equal weight. This single variable might now be used to predict occupational attainment as an adult, for example.

The mean and standard deviation could have been used just as easily to create these standardized scores. Exercise 3.4 has been set to allow you to try using means and standard deviations for all 238 cases in the dataset EDUCATE.

Standardizing the variables was a necessary but not a sufficient condition for creating a simple summary score. It is also important to have confidence that the components are both valid indicators of the underlying construct of interest. This could be gauged by inspecting the type of items included in the tests; critics of IQ tests, for example, argue that the items selected often reflect cultural knowledge rather than underlying intelligence. It is very hard to *prove* that a test is valid. Item validity is usually assessed only with reference to other items; in this case, we might plot the joint distribution of the two items to see if there was an association between them.

3.6 The Gaussian distribution

We are now ready to turn to the third feature of distributions, their shape. With level and spread taken care of, the shape of the distribution refers to everything that's left.

In order to summarize the shape of a distribution succinctly, it would need to be simple enough to be able to specify how it should be drawn in a very few statements. If the distribution was completely flat (a **uniform distribution**), for example, this would be possible; we would only need to specify the value of the extremes and the number of cases for it to be reproduced accurately, and it would be possible to say exactly what proportion of the cases fell above and below a certain level.

In fact, distributions are almost never flat. Even age distributions, which one might expect to be fairly flat, turn out to be quite lumpy: in Britain, those born in 1976 are 36 per cent fewer in number than those born in 1965, for example. However, many distributions do have a characteristic shape – a lump in the middle and tails straggling out at both ends. How convenient it would be if there was an easy way to define a more complex shape like this and to know what proportion of the distribution would lie above and below different levels.

One such shape, investigated in the early nineteenth century by the German mathematician and astronomer, Gauss, and therefore referred to as the **Gaussian distribution**, is commonly used. It is possible to define a symmetrical, bell-shaped curve which looks like those in figure 3.4, and which contains fixed proportions of the distribution at different distances from the centre. (Turn the figure clockwise through 90° if you prefer, to compare the shapes to those of the stem and leaf displays we have considered up to now.) The two curves in figure 3.4 look different – (a) has a smaller spread than (b) – but in fact they only differ by a scaling factor.

Any Gaussian distribution has a very useful property: it can be defined uniquely by its mean and standard deviation. Given these two pieces of information, the exact shape of the curve can be reconstructed, and the proportion of the area under the curve falling between various points can be calculated (see figure 3.5). (The Gaussian is not the only family of distributions with this property, you should note, but it is the one which, when used to represent a sample, involves the simplest calculations from sample values.)

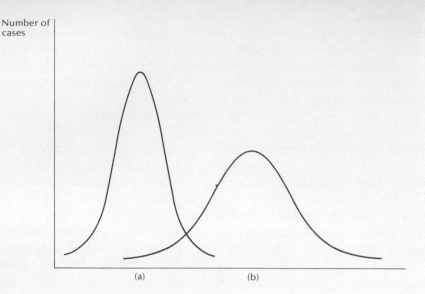

Figure 3.4 The Gaussian distribution

The Gaussian distribution is a hypothetical entity. Up to now, we have used the stem and leaf display to look at empirical distributions; the length of the leaves indicated the frequency of that stem. The Gaussian distribution is defined theoretically; you can think of it as being based on an infinitely large number of cases. For this reason it is perfectly smooth, and has infinitely long tails with infinitely small proportions of the distribution falling under them. The theoretical definition of the curve is given by an equation; you do not need to know it for most purposes but it will be found in any set of mathematical tables.

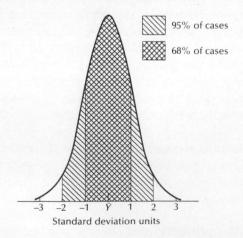

Figure 3.5 Fixed proportions under the Gaussian curve with mean 0 and standard deviation 1

This bell-shaped curve is often called 'the normal distribution'. Its discovery was associated with the observation of errors of measurement. If sufficient repeated measurements were made of the same object, it was discovered that most of them centred around one value (assumed to be the true measurement), quite a few were fairly near the centre, and measurements fairly wide of the mark were unusual but did occur. The distribution of these errors of measurement often approximated to the bell-shape in figure 3.4.

When social accounting became widespread in the nineteenth century, and crime statistics, education statistics and so on became available for the first time, early social statisticians became very excited: it seemed as though the social world yielded distributions that looked very like those of the natural world. A Belgian astronomer-cum-social-scientist, Adolphe Quetelet, hypothesized the existence of *l'homme moyen*, the average human type about whom laws as firm as those of planetary motion could be framed. The Gaussian distribution became known as the 'normal distribution', as if it were a distribution which was normally found empirically.

Some empirical distributions are reasonably well described by this shape: heights, for example, are approximately Gaussian in shape, as you can confirm by looking back to figure 2.2. Others, such as IQ, are human constructs, carefully fashioned to make sure that they are close to Gaussian in their shape; the items are selected to ensure a reassuring bell-shaped distribution when they are scored over a large sample. But, in general, it is not all that common to find variables whose distribution approximates closely to the Gaussian shape. For this reason the term 'normal distribution' is something of a misnomer, and is not used here.

How is the distribution to be used if we are not going to define it mathematically? The answer is that tables exist to allow one to look up what proportion of the distribution falls within given distances from the mean. Now the link with the previous section becomes clear. It would be impossible to do this for every conceivable Gaussian distribution – with every possible mean and standard deviation. The tables are therefore presented for a standardized distribution where the mean is 0 and the standard deviation 1.

To know if the shape of a particular empirical distribution approximates the Gaussian shape, it is first standardized, and then examined to see if the proportion of the cases which lie given distances from the mean agrees with the proportion given in the tables. If it is, the tables predict that approximately:

- 68 per cent of the cases lie within one standard deviation unit of the mean
- 95 per cent of the cases lie within two standard deviations units of the mean

- 99.7 per cent of the cases lie within three standard deviation units of the mean

So, for example, in a Gaussian distribution with a mean of 100 and a standard deviation of 15, 95 per cent of all the cases would lie between 70 and 130.

The Gaussian distribution may not be 'normal', in the sense of commonly occurring as an empirical distribution, but this does not stop it being useful. It acts as a benchmark for comparison, a standard shape against which to compare the particular shape in hand. Although few empirical distributions start life with a Gaussian shape, we shall discover in chapter 11 that they can often be transformed to help them approximate to it. Once this has been achieved, their approximate shape can be described succinctly. Moreover, distributions which started out with different shapes can, once they have been transformed into similar characteristic shapes, be better compared.

The Gaussian curve also has an important role to play in statistical inference, which is not covered in this text. It turns out that many theoretical distributions are Gaussian in shape; exercise 3.6 illustrates this idea. You will come across this shape again as you acquire more experience with data analysis.

3.7 Standardizing with respect to an appropriate base

In the scaling and standardizing techniques considered up to now, the same *numerical* adjustment has been made to each of the values in a batch of data. Sometimes, however, it can be useful to make the same *conceptual* adjustment to each data value, which may involve a different number in each case.

A batch of numbers may be reworked in several different ways in order to reveal different aspects of the story line they contain. A dataset which can be viewed from several angles is shown in figure 3.6: the value of the lower quartile, the median and the upper quartile of male and female earnings in the period 1972–86. The data is drawn from the New Earnings Survey, a survey which collects information about earnings in a fixed period each year from the employers of a large sample of employees; more information about the survey is given in the appendix to chapter 2.

As the figures stand, the most dominant feature of the dataset is a rather uninteresting one: the change in the value of the pound. While the median and midspreads of the money incomes each year have quadrupled in this period, real incomes and differentials almost certainly have not. How could the data be cast in order to focus on the trend in real income differentials over time?

Figure 3.6 Male and female earnings 1972–86: gross earnings in pounds per week for full-time workers whose pay was not affected by absence

	Male earnings			Female earnings		
	Q_L	M	Q_U	Q_L	M	Q_U
1972	27	33	42	15	19	24
1973	31	38	48	17	21	27
1974	35	44	55	20	25	31
1975	45	56	70	28	34	43
1976	53	66	83	34	42	53
1977	59	72	90	39	47	58
1978	66	82	103	43	52	65
1979	75	94	117	48	58	73
1980	91	113	143	59	72	91
1981	101	126	164	66	82	107
1982	110	139	180	72	90	116
1983 (old)	118	150	195	79	99	128
1983 (new)	116	148	193	80	99	129
1984	124	161	210	85	107	139
1985	133	173	226	91	115	151
1986	142	185	244	95	123	164

Source: New Earnings Survey 1986 part B: 29–30; from 1983 the results are based on adult earnings

If we suspect that inflation has acted similarly on all these points in the distribution, multiplying incomes by a constant amount every year, one solution might be to log the data, as was done in figure 3.2, and then look at differences in the logs. If the suspicion is correct, the distributions will have the same shape and scale, but differ only in level. The reader is left to try this as an exercise.

Another solution would be to treat the distribution of incomes for each sex in each year as a separate distribution, and express each of the quartiles relative to the median, as shown in section 3.3. The result is given in figure 3.7. The figure of 82 for the Q_L in 1972, for example, was obtained by dividing £27 by £33 and multiplying the result by 100.

The internal differentials within each income distribution in each year can now be compared, although any overall growth or decline in the purchasing power of the incomes has been lost. The stability of earnings differentials over time is quite apparent; not only are the quartiles very stable in relation to the median, but the proportion of the male quartiles to the male median is remarkably similar to the proportion of the female quartiles to the female median. Closer scrutiny suggests that there has been some widening of the differentials between the lower and upper quartiles in the later period. Interested readers might like to explore this further by consulting the New Earnings Survey to obtain information on other quantiles of the distribution.

Figure 3.7 Male and female earnings relative to medians for each sex

	Male earnings			Female earnings		
	Q_L	M	Q_U	Q_L	M	Q_U
1972	82	100	127	79	100	126
1973	82	100	126	81	100	129
1974	79	100	125	80	100	124
1975	80	100	125	82	100	126
1976	80	100	126	81	100	126
1977	82	100	125	83	100	123
1978	80	100	126	83	100	125
1979	80	100	124	83	100	126
1980	81	100	127	82	100	126
1981	80	100	130	80	100	130
1982	79	100	129	80	100	129
1983 (old)	79	100	130	80	100	129
1983 (new)	78	100	130	81	100	130
1984	77	100	130	79	100	130
1985	77	100	131	79	100	131
1986	77	100	132	77	100	133

Source: re-expression of data in figure 3.6

3.8 Did the Equal Pay Act work?

In re-expressing the male earnings relative to the male median and the female earnings relative to the female median, we lost the ability to compare male and female earnings. One way to facilitate such a comparison in the original money earnings would be to correct the money incomes in each year for inflation, to express them all in real terms. Exercise 4.4 is designed to show you how to do this.

But if we were concerned to focus on the relativities between male and female earnings, irrespective of the value of real earnings, the female earnings could be expressed relative to the male earnings at the same point in the distribution.

The Old Testament prescribed a stable relationship between the value of men and women when it came to death duties: men were worth fifty shekels and women worth thirty (*Leviticus* 27:3–4). The British Labour Party in 1970 passed an Equal Pay Act, which aimed to promote equality of earnings between men and women. The Act came into force in 1975; employers thus had five years to make any adjustments necessary to bring the pay of their male and female employees into line. How successful was this challenge to the divine order of things?

Figure 3.8 shows the value of the female earnings each year at the three points on the distribution relative to male earnings at the same

Figure 3.8 Female earnings relative to male earnings at the same quantile: corresponding male earnings are 100

	Q_L	M	Q_U
1972	56	58	57
1973	55	55	56
1974	57	57	56
1975	62	61	61
1976	64	64	64
1977	66	65	64
1978	65	63	63
1979	64	62	63
1980	65	64	64
1981	65	65	65
1982	65	65	64
1983	67	66	66
1984	69	67	67
1985	68	66	67
1986	67	66	67

Source: re expression of data in figure 3.6

point. The value of 56 for Q_L in 1972, for example, was obtained from figure 3.6 by dividing £15 by £27 and multiplying the result by 100.

The data suggests that the Equal Pay Act had some impact, albeit only raising women's earnings relative to men from 5 per cent less than the biblical recommendation to around two-thirds of male earnings. The figures suggest that the impact was greatest immediately following the implementation of the Equal Pay Act: employers waited until the last minute to change their pay practices. The movement towards equality then reached a plateau at around 67 per cent of the equivalent point in the male distribution.

The earnings in figure 3.6 include earnings from overtime. Since men work much more overtime than women, it could be argued the differential in pay *rates* would not be as great as this. However, in compensation, published data from the New Earnings Survey excludes the earnings of part-time workers, who comprise two in five of the female labour force in Britain, and whose pay rates are particularly poor.

Why did women's earnings relative to men not get nearer 100 following the passing of the Equal Pay Act? Critics have argued that, by allowing a five year period between passing and implementing the legislation, the government gave employers time to ensure that women and men were doing distinctively different jobs. The major problem with equal pay legislation is that men and women in all societies tend to be found in very different jobs. Decreeing that there shall be the same pay for the same work fails to address this problem; for women who do 'women's work', there is often no male comparison, especially working for the same employer.

The Act was amended with effect from the beginning of January 1984, to bring Britain in line with European law, and to specify equality of pay for 'work of equal value'. It is too early to assess the effect that this amendment will have on earnings.

3.9 Conclusion

The important lesson of this chapter is that numbers are not given in any divine and unchangeable form. One of the most fruitful things for the data analyst to do before searching for any associations between variables is to see if some re-expression would make the numbers more suitable for the problems in hand.

Subtracting a constant from each value in a dataset alters the level of the distribution. Multiplying or dividing by a constant alters the spread. Standardized scores are constructed by altering both the level and the spread to a norm of zero and one respectively. Each value in a dataset can often usefully be expressed relative to some appropriate base for comparison; the effect of this on the distribution varies. You should routinely think if any of these re-expressions would help in analysing data in exercises from now on.

The aim of the data analysis game is comparison. The Gaussian shape is a useful hypothetical distribution with which the shape of particular empirical distributions can be compared. Gaussian distributions are bell-shaped, and have the convenient property of being reproducible from their mean and standard deviation: if the Gaussian distribution is expressed in standardized form (with a mean of zero and a standard deviation of one), tables exist to establish how much of the distribution falls a given number of standard deviation units from the mean.

The distribution is a convenience, however, not a gift from God. Scientists and mathematicians tend to be over-reverent towards the 'normal distribution', the scientists because they think it has been proved mathematically and the mathematicians because they think it is a scientific fact.

Exercises

3.1 The average monthly earnings of men and women in different occupational groups in Britain and Italy in 1972 is shown below. The British data comes from the NES, and the Italian data from a European-wide investigation into average earnings.

	Italy (000 lire)		Britain (£)	
	Men	Women	Men	Women
Higher management	595.6	319.6	338.9	164.0
Executives	353.4	275.2	214.1	129.3
Assistants	250.9	216.0	152.7	103.1
Clerical	219.5	145.0	129.6	83.5
Foremen	277.7	165.5	172.3	110.9
Skilled manual	170.2	115.2	147.0	73.5
Semi-skilled manual	146.0	112.8	135.8	76.6
Unskilled manual	152.2	116.7	119.7	71.3

Source: Saunders and Marsden (1981: table 4.3)

Describe the similarities and differences in the structure of rewards in British and Italian society in 1972. Do the similarities or the differences strike you more forcibly?

3.2 If you were told that the distribution of a test of ability on a set of children was Gaussian with a mean of 75 and a standard deviation of 12, what proportion of children would have got scores between 51 and 99?

3.3 The data below is drawn from the dataset EDUCATE (columns 4 to 6), and shows the scores obtained by nine respondents on three different tests which claim to be measuring general intelligence.

Draw-a-man test	Verbal ability	Non-verbal ability
18	25	23
25	16	12
27	38	31
1	8	15
26	30	20
19	19	12
26	16	15
24	24	24
16	11	17

The first test was administered at age 7; the children were asked to draw a picture of a man, and the result was scored for indications of the child's general mental and perceptual ability (Goodenough 1926). The second and third are tests of verbal and non-verbal abilities respectively, administered at age 11 (Douglas 1964). Convert these three scores into one general IQ score.

3.4 Read the full dataset EDUCATE into Minitab, and standardize the two tests of attainment at age 16 using means and standard deviations instead of medians and midspreads as in this chapter. Sum the standardized measures into a composite score and present the result as a stem and leaf display. The command LET is used for arithmetic operations on columns.

3.5 Minitab allows you to generate random samples drawn from a hypothetical Gaussian distribution, using the command NRAN. Experiment with creating and displaying different Gaussian distributions in this way. In particular, try creating the standard Gaussian distribution with a mean of 0 and a standard deviation of 1.

3.6 Look back at the sample means and medians you obtained in exercise 2.6. Would you say that the shape of the distribution of sample means or medians was approximately like the Gaussian distribution?

Appendix: the National Child Development Study

Three birth cohort studies have been undertaken in Britain. The first, the National Survey of Health and Development, was of babies born in a particular week in 1946 (Douglas 1964). The second, the National Child Development Study, followed up babies born in a week in 1958, and a third followed through a week's births in 1970 (Chamberlain et al. 1975). Each of the three studies was initiated because of concern with the effects of events surrounding pregnancy and childbirth, and then the children were followed up to trace aspects of their physical, social and psychological development. Their prospective design and large sample size makes them a particularly rich source of information about development in childhood and adulthood. Data has been drawn from the second of them for this book.

In 1958, a Perinatal Mortality Survey was mounted by the National Birthday Trust Fund of the seventeen thousand births in England, Scotland and Wales in the week 3 to 9 March 1958. It achieved a 98 per cent response rate and led to important advances in understanding why some thirty-five babies per thousand were either stillborn or died within seven days of birth (Butler and Bonham 1963). However, paediatric and educational researchers persuaded the Plowden Committee, which was investigating primary school education at the time, that the development of these children should be followed up. The study became known as the National Child Development Study at the first follow-up in 1965, when the cohort was aged seven (Pringle et al. 1966). The study has since been extended to return to respondents at age eleven, sixteen and twenty-three, and information on them has been collected from their schools. Each sweep has been augmented with a sample of immigrants born in the same week.

For the birth survey, information was collected from the mother and from medical records by the midwife. In the surveys at seven, eleven and sixteen, interviews were conducted with the parents by health visitors, the children were given various tests of ability and attainment, and questionnaires were administered to the children, their teachers and local authority medical officers (who carried out medical examinations). In 1978, when the respondents were twenty, a questionnaire was sent to their last school or FE college to obtain details of their examination passes. When the respondents were aged twenty-three, professional survey research firms were employed to trace them and interview them. Moreover, summary information about the locality in which they were living at age twenty-three, derived from Census data, was added to the file.

The very high original response rate is testament to the support and cooperation of the vast health service network that undertook the original perinatal mortality survey, which enabled briefing meetings to be organized, careful checks on the quality and reliability of the data to be carried out, and so on. At each subsequent sweep, an attempt was made to trace all surviving respondents. In the first three follow-ups, this was done through schools, and, if that failed, by writing to the last known address, contacting the health and social services and by making public appeals. At age twenty three, an attempt was made to follow up all respondents who still lived in Britain and who had taken part in at least one earlier sweep. The starting point was the last address on file, but attempts were also made by a number of other methods, such as attempting to trace them through their National Health number. Wastage of course occurred, and inevitably increased as time went by (figure 3.9).

Figure 3.9 Response to NCDS follow-ups

Cohort age	Target sample	Some data (%)	Refused (%)	Others with no data (%)
Birth	17,733	98	–	2
7	16,883	91	1	8
11	16,835	91	5	4
16	16,915	87	7	6
20	16,906	85	–	15
23	16,457	76	7	17

Source: Shepherd (1985: 17)

One advantage of longitudinal surveys is that one knows a lot more about the characteristics of non-respondents than is usual in cross-sectional surveys. Up to the age of sixteen, non-response bias on indices of educational or health development are negligible. In the sweeps at age sixteen and twenty-three, there is some evidence that the coverage among disadvantaged groups of various types declined. These biases are small, except with respect to ethnic status; respondents of Caribbean origin are underrepresented by about one-third, from the Indian subcontinent by about one-quarter and from Ireland by about one-tenth.

The survey covers a wide range of medical, educational and developmental topics. During their school years, several tests of ability and attainment were administered to the children; some were standard tests, others were devised specially for the study. Success in formal examinations was also recorded. The respondents' views on many topics have been sought, including schooling, the family, occupational opportunities, income, leisure and health. Details of their parents' circumstances, jobs, health and housing have been obtained, along with parental reports of any major illnesses and accidents suffered by the children, or difficulties at school. The medical information obtained from examinations covers the normal development of the children, their vision, speech, motor coordination, height and weight, as well as information on any ongoing illnesses or defects. Information about the schools the child attended and the neighbourhood in which they lived have also been appended to the file.

There has been no single sponsor of the NCDS. The majority of sponsorship has come from public funds, with government departments bearing the largest part of the expense, but some private funds have also contributed.

The dataset has been exploited for a very wide variety of analyses, relating to the children's physical, social and educational development. The best general guides to these are given by Davie et al. (1972) and Fogelman (1983). There have also been a number of specialist studies which have drawn their sample from the NCDS, and collected more information than was obtained in the original sweeps. These include studies of children in care, adopted children, gifted children, children living in one parent families, handicapped schoolleavers, epileptics and smokers.

A User Support Group for the NCDS has been set up in the Social Statistics Department of City University, funded by the Economic and Social Research Council, to promote use of and to facilitate access to the data. Information from all the sweeps of the survey, apart from the raw examination results, is maintained as a merged database on the University of London Computer by the Support Group. The ESRC Data Archive at the University of Essex also has the survey information on separate files, but will create merged files of information for individual users.

4 Price Indices

4.1 Introduction

In the previous chapter we looked at various ways to recode data in order to render it in a form most suitable for analysis. The techniques involved simple additive or multiplicative operations. We then saw how standardized variables could be summed in order to obtain composite scores; children's standardized scores on mathematics and reading tests, for example, were summed into a composite measure of general attainment.

In forming an IQ score by summing two equally scaled components, the implicit assumption made was that attainment is composed of two equal parts, a component reflecting mathematical ability and one reflecting reading ability. In this chapter, we look at a way of forming a complex measure – a price index – where such a simple assumption would not be satisfactory, and where the weight that should be attached to different components varies; when monitoring price inflation, some account has to be taken of the fact that people tend to buy more loaves of bread than televisions. As we shall see, the choice of weights very much affects the interpretation we give to the index.

In chapter 14, attention is paid to standardized mortality ratios (SMRs), which bear a great technical similarity to price indices, although the logic of their construction makes them better suited to the third part of this book. This chapter is relatively free-standing, and could be read at any point.

4.2 Price inflation

One of the earliest attempts to summarize price inflation was made in the eighteenth century by a certain Bishop Fleetwood, who faced a problem (Kendall 1969). The statutes of All Souls College, Oxford, required that a Fellow should swear, on admission to his Fellowship, to vacate it if he came into an estate worth more than £5 per annum. By Fleetwood's time, the quantity of goods which £5 would buy had fallen, with the general increase of prices. Could the oath still be taken, therefore, in all conscience, by someone whose estate was now worth more than this?

Fleetwood started by investigating the level of prices of four commodities, corn, meat, drink and cloth, over the preceding 600 years. As is typically the case, he found that prices had risen, but not by the same amount for each commodity; to buy £5 worth of each at 1440 prices would cost, in 1700, £30 for corn, £30 for meat, somewhat above £25 for drink and somewhat less than £25 for cloth. He concluded that £28 to £30 per annum should not be accounted a greater estate than was £5 per annum at the time of the foundation of the College. Accordingly, an income of £30 or less 'may be enjoyed, with the same innocence and honesty, together with a Fellowship, according to the Founder's Will' (Kendall 1969:1).

Fleetwood's investigations and calculations are forerunners of those required to construct what is now called a **price index**, although this invariably requires information concerning the price of more than just four commodities. Such indices are of use whenever it is necessary to describe how much the purchasing power of money has changed.

Official price indices do more than summarize economic reality, however; they play a part in creating it. They are used in wage bargaining, in indexing pensions, by foreign investors as a guide to the rate of domestic inflation, in assessing the performance of the economy and so on. It is therefore important to understand how such index numbers are defined and constructed.

Although anyone who takes more than a passing interest in political and economic affairs will have an intuitive understanding of what an **index number** is, a precise definition is really quite difficult. Kendall and Buckland, in their *Dictionary of Statistical Terms* (1971:71), offer the following:

> An index number is a quantity which shows by its variations the changes over time or space of a magnitude which is not susceptible of direct measurement in itself or of direct observation in practice.

They then proceed to give some examples of these 'magnitudes', mentioning business activity, production and prices, and conclude by saying:

> It is . . . somewhat tendentious to define an index number as the measure of a magnitude when that magnitude relates to an ill-defined concept such as 'business activity'. It is perhaps preferable to regard the index number as not relating to a specific quality but as a measure of location in a complex of concomitant variation.

The first part of this definition draws our attention to the fact that the·

index is merely an indicator of an underlying theoretical concept. The final part of the definition – the idea that an index is a 'measure of location' – gives the first clue to how it is in practice constructed.

4.3   A price index as a weighted average

Consider an example involving a hypothetical college that wanted to construct a price index to measure the increase in the cost of the educational services it provides. To keep the exposition simple, we will assume the college has a staff of 100 who are all paid the same and that the only items of expenditure are staff costs, books and equipment. In the year which will be regarded as the **base year** for the index (year 0), the following items are purchased at the prices shown:

> 100 staff at £10,000 p.a. each
> 1000 books at £20 per book
> 5 pieces of equipment at £15,000 each

During the following year (year 1) costs rise. Staff receive a pay award which increases their salaries to £11,000 per annum, books increase to £30 each and equipment becomes £20,000 per item. It is straightforward to calculate and tabulate the relative change in the price of each commodity. It is conventional to take the price in the base year as 100 to avoid decimal points.

> Staff: $(11,000/10,000) \times 100 = 110$
> Books: $(30/20) \quad\quad\quad \times 100 = 150$
> Equipment: $(20,000/15,000) \times 100 = 133$

The relative changes, which are called **price relatives**, are very different for the three items. We have, in simple form, Kendall and Buckland's 'complex of concomitant variation', and a measure of location must now be found to summarize these three price relatives.

One such measure might be the arithmetic mean. This is easily calculated: $(110 + 150 + 133)/3 = 131$. A little reflection, however, will suggest that this proposal is too simple minded and therefore potentially misleading. To shed further light on why, look at the distribution of the base year expenditure across the different purchases (figure 4.1). The biggest proportion of the college's expenditure is on staff, where costs have only gone up by 10 per cent. The simple average gives the impression that the cost of the base year mix of items has risen by nearly one-third – from a base of 100 to a value of 131.

If we wish the summary to reflect the relative importance of each commodity to the functioning of the college, we need a **weighted average**. (The simple average gives an equal weight – one-third – to each price

Figure 4.1 Breakdown of college expenditure in base year

1 Item	2 Quantity	3 Price (£)	4 Expenditure col. 2 × col. 3 (£)	5 Proportional expenditure col.4/Σ (col. 4)
Staff	100	10,000	1,000,000	0.91
Books	1000	20	20,000	0.02
Equipment	5	15,000	75,000	0.07
Sum			1,095,000	1.00

relative.) To form a weighted average, each component is multiplied by an amount, a weight, to reflect its relative importance, and then the total is divided by the sum of the weights.

One choice of weights is the proportional expenditures, which conveniently sum to one. Weighting price increases in this way indicates how much more would need to be spent to buy this particular set of goods and services a year on; this is not the same as indicating how much less the goods bought now cost a year ago, as we shall see later. Recalculating the measure of location as a weighted average of the price relatives is straightforward (figure 4.2). This calculation shows a typical rise of about

Figure 4.2 Worksheet for calculating an index as a weighted average

1 Item	2 Weights from base period	3 Year 1 price relative to year 0	4 Weighted relatives col. 2 × col. 3
Staff	0.91	110	100.1
Books	0.02	150	3.0
Equipment	0.07	133	9.3
Sum	1.00		112.4

12 per cent. It reflects the fact that staff costs have risen 10 per cent and other items rather more; the latter, however, are a much smaller proportion of the total expenditure.

In general, the form of a price index is given as follows:

$$\text{Index number} = \frac{\text{Sum of the weighted relatives}}{\text{Sum of the weights}} = \frac{\Sigma(Rw)}{\Sigma w}$$

where R are the price relatives and w the weights taken from the base period.

We have seen, then, that one way of constructing a price index is to compute a weighted average of price relatives, taking as weights the proportional expenditure in a base year; such a number is called a **base-weighted index**, or a **Laspeyres index**, after its originator. It can be summarized as follows:

$$\frac{\text{Present cost of base year package}}{\text{Base year cost of base year package}} \times 100$$

In order to manipulate the weights and price relatives used in forming the Retail Prices Index, the official index for the UK, this simple formula using weighted averages is quite sufficient.

4.4 The Retail Prices Index

The first official attempt to construct a price index in 1914 had, as its object, to 'show the average percentage increase in the cost of maintaining unchanged the standard of living prevailing in working class families prior to August 1914' (*Department of Employment Gazette* October 1975:971).

'Cost of living' and 'standard of living' are complex concepts, and hard to operationalize. In the period before the Second World War, a few goods, considered by experts to be necessary for the maintenance of a basic standard of living, were selected – potatoes, clothing, materials, candles – and changes in their prices were monitored. But after the last war, when a new index was started, this judgemental method was abandoned, and the prices of all types of goods and services that are actually bought was monitored.

The Retail Prices Index (RPI) has been constructed since 1947. It is a complex Laspeyres index, calculated in three stages. The first consists of establishing what goods and services are typically bought at any one time to form the weights, the second is to discover how the prices of these things change over time, and the third is to combine them into one overall index.

The index aims to monitor the price of any good or service bought for current consumption. All forms of saving are excluded, even less obvious ones like the capital element of mortgage repayments and pension contributions. And some other items are excluded 'because of the variable or non-measurable nature of the services acquired in return for the payments made' (*Department of Employment Gazette* October 1975:972), such as betting payments and cash gifts. More importantly, all forms of direct tax are excluded. In sum, alterations to the cost of living which result from changes in things other than consumer prices are ignored.

The Family Expenditure Survey (FES) provides the data on the items which are typically bought; the appendix to this chapter deals with the origins, purposes and methods of this important survey. Respondents to the FES are asked to note in a diary details of every expenditure they make in a two-week period. The FES is a continuous survey carried out by the Office of Population Censuses and Surveys for the government, and the results are aggregated each year within various categories of expenditure to show what households typically spend their money on. The richest 4 per cent of households are excluded when the weights for the RPI are calculated, however.

The items of expenditure are grouped into broad categories; those in use in 1986 are shown in exercise 4.1. Each group is then subdivided into subgroups and sections; there are several hundred such sections. The information obtained from the FES is used to weight each group and section within each group in the proportion in which it is bought. The weights sum to 1000. (Interested readers will find the weights for the subgroups in 1985 in the *Employment Gazette*, March/April 1986: 103–5).

The second stage of the process is to monitor the prices charged for items in each section. Some sampling of goods within sections is necessary to make this a practicable task; in group 1 section 111, for example, the representative items selected might be pork sausages, beef sausages, corned beef, pork luncheon meat, calf liver, ox liver and roasting chicken.

While the groups and sections correspond precisely to predefined expenditure groups and can be assigned appropriate weights, the selection and weighting of indicator items is less straightforward. It is relatively easy where homogeneous commodities are involved, such as white bread or petrol, but, in the case of some items such as consumer durables, the wide range of models available makes it hard to pick a representative item. (In countries where the official price index has many fewer sections, moreover, the possibility exists for governments to depress the official inflation rate artificially by subsidizing the items currently selected within sections.)

Inspectors are employed to collect information on how much these items cost. Department of Employment staff from about 180 local offices visit a selection of shops on a predetermined Tuesday in the middle of the month and note the prices being charged for the products specified. They then return once a month to the same shops and note any price changes on the same product. The shops that they visit are chosen to be typical of those used by consumers.

Problems can arise where quality changes over time. The price collectors monitor exactly the same items during the course of a year, but if manufacturers of a brand of fish fingers respond to rising wholesale prices by including less fish in the recipe, and fail to declare this on the packet, the prices monitored will relate to a product whose quality has changed. The problem of allowing for changes in quality is inherent in the construction of any price index; there is no easy solution.

Finally, the price changes in these several hundred items (actually 130,000 price quotes from different shops) are combined into one index. An average price or price relative for each item is first calculated across all the shops where prices have been collected, sometimes distinguishing between shops of different types or in different regions. Price indices are then calculated for each section, the section indices are weighted and combined to form subgroup and group indices, and finally the groups are combined into one general index. Exercise 4.1 enables you to recapitulate the final stage of the process.

4.5 General expression for index numbers

It would be pleasing if one could say that *all* indices were straightforward weighted averages. Unfortunately the position is a little more complicated than this, and we now need to consider an alternative interpretation of price indices and show how this leads to other methods for their construction.

Let us first pose the index number problem in a slightly different way and introduce a little notation. As we saw, the hypothetical college administrators selected a certain mix of items to fulfil their educational objectives in the base year, namely:

> 100 staff
> 1000 books
> 5 pieces of equipment

We will denote the base year as year 0 and the quantity of each commodity in the base year as Q. We can now define three quantities:

> Q_{01} quantity of staff
> Q_{02} quantity of books
> Q_{03} quantity of equipment

where the first subscript 0 reminds us that we are referring to the base year and the second (1–3) reminds us which commodity we are talking about. Let the corresponding prices per unit of each of these commodities be denoted by P_{01}, P_{02}, and P_{03}. Then, algebraically, the total expenditure in the base year is:

$$P_{01}Q_{01} + P_{02}Q_{02} + P_{03}Q_{03}$$

or, more succinctly:

$$\Sigma \, P_{0i}Q_{0i}$$

The i subscript varies from $i = 1$ to $i = 3$ in this case, but the form of the equation allows us to move easily to the more realistic case of many items rather than just three.

Prices will typically change during the year. Let us write P_{11}, P_{12} and P_{13} to denote the unit prices of each of the commodities at the end of year 1. To purchase the same quantity of staff as one year earlier will cost $P_{11}Q_{01}$. Similar bits of algebra can express the cost of books and equipment. The total outlay required, therefore, to preserve the same mix of commodities may be written as $P_{1i}Q_{0i}$. Now we can construct the index by dividing this by the actual cost of these items in the base year. The value of the base-weighted index at the end of the first year can therefore be expressed formally as:

$$\frac{\Sigma P_{1i}Q_{0i} \times 100}{\Sigma \, P_{0i}Q_{0i}}$$

It is easy to show algebraically that this index is identical to the weighted average of price relatives presented earlier.

Let us demonstrate this new approach with the college data. We have all the necessary information to lay it out in a worksheet as in figure 4.3. From this worksheet we can see that $\Sigma P_{0i}Q_{0i} = £1,095,000$ (the total base year expenditure) and $\Sigma P_{1i}Q_{0i} = £1,230,000$ (what it would cost in year 1 to buy again the goods purchased in year 0). Then

$$\frac{\Sigma P_{1i}Q_{0i} \times 100}{P_{0i}Q_{0i}} = \frac{1,230,000 \times 100}{1,095,000}$$

$$= 112 \quad \text{(as before)}$$

Figure 4.3 Worksheet for the general form of a base-weighted index

Item	Year 0 price P_{0i}	Year 0 quantity Q_{0i}	Year 1 price P_{1i}	Year 0 expenditure $P_{0i} \, Q_{0i}$	Year 1 hypothetical expenditure $P_{1i} \, Q_{0i}$
	(£)		(£)	(£)	(£)
Staff	10,000	100	11,000	1,000,000	1,100,000
Books	20	1000	30	20,000	30,000
Equipment	15,000	5	20,000	75,000	100,000
Sum				1,095,000	1,230,000

4.6 Base-weighted versus current-weighted index numbers

We often want a price index to tell us how much it would cost at various points in time to meet a given standard of living, or standard of service, regardless of precisely how that is achieved; up to now we have not considered the possibility of substitution of purchases. Why, however, should the college necessarily continue with exactly the same items to fulfil its educational goals, to maintain the same standard of educational provision? Why should a consumer continue to consume beef and lamb in the same proportion as before if beef has risen far more in price than lamb? Economic theory in fact predicts that rational consumers will change their behaviour when costs rise by substituting cheaper items when they can equally well meet their needs. Base-weighted index numbers will, if this theory is correct, tend to overestimate the rate of price inflation in the goods that are normally bought, as we shall see from continuing the college example.

Let us now project the example into the next year (year 2). At the start of the year, the cost of books has risen astronomically, and the college administration faces the following array of prices:

> Staff: £12,100 per annum
> Books: £50 each
> Equipment: £25,000 per piece

The value of the price index, relative to the base year, is a weighted average of prices in year 2 relative to year 0. These price relatives are:

> Staff: 121
> Books: 250
> Equipment: 166

and the weights are as before: 0.91, 0.02 and 0.07 respectively. By the end of the second year, therefore, the value of the index is:

$$(0.91 \times 121) + (0.02 \times 250) + (0.07 \times 166) = 127$$

In other words, to buy the same goods two years later would cost 27 per cent more.

But suppose that the administrators decide to purchase no more books during the second year and take on three extra staff instead? It is clearly possible to argue that to give any weight to an item – books – which have now been priced out of the budget, is misleading, leading to an unrealistically high picture of the rise in costs actually experienced by the college.

We can tackle the problem of monitoring cost increases in maintaining a fixed standard of living in a different way, and ask: if the college had bought this current mix of items in the base year, what would it have cost then, and by how much would costs have gone up over two years? The answer to this question is a **current-weighted index**, or a **Paasche index**, after its inventor:

$$\frac{\text{Present cost of present package}}{\text{Base year cost of present package}} \times 100$$

Note that, although the alternative names for both Laspeyres and Paasche indices both use the term 'weighted', it is not possible to write the latter neatly as a weighted average; the word 'weight' as used here rather refers to the date on which the package of purchases is selected.

The construction of a current-weighted index is laid out in figure 4.4. In terms of our example, by the end of the second year, the value of this index is

$$\frac{1,371,300}{1,105,000} \times 100 = 124$$

In other words, the cost of goods typically bought today is 24 per cent more than it was two years ago. The index value is lower than that previously calculated because books have been removed from the list of purchases. However, this is now something of an underestimate of price rises experienced by the college in a two year period, since books did feature among the items bought by the college in the first year.

Laspeyres and Paasche were both German economists; their proposals date back to articles written in 1864 and 1874 respectively (Kendall 1969). There has been much debate since they wrote about how to deal with the inherent exaggeration in the first index and underestimation in the second. Clearly, the problem of what to use as weights increases as the index attempts to measure inflation over longer periods. As cars

Figure 4.4 Worksheet for a current-weighted index

Item	Year 2 price P_{2i}	Year 2 quantity Q_{2i}	Year 2 expenditure $P_{2i} Q_{2i}$	Year 0 price P_{0i}	Year 0 hypothetical expenditure $P_{0i} Q_{2i}$
	(£)		(£)	(£)	(£)
Staff	12,100	103	1,246,300	10,000	1,030,000
Equipment	25,000	5	125,000	15,000	75,000
Sum			1,371,300		1,105,000

replace horses and light bulbs replace gas mantles, so the difference between Laspeyres and Paasche index numbers grows. One compromise index was proposed by Fisher (1922), which was to combine the Laspeyres and Paasche index numbers.

However, there is a further practical difficulty to consider with respect to Paasche indices: they tend to be difficult to calculate since they require information on the current distribution of consumption, which may take a long time to acquire. The Fisher index therefore also suffers from this practical problem.

An alternative solution is to calculate a Laspeyres index with frequently updated weights, and to link all the small price changes thus noted together. Such an index is called a **chained Laspeyres index**. The RPI is a chained Laspeyres index. The weights for all goods are altered yearly, but with a lag to allow time to process the mass of information from the FES; expenditures from July in year 0 to June in year 1 are used as weights throughout year 2. (The weights for those items which are purchased infrequently or whose sales fluctuate violently are averaged over three years.)

Because the weights are always between six and eighteen months out of date, the RPI always slightly exaggerates the rate of increase in prices of goods currently being bought. In 1978 this exaggeration was at its worst, and led to a 0.8 per cent overestimate of the annual rate of inflation (Fry and Pashardes 1986); the researchers point out that such an overestimate, while slight, cost the Exchequer at least £400 million (in 1986 prices) in over-indexation of government expenditures statutorily linked to the RPI.

4.7 Whose cost of living?

The basket of goods used in calculating the RPI is typical of items that are bought in the UK in any one year. It does not measure the basket of goods bought by an average household: wealthier families buy more and therefore are more heavily represented (although this is somewhat offset by the goods bought by the wealthiest 4 per cent being excluded altogether). Nor, being a summary measure of level, does it tell us anything of the differential impact of inflation on different groups in society.

One of the most robust laws in economics is Engel's law: as incomes rise, the proportion spent on food drops. If price inflation is faster in food, then lower income groups will experience more inflation. Several studies have shown that inflation has indeed been faster on food and fuel, which form a larger part of the budgets of the poor. In the ten year period from 1956 to 1966, for example, during which time the RPI showed an increase of 37 per cent, the true rate of inflation for people at the fifth percentile of income has been variously calculated as 44 per cent

(Tipping 1970) and 48 per cent (Piachaud 1978). More recently, Fry and Pashardes (1986) showed that the poorest 10 per cent of households faced an increase in prices between 1974 and 1982 which was on average 8 per cent higher than that faced by the richest 10 per cent.

The implication of such studies is clear: since so many of the lowest income groups in society live on welfare benefits, indexing such benefits to the RPI leads to a fall in their real value.

The special experience of one group in society – pensioners who are mainly dependent on state benefits – has been recognized, and separate official price indices are calculated for them. But there are many household characteristics which lead to different inflation experience: we have discussed level of income, but the number of children in the household, the employment status of adults in the household, whether the household lives in mortgaged accommodation or not, in London or not and so on are also important. It might be impractical to create a multitude of separate summaries for each household type, but Fry and Pashardes (1986) suggest that instead an estimate could be made of the average effect of being in different groups, and that the change shown by the RPI could be adjusted by the appropriate amount to calculate the effect of rising costs on subgroups.

4.8 Conclusion

In this chapter, we have seen how a price index is constructed. Two methods were presented. A base-weighted index can always be expressed as a sum of weighted price relatives. However, a more general form of expression was needed to show how one could also calculate a current-weighted index. The RPI is a chained base-weighted index, and its method of construction was explained in some detail.

Exercises

4.1 The expenditure weights for the year up to June 1985 and the price movements of the various groups in the RPI during the first five months of 1986 are shown in the accompanying table.

	Weights based on expenditure to June 1985	Prices 15 January 1986	Prices 15 May 1986
		15 January 1974 = 100	
Food	185	341	349
Alcohol	82	424	429
Tobacco	40	546	594
Housing	153	464	483
Fuel/light	62	507	504
Household durables	63	265	269
Clothing	75	225	228
Transport	157	393	384
Miscellaneous goods	81	403	408
Services	58	393	400
Meals out	44	427	436

Source: *Employment Gazette* July 1986

Calculate the increase in the RPI during the first five months of 1986. What can you infer about changes in the cost of living experienced by British people from these figures?

4.2 There has been some controversy in recent years about the representation of housing costs in the RPI. How do you think the weights for the housing element in an index of retail prices ought to be calculated?

4.3 The data below shows the annual averages of the RPI with a revision of the base date in 1974. Convert it into a series with the same base date. What is the effect of such changes of base date?

	16 Jan. 1962 = 100		15 Jan. 1974 = 100	
	1962	101.6	1974	108.5
	1963	103.6	1975	134.8
	1964	107.0	1976	157.1
	1965	112.1	1977	182.0
	1966	116.5	1978	197.1
	1967	119.4	1979	223.5
	1968	125.0	1980	263.7
	1969	131.8	1981	295.0
	1970	140.2	1982	320.4
	1971	153.4	1983	335.1
	1972	164.3	1984	351.8
	1973	179.4	1985	373.2
(15 Jan.	1974	191.8)		

4.4 The dataset ECONOMY contains monthly data about the economy from January 1977 to December 1985. Column 9 contains an estimate of median gross household income per week derived from the General Household Survey, while column 11 shows the value of the Retail Prices Index. Deflate the incomes by the value of the RPI to obtain an estimate of the movement in real income, and print out the result. You may find it helpful to PLOT the results.

Appendix: the Family Expenditure Survey

Expenditure surveys

The nineteenth century pioneers of budget studies were the French sociologist Frederick Le Play and his student, the German statistician Engel. Their methods were emulated in Britain at the turn of the twentieth century by Seebohm Rowntree in his study of poverty in York (Rowntree 1901); he discovered that industrial labourers were purchasing a diet substantially inferior to that found in the prisons and workhouses of the time.

The first official expenditure survey in Britain was conducted by the Board of Trade in 1904 on around two thousand working class families; the budget information collected formed the basis of the first cost of living index in 1914. The next major survey was conducted thirty-three years later by the Ministry of Labour, and in 1953–4 the exercise was repeated. But clearly, such irregularly conducted research was not a satisfactory basis for estimating trends in expenditure patterns or the inflation rate. The Ministry of Labour's Cost of Living Advisory Committee therefore recommended that a series of annual budget surveys be started, principally to collect information to form the weights of a reliable price index.

The annual Family Expenditure Survey (FES) series began in 1957, on a sample of around 3500 households, and has continued ever since; the sample size was doubled in 1967 to around 7000 households. It is a voluntary survey, conducted continuously by the Social Survey Division of the Office of Population Censuses and Surveys for the Department of Employment. Detailed information on expenditure is collected to form the weights for the Retail Prices Index, but it is also an important source of information on household incomes, and is used by many government departments – the Central Statistical Office in compiling the National Income Accounts, and the Department of Health and Social Security in formulating policy on housing benefit and sick pay. It is also widely used by academics and market researchers. The sample is not as large as the New Earnings Survey, but it has the important advantage of collecting data on total income, rather than earnings.

Sample design and response rate

All private households in Great Britain are covered in the sample. The exclusion of inhabitants of institutions means that some of the very poorest people in

Britain (those resident in hospitals, hostels, prisons and similar places – 1.5 per cent of the population according to the 1981 Census) are also excluded.

The sample is drawn in a manner very similar to that of the GHS. It is taken from the Postcode Address File of small users; this consists of addresses ('delivery points') at which fewer than 25 letters are delivered each day. The primary sampling units are postcode sectors, and these are stratified by region and urban type. From each of some 660 sectors, a random sample of 17 postal delivery points is drawn, yielding some 11,400 delivery points in total. At most addresses there is only one household present, and all adults within that household are then interviewed. Multi-household addresses are more complex, and readers are referred to Kemsley et al. (1980) to see how they are treated.

Only households in which all adults agree to take part and complete diaries are included. This leads to around 30 per cent non-response (overwhelmingly refusals), which is high in comparison with other government surveys such as the GHS, but extremely low in comparison with similar expenditure surveys in other countries (Eurostat 1980). The biases due to non-response can be studied by comparing characteristics of respondents to the FES with characteristics of residents of private addresses at the census. Although income information is not collected at the census, and bias on this key variable cannot be assessed directly, households registering two or more cars at the census are less likely to respond to the FES. Moreover, households with dependent children are the most likely to respond and those with non-dependent children least likely. Characteristics of heads of households which prove disproportionately hard to persuade to respond are: highly educated males, widowed females, the old, self-employed, ethnic minorities and unskilled manual workers (Redpath 1986).

Data collection procedures

The FES aims to collect detailed information on all current expenditure of private households (as defined in section 4.4). All adults in participating households are interviewed to obtain personal details, income information, and details on larger or irregular items of expenditure. Wherever possible, interviewers ask respondents to check information from receipts, payslips, accounts and so on. The bulk of regular expenditure information, however, is collected by means of diaries. Every member of each cooperating household aged 16 or more is asked to keep a complete record of their expenditure during a two-week period. A token payment (£5 in 1985) is made to each person who keeps a diary.

'Family Expenditure Survey' is something of a misnomer, since the unit of analysis is the household, a group assumed to share expenditure rather than genes or marriage vows. The household is defined as one person living alone or a group of people who live at the same address, who share at least one meal a day, and who make common housekeeping arrangements. (They do not need to be members of the same family.) The person in the household in whose name the accommodation is rented, mortgaged or owned is designated the head of household, and the person who does most of the domestic duties is nominated the housewife, regardless of sex.

The gross normal income of the household is collected. This includes earnings from employment and self-employment, income from pensions and investments, welfare allowances and benefits, in fact any regular source of monetary income;

only 'windfall income', such as a win at the horses or at the Stock Exchange, is excluded. Gross income from employment is taken before deduction of National Insurance contributions or income tax.

It is always very hard to get respondents to estimate what happens 'normally' (Moss and Goldstein 1979); in most cases, asking what happened in a fixed reference period is preferable to asking for habitual data. Ideally, respondents would provide data for the last twelve months, but this is very difficult to obtain (Kemsley et al. 1980); the approach generally adopted on the FES is to ask what happened in a recent reference period. With earnings, however, the interviewer asks if the pay for the last pay period is considered to be normal, and if not respondents are asked to make an estimate of their normal income. If respondents have been unemployed for less than thirteen weeks, their normal earnings when last employed are included in gross normal income, rather than their current income, on the assumption that the lifestyle of an unemployed person would be maintained for that time.

The accuracy of the data

Certain categories of expenditure are known to be underreported. The worst biases occur with the consumption of alcohol and tobacco; the quantity of alcohol reported in the FES diaries grossed up to population estimates, for example, falls short by between 30 and 40 per cent of the amount on which excise duties are paid. Several experiments have been conducted to attempt to improve the reliability and validity of the method of recording these sensitive items of consumption, but none has significantly reduced the bias (Kemsley et al. 1980). The consumption of alcohol is known (from GHS) to be very unequally distributed; a small number of heavy drinkers account for a large amount of the alcohol consumed. One plausible explanation for the underrecording of alcohol on the FES is that a high proportion of such drinkers refuse to cooperate.

Several aspects of income are also known to be underrecorded: income from self-employment, investment income and the earnings of part-time workers and very high earners (Kemsley et al. 1980; Atkinson and Micklewright 1983). In the case of the self-employed the problem is in part a response bias, since fewer self-employed agree to be interviewed, and in part it seems to stem from respondents' genuine difficulty in knowing the right answer, since answers to the question have low retest reliability.

Publications and availability of the data

The main findings are summarized in an annual volume published by the Department of Employment (e.g. 1986c). In most of the tables, households are classified by their gross normal income, rather than income per capita; since the size and composition of income groups is not constant, it is not possible to use the information readily to study poverty (Fiegehan et al. 1977). The methodology and sampling techniques used are described more fully by Kemsley et al. (1980) and in a guide (Department of Employment 1986b) which will be supplied on request.

Other unpublished analyses are sometimes available from the Department of Employment. The survey data from 1961 to 1963 and from 1968 onwards is deposited at the ESRC Data Archive at the University of Essex in an anonymous form to prevent people from being able to identify individual households, and is distributed for research purposes.

5 Inequality

Students of income inequality have traditionally used techniques of displaying income distributions and summarizing their degree of spread which are rather different from the methods outlined in chapters 1 and 2. This chapter provides an introduction to these techniques. Like chapter 4, it is somewhat separate from the cumulative structure of the book: it does, however, build on the discussion of quantiles in chapter 2 and of re-expressing data relative to a particular quantile in chapter 3.

5.1 The British religion

The British, according to R. H. Tawney, make something of a religion of inequality. It is not just a question of the rich defending their privileges either, he maintained; the middle classes and even the disadvantaged in Britain seem to accept the justice of handing out goods and services to individuals in a grossly unequal way. The arguments, written in the 1930s, still stand as one of the most eloquent polemics against the religion that Tawney so detested.

The British Labour Party has, from its inception, been committed to ensuring that the distribution of income and wealth in society was moving in an equitable direction, and that the religion of inequality would be replaced with a commitment to principles of social justice. Clause IV of the party constitution states that a basic party aim is: 'To secure for the workers by hand or by brain the full fruits of their industry and the most equitable distribution thereof that may be possible upon the basis of the common ownership of the means of production.'

In 1974, the party went to the country with a manifesto to 'achieve far greater economic equality – in income, wealth and living standards' (Bosanquet and Townsend 1980: 5). In the course of this chapter we shall assess the extent to which this had been achieved by 1979, at the end of Labour's term of office, presenting and using techniques which have been specially devised for studying inequality in the distribution of income and wealth.

One of the first acts of the 1974 Labour administration was to institute research into the nature and causes of the problem of economic inequality. On 23 August 1974, it set up the Royal Commission on the Distribution of Income and Wealth, with the following terms of reference (1975: v):

> To help secure a fairer distribution of income and wealth in the community there is a need for a thorough and comprehensive enquiry into the existing distribution of income and wealth. There is also a need for a study of past trends in that distribution and for regular assessments of the subsequent changes.
>
> The Government therefore ask the Commission to undertake an analysis of the current distribution of personal income and wealth and of available information on past trends in that distribution.

Lord Diamond was appointed to be its chairman.

In the following five years, the result was a stream of evidence, general and specialized reports, popular articles, background papers and discussion documents, either produced by the Commission's permanent staff or written for the Commission by academics or members of government departments. These papers brought together information about the distribution of income and wealth on a scale not seen before in Britain or any other country. Moreover, discussions with the Central Statistical Office and the Inland Revenue led to these bodies producing routine statistics on income and wealth more regularly and in a form more suitable for answering questions about economic inequality. The discussion which follows draws heavily on the Commission's initial report cited above.

One of the first acts of the 1979 Conservative administration was to abolish the Royal Commission. The Central Statistical Office had so improved its reporting of inequality, the Secretary of State argued, that the Royal Commission did not need to produce reports as well. Shortly after, however, in a review of statistical procedures within government, the CSO was also instructed to stop producing so many reports on inequality; the main statistics on the distribution of income in the UK are now to be produced at three-yearly intervals.

5.2 Studying the distribution of income

Considered at the most abstract level, income and wealth are two different ways of looking at the same thing: both concepts try to capture ways in which members of society have different access to the goods and services that are valued in that society. Wealth is measured simply in pounds, and is a snapshot of the **stock** of such valued goods that any

person owns, regardless of whether this is growing or declining. Income
is measured in pounds per given period, and gives a moving picture,
telling us about the **flow** of revenue over time.

In this chapter we restrict our focus to the distribution of income, for
the sake of simplicity. We shall look in detail at the problems of
measuring income and then consider some of the distinctive techniques
for describing and summarizing inequality that have evolved in the
literature on economic inequality.

There are four major methodological problems encountered when
studying the distribution of income:

1 How should income be defined?
2 What should be the unit of measurement?
3 What should be the time period considered?
4 What sources of data are available?

Definition of income

To say that income is a flow of revenue is fine in theory, but we have to
choose between two approaches to making this operational. One is to
follow accounting and tax practices, and make a clear distinction between
income and additions to wealth; on this approach, capital gains in a given
period, even though they might be used in the same way as income,
would be excluded from the definition. This is the approach of the Inland
Revenue, which has separate taxes for income and capital gains.

The second approach is to treat income as the value of goods and
services consumed in a given period plus net changes in personal wealth
during that period. This approach involves constantly monitoring the
value of assets even when they do not come to the market, a very hard
task. So, although the second approach is theoretically superior, it is not
very practical and the first is usually adopted.

The phrase 'the value of goods and services' rather than 'money' was
used above, to indicate that incomes both in cash and in kind should be
considered; if an employee gets the free use of a company car, this has an
important bearing on his or her standard of living, freeing income for
other goods. It is, however, hard to get good data on non-cash benefits.
The Royal Commission pointed out that very little is known, for
example, about the value of employees' fringe benefits, although they
surmised that the value of such benefits had increased during the 1970s
when there were formal constraints to stop employers giving pay rises
above a certain level.

The definition of income usually only includes money spent on goods
and services that are consumed privately. But many things of great value
to different people are organized at a collective level: health services,
education, libraries, parks, museums, nuclear warheads. The benefits
which accrue from these are not spread evenly across all members of
society; if education were not provided free, only families with children

would need to use their money income to buy schooling. Some sophisticated studies of the distribution of income (such as that by Nicholson 1974) have extended the definition of income and estimated the likely benefits accruing from welfare provision using information about different families' circumstances. This is not done in the principal estimates of income distribution to be discussed in this chapter; the Central Statistical Office does, however, publish other analyses which address this issue (CSO 1986, for example).

Sources of income are often grouped into three types: **earned income**, from either employment or self-employment; **unearned income** which accrues from ownership of investments, property, rent and so on; and **transfer income**, that is benefits and pensions transferred on the basis of entitlement, not on the basis of work or ownership, mainly by the government but occasionally by individuals (e.g. alimony). The first two sources are sometimes added together and referred to as **original income**. While earnings form some three-quarters of the total income in the UK, they form a much higher proportion among higher quantiles of the income distribution. Conversely, transfer payments constitute a very large proportion of the income of those at the bottom of the income distribution.

Deciding what to count as income for current consumption has proved problematic, especially in the area of National Insurance and pension contributions; if people use part of their current income to purchase an insurance of income in the future, should their current income be considered before or after that outlay? If income is measured before deductions, the savings element will eventually be counted twice – now while it is being bought and later when it is being used as income. But if it is ignored, two individuals who have the same income after deductions will be considered to be in the same boat; this may not seem sensible when one has some guarantee in the future and the other has none. The Royal Commission decided that the arguments both ways were so strong that it was important to present income distributions based on both assumptions separately.

There are a large number of other detailed difficulties in the fine grain definition of income. How are benefits in kind, such as access to company clubs, to be valued, for example, or what should be done about the value of living in a house that is owned outright? The latter question was considered in the answer to exercise 4.2. The appendix to this chapter gives a brief summary of the income definition in the Survey of Personal Incomes; the Royal Commission report (1975) and Atkinson (1983) give the matter a more detailed discussion.

The unit of income

While nominally most income accrues to individuals, the benefits of that income are shared across broader units. Ideally, we should like to study the distribution of income across those who receive the benefits of that income. As we have noted before, too little is known about effective income sharing for us to be able to do this very well.

Many different units are candidates for the study of income. The individual is certainly the easiest to make operational, but probably the least satisfactory, because so many people in society would be deemed as having no income. The family unit as defined for welfare purposes was introduced in chapter 1, but there are other different definitions of family that are sometimes used. However, the links of blood are not necessarily the links of revenue. The household, often defined as a group of people who live at the same address and make common catering arrangements, is perhaps the ideal unit to study. Unfortunately, none of the large administrative sources of income data is available on a household basis.

Because knowledge of income is required to administer the tax and benefit systems, researchers have a great deal of data available to them if they accept the units used by these institutions. In this chapter, the incomes of tax units will be considered. The Inland Revenue treats husbands and wives as in the same unit (whether they are taxed separately or not). All children with an income above the personal allowance threshold count as a unit on their own; dependent children with an income below this level are included with their parents.

It is rare, however, to find published income data on either households or tax units which lists the actual income received by individual units. It is nearly always published in a condensed form, grouped into classes of income; figure 5.1 shows the way the distribution of income was published in *Economic Trends* for the tax year 1978–9, the last year of the 1974 Labour administration.

The period

It is difficult to decide what the appropriate period should be for the assessment of income. It is usually important to distinguish inequalities between the same people over the course of their life-cycle and inequalities between different people. If a short period, like a week, is chosen, two people may appear to have identical incomes even though they are on very different lifetime career paths; conversely, two individuals who appear to have very different incomes may be on identical lifetime career paths but just be at different ages. In general, income inequality will appear greater the shorter the time period considered.

The solution might be to take a longer period – ideally a lifetime, perhaps. However, either guesses will have to be made about what people will earn in the future, or definitive statements will only be possible about the degree of inequality pertaining in society many decades previously. For most purposes, one tax year is used as the period over which information about income is collected.

Figure 5.1 Distribution of income before and after tax: 1978–9

Range of income (lower limit) (£ p.a.)	Before tax Number of units (thousands)	After tax Number of units (thousands)
0	1,411	1,446
1,000	3,670	3,895
1,500	2,974	3,685
2,000	2,701	3,320
2,500	2,263	2,691
3,000	1,975	2,340
3,500	1,815	2,090
4,000	1,698	1,961
4,500	1,652	1,714
5,000	2,855	2,593
6,000	2,173	1,602
7,000	1,460	791
8,000	1,394	595
10,000	458	199
12,000	310	94
15,000	160	47
20,000	76	11
30,000	31	2
	29,076	29,076

Source: *Economic Trends* no. 328, February 1981: 88

In any empirical study of incomes, some individuals will be found who register an income of zero, and the shorter the period over which income is measured, the more zeros there will be. These individuals are important theoretically; they clearly cannot be living on air, and it is usually of interest to find out if they are experiencing a foreseeable period without income for which they have made alternative provision, or whether this fluctuation in their fortunes is unforeseen and causes major hardship. (The zeros may also cause technical difficulties, particularly if the researcher wants to express the data in logs, as we shall see.)

Sources of data on income

In Britain, the Central Statistical Office is responsible for collating and publishing the estimates of the nation's wealth in an annual volume of statistics, *United Kingdom National Accounts*, known popularly as the Blue Book (see for example Newman 1985). Details of the sources from which the information is collected, and the precise definitions and methods used to compile the statistics, are given in a separate volume entitled *Sources and Methods*, which should always be consulted along with the data (CSO 1985).

An important part of the National Accounts is the total income of the personal sector. The major source used in compiling these estimates is the Survey of Personal Incomes (SPI), which is detailed more fully in the appendix to this chapter. This is a large annual survey drawn from the Inland Revenue's tax records; it is therefore restricted to the Inland Revenue's definition of income, to treating tax units, and to extending coverage only to those who pay tax. The CSO supplements this information by turning to other sources for data on income which is not reported to the Inland Revenue; the principal addition is the amount that central and local government pay out in benefits (mainly cash benefits) which are not liable to tax.

The Blue Book only presents totals of income before and after tax. In order to estimate how equally or unequally income is spread across the population, the CSO supplements the Blue Book estimates with information from the Family Expenditure Survey (see appendix to chapter 4). There are, however, some items of income that are not covered in either the SPI or the FES, and so only 88 per cent of the total Blue Book estimate of personal income can be allocated to tax units at particular points in the income distribution; the major source of unallocated income is employees' contributions to and lump sum benefits from pension schemes. The summary tables (such as figure 5.1) are published in *Economic Trends*.

5.3 Quantiles and quantile shares

A great deal of information is packed rather indigestibly into tables such as figure 5.1. As we saw in chapter 3, clarification can often be obtained if the value of the incomes held at different quantiles of the distribution is expressed relative to the median income. The quantiles conventionally considered are the quartiles, the top and bottom deciles, the top quintile and the top percentile. To calculate the precise value of these points, we would need to go back to the incomes received by the tax units before they were grouped. Since this technique has already been illustrated in figure 3.7, it will not be repeated here.

However, these summaries only capture what is happening at the particular points which are used to divide up the distribution; the incomes of all units that lie above the top percentile could double, for example, without the value of the top percentile changing. To avoid this problem, the **quantile shares** approach can be adopted. The income of all

Figure 5.2 Quantile shares of income: 1978–9

Quantile	Percentage of total income received by the quantile	
	Pre-tax	Post-tax
Top 1%	5.3	3.9
2–5%	10.7	9.8
6–10%	10.1	9.7
Top 10%	26.1	23.4
11–20%	16.5	16.3
21–30%	13.5	13.5
31–40%	11.2	11.3
41–50%	9.2	9.3
51–60%	7.3	7.7
61–70%	5.8	6.4
71–80%	4.5	5.1
81–90%	3.5	4.1
Bottom 10%	2.4	2.9

Source: *Economic Trends* no. 328, February 1981, table A: 82

units falling in a particular **quantile group** – all those with income above the top percentile, for example – is summed and expressed as a proportion of the total income received by everyone.

It is then possible to trace trends in inequality by considering changes over time in the share of total income received by particular quantile groups. It is important to remember, however, that the individuals who make up the top 1 per cent of the income distribution may have changed over time.

The quantile share approach is regularly used by the Central Statistical Office in the figures it reports, and is illustrated for the same year, 1978–9, in figure 5.2. Notice that the information about how much is received by the top 10 per cent of earners is given twice; the top three lines of the table show in detail how the 26 per cent of pre-tax income is distributed within the top decile group, for example.

Governments can affect the distribution of income in two ways – they can alter pre-tax income through macro-economic policies, and they can alter post-tax income through fiscal policies. The Labour administration of 1974–9 had not managed to eradicate inequality in pre-tax incomes, as the first column of figure 5.2 shows; the top 10 per cent of income units had over ten times as much income as the bottom 10 per cent of units, for example.

Perhaps it is more fair to judge the record of the administration by the extent to which it managed to alter the distribution of income through its fiscal policies. However, the information in the post-tax column of figure 5.2 is not much more impressive. Even after tax, the differences between top and bottom are almost as large; the overall distribution of incomes does not change dramatically before and after tax. The question of change over time during the Labour administration is postponed for the moment.

Of course, assessing the total effect of government policy in this way is very crude for several reasons. The column of pre-tax income already includes some transfer income; the income share of the bottom 10 per cent of the distribution is almost wholly composed of state benefits to those who have little or no income. Figure 5.2 also ignores the effect of the indirect taxes levied on certain goods and services, such as value added tax and customs and excise taxes, and the redistributive effect of non-cash benefits such as health services and education.

5.4 Cumulative income shares and Lorenz curves

Neither quantiles nor quantile shares lend themselves to an appealing way of presenting the distribution of income in a graphical form. This is usually achieved by making use of **cumulative distributions**. The income distribution is displayed by plotting cumulative income shares against the cumulative percentage of the population.

The cumulative distribution is obtained by counting in (explained in chapter 1) from one end only; income distributions are traditionally cumulated from the lowest to the highest incomes. To see how this is done, consider the worksheet in figure 5.3. The bottom 10 per cent receive 2.4 per cent of the total pre-tax income, and the next 10 per cent receive 3.5 per cent; summing these, we can say that the bottom 20 per cent receive 5.9 per cent of the total income. We work our way up through the incomes in this fashion.

The cumulative percentage of the population is then plotted against the cumulative share of total income (plotting data will be discussed more fully in chapter 10, which also has an appendix listing some aesthetic considerations). The resulting graphical display is known as a **Lorenz curve**; it was first introduced in 1905 and has been repeatedly used for visual communication of income and wealth inequality. The Lorenz curve for pre-tax income in the UK is shown in figure 5.4.

Lorenz curves have visual appeal because they portray how near total equality or total inequality a particular distribution falls. If everyone in society had the same income, then the share received by each decile group, for example, would be 10 per cent, and the Lorenz curve would be completely straight, described by the diagonal line in figure 5.4. If, on the other hand, one person received all the income and no-one else got

Figure 5.3 Cumulative income shares: 1978–9

Cumulative percentage of population	Percentage of total income received by the quantile		Cumulative share of total income	
	Pre-tax	Post-tax	Pre-tax	Post-tax
100	5.3	3.9	100.0	100.0
99	10.7	9.8	94.7	96.1
95	10.1	9.7	84.0	86.3
90	16.5	16.3	73.9	76.6
80	13.5	13.5	57.4	60.3
70	11.2	11.3	43.9	46.8
60	9.2	9.3	32.7	35.5
50	7.3	7.7	23.5	26.2
40	5.8	6.4	16.2	18.5
30	4.5	5.1	10.4	12.1
20	3.5	4.1	5.9	7.0
10	2.4	2.9	2.4	2.9

Source: cumulating columns from figure 5.2

anything, the curve would be the L-shape described by the two axes. The nearer the empirical line comes to the diagonal, the more equally distributed income in society is.

The degree of inequality in two distributions can be compared by superimposing their Lorenz curves, as in figure 5.4. The fact that the post-tax curve lies nearer the diagonal shows that income tax does have

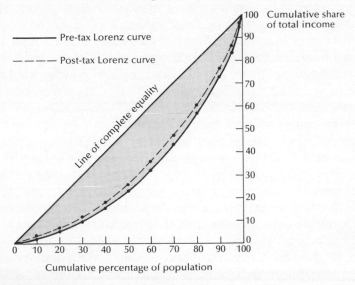

Figure 5.4 Lorenz curves of income 1978–9
Source: figure 5.3

some, albeit quite small, effect in redistributing income from the rich to the poor in society. If the two lines represented income inequality in two different societies, it is quite possible that the two lines would intersect; one society might have more equality at the lower ends of the distribution, and another more at the higher ends.

5.5 Desirable properties in a summary measure of inequality

In the previous section, we saw how the whole of an income distribution is conventionally presented in both numerical and graphical form. In order to trace trends in income inequality over time, or in order to make comparisons across nations, or in order to compare inequalities in income with inequalities in wealth or housing or health, however, a single numerical summary is desirable. Very many different measures have been proposed. Before we consider any of them in detail, it is useful to ask what properties we would want such a measure to have.

Scale independence

We have already come across two measures of the spread of a distribution – the standard deviation and the midspread. Unfortunately, if money incomes change because they are expressed in yen rather than pounds, or, less obviously, if they increase simply to keep pace with inflation, the standard deviation and midspread of the distribution will also change; as we saw in chapter 3, the dominant source of variation in income over time is usually the purchasing power of the currency. We want a measure of inequality that is insensitive to such scaling factors.

However, it is important that the measure be sensitive to the level of the distribution. Imagine a hypothetical society containing three individuals who earned £5000, £10,000 and £15,000 respectively. If they all had an increase in their incomes of £1 million, we would expect a measure of inequality to decline, since the differences between these individuals would have become trivial. The standard deviation and midspread would, however, be unaffected.

A popular approach is to log income data before calculating the numerical summaries of spread. As we saw in section 3.4, if two distributions differ by a scaling factor, the logged distributions will differ only in level. However, if they differ by an arithmetic constant (£1,000,000 in this example), they will have different spreads when logged. The existence of units with zero incomes leads to problems, since the log of zero cannot be defined mathematically. An easy technical solution to this problem is to add a very small number (£0.50, for example) to each of the zeros. If a numerical summary of spread in a logged distribution met the other desirable features of a measure of inequality, we could stop here. Unfortunately, it does not.

The principle of transfers

It makes intuitive sense to require that a numerical summary of inequality should decline whenever money is given by a rich person to a poor person, regardless of how poor or how rich, and regardless of how much money is transferred (provided of course that the amount is not so big that the previously poor person becomes even richer than the previously rich person).

One numerical summary – the income share of a selected quantile group – fails to meet this principle. By focusing on one part of the distribution only, perhaps the top 5 per cent, it would fail to record a change if a transfer occurred elsewhere in the distribution. Similar objections apply to another commonly used summary, the **decile ratio**, which simply expresses the ratio of the upper decile to the lower decile.

Much less obviously, this appealing principle of transfers also rules out simply using a conventional measure of spread based on the logged income distribution. The standard deviation of the logs behaves as one would wish at lower levels of the income distribution, but a transfer from one extremely rich individual to one only slightly less rich can actually result in the measure of spread increasing.

Other inequality measures meet this principle, and so are to be preferred. However, they unfortunately still fail to agree on an unambiguous ranking of different societies in terms of income inequality, because they are sensitive in different ways to transfers of varying amounts and at different points in the income scale. Cowell (1977) argues that the principle of transfers should be strengthened to specify that the measure of inequality should be sensitive only to the distance on the income scale over which the transfer is made, not to the amount transferred. He also adds a third principle to the two considered here, that of decomposition: a decline in inequality in part of a distribution should lead to a decline in inequality overall. We shall return to these more stringent criteria below.

5.6 The Gini coefficient

A measure that summarizes what is happening across all the distribution is the **Gini coefficient**. An intuitive explanation of the Gini coefficient can be given by looking back at figure 5.4. The area between the Lorenz curves and the line of total equality was shaded; the Gini coefficient expresses the ratio between the shaded and the total area in the triangle formed between the perfect equality and perfect inequality lines. It therefore varies between 0 (on the line of perfect equality) and 1 (on the L of perfect inequality), although it is sometimes multiplied by 100 to express the coefficient in percentage form.

The Lorenz curve of pre-tax income in figure 5.4 represents a Gini coefficient of 0.375. Is this a large or small amount of inequality? It is certainly greater than 0, the value it would take if incomes were equally distributed. But beyond that, we have to compare it with something before we can decided whether it is high or low. For example, it is bigger than the post-tax coefficient of 0.335, as one would expect.

These Gini coefficients were not calculated from the data as given in figure 5.3, but from the original ungrouped distribution of income not shown here. There is a measure of spread (which was alluded to but not developed in chapter 2) which can be calculated by taking the mean of the difference between the value of every individual compared with every other individual. The Gini coefficient is one-half of this amount.

As you might expect, a measure which requires you to look at every possible pair of incomes is tremendously laborious to calculate; even a mainframe computer feels the strain when the sample size begins to get large. Because income distributions are so often presented in grouped form, the intuitive definition based on the Lorenz curve is usually sufficient. A rough guide to the numerical value of the Gini coefficient can always be obtained by plotting the Lorenz curve on to squared paper and counting the proportion of squares that fall in the shaded area.

However, since we live in an era where we expect computers to be able to take a bit of strain, and since a computationally convenient version of the formula for the Gini coefficient exists (Cowell 1977), the formula is presented here:

$$\text{Gini coefficient} = \frac{2}{YN^2} \Sigma i Y_i - \frac{N+1}{N}$$

(The symbols were introduced in section 2.4.) Notice that the key term $(\Sigma i Y_i)$ involves a weighted sum of the data values, where the weight is the unit's rank order in the income distribution. You are not expected to be able to manipulate this formula in hand calculation, but exercise 5.4 has been set to give you the opportunity to try translating it into a Minitab program.

Perhaps a fairer way to evaluate the record of the 1974–9 Labour administration in reducing inequality is to see if the Gini coefficients while it was in office differed from those before or after. To put the 1978–9 coefficient in context, figure 5.5 shows the trend in inequality as measured by the Gini coefficient of both pre-tax and post-tax income across time, from 1949 to 1981–2.

The definition of income underwent a major revision in the middle of the 1974–9 period. The most important change involved mortgage payments; before 1976, income was recorded net of such payments. When they were added in, the Gini coefficients went up, especially in post-tax incomes, because mortgage payments form a greater proportion of higher incomes and are untaxed. The two data values for 1975–6 in figure 5.5 show the Gini coefficients both on the old definitions and the new. (There was also a change of method after 1967, but this is thought to have had less impact.)

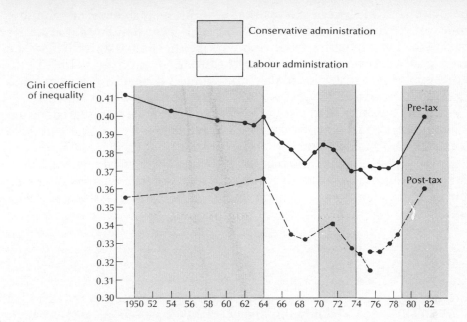

Figure 5.5 Trends in income inequality: 1949 to 1981–2

Source: Royal Commission (1975: table 15); *Economic Trends* May 1978, February 1979 and July 1984

Focusing on the 1974–9 period in figure 5.5, there was very little change indeed in the distribution of pre-tax income, and there was even an increase in inequality in post-tax incomes after 1977. It would seem that the Labour administration had failed by the standards of its own manifesto. The previous Labour administration, in 1964–70, presided over a much greater fall in income inequality, reversing a trend of a gradual increase in inequality in post-tax incomes after the war.

However, a more striking change in inequality occurred after 1979, in the first three years of the ensuing Conservative administration, when the Gini coefficients increased sharply. The quantile shares (not shown here) suggest that the top 10 per cent gained at the expense of everybody else between 1978–9 and 1981–2. Note that this information is not revealed by the Gini coefficient; like all numerical summaries, it has to throw a lot of information away in order to clarify the picture.

The Gini coefficient does meet the criteria of scale independence and the principle of transfers discussed above. It does not, however, meet the principle of decomposition. It is also more sensitive to transfers that displace the rank orders of more individuals; it is therefore more sensitive to changes in the middle of the distribution than to changes at either the top or the bottom.

It is now generally recognized, furthermore, that the Gini coefficient is not a technical, value-free measure of inequality. It should be clear from the discussion of Lorenz curves that two different income distributions could yield two identical Gini coefficients. It may well be that a society would care more about gross income inequalities in the lower half of the income distribution than about inequalities higher up; the Gini coefficient implicitly treats inequality the same wherever it occurs, thus applying one particular set of values to the discussion of inequality.

Atkinson has proposed a set of measures which allows researchers and policy-makers to make their social value judgements explicit and to give increased weight to inequality at the bottom end of the distribution if they wish. These indices of inequality, while far less widely used than Gini coefficients, meet all the criteria for numerical summaries discussed above. A clear and non-technical discussion is given in Atkinson (1983: 56–9).

5.7 Conclusion

In this chapter, special attention has been given to ways of conceptualizing, displaying and summarizing inequalities in the distribution of personal incomes. In terms of techniques, the chapter followed on from those presented in chapter 3, building especially on the analysis of different quantiles of a distribution; the share of income received by a quantile group is the primary way in which information about the distribution of incomes is usually presented. When these income shares are cumulated, they can be presented effectively as Lorenz curves, and summarized by Gini coefficients.

Lorenz curves and Gini coefficients have been most widely applied to the study of inequality in income and wealth. But they have not been restricted to that field. They have been used to describe inequalities in other areas – in the allocation of housing (Robinson et al. 1985), and in health (Le Grand 1985), for example. In the latter case, the trend in individual inequalities in life expectancy over time runs counter to the trends observed in social class mortality differentials; the Gini coefficients have declined where class differentials have, if anything, increased. We shall come back to this topic in chapter 14.

However, inequalities have far from disappeared in any of these areas. The depressing conclusion of most studies is that Tawney's verdict from 1931 (1964: 73) still holds true today:

> Not only are there the oft-cited disparities of financial resources, which are susceptible of statistical measurement, but, what is more fundamental, education, health, the opportunities for personal culture and even decency, and sometimes, it would seem, life itself, seem to be meted out on a graduated scale.

Exercises

5.1 Data about the distribution of income is not published as regularly in the USSR as it is in the UK. There is an equivalent to the Family Expenditure Survey, but the results are published less often and in less detail. For this reason, those who study the USSR prefer to use the one-off housing surveys that are conducted from time to time, which collect quite detailed income information; there have been three since the Second World War, and the latest at the time of writing relates to 1967. The survey sample is drawn from employment records, and covers the non-agricultural population. Respondents were asked about money income from all sources that accrued to households in April 1967; the distribution of gross incomes is shown below alongside data from the UK for 1967.

Quantile Group	USSR	UK
Top 10%	21	28
Top 20%	35	43
21–40%	22	24
41–60%	18	17
1–80%	14	11
Bottom 20%	10	6
Unit	individual	tax unit

Sources: USSR data in McAuley (1985: 10); UK data in Royal Commission on the Distribution of Income and Wealth (1979, table 2.3)

Construct cumulative income distributions for the USSR and the UK and from these plot the data as two superimposed Lorenz curves. What can you say as a result about inequality in the two countries?

5.2 The Gini coefficient of 0.375 for 1978–9 was based on all incomes, including those which were only for a part-year (as explained in the appendix). Would you expect the Gini coefficient to increase or decrease if part-year incomes were excluded? Which portion of the distribution would you expect to be most affected?

5.3 The income share of the top 10 per cent of households is given in the dataset WORLD; the information is not available for many of the poorer countries, unfortunately. Write a Minitab program to construct a stem and leaf display of these decile shares.

5.4 Using the income data in column 1 of POVERTY, write a Minitab program to calculate the Gini coefficient of inequality, using the formula in section 5.6. You will need to order the values in the column first (Minitab command ORDER) and generate a new column of rank orders (GENERATE).

Appendix: the Survey of Personal Incomes

The Inland Revenue, which is responsible for levying income tax, conducts the largest investigation into incomes in Britain, known as the Survey of Personal Incomes. About 80 per cent of the adult population of Britain is in a tax unit recorded by the Inland Revenue; the other 20 per cent are mainly the elderly whose incomes are not high enough to be taxable.

From the total population of tax units, a sample is drawn. Until 1982–3, the sample size was around 120,000 tax units per year, but this was reduced to something around 70,000 from 1983–4. A simple random sample of the returns would include only a few very wealthy individuals, and would mean that the estimates from the survey of the incomes received by the rich were very unreliable. The incomes are therefore first stratified into groups, depending on both type of income and amount, and then a **disproportionate** stratified sample is drawn; in other words, the sampling fraction varies depending on which group a particular tax unit is in. For example, in 1981–2, the highest sampling fraction was one in three for the highest band of incomes, and the lowest was one in 2000 for employees and pensioners on the lowest incomes.

The sample is selected at the local tax offices, where a survey form is completed about each selected case. Information is available for between 92 per cent and 97 per cent of the cases, but only for about 85 per cent in the case of employed married women; it is not always possible from the tax record to know which tax office holds a spouse's file.

The definition of income used is the type of income that is assessed for tax purposes; forms of income that are exempt from tax (such as National Savings Bank interest) or that have been taxed at source are excluded. From the total income reported to the Inland Revenue, any allowable deductions – such as contributions to approved pension schemes – are first subtracted; however allowances against tax such as the blanket personal allowances are not deducted. The result is rather misleadingly referred to by the Inland Revenue as **total net income**, but this is not net of tax, merely net of allowable deductions.

The period over which income is calculated is the last tax year for employees; for the self-employed, it can be the year preceding that. Some of the units only have **part-year incomes**, because the units only came into being during a particular year (those who start work or are widowed during the period, for example). No attempt is made to multiply these part-year incomes up to their annual equivalent.

The principal use to which the survey is put is to provide the data for a model of the tax system which can be used to estimate the costs and yields of changes when the Chancellor is planning a new Budget. However, it is also used in the construction of a combined Taxes and Prices Index, and, as we have seen in this chapter, is also used by the Central Statistical Office in estimating the distribution of personal incomes.

The Royal Commission on the Distribution of Income and Wealth noted, in their first report, that there are a number of characteristics of this data which limit its usefulness in studying distribution of income (1975: 195). Total net income, as defined above, excludes certain important parts of income; very little allowance is made for income which is not received in cash, such as the value of living in an owner-occupied building, or income received in kind. One of the most important parts of the work of the Royal Commission was to study the distribution of income using different definitions of income, adding back in mortgage interest allowed against tax, for example.

Most importantly, the data is a by-product of the taxation system, and carries its hallmarks. When the tax rules change, the data changes. To the extent that tax evasion and underreporting of income occur, the data is biased. Investment income is probably understated.

The main results are published annually, showing pre- and post-tax income by standard regions (for example, Board of Inland Revenue 1985). The data is held in anonymous form by the ESRC Data Archive at the University of Essex.

Part II   Relationships between Two Variables

In the first five chapters of this book we looked in detail at how single variables could be measured, displayed and summarized. Most of the interesting questions about those variables, however, involved bringing another variable into the picture. Do the heights of people in different classes vary? How does the pay of men compare with the pay of women? What has been happening to the distribution of incomes over time?

Relationships between two variables (**bivariate** relationships) are of interest because they can suggest hypotheses about the way in which the world works. In particular, they are interesting when one variable can be considered a cause and the other an effect. It is customary to call these variables by different names. We shall call the variable that is presumed to be the cause the **explanatory** variable (and denote it X) and the one that is presumed to be the effect the **response** variable (denoted Y); they are termed independent and dependent variables respectively in some textbooks.

In different chapters in this part of the book we shall look at a variety of techniques for examining bivariate relationships, to see if the explanatory variable seems to have an effect on the response. In order to do this, it will be helpful to introduce some terms and graphical devices used by social scientists analysing relationships between variables.

Causal reasoning is often assisted by the construction of a schematic model of the hypothesized causes and effects: a **causal path model**. If we believe that the class a child comes from is likely to have an effect on its school performance, we could model the relationship as in the accompanying sketch.

Such models are drawn up according to a set of conventions:

1 The variables are represented inside boxes or circles and labelled; in this example the variables are class background and performance at school.
2 Arrows run from the variables which we consider to be causes to those

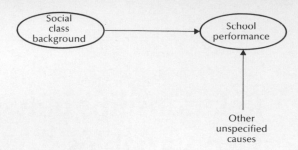

we consider to be effects; class background is assumed to have a causal effect on school performance.

3 Positive effects are drawn as unbroken lines and negative effects are drawn as dashed lines.

4 A number is placed on the arrow to denote how strong the effect of the explanatory variable is.

5 An extra arrow is included as an effect on the response variable, often unlabelled, to act as a reminder that not all the causes have been specified in the model.

There is no arrow running into class background because it is the explanatory variable, and we are not interested, in this instance, in causal factors affecting it. The general model is therefore as shown in the accompanying diagram.

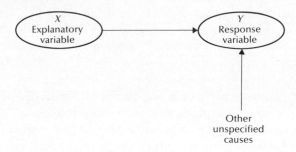

It is good to get into the habit of constructing hypothetical causal path models before turning to examine data; it nearly always clarifies one's analytic strategy to think through the relationships one would expect to be present before seeing if they exist as predicted. In non-experimental research, when many variables may be operating simultaneously, such models can prove invaluable in helping the researcher keep a clear head.

The task in this part of the book is to learn how the effects of an explanatory variable on a response variable may be quantified and summarized. Chapter 6 deals with situations where the explanatory variable is a nominal scale and the response variable is interval. The next two chapters deal with the relationship between two nominal scale variables. In chapter 9 the special case where time is the explanatory variable is discussed, and techniques for smoothing time series are presented. Chapter 10 deals with situations where both explanatory and response variables are measured on interval scales, and linear models can be fitted. Finally, chapter 11 discusses the use of power transformations to change the scale of a variable.

Throughout this part, it is important to remember that statistical effects need not be true causal effects. The birth rate in different counties in Sweden can be predicted moderately well from the number of storks observed in that county. Is this because storks cause babies? Clearly not. What, then, is the point of looking at statistical effects, especially when they produce such seemingly nonsensical links as that between storks and babies? The answer is that, by making a set of careful judgements about the operation of other variables, we can reason about likely patterns of causation. How that is done is the subject of the third part of this book. Previewing the argument, it turns out that, if we control for how rural a particular county in Sweden is, the association between storks and babies disappears; the bivariate association exists because there are both more babies and more storks in rural communities.

6 Handling Several Batches

When the response variable under analysis is measured on an interval scale and the explanatory variable is on a nominal scale, the joint association between the two variables is examined by looking at the distribution of the response variable within each category of the explanatory variable. In this chapter we shall examine the distribution of local unemployment rates within each region of the country. Instead of fitting numerical constants, as we did in the first part of the book, conditional fits will be introduced. A new graphical method will be presented which facilitates comparisons between distributions, and the idea of an unusual data value will be given more systematic treatment than hitherto. This chapter builds directly on the subject matter of the first two chapters.

6.1 Unemployment – an issue of concern

Unemployment is viewed as a personal catastrophe by most of its victims, even those who are relatively quickly back in work. In a survey of the unemployed in 1981, respondents were asked to rate how they felt about being out of work on a nine point scale, where nine indicated 'about the worst thing that ever happened to me'; 44 per cent gave the maximum score and nearly three-quarters gave a score of six or more (Daniel 1981: ix). Being deprived of work, the unemployed lack not only access to an adequate income, but also access to a routine to organize their lives around, and to one of the most important sources of personal and social esteem.

Unemployment is also viewed as a major national problem by the overwhelming majority of adults in Britain, whether unemployed or employed. Every upward spiral of the unemployment figures has brought a corresponding increase in the number of people who say, in response to being asked what they think are the most urgent problems facing the country today, that unemployment is top or second from the top, as figure 6.1 shows. In the 1980s, the proportion endorsing it as an important problem reached over 80 per cent, although concern reached some kind of a plateau at this level; there seems to be a hard core of around 20 per cent who are not influenced by rising levels of unemployment.

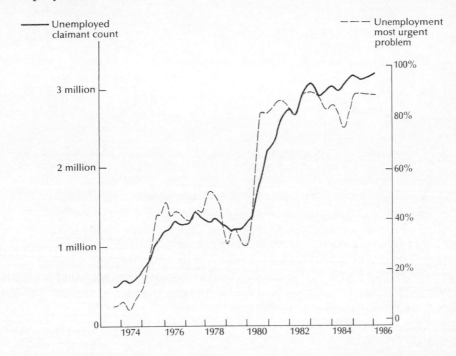

Figure 6.1 Unemployment as a problem in Britain: actual and perceived

Sources: unemployed claimant count: *Employment Gazette* December 1982 and May 1986. Percentage naming unemployment as most or second most urgent problem facing the country: *Gallup Political Index* monthly

It is striking how closely increases in concern over unemployment track over time with increases in the rate of unemployment in Britain. If one makes cross-national comparisons, however, it is not the case that those countries with the highest unemployment levels have the highest degree of concern, as figure 6.2 demonstrates. Norwegians, living in a country that used its oil bonanza to expand other sectors of its economy and with a very low unemployment rate, are nevertheless more concerned about unemployment than are Americans, who tolerate a much higher unemployment rate.

These two figures suggest that people are aware of the numbers of unemployed and how they are changing over time, and that unemployment as a political problem is inescapably viewed within a national frame of reference. These conclusions combine to make national unemploy-

Figure 6.2 Unemployment as a concern in eight countries

	1 Concern (%)	2 Rate (%)
Spain	75	21.6
Netherlands	70	14.3
Britain	68	11.7
Italy	61	11.4
France	69	10.6
West Germany	75	8.7
United States	42	6.7
Norway	50	2.0

Column 1   Percentage who answered 'unemployment' when asked which were their greatest concerns for themselves and their country.
Column 2   Actual rate of unemployment in each country.

Source: concern data from *International Herald Tribune* 25 October 1982; comparative rates from *Employment Gazette* September 1982

ment statistics a matter of great political sensitivity. In this chapter, some of the problems of using the official unemployment statistics will be discussed.

6.2 Counting the unemployed

Unemployment statistics serve several functions. They are used, along with employment, vacancies, output and earnings statistics, as indicators of the level of economic activity. They are interpreted as an indicator of the size of the potential labour reserve. They suggest levels of social distress in a community. And they have operational uses in guiding the management of employment services, and administrative uses in helping determine, for example, which areas should be granted assisted area status to qualify for various forms of government relief. No single statistical series could hope to serve all these functions at once; there is, therefore, no unique answer to the question of how unemployment should be defined.

The employed and the unemployed between them comprise the **labour force**; the unemployed should ideally be distinguished from the **economically inactive** who would not accept a job in the formal economy if it were offered to them. The line between the unemployed and the inactive is in practice, however, a hard one to draw: how is one to know what would happen in hypothetical situations? Even the unemployed themselves may not be very good informants about their likely behaviour under different labour market conditions.

The most commonly used unemployment statistics are those published by the Department of Employment each month. They are based on the numbers claiming benefit because they are unemployed. Like other statistics that arise as a by-product of an administrative process, there are problems with matching them to the concept as defined theoretically. Some of the people claiming benefit are not actually looking for work. And some who seek work are not claiming benefit (Department of Employment 1986a and 1986d). The appendix at the end of this chapter tries to estimate how big these different biases are.

Unemployment is another instance where an important distinction must be made between stock and flow; the distinction between wealth and income in the last chapter was similar. The Department of Employment's monthly count of the unemployed represents the stock of those claiming benefit when the records are summarized on the second Thursday of each month. The monthly change in the count is not great; in the year to June 1986, for example, the median monthly change was around 50,000.

However, this disguises the fact that there are huge inflows to and outflows from the cumulated total of claimants each month. Typically, in the year to June 1986, 403,000 new people started claiming benefit each month and 396,000 people stopped claiming. As a result, while the unemployment rate at any one point in time in this year was around 12 per cent, many more experienced unemployment at some point during the year; the 1986 Social Attitudes Survey suggests that 30 per cent of people in the labour force in 1986 had some experience of unemployment in the previous five years.

The unemployed stock is composed disproportionately of unskilled workers; 40 per cent of them were unskilled in 1981, as compared with 7 per cent of the workforce as a whole (Daniel 1981: II.7). However, we cannot tell from the stock statistics alone if this is because unskilled workers are more likely to lose their jobs than others, or because, once they are out of work, the unskilled take much longer to find work than others, or both.

Generally, until the 1980s, the only detailed descriptive statements that could be made about the unemployed referred to the unemployed stock. As special studies have been conducted of the unemployed flow (Daniel 1981), and the Department of Employment has published more detailed flow statistics (Department of Employment 1983), several important differences have emerged between the characteristics of the unemployed stock at any point in time and those who become unemployed at some point during a period. For example:

1 Unskilled workers are more likely to lose their jobs and less likely to find another when unemployed.

2 The young are more likely to lose their jobs but more likely to get
  another.
3 Areas of high unemployment are places where people are both more
  likely to lose their jobs and less likely to get another; the exception is
  the West Midlands where the risk of job loss is the national average,
  but the chance of finding another job is lower.

We have become accustomed to describing unemployment by summarizing features of the unemployed stock; indeed, the example to be used in
the rest of this chapter looks at the relative size of the stock in different
areas. Nevertheless, more sophisticated analyses of either the causes or
consequences of unemployment increasingly study entry to and exit from
the unemployment queue as separate processes.

6.3 Regional variation in unemployment rates

In the 1920s, the unemployed were required to show that they were
'genuinely seeking work' before they could claim benefit. People from
Liverpool travelling to Manchester to look for work would pass
Mancunians travelling to Liverpool for the same reason, when there was
little prospect of work in either place. The futility of this exercise was
deeply resented by the unemployed, and campaigning against this rule
was one of the principal activities of the National Unemployed Workers'
Movement at the time.

Although nothing like this is now enforced, there are still plenty of
people who believe that the problem of unemployment would be
lessened if the unemployed moved around more. The exhortation of the
Secretary of State for Employment in 1981 that the current unemployed
should 'get on their bikes', like those in the depression, to look for work,
has become an emotionally charged slogan. In this chapter, by looking at
regional and local unemployment rates, we investigate what the
unemployed in 1985 would have found if they had got on their bikes – if
they had one, that is; the unemployed are much less likely to own a
bicycle than the employed (Miles 1983: 64).

One of the geographical units into which the Department of
Employment summarizes unemployment information is the **travel-to-
work area**. This is not an administrative unit, but an area which the
Census shows to be a relatively self-contained labour market. The
unemployment rate within each area is calculated by dividing the
numbers unemployed by the most recent estimate of the size of the
labour force in the area. The workforce in each area in May 1985, for
example, was estimated by taking the 1981 Census of Employment
figures as the baseline, and adjusting them on the basis of their industrial
composition and of changes in the industrial composition in that region
since 1981 known from other more up-to-date sources.

Figure 6.3 Sample of unemployment rates by local area in May 1985

Area	Region	%
Wolverhampton	West Midlands	17.3
Nottingham	East Midlands	13.2
Braintree	South East	11.1
Harlow	South East	9.5
Reigate	South East	6.2
Cwmbran	Wales	14.8
Birkenhead	North West	24.0
Oldham	North West	14.3
Aberdeen	Scotland	7.3
Truro	South West	13.2
Boston	East Midlands	17.4
Chesterfield	East Midlands	13.6
Dundee	Scotland	15.9
Dover	South East	9.4
Oban	Scotland	15.9
Goole	Yorkshire/Humberside	16.1
Isle of Wight	South East	14.4
Loughborough	East Midlands	7.8
Ffestiniog	Wales	15.8
Nelson and Colne	North West	13.4
Stamford	East Midlands	12.8
Swindon	South West	10.6
Stirling	Scotland	13.4
Workington	North	15.8
Gosport	South East	13.1
Peterlee	North	18.9
Worthing	South East	9.6

Source: drawn from the dataset TOWNS, column 5

The data to be used in this chapter, however, is drawn from the dataset TOWNS at the end of this book. Strictly, towns are defined somewhat differently from the Department of Employment's travel-to-work areas. However, they also aim to delineate self-contained labour markets on the basis of data on commuting flows from the 1981 Census of Population.

To get a feeling for how variable the experience of unemployment is in different parts of the country, we shall start by examining a sample of towns; figure 6.3 shows the unemployment rate for a systematic sample of one in ten of the areas listed in TOWNS. Ignore for now the fact that we know which region each town is in, and treat the data as a single batch.

The stem and leaf display and the five number summary of median, quartiles and extremes are shown in figure 6.4. As usual, we focus in turn

Figure 6.4 Local area unemployment in May 1985: stem and leaf display

leaf unit = 0.1%
6 2 denotes 6.2%

```
 1     6 | 2
 3     7 | 38
       8 |
 6     9 | 456
 7    10 | 6
 8    11 | 1                M 14.0                  13.4
 9    12 | 8                Q  7.5      10.8              15.8   dQ 5.0
(6)   13 | 122446           X  1.0       6.2              24.0
12    14 | 348
 9    15 | 8899
 5    16 | 1
 4    17 | 34
 2    18 | 9

      HI    24.0
```

Source: data in figure 6.3

on four different aspects of the distribution, the level, spread, shape and outliers. Typical local unemployment rates in May 1985 were around 13 per cent, and the middle 50 per cent of areas varied between 11 and 16 per cent. The main body of the data is roughly symmetrical, and there is one point, Birkenhead, that is quite a distance from the rest of the data.

Even the lowest rate (Reigate, at 6.2 per cent) is high enough to make the unemployed pause before jumping on their bikes. The ordering of the points does, however, suggest that there is a fairly strong regional effect in unemployment; areas in the South East generally have lower unemployment rates than areas in the North West, for example.

In order to investigate whether and to what extent unemployment rates are associated with region, we must turn to the distribution of unemployment within regions, rather than over regions. Figure 6.5 shows the detail of the rates in May 1985 for all the local areas in the East Midlands, for example.

By comparing figures 6.4 and 6.5, two indications may be gained that unemployment is associated with region. The regional median is not the same as the national average; it is lower. There is also much less variation in the unemployment rates experienced by towns in the same region than there was in the sample of areas drawn from all over the country. An area that appeared normal in the context of the national spread of unemployment rates, Boston, is seen from figure 6.5 to be high for the East Midlands.

Figure 6.5 Unemployment rate in the East Midlands in May 1985

Area	%	Area	%
Mansfield	12.3	Kettering	11.1
Nottingham	13.2	Loughborough	7.8
Newark	16.6	Leicester	10.9
Heanor	16.4	Melton Mowbray	12.0
Buxton	10.2	Lincoln	13.5
Boston	17.4	Northampton	10.9
Chesterfield	13.6	Spalding	12.0
Coalville	10.1	Stamford	12.8
Corby	16.5	Wellingborough	11.2
Derby	11.6	Worksop	12.7
Matlock	7.4	Hinckley	11.1
Grantham	12.6		

leaf unit = 0.1%
7 4 denotes 7.4%

```
      6 |
 2    7 | 48
      8 |
      9 |
 6   10 | 1299
10   11 | 1126
(6)  12 | 003678
 7   13 | 256
     14 |
     15 |
 4   16 | 456
 1   17 | 4
```

M 12.0		12.0	
Q 6.5	11.0	13.3	dQ 2.3
X 1.0	7.4	17.4	

Source: data in TOWNS columns 5 and 7

The exercise can now be repeated for all regions in the country. However, since it is too cumbersome to construct stem and leaf displays of ten batches of data at once and to compare their essential features, we will first introduce a new graphical device, and a more formal way of identifying outliers.

6.4 Outliers

Some, but not all, datasets contain points which are a lot higher or lower than the main body of the data; they are called **outliers**. They are always points that require the data analyst's special attention. They are important as diagnostics, and they can arise for one of four reasons:

1 They may just result from a fluke of the particular sample that was drawn; the probability of this kind of fluke can be assessed by traditional statistical tests, if sensible assumptions can be made about the shape of the distribution.
2 They may arise through measurement or transcription errors, which can occur in official statistics as well as anywhere else. We always want to be alerted to such errors, so that they can be corrected, or so that the points can be omitted from the analysis.
3 They may occur because the whole distribution is strongly skewed. In this case they point to the need to transform the data. As we shall see in chapter 11, transformations such as logging or squaring the values may remove these outliers.
4 Most interesting of all, they may suggest that these particular data points do not really belong substantively to the same data batch.

Up to now the idea of a data point being unusually large or small has been judgemental. It is useful to formalize the idea and define just how far away any case needs to fall from the main body of the data before we will decide that it may be particularly unusual.

We could declare the extremes, or the outside 5 per cent of the distribution, to be outliers. This would be totally unsatisfactory, however, as it would result in all distributions containing some, indeed the same proportion of, outliers. A rule is needed which highlights real differences between empirical distributions in the proportion of unusual data points they contain.

It makes sense to use the information about the spread in the main body of the data to define a point that is a long way away. The following has proved a useful rule of thumb: we define the main body of the data as spreading from one and a half times the dQ higher than the upper quartile to one and a half times the dQ lower than the lower quartile. Values further out than this are outliers. Moreover, it is also useful to define a cut-off for even more unusual points: we treat as a **far outlier** any point which is more than three times the dQ higher than the Q_U or lower than the Q_L.

Experience has shown that, in most instances, this rule identifies outliers only when there really is something worthy of attention. If we only selected one dQ either side of the quartile, then we would often be scratching our heads to explain relatively common occurrences. If, on the other hand, we selected two dQs either side of the quartiles, we might too often fail to detect the existence of some points that were genuinely different from the rest, or that would benefit from some kind of re-expression.

There is nothing hard and fast about this definition; it is not intended to replace human judgement. If an extreme data point only just qualified as an outlier and there were many other points close to it which did not, we might choose not to so label it. On the other hand, if a point technically just failed to qualify but resembled other outliers more than the rest of the data, or was separated from the rest of the data by a big gap, we might choose to call it an outlier.

Extended number summaries

To identify the outliers in a particular dataset, a value 1.5 times the dQ, or a **step**, is calculated; as usual, fractions other than one-half are ignored. Then the points beyond which the outliers fall (the **inner fences**) and the points beyond which the far outliers fall (the **outer fences**) are identified; inner fences lie one step beyond the quartiles and outer fences lie two steps beyond the quartiles.

It is helpful to lay out the calculations for detecting outliers in a standardized format, identifying the fences, how many outliers lie beyond them, and naming them. Such a format is often called an **extended number summary**.

The extended number summary for the distribution of unemployment in the East Midlands is shown in figure 6.6. The dQ is 2.3, so the step is 3.4; the inner fences lie at 7.6 and 16.7. Similarly, the outer fences lie 3.4 points further out, at 4.2 and 20.1. Boston is now seen to lie beyond the upper inner fence and Matlock is just beyond the lower inner fence. Both are deemed to be unusual according to the rules enunciated above.

Figure 6.6 Unemployment in East Midlands in May 1985: extended
            number summary

		3.4		
Inner fences	7.6		16.7	
Points beyond	1		1	Matlock, Boston
Outer fences	4.2		20.1	
Points beyond	0		0	

Source: read off figure 6.5

In fact, an argument could be made from figure 6.5 that there are four towns in the East Midlands with unusually high unemployment rates – Boston, Corby, Newark and Heanor – and two with low rates — Matlock and Loughborough — which should be investigated together to see if there are special reasons which make their experience different from nearby areas, since they are separated from the main body of the data by fairly wide gaps. The upper groups is not very homogeneous, however; Boston is the area in Britain with the highest proportion of agricultural workers, while Corby used to be a one-industry steel town before it faced massive closures.

Boston was in the original 5 per cent sample. It was not considered an outlier in the context of unemployment rates across the whole of Britain. However, our rule suggests that it is unusually high for an East Midlands town. In the context of the original batch, we say that Boston was a **hidden outlier**, in that its unusual features could not be seen until the batch was split up into categories of an explanatory variable.

6.5 Boxplots

Most people agree that it is important to display data well when communicating it to others; pictures are better at conveying the story line than numbers. However, visual display also has a role that is less well appreciated in helping researchers themselves understand their data and in forcing them to notice features that they did not suspect. We have already looked at one pictorial representation of data, the stem and leaf display. Its advantage was that it preserved a great deal of the numerical information. For some purposes, however, it preserves too much.

The **boxplot** is a device for conveying the information in the five number summaries economically and effectively. The important aspects of the distribution are represented schematically as shown in figure 6.7.

The middle 50 per cent of the distribution is represented by a box; the median is shown as a line dividing that box. Whiskers are drawn connecting the box to the end of the main body of the data. They are not drawn right up to the inner fences because there may not be any data points that far out; they extend to the **adjacent values**, the data points which come nearest to the inner fence while still being inside or on them. The outliers are drawn in separately; they can be coded with symbols (such as those in figure 6.7) to denote whether they are ordinary or far outliers, and are often identified by name.

The boxplot of unemployment in the East Midlands is shown in figure 6.8. It contains the same data as figures 6.5 and 6.6, but in a schematic form, highlighting the summary features, and drawing the eye's attention to Boston and Matlock. It seems more natural for the scale to ascend the page in boxplots (stem and leaf displays are shown with values descending in this book). Computers which use line printers to make graphical displays have difficulty drawing vertical lines, and so computer boxplots tend to be horizontal.

6.6 Multiple boxplots

The ordering of the areas in figure 6.4 suggested the hypothesis that the unemployment rate in a local labour market might be a function of which

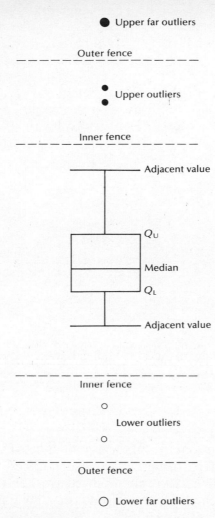

Figure 6.7 Anatomy of a boxplot

region it is in. We can now proceed to display unemployment in each region separately, to investigate this.

Boxplots, laid out side by side, as shown in figure 6.9, permit comparisons to be made with ease. The figure has been drawn according to the rule of thumb, not using any local knowledge or judgement to decide whether a point should be treated as an outlier. The order in which the regions are drawn is not fixed, since region is measured on a nominal scale; in the absence of any other rationale, it is helpful to order batches by their medians. The boxplot for all the areas is also included, for comparison.

The principal features of unemployment in each region now stand out clearly. The standard four features of each region's distribution can now be compared:

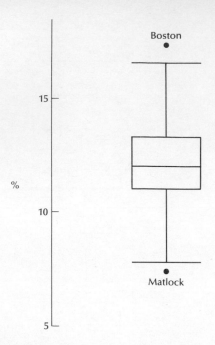

Figure 6.8 Unemployment in the East Midlands in May 1985: boxplot
Source: data in figures 6.5 and 6.6

The level The median unemployment rate varies from 8.6 per cent in the South East to 16.3 per cent in Wales. The original hypothesis was therefore correct: one source of the variation in local area unemployment rates is a regional effect; if there was no such effect, the medians would all be roughly the same. An unemployed worker who travelled from region to region in search of work would certainly find different average levels of unemployment prevailing.

The spread The lowest local unemployment rate in any region (Winchester) is above 4 per cent and the highest (Dingwall) over 26 per cent. There is some regional variation in spread; the East Midlands has a smaller midspread than other areas, and the North has a larger mid-spread. The differences, however, are not very marked (it is not unusual to find batches of data where the midspread of one batch is ten times the midspread of another). Importantly, there is no systematic evidence that the spread increases as the median increases, although this could be checked by plotting midspreads against medians. We should always watch out for such a pattern, as it usually suggests that looking at the data on a transformed scale might be better, as we shall see in chapter 11.

The shape The datasets seem about as symmetrical as batches of data ever are. If we had looked at unemployment in an earlier period, however, we might have found the batches had longer upper tails than

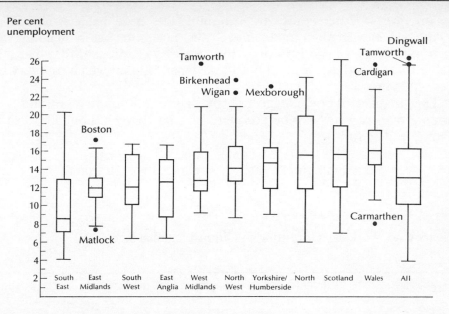

Figure 6.9 Local unemployment within regions in May 1985: multiple boxplots
Source: data in TOWNS columns 5 and 7

lower tails, because unemployment overall was lower; the floor of zero unemployment would prevent the possibility of a long lower tail at a time when median unemployment was lower.

Outliers   Our attention is then drawn to several towns which do not fit the pattern of unemployment exhibited in the rest of the data. Many of those that have unusually high unemployment rates for their region appear to be one-industry towns in which there have been major redundancies; perhaps degree of employment mix is another variable which predicts how an area fares during recession. The regional outliers are generally not the same as the outliers in the whole batch; Dingwall, for example, appears to be an outlier when viewed in the context of the country as a whole, but is seen to be almost normal in the context of Scotland's unemployment rate.

6.7 Decomposing the variation in unemployment rates

The boxplot of unemployment rates in all local areas in Britain (figure 6.9) is longer than the plots for any of the individual regions. This indicates that the variation in unemployment rates in the country as a whole could be broken down into two components: between region variation and within region variation.

You will remember the DFR equation:

$$\text{Data} = \text{Fit} + \text{Residual}$$

In previous chapters only single number fits have been discussed; in chapter 1 the median male wage was fitted to family income, for example. Now we can introduce the idea of a **conditional fit**, where the value to be fitted is not fixed but itself depends upon which category the case falls in.

The implicit model suggested by figure 6.9 is that variation in unemployment rates can be accounted for partly by region. This can be formalized as follows:

$$\text{Unemployment rate} = \text{Regional fit} + \text{Residual}$$

Figure 6.10 Worksheet for fitting conditional regional medians

Area	Region	Data	Fit (regional) (median)	Residual
Wolverhampton	West Midlands	17.3	12.9	4.4
Nottingham	East Midlands	13.2	12.0	1.2
Braintree	South East	11.1	8.6	2.5
Harlow	South East	9.5	8.6	0.9
Reigate	South East	6.2	8.6	−2.4
Cwmbran	Wales	14.8	16.3	−1.5
Birkenhead	North West	24.0	14.3	9.7
Oldham	North West	14.3	14.3	0.0
Aberdeen	Scotland	7.3	15.9	−8.6
Truro	South West	13.2	12.1	1.1
Boston	East Midlands	17.4	12.0	5.4
Chesterfield	East Midlands	13.6	12.0	1.6
Dundee	Scotland	15.9	15.9	0.0
Dover	South East	9.4	8.6	0.8
Oban	Scotland	15.9	15.9	0.0
Goole	Yorkshire/Humberside	16.1	14.9	1.2
Isle of Wight	South East	14.4	8.6	5.8
Loughborough	East Midlands	7.8	12.0	−4.2
Ffestiniog	Wales	15.8	16.3	−0.5
Nelson and Colne	North West	13.4	14.3	−0.9
Stamford	East Midlands	12.8	12.0	0.8
Swindon	South West	10.6	12.1	−1.5
Stirling	Scotland	13.4	15.9	−2.5
Workington	North	15.8	15.8	0.0
Gosport	South East	13.1	8.6	4.5
Peterlee	North	18.9	15.8	3.1
Worthing	South East	9.6	8.6	1.0

Source: sample as figure 6.3, drawn from dataset TOWNS

This model says that part of the reason for variation in all the local areas in the country stems from the fact that they are in different regions, and part stems from other factors unconnected with region. The unemployment rate in Wolverhampton, for example (17.3 per cent), can be decomposed into a typical rate for the West Midlands (12.9 per cent) and a residual of +4.4 per cent.

The regional medians could themselves be decomposed into two parts: a grand median and a regional effect, which indicates how far the median rate in a particular region deviates from the grand median:

Unemployment rate = Grand median + Regional effect + Residual

The median unemployment rate in the whole of Great Britain was 13.4 per cent, so the West Midlands regional median of 12.9 per cent was 0.5 per cent lower. The unemployment rate in Wolverhampton can therefore also be decomposed as $13.4 - 0.5 + 4.4$, or 17.3 per cent as before.

An **effect** is here calculated as the difference between a conditional fit and the grand median. It is the value that is entered on the arrows in causal path models. If we ask 'What is the effect of region on local unemployment rates?', ten answers would have to be given, one for each region.

To quantify how much of the variation in unemployment rates is accounted for by region, the regional median is fitted to each value, residuals from the fit are calculated, and the variation in the residuals is compared with the original variation. Figure 6.10 shows a worksheet where this is done for the sample of local areas. The residuals from the regional fit show the variation in unemployment rates not accounted for by region; Aberdeen, for example, has a very low unemployment rate for Scotland.

The residuals can be displayed in the usual manner (figure 6.11). Whereas the midspread in the original sample batch was 5.0, the residual midspread is now only 2.7, little more than half its original size. This corresponds with the feature observable in figure 6.9 that the variation in all areas taken together is substantially larger than that in the regions taken separately. This reduction in midspread is an indicator of the strength of the effect of the explanatory variable on the response variable; exercise 6.1 invites you to reflect on how such a measure might be bounded.

6.8 Conclusion

This chapter had three methodological aims. First, a useful graphical device known as the boxplot was introduced, which facilitated focused comparison. Secondly, a rigorous definition of an unusual data point was

Figure 6.11 Displaying residuals from conditional regional fit

leaf unit = 0.1%
−4 2 represents −4.2%

1	LO	−8.6			
2	−4	2			
	−3				
4	−2	54			
6	−1	55	M 14.0		0.0
10	−0	9500	Q 7.5	−0.7	2.0 dQ 2.7
(5)	0	00889	X 1.0	−8.6	9.7
12	1	01226			
7	2	5			
6	3	1			
5	4	45			
3	5	48			
1	HI	9.7			

Source: data in final column of figure 6.10.

given; a rule of thumb for identifying unusual values relative to the midspread in the main body of the data was advanced.

The third goal was to show how effects are calculated when the response variable is measured on an interval scale and the explanatory variable on a nominal scale. This is done by decomposing each data value into a grand median, a category effect and a residual; the larger the effects (the explained component), the smaller the residuals (the unexplained component). The idea of analysing variation in a single batch of data into two components, a fitted and an unexplained component, is fundamental to data analysis. (There is an analogous technique, known as **analysis of variance**, which decomposes the sum of the squared distances of each data value from the grand mean.)

The substantive theme of the chapter was the rate of unemployment in Britain. No labour market in 1985 had anything approaching full employment. There was, however, a wide variation in rates, both between and within regions; those who seek to blame the unemployed's immobility for their condition may have felt that this vindicated their views. But, as usual, policy conclusions cannot be directly read off from the data. It would be important to know other basic facts about Winchester – the number of unfilled vacancies and the type of skills required, and the type and cost of available housing – before it would be worthwhile for the unemployed of Dingwall, Tamworth and Boston to cycle there when the unemployment statistics were announced.

Exercises

6.1 The midspread of the sample of unemployment rates drawn from all regions was 5.0 per cent (figure 6.4). If region had no effect on unemployment, what would you expect the residual midspread to be once the regional median was fitted? At the other extreme, what would the residual variation be if an area's unemployment level could be predicted perfectly from its region?

6.2 The Registrar-General's social class scheme claims to group occupations on the basis of their general standing in the community. Goldthorpe and Hope (1974) asked a random sample of the population to rank various occupations in terms of their social standing; from their responses, they constructed a scale of occupations ranging from 17 (lowest social standing) to 82 (highest social standing). The scores of some occupations are shown below, grouped under the appropriate social class as in the 1971 Census.

Class I (higher professional and managerial)		*Class II* (lower professional and managerial)	
Chartered accountant	82	Film producer	66
Computer designer	70	Garage proprietor	56
Dentist*	74	Hedger and ditcher*	30
University teacher	76	Laboratory assistant	64
Vicar	62	Local union official	55
		Building society manager	52
		Personnel manager	66
		Riding instructor*	65
		Stockbroker*†	71

Class IIIN (routine non-manual)		*Class IIIM* (skilled manual)	
Audit clerk	39	Building site foreman	46
Betting shop owner	60	Clay-pit owner†	66
Bookshop assistant	34	Coal miner (face)	35
Butler	36	Machine shop foreman	48
Estate agent*‡	56	Head keeper in zoo	40
Head waiter	36	Knife grinder	33
Insurance agent	30	Jewellery engraver	39
Security manager†	67	Railway guard	27
Police constable	64	Swimming instructor	50
Shop security officer	47	Taxi owner	63
Supervisor in Post Office	56	Ticket inspector	42
Technical illustrator	63		

Class IV (semi-skilled manual)		*Class V* (unskilled manual)	
Car assembly worker	35	Dock labourer	28
Coal miner (surface)	32	Docker (own gang)‡	40
Dry cleaner*†	53	Industrial cleaner	52
Fisherman	43	Ticket collector	18
Jobbing gardener	17	Window cleaner	30
Press photographer	32		
Scrap metal dealer†	55		
Slate maker†	61		
Traffic warden	27		

* Self-employed
† Manager or owner of large firm
‡ Manager or owner of small firm

Select two of the classes and display the information as parallel boxplots. What do you learn about the validity of the Registrar-General's social classes as a measure of social standing in the community?

6.3 The file TOWNS contains information about how fast employment has grown or declined in each of the local areas in two separate periods; 1971–78 in column 3 and 1978–81 in column 4. (Growth in unemployment is not just the inverse of decline in employment, since the size of the labour force also alters significantly over time.) Display the regional variation in growth rates in these two periods. The Minitab instruction is BOXPLOT.

Appendix: sources of unemployment statistics

The poor may have been with us always, but the unemployed have not. The concept of unemployment seems to have entered the vocabulary at about the same time as insurance schemes made it possible for those without work to claim benefit. Before then people could not afford the luxury of an unemployed identity; many of them would have been referred to as 'casual labourers'. It therefore seems natural to turn to the benefit system for an estimate of how many people are unemployed.

Until October 1982, monthly counts were made of unemployed persons who were registered as 'seeking employment'. Unemployed people had two motivations for registering: to try to find work and to gain entitlement to unemployment benefit. Staff at employment offices or careers offices accepted people on the register if they were capable of and available for work, whether they were entitled to unemployment benefit or not; they denied registration to those who refused an offer of suitable employment without good cause. The numbers registered were tallied clerically in each employment office, and aggregate statistics were published monthly by the Department of Employment.

As a result of a review of these procedures, however, registration became voluntary in October 1982, and the count of those registered became incomplete as an estimate of the numbers unemployed. The basis of the statistics therefore changed to those receiving at least one of three types of benefit available to the unemployed: unemployment benefit, which is paid to everyone with relevant insurance contributions as of right; supplementary benefit, which unemployed people may be entitled to claim if they can show they need it; and credits of National Insurance contributions. There are some groups who claim benefit but who are not included when unemployed claimants are counted, such as the temporarily stopped and adult students seeking temporary work. Those seeking part-time work may be undercounted because their entitlement to sup-plementary benefit may be affected if the hours for which they are available restricts their chances of finding a job.

The payment of benefits to most claimants is handled by computer, which makes the process of compiling the statistics much simpler and cheaper. The stock statistics are based on a count of the total claiming benefit on a fixed day, usually the second Thursday, in every month. They are broken down in the published statistics by region and area, as in this chapter, and also by age, sex and duration of unemployment; unfortunately, the occupation and industry of the unemployed person's last job is no longer recorded. But some more sophisticated analyses have become possible; a more detailed tally of the numbers flowing on to and off the stock of claimants can now regularly be made, and a cohort sample is being followed through to see how often the same people appear on the books over time.

How well does the number of claimants represent the theoretical idea of the extent of the labour force who would work if work was available?

Some have argued that it contains false inclusions: the 'voluntary unemployed' (who are paid more on the dole than they would be in work); older people who have effectively retired but who claim National Insurance credits until they become eligible for pensions, the 'fraudulently unemployed', the subject of so much media attention, the 'frictionally unemployed' who are between jobs (usually recognized by being very short-term unemployed), and even the 'unemployable', a cruel categorization which would enable the very long-term unemployed to be deleted from the list simply by virtue of their length of unemployment. Others have argued that it makes false exclusions: all those who would like to work but who are not entitled to benefit, and those who do not claim the benefits to which they are entitled.

While there will continue to be debate about precisely which groups should be counted in definitions of unemployment for different purposes (Department of Employment 1986a), we can get important insight into the number of people who would have been in work if jobs had been available by turning to survey evidence, to the 1985 Labour Force Survey in particular. In this large annual survey, involving one in every 350 households in the United Kingdom, all respondents without jobs are asked whether they would like a job, whether they are currently available for work, and whether they have looked for work in the last week and the last month. Those who have not looked for work are asked why not.

One common survey-based definition of the unemployed, used by the

Organization for Economic Cooperation and Development following the guidelines of the the International Labour Organization, includes those who were available for work and had looked for work in the last four weeks. This is quite a stringent indicator of labour surplus; it excludes those in better times who might have made themselves available for work (rather than studying or keeping house) or who might have felt it worthwhile to look for work. It is a useful comparative baseline, however. Figure 6.12 compares estimates of the number who would be counted as unemployed by that definition with the claimant count.

Figure 6.12 Alternative definitions of the unemployed: estimates from Labour Force Survey in spring 1985

	All	Men	Women
		(thousands)†	
'Unemployed' by survey criteria*	2970	1790	1180
of whom:			
Claiming benefits	2140	1600	540
Not claiming benefits	830	180	640
Claimant count	3130	2170	960
of whom:			
'Unemployed' by survey criteria*	2130	1600	530
Not 'unemployed' by survey criteria	800	460	340
Worked during last week	200	110	90

Source: Department of Employment 1986d: 419

* Unemployed by survey criteria are those who were available for work in the next fortnight and who had sought work in last four weeks.

† These figures are estimated to the nearest 10,000, and totals will therefore not always tally.

The number of people who were not picked up in the claimant count in spring 1985 but who were available for and had sought work in the last month is 830,000. However, this cannot simply be added to the count of claimants, since there were claimants who on these survey criteria were not unemployed; 800,000 said they either had not looked for work in the last four weeks or had looked but were not available for work. Another 200,000 claimants had done some paid work in the survey reference week. Since two-thirds of them were not looking for work, some feel it is correct to exclude them from the unemployed count. On the other hand, since only a very limited amount of work can be done while benefit is being claimed (and since it is unlikely that much illegal work will be reported to government interviewers) this last group should arguably be included the with unemployed. They are shown separately to allow other calculations. On this latter basis, we may say that the count has 830,000 false exclusions and 800,000 false inclusions, a net undercount of 30,000.

There are additions we might wish to make to this, however. From the same survey evidence, it is clear that there were also a large number of people without jobs who said that they would like a job and were ready to start work within two weeks if one was available, but who did not count in the survey definition of unemployed because they had not looked for work recently. There were an estimated 916,000 such people in spring 1985, three-quarters of whom were women. One way of judging how committed they might in reality be to the labour market is to subdivide them by their reason for not looking for work in the last week, as shown in figure 6.13. It is futile to argue about how many of these individuals should be counted as 'truly unemployed'; we cannot know how many of them would actually take a job if one were offered to them.

Figure 6.13 Reasons for not looking for work in previous week, among those who would like work and are available for work, but had not looked in last four weeks

	All	Men	Women
		(thousands)†	
Looking after family/home	490	10	490
Retired from paid work	130	80	50
Believes no jobs available	90	30	60
Long-term sick	70	40	30
Students	60	30	30
Other	80	20	60
All	916	204	712

† These figures are estimated to nearest 10,000, and totals will therefore not always tally.

Source: Estimates based on spring 1985 Labour Force Survey; kindly supplied by the Department of Employment

Neither the claimant count nor the survey estimates of the numbers of people who would work if work were available take account of whether the individual in question wants a full-time or a part-time job. For certain purposes we might wish to refine these estimates into demand for full-time equivalent jobs, but we should also then have to add to these calculations the number of employed people who say they would like to be working more hours per week than they are working at present.

Finally, we might question whether it is right to exclude those on special government training or employment schemes from the count of the unemployed. There were 587,000 such people in spring 1985. People on such schemes cannot be treated like others in full-time higher education, since there is evidence that many of them would leave if they could get any kind of job. Some argue that the schemes do not provide real jobs, and that, if they were not available, most people on them would be unemployed, while others believe that the schemes have allowed employers to remove real jobs. The Department of Employment estimates that 425,000 of them would have been claimants in spring 1985 if they were not on such schemes (DE Press Notice July 1985). Estimates of youth unemployment vary widely depending on whether young people on schemes are included or omitted from either the numerator or denominator of the unemployment rate (Raffe 1985).

The change in the numbers unemployed over time is of great political significance, as figure 6.1 showed. Between summer 1979 and summer 1986, many changes were made either to the benefit system or in counting the unemployed, almost all of which, critics claim, kept the monthly claimant count down (Unemployment Unit 1986). However, the criticism is rejected as exaggerated by the Department of Employment, and they have produced a consistent series of the claimant count back to 1971 adjusted for the effect of these changes (1985).

7   Percentage Tables

7.1 Introduction

In the previous chapter, we looked at the relationship between two variables when the response variable was measured on an interval scale (unemployment rate) and the explanatory variable on a nominal scale (region). The strategy used to obtain effects was to decompose individual values; local unemployment rates were broken into three parts, a national average, a typical regional effect or deviation from the national average, and a residual amount or deviation from the regional average.

In this chapter and the next we shall consider ways of dealing with the relationship between two variables when both of them may only be measured at the nominal level. There is no way in which the individual data can be decomposed into a fitted value and a residual value; if the number 4 is used to denote attendance at grammar school, for example, any individual either is or is not coded 4. The strategy for nominal level variables therefore has to be different, and involves looking at groups of cases. We can calculate the chances of going to grammar school for a group of people, for example, and attempt to decompose this into chances conditional upon being from a working class family, a middle class family and so on.

There has been some controversy in recent years about the techniques of analysis best suited to this type of data; inferential techniques based on log-linear models have become very fashionable, but humble old percentages survive because of their intuitive intelligibility. In this chapter we shall take a close look at percentage tables, their construction and interpretation. In the next we shall look at how percentages may be used to summarize the effect of one variable upon another, and at alternative summaries based on the concept of odds. The two chapters should be read together sometime after chapter 3 and before chapter 12.

The relationship which forms the subject matter of these two chapters is that between the type of school a child attends and the child's class background. School type is a nominal level variable; schools in Britain may be categorized into several different types, and, even though these categories may be ranked in terms of some property such as social status, they have no inherent ordinal properties suitable for all purposes. Social class is more debatable. If one views it as a classification of people according to their conditions of employment (the method of classification used here), then it should arguably be treated as a nominal scale variable. However, many view these class divisions as ranked divisions on a dimension of social status, and treat class as measured on an ordinal scale. Since the techniques of analysis to be discussed in these two chapters are suitable for both nominal and ordinal variables, the distinction is not important.

7.2 Secondary education in England and Wales

Most adults in Britain attended state schools when they were young. Education in 'elementary schools' became compulsory after the passing of the 1870 Education Act. Many stayed in these schools beyond the age of 11, and in 1921 staying on until 14 became compulsory. In 1902 a national system of state secondary schools was established. These were grammar schools, and entry to them was selective, based on a competitive examination for one of the free places, paid for by the local authority. Demand from students who were willing and able to take up such places always outstripped supply, and calls for the expansion of state secondary education for all were heard both before and during the Second World War.

The Education Act of 1944 was designed to meet these demands. It instituted two main reforms. First, it made secondary education compulsory for all. Secondly, it established a 'tripartite system' in which three different types of school, supposedly of equal value, would meet the needs of different children. The grammar schools would be expanded for children with academic aptitudes, the secondary modern schools were to give a more general education for life, and the technical schools recruited children who had shown particular practical skills to prepare them for jobs in industry.

The plan was that placement in one of these schools would be based purely on the child's aptitudes and the parents' wishes. However, even though the supply of grammar school places was expanded, there were never enough to meet the demand; grammar school places were therefore still effectively rationed after 1944 by an examination taken at age eleven.

There had always been those who advocated a more comprehensive system of secondary education; in 1951, the Labour Party committed itself to this philosophy. When it came to power in 1964, it set about a further reorganization of secondary education, replacing the tripartite system with comprehensive schools to which all children would go.

About 6 per cent of the population have in the past been educated outside the state system, thus preventing the state schools ever being truly comprehensive by taking all children. Private schooling in Britain takes place in obtusely termed 'public schools'. These split into approximately two equal halves: those where the Head Master is a member of a symbolically significant club known as the Head Masters' Conference (HMC), and the rest. In the past some children were also educated in direct grant schools, private foundations which used to receive a grant from central government in return for taking some scholarship entrants.

7.3 Proportions, percentages and probabilities

How is information about the distribution of school backgrounds in the population to be presented? Bar charts were introduced in chapter 1 as a way of displaying the distribution of a nominal scale variable; the height or length of the bar was used to represent the number of cases in a category, thus making the relative size of categories clear. The same effect can be achieved numerically by means of proportions or percentages; to express a variable in proportional terms, the number in each category is divided by the total number of cases N. Percentages are proportions multiplied by 100.

Figure 7.1 shows the proportions of men in 1972 who had attended various different types of school; the survey from which the data comes will be described shortly. Some people in the sample had received no education at genuinely secondary schools, but, if they stayed on at a

Figure 7.1 Educational background of men aged 20–59 in 1972

	Number of cases	Proportion	Percentage
Secondary modern	5083	0.634	63.4
Comprehensive	119	0.015	1.5
Technical	937	0.117	11.7
Grammar	1355	0.169	16.9
Direct grant	132	0.016	1.6
Private: non-HMC	197	0.024	2.4
Private: HMC	191	0.024	2.4
Total	8014	1.000	100.0

Source: Halsey et al. (1980: table 4.4)

non-selective elementary school beyond the age of 11, they were coded with those attending comprehensive schools (a decision we shall question below).

Since proportions and percentages can only be converted back to raw frequencies if we know the total number of cases (the **base** *N*), the reader should always be given at least this figure. A spurious air of scientific precision can be created by presenting results in proportional terms, perhaps even correct to several decimal places, when the total sample size is very small. It is good practice to draw the reader's attention to proportions based on a sample of less than 50, and not to calculate them at all on a sample of less than 20.

Proportions and percentages are **bounded numbers**, in that they have a floor of zero, below which they cannot go, and a ceiling of 1.0 and 100 respectively. (People do sometimes talk of '300 per cent', but this is just a shorthand way of saying that one value is three times another; percentages over 100 are called 'relatives' in this book.) Distributions which are effectively bounded at the bottom by the zero point, such as income, tend to straggle up. When numbers are bounded at the top and the bottom, as percentages are, this can cause problems in an analysis based on very small or large percentages, which may need to be taken into account.

Proportions can be used descriptively as in figure 7.1 to represent the relative size of different subgroups in a population. But they can also be thought of as probabilities; we can, for example, say that the probability of a man aged between 20 and 59 in 1972 having attended a secondary modern school was 0.634, and the probability of his being from the working class was 4470/8014 or 0.558 (figure 7.5). Probabilities can, under certain conditions, be multiplied together; if class background was unrelated to the type of school one attended, then the probability of both being working class and having attended a secondary modern would be 0.634 × 0.558, or 0.354. (The numerically trivial difference between proportions and percentages becomes important in this respect; percentages must be divided by 100 after they are multiplied together.)

Probabilities are not the only way of giving numerical expression to the idea of chance. As well as saying that there is a 0.67 probability that something will happen, we could say that the odds of it happening are 2 to 1. In the first case, the number of cases in one category is divided by the total, in the second it is divided by the number of cases not in the category; if proportions are denoted p, then odds are $p/(1-p)$. We shall take up the idea of odds in the next chapter.

7.4 Educational mobility

There are two views of the function of education. Reformers from John Stuart Mill to the present day have viewed it as a mechanism capable of promoting social equality; if there was equal access to education, they argue, individuals would be able to move out of the social class in which they were born. Others have been less sanguine, viewing education as a mechanism for transmitting social inequalities rather than reducing them.

In a major contribution to educational sociology, Halsey et al. (1980) analysed the educational patterns of respondents to the Oxford Mobility Survey. This was a survey of men aged 20 and above in England and Wales, conducted in 1972 by researchers at Nuffield College, Oxford. There were 10,309 men in the original sample, which makes it one of the largest academic social surveys ever undertaken in Britain. Details of the sampling procedure are given in Goldthorpe and Llewellyn (1980).

The decision to restrict the respondents to men was taken partly because one purpose of the study was to replicate earlier mobility studies. Halsey et al. (1980:20) explain:

> Given the unavoidable historical character of mobility studies, male occupations were the major articulation between on the one hand nuclear families and on the other the class and status structure of Britain in the period with which we are concerned.

The authors admit that if the survey had been designed purely to look at educational experiences, the omission of women would have been unjustifiable.

The fieldwork was conducted in the early summer of 1972, which means that there were very few men in the sample who had attended comprehensive schools. The focus of the study was therefore restricted to an evaluation of the effect of the 1944 Education Act. Those aged 60 or more, and those not resident in England or Wales when they were 14, were excluded from the analysis in order to be able to compare the educational system in two distinct periods: as it functioned between the two World Wars, and after the Act was passed.

One of the important variables used in the analysis was the class of the respondent and that of his father. The research team felt that the social class scheme of the Registrar-General was not constructed sufficiently rigorously for use in a mobility study (as you discovered in exercise 6.2), so they constructed their own system; the scheme is described fully by Halsey et al. (1980: 17–18).

The original scheme had eight categories, but for much of the data analysis these were grouped into three. Groups I and II form the service class (13 per cent of respondents in 1972) – the professionals, administrators, officials and managers who run the capitalist economy on behalf of, servicing, the corporate authorities. Groups VI, VII and VIII comprise the working class (56 per cent in 1972) – manual workers, whether skilled or unskilled, industrial or agricultural. The remaining three groups together form the intermediate class (31 per cent in 1972) – routine non-manual workers, small proprietors, lower-grade technicians and foremen.

If there were plenty of able children in all social classes (a reasonable assumption), if parental ambitions were the same in all classes (a more questionable assumption), and if access to education was open, then similar proportions of children from each social class would appear in the high status education types. If, on the other hand, education serves to reproduce the patterns of inequality of the previous generation, the children from the higher social classes would be disproportionately represented in higher status schools. We shall investigate these rival hypotheses by looking at the relationship between class of father and the secondary schooling of the son; primary education is of less interest since it predominantly takes place in the state sector, even among the sons and daughters of the service class.

7.5 Contingency tables

The distribution of a single variable can, as we saw in chapter 1, be represented graphically as a bar chart. The univariate distribution of the class backgrounds and educational backgrounds of the respondents to the 1972 survey is shown in figure 7.2.

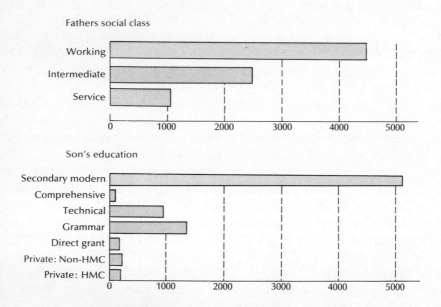

Figure 7.2 Background of respondents in 1972
Source: Halsey et al. (1980: table 4.4)

These two distributions must be interpreted with care. The class distribution, for example, tells us about the jobs performed by the fathers of men who were between 20 and 59 in 1972 when the sons were aged 14. It does not strictly represent the occupational structure at any fixed point in the past, since the respondents are all of different ages. It is not even a simple average of past occupational distributions, since classes have different fertility and mortality rates: current respondents overrepresent those classes who, a generation ago, were relatively more fertile. Similarly, the educational distribution does not represent proportions actually attending such schools at any one point in time.

These two distributions, then, describe two separate features of a sample of men in 1972. By looking at both the bar chart of school types and the bar chart of class background, however, nothing can be inferred about the relationship between the two. For that purpose, we need some kind of three-dimensional bar chart, showing the joint distribution of the two variables, as shown in figure 7.3.

A **contingency table** does numerically what the three-dimensional bar chart does graphically. The *Concise Oxford Dictionary* defines contingent as 'true only under existing or specified conditions'; a contingency

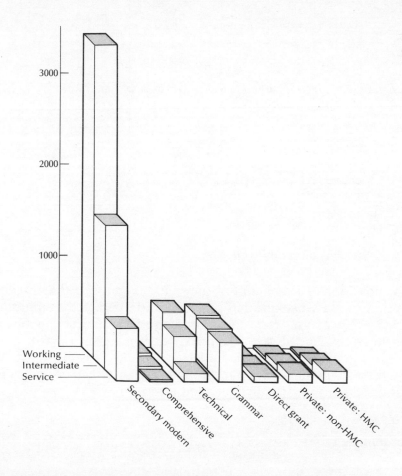

Figure 7.3 Three-dimensional bar chart: school type by class background
Source: Halsey et al. (1980: table 4.4)

table shows the distribution of each variable conditional upon each category of the other. The categories of one of the variables form the **rows**, and the categories of the other variable form the **columns**. Each individual case is then tallied in the appropriate pigeonhole depending on its value on both variables. The pigeonholes are given the more scientific name **cells**, and the number of cases in each cell is called the **cell frequency**. Each row and column can have a total presented at the right-hand end and at the bottom respectively; these are called the **marginals**, and the univariate distributions can be obtained from the **marginal distributions**. Figure 7.4 shows a schematic contingency table with four rows and four columns (a four by four table).

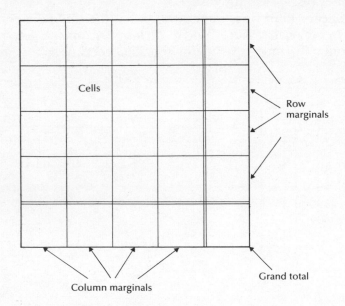

Figure 7.4 Anatomy of a contingency table

Let us now look at a real contingency table. Figure 7.5 shows the joint distribution of class background and education depicted graphically in figure 7.3. The contingency table in figure 7.5 depicts the bivariate relationship between the two variables, but it is hard to grasp; gaze as you will, it is extremely difficult to decide, on the basis of raw numbers such as these, whether class background has an effect on educational destination. Something further is called for.

7.6 Percentage tables

The commonest way to make contingency tables readable is to cast them in percentage form. There are three different ways in which this can be done, as shown in the three panels of figure 7.6.

Figure 7.5 School type by class background: frequencies

Son's school	Father's class			
	Service class	Intermediate class	Working class	Total
Secondary modern	285	1459	3339	5083
Comprehensive	16	32	71	119
Technical	109	319	509	937
Grammar	376	484	495	1355
Direct grant	66	44	22	132
Private: non-HMC	94	81	22	197
Private: HMC	126	53	12	191
Total	1072	2472	4470	8014

Source: reconstructed from Halsey et al. (1980: table 4.4)

The first table, shown in panel (a) of figure 7.6, was constructed by dividing each cell frequency by the grand total; we now know that the 3339 respondents with working class fathers who attended secondary modern schools represented 42 per cent of the total population aged between 20 and 59 in 1972. But the table as a whole is scarcely more readable than the raw frequencies were, because there is nothing we can compare this 42 per cent with. For this reason, total percentage tables are not often constructed.

Figure 7.6 School type by class background

(a) Total percentages

Son's school	Father's class			
	Service class	Intermediate class	Working class	Total
Secondary modern	3.6	18.2	41.7	53.4
Comprehensive	0.2	0.4	0.9	1.5
Technical	1.4	4.0	6.4	11.7
Grammar	4.7	6.0	6.2	16.9
Direct grant	0.8	0.5	0.3	1.6
Private: non-HMC	1.2	1.0	0.3	2.4
Private: HMC	1.6	0.7	0.1	2.4
Total	13.4	30.8	55.9	100.0 (N=8014)

(b) Column percentages (outflow)

Son's school	Father's class		
	Service class	Intermediate class	Working class
Secondary modern	26.6	59.0	74.7
Comprehensive	1.5	1.3	1.6
Technical	10.2	12.9	11.4
Grammar	35.1	19.6	11.1
Direct grant	6.2	1.8	0.5
Private: non-HMC	8.8	3.3	0.5
Private: HMC	11.8	2.1	0.3
Total	100.0	100.0	100.0
	(N=1072)	(N=2472)	(N=4470)

(c) Row percentages (inflow)

Son's school	Father's class			
	Service class	Intermediate class	Working class	Total
Secondary modern	5.6	28.7	65.7	100.0 (N=5083)
Comprehensive	13.4	26.9	59.7	100.0 (N=119)
Technical	11.6	34.0	54.3	100.0 (N=937)
Grammar	27.8	35.7	36.5	100.0 (N=1355)
Direct grant	50.0	33.3	16.7	100.0 (N=132)
Private: non-HMC	47.7	41.1	11.2	100.0 (N=197)
Private: HMC	66.0	27.7	6.3	100.0 (N=191)

Source: As figure 7.5

Panel (b) of figure 7.6 shows the percentage of people within each class who went to each type of school; it was constructed by dividing each cell frequency by its appropriate column total. The first column, for example, shows what happened to children of the service class; of the 1072 respondents in this category, 285, or 27 per cent of them, went to secondary modern schools, 1 per cent went to comprehensives, 10 per cent went to technical schools and so on. The second and third columns show in a comparable form what happened to children of the intermediate and working classes, regardless of the fact that there were many more of them.

Tables that are constructed by percentaging the columns are usually read across the rows (reading down the columns would probably only confirm two things we already know: the broad profile of the marginal distribution and the fact that the percentages sum to 100). Reading across the first row of panel (b), we see that 27 per cent of service class children went to secondary modern schools, whereas 59 per cent of intermediate class children did and 75 per cent of working class children did. Similarly, looking at the last row, 12 per cent of service class children went to HMC schools, 2 per cent of intermediate class children did, and only a fraction of a per cent of working class children did. By making comparisons along the rows, and by interpreting percentages as probabilities, we can see that people from different class backgrounds had very different chances of getting to particular types of school.

Mobility analysts call tables such as that in panel (b) 'outflow mobility tables', since they show where people from the same origins go to. The outflow table in panel (b) suggests that there was no equality of access to selective schools in the period as a whole; one cannot, of course, tell whether the situation improved significantly after the passing of the 1944 Education Act, since all the age groups have been added together in this table; the trends in the relationship will be examined later.

It is also possible to tell the story in a rather different way, and look at where people who ended up in the same place came from: the 'inflow table'. This is shown in panel (c) of figure 7.6. Inflow tables describe the class composition of each of the school types. Of the 5083 people who attended secondary modern schools, 6 per cent came from the service class, 29 per cent from the intermediate class and 66 per cent from the working class. Tables that have been constructed by percentaging the rows are usually read down the columns. Looking at the last column, we can see that the proportion of working class children in various school types ranges from 66 per cent in secondary moderns to 6 per cent in HMC schools.

The inflow and outflow tables focus attention on the data in rather different ways, and the researcher would have to be clear about what questions were being addressed in the analysis. Consider the critical case for the 1944 education reformers: the working class boys who got to grammar school. The inflow figures tell us that working class boys were the largest single group (the **plurality**, although not the majority) at grammar school; the character and ethos of grammar schools must have been affected by this. However, the outflow figures tell us that this only represented a ninth of all working class boys; as a group, they did not have a very big chance of getting to such a school.

Running the percentages the other way round can cast a table in a different light, and there are many considerations that might be taken into account before deciding which percentages to construct; exercise 7.2 illustrates this point more fully. There is, however, a firm rule when we have a causal hypothesis about the relationship between the two variables; tables of the outflow variety are better suited for exploring causal ideas. This will be fully discussed in the next chapter.

7.7 Collapsing categories

To examine trends in the relationship between class background and access to education, the table in figure 7.5 would have to be further subdivided by age groups. We would, however, soon run into the case base problem. Even in this sample of over eight thousand people, only twelve of them were working class boys who had attended HMC schools. If we tried to subdivide each category into different age groups, the cell frequencies would be very small and, in some cases, zero. Furthermore, even if we had enough cases, splitting a seven by three table into several age groups would make it very fussy and complicated to follow. It would be better if we could distil the story line first.

Cutting down the number of categories would reduce the complexity of the table considerably. The authors, you will notice, have already collapsed the social class groupings into three. Can something similar be done with the school types?

There are several factors to consider when deciding how to **collapse** the number of categories in a variable. Most importantly, a substantive judgement must be made that categories are similar. Obviously, if a variable is ordinal, it only makes sense to collapse adjacent categories. With a nominal variable like school type, the HMC and non-HMC schools could be grouped into a category representing the private sector, and secondary moderns and comprehensives as the non-selective state sector (non-selective in the sense that they will admit anybody who wishes to go to them). The direct grant schools, a small group, are more ambiguous; an argument could be made for grouping them with either private schools, or with state selective schools. Or we could just group all the selective schools (which select on either financial or examination criteria), and compare them with all the non-selective.

Since one aim of collapsing tables is to produce cells with adequate frequencies for analysis, a second, more technical, consideration must be the size of the marginals. This is highly relevant here, since some of the school types have very few cases; however dissimilar we may feel direct grant schools and private schools to be, and however interesting it might be to compare them, it cannot be done if there are not enough cases. We have to make the best decisions we can; it is nearly always preferable to put together things that are not exactly the same than leave categories out completely.

A third consideration is to ensure that we do not obscure the relationship between the variable whose categories we wish to reduce and another important variable. To take an extreme example, we would not want to combine secondary modern schools, which working class boys had an above average chance of attending, with HMC schools, which they had a below average chance of attending; any differences between working class and service class boys in their likelihood of attending this joint category would be severely attenuated. We would therefore be advised to inspect the bivariate percentage table as well as the marginals before deciding how to form the categories. For this reason, it is best to plan for more rather than fewer categories when collecting the data; they can then be collapsed on the basis of their relationship with other variables.

In order to collapse the number of columns in a table of row percentages such as that shown in panel (b) of figure 7.6, the raw frequencies must be reworked. The result of reducing the school types to three – the elite (private and direct grant) sector, state selective (grammar and technical) schools and non-selective schools – is shown in figure 7.7.

Figure 7.7 Reducing school types to three categories

Son's school	Father's class		
	Service class	Intermediate class	Working class
Elite	26.7	7.2	1.3
State selective	45.2	32.5	22.5
Non-selective	28.1	60.3	76.3
Total	100.0	100.0	100.0
	(N=1072)	(N=2472)	(N=4470)

Source: collapsing categories of figure 7.5

If we wanted to go even further and form only two educational categories, the elite schools (which are broadly financially selective) could be grouped with the state selective schools into a 'selective education' category: they both are less likely to be attended by children lower down the social ladder. The resulting table is shown in figure 7.8. The percentages attending the non-selective schools have been bracketed; once a variable has been reduced from a **polytomy** (a variable with many categories) to a **dichotomy** (a variable with two categories), the reader can easily derive the shadow proportion in the second category by subtracting the first percentage from 100. Such shadow percentages are often dropped from show; it then becomes very important to label the table well, to explain exactly what each percentage is based on.

Collapsing is a one-way process; the reader will not be able to re-create the original categories. If decisions about grouping are controversial or involve significant loss of information, the full table should be given in an appendix. In this example, it might have been preferable to group respondents who had only attended an elementary school with those who had attended secondary moderns; this cannot be done on the published

Figure 7.8 Reducing school types to two categories

Son's school	Father's class		
	Service class	Intermediate class	Working class
Selective	71.9	39.7	23.7
(Non-selective)	(28.1)	(60.3)	(76.3)
Total	100.0	100.0	100.0
	(N=1072)	(N=2472)	(N=4470)

Source: collapsing categories of figure 7.5

data in Halsey et al.'s book, as they took the decision to group them with those who had attended comprehensives.

The story line in figure 7.8 can be boiled down to a very simple statement; 48 per cent more children from the service class attended selective schools than those from the working class (71.8 per cent – 23.7 per cent). The relationship in this streamlined form is now highly suitable for examining trends over time.

In order to examine how educational opportunities changed, different **birth cohorts** – people who were all born at around the same time – must be compared. Halsey et al. grouped respondents into four ten-year birth cohorts: 1913–22, 1923–32, 1933–42 and 1943–52. The oldest cohort entered school just after World War I; the last two had their secondary schooling after 1944 and some of the last group experienced comprehensive education.

The experience of these four groups is shown in figure 7.9. There is a table shadowing this one – showing the percentage of sons attending non-selective schools – which would make each cell total to 100; these figures have been omitted in the interests of clarity. Notice how superficially similar the layout is to the panels in figure 7.6. It is especially important to provide good titles and labels for tables where the percentages shown do not sum to 100; care should be taken when reading other people's tables that you understand the base upon which every percentage has been calculated.

What can be seen from figure 7.9? Since it is a table neither of row percentages nor of column percentages, comparisons must be made both across rows and down columns. Reading first across the rows, we can see that attendance at selective secondary schools rose until the post-war generation; the proportions attending then fell.

One way to read the columns would be to look at the difference between the proportion of the service class attending selective schools and the proportion of the working class attending them. These class

Figure 7.9 Trends in school attendance: percentages attending selective schools

Father's class	Year of birth			
	1913–22	1923–32	1933–42	1943–52
Service	69.9	76.8	79.4	66.4
	(N=186)	(N=211)	(N=243)	(N=435)
Intermediate	34.9	44.0	43.3	37.1
	(N=579)	(N=562)	(N=591)	(N=744)
Working	20.2	26.1	27.1	21.6
	(N=1116)	(N=1127)	(N=1060)	(N=1174)

Source: reconstructed from Halsey et al (1980: figures 4.4 and 4.9)

differences increased for the first three ten-year groups and then fell. On the face of it, we might conclude that this was because it was the post-war cohort who first felt the full impact of the 1944 Education Act. Actually, it is more complex than that, because there were simultaneous changes in birth cohort sizes and class structure; interested readers should follow the discussion up in Halsey et al.'s book (1980: 62–9).

7.8 Conclusion

In this chapter we have looked at the basic apparatus for constructing contingency tables and casting them into probabilistic or percentage terms; further aspects of layout and presentation in tables are discussed in the appendix. We have seen that the same frequencies can be expressed in many different ways, and that the data analyst must judge which is required to answer the question at hand.

It can be useful to collapse the number of categories in a variable. There are several factors to take into consideration when collapsing a variable: categories that are substantively similar, categories with small marginal frequencies, and categories which behave in a similar fashion with respect to a second variable are all good candidates for combining. It is usually bad practice to leave categories out completely when collapsing a variable. We have not yet shown how to quantify the effect of one variable upon another: that is the subject of the next chapter.

Exercises

7.1 The dataset CLASS contains information about the social class of respondents and the social class of their wives; codes 1 to 6 stand for the Registrar-General's classes I, II, IIIN, IIIM, IV and V respectively, and −1 denotes a missing value. The last ten cases in the file are as follows:

Class of husband	Class of wife
4	−1
4	3
4	3
3	3
3	6
3	−1
5	−1
2	5
4	2
2	−1

The cross-tabulation of husband's class by wife's class without these ten cases is shown below.

Husband's class	Wife's class						
	I	II	IIIN	IIIM	IV	V	Total
I	0	0	5	0	2	0	7
II	0	5	16	2	3	1	27
IIIN	0	1	16	3	7	1	28
IIIM	1	3	22	6	23	6	61
IV	0	2	3	1	5	3	14
V	0	0	1	0	2	0	3
Total	1	11	63	12	42	11	140

Missing cases = 50

Complete the table by tallying the last ten cases in the appropriate cells. What does the result tell you about the practice of using the class position of the husband to indicate the class position of the wife?

7.2 The following table is adapted from Fiegehan et al. (1977); the authors set out to investigate both the causes of poverty and the type of social policy that would best alleviate it. In order to discover whether household size had any effect on poverty, they re-analysed some data originally collected for the Family Expenditure Survey, and got a table something like that shown.

Number in household	In poverty	Not in poverty	Total
1	259	991	1250
2	148	2159	2307
3	45	1319	1364
4	21	1272	1293
5	16	573	589
6 or more	21	324	345
Total	510	6638	7148

Construct two tables running the percentages both ways and say how each table might contribute to understanding the relationship between poverty and household size. What advice would you give to a policy-maker about where to concentrate resources to alleviate poverty on the basis of these figures?

7.3 The dataset EDUCATE contains information on the social class of a sample of men aged twenty-three and the social class of their father when they were born. Construct both an inflow and an outflow mobility table and discuss the results. Since there are not many cases, you should collapse categories, using the CODE instruction, taking care with the missing values. The Minitab command TABLE takes subcommands, such as ROWPERCENTS and COLPERCENTS.

7.4 In exercise 7.1, ten cases were omitted from a file containing two hundred cases. Using Minitab, try leaving out a different random ten cases and see how different the table you obtain is.

Appendix: good table manners

Effective presentation is an art that conceals art. A well-designed table is easy to read, but takes effort, time and perhaps many drafts to perfect. Clear display of data not only aids the final consumer of the research but also helps the data analyst. It pays to take care over the presentation of your own working and calculations, however preliminary; this can help reveal patterns in the data, and can save time at a later stage. Here are some guidelines on how to construct a lucid table of numerical data; some of the hints, those about labelling for example, apply to all illustrations, whether tabular or pictorial. Comments about constructing a lucid picture of the data will be reserved for an appendix to chapter 10.

Reproducibility versus clarity

We are often trying to do two jobs at once when we present data: to tell a story while also allowing readers to check the conclusions by inspecting the data for themselves. These two jobs tend to work against one another, although the techniques of exploratory data analysis allow the researcher to pursue both at once to a much greater extent than more traditional techniques. For clarity we prefer visual displays, and we leave out extraneous detail to focus attention on the story line. To allow others to inspect and possibly reinterpret the results we want to leave as much of the original data as possible in numerical form. Think hard about which job any particular table is aiming to achieve. Dilemmas can often be solved by simplifying a table in the text and placing fuller details in an appendix, although in general it is desirable to place a table as near as possible to the text which discusses it. There are some elementary details which must always appear.

Labelling

The title of a table should be the first thing the reader looks at (although many readers of data often neglect this obvious first step). A clear title should summarize the contents; it should be as short as possible while at the same time making clear when the data was collected, the geographical unit covered, and the unit of analysis. You may find it helpful to number figures so that you can refer to them more pithily in the text. Other parts of a table also need clear, informative labels; the variables included in the rows and columns must be clearly identified. Don't be tempted to use mnemonics in computerese; you may have called household income 'HHINC' so many times you think everyone will know what it means – they won't.

Sources

The reader needs to be told the source of the data. It is not good enough to say that it was from *Social Trends*; the volume and year, and either the table or page, and sometimes even the column in a complex table must be included. When the data is first collected from a published source, all these things should be recorded, or a return trip to the library will be needed.

Sample data

If data is based on a sample drawn from a wider population it always needs special referencing; the reader must be given enough information to assess the adequacy of the sample. The following details should be available somewhere: the method of sampling (for example 'stratified random sample' or 'sample based on interlocking age and sex quotas'), the achieved sample size, the response rate or refusal rate, the geographical area which the sample covers and the frame from which it was drawn.

Missing data

It is important to try to present the whole of a picture. One of the commonest ways in which data can mislead people is for some unstated principle of selected to have been used. Don't exclude cases from analysis, miss out particular categories of a variable or ignore particular attitudinal items in a set without good reason and without telling the reader what you are doing and why.

Providing details of the overall response rate in a survey does not usually tell the whole story about missing information. Many particular items in a survey attract refusals or responses that cannot be coded, and the extent of such **item non-response** should be reported.

Definitions

There can be no hard and fast rule about how much definitional information to include in your tables; they could become unreadable if too much were included. Err on the side of repeating definitions in a table when in doubt; if complex terms are explained elsewhere in the text, include a precise section or page reference.

Opinion data

When presenting opinion data, always give the exact wording of the question put to respondents, including the response categories if these were read out. There can be big differences in replies to open questions such as: 'Who do you think is the most powerful person in Britain today?' and forced choice questions such as 'Which of the people on this card do you think is the most powerful person in Britain today?'

Ensuring frequencies can be reconstructed

It should always be possible to convert a percentage table back into the raw cell frequencies. To retain the clarity of a percentage table, present the minimum number of base Ns needed for the entire frequency table to be reconstructed.

Showing which way the percentages run

Proportions add up to 1 and percentages to 100. At least they do in theory; in practice, rounding may mean that they are slightly out. In a table where it is not clear whether the percentages have been calculated on rows or columns, it can be infuriating not to be able to make either rows or columns sum exactly to the expected figure. One solution is to point out every time the total comes to something other than the expected figure because of rounding error. It is usually helpful to include an explicit total of 100 as in figures 7.6(b) and 7.6(c).

However you achieve it, check that frequencies and proportions or percentages can be clearly differentiated.

Layout

The effective use of space and grid lines can make the difference between a table that is easy to read and one which is not. In general, white space is preferable, but grid lines can help indicate how far a heading or subheading extends in a complex table. Tables of monthly data can be broken up by spaces between every December and January, for example. Labels must not be allowed to get in the way of the data. Set variable headings off from the table, and further set off the category headings. Avoid underlining words or numbers.

Clarity is often increased by reordering either the rows or the columns. It can be helpful to arrange them in increasing order of size, or size of effect on another variable: the schools in figures 7.1, 7.5 and 7.6, for example, were ordered by the proportion of working class children who attended them (except for comprehensives). Make a decision about which variable to put in the rows and which in the columns by combining the following considerations:

1 closer figures are easier to compare
2 comparisons are more easily made down a column
3 a variable with more than three categories is best put in the rows so that there is plenty of room for category labels.

Further reading

Clarity is the goal of all communicators. Millions of people have been encouraged into good writing habits by Sir Ernest Gowers (1973), whose *Complete Plain Words* has run into many editions. The governmental statistical service has more recently encouraged the preparation of a book along similar lines to cover clarity of presentation of numerical data. Called *Plain Numbers*, it is recommended to all data analysts (Chapman 1986). Ehrenberg (1975) has also written a useful text with examples drawn from business studies which gives many good tips about the effective presentation of tabular data.

8 Analysing Contingency Tables

In the previous chapter, percentage tables were introduced as a way of making contingency data more readable. This chapter follows on directly; the properties of percentages and proportions will be scrutinized more closely, and other ways of analysing contingency data considered in the quest for a summary measure of the effect of one variable upon another. First, however, we must come back to the question of how to read a contingency table when one variable can be considered a cause of the other. (We shall shift from percentages to proportions from now on, since we need measures of effect which can be multiplied together.)

8.1 Which way should proportions run?

When we have a hypothesis about the causal relationship between variables, this can be conveyed by which of the proportions one uses in the analysis. Fiegehan and his colleagues (1977) found age to be closely related to poverty: old people in Britain often subsist on very small incomes indeed. The causal explanation must be that old age causes poverty, not that poverty causes people to be old; in a cross-tabulation of age by poverty, it is more natural to examine the proportion of each age group who are poor rather than the proportion of each income category who are old.

This can be formalized into a rule when dealing with contingency data:

Construct the proportions so that they sum to one within the categories of the *explanatory* variable.

This rule is worth memorizing. The idea is directly analogous to the treatment of interval level variables in chapter 6: we looked at the distribution of unemployment, the response variable, within each region, the explanatory variable. The response variable thus provides the proportions, and the explanatory variable the categories.

Response variable

				1.00
				1.00
				1.00
				1.00

Explanatory
variable

The rule is illustrated by the accompanying diagram. Note that it cannot be formulated as 'always calculate proportions along the rows'; this would only work if the explanatory variable was always put in the rows, and no such convention has been established. This is illustrated in exercise 8.4.

8.2 The base for comparison

In chapter 6, each individual value of a response variable (data) was decomposed into a conditional median (fit) and an unexplained component (residual). Effects were then defined as the difference between the grand median and the conditional fit. The same idea can be used with contingency tables, but the effects are usually derived by making comparisons not with a typical value such as the grand median but with one of the categories that has been chosen as the base for comparison.

To illustrate this, consider once more the example used in the previous chapter. Inflow and outflow mobility tables were introduced in that chapter without reference to any causal hypothesis. However, it is plausible to imagine that class background has a causal effect on the type of school that the son attends. The explanatory variable is therefore father's class, a three-category variable. In accordance with the rule propounded in the previous section, the proportions attending each school type should be calculated first within the service class, then within the intermediate class, then within the working class. Figure 8.1 repeats the cross-tabulation of class background and a collapsed version of school type first shown in figure 7.8; the full raw frequencies have been included as they will be helpful in the following discussion.

Numbers only have meaning in comparison with other numbers. To decide whether 0.237 of working class children attending selective secondary schools is high or low, it can be compared with the 0.397 of intermediate class children and 0.719 of service class children who attend those schools. One category is picked to act as the **base** for comparison with all other categories. The base category acts in analogous manner to the fitted median with interval level data. By making comparisons with

Figure 8.1 Attendance at selective secondary school

Father's class	Attended		Did not attend		Total	
	N	p	N	p	N	p
Service	771	0.719	301	0.281	1072	1.000
Intermediate	981	0.397	1491	0.603	2472	1.000
Working	1059	0.237	3411	0.763	4470	1.000
Total	2811		5203		8014	

Source: Halsey et al. (1980: table 4.4)

this base, quantitative estimates of the causal effect of one variable on another can be made, and positive and negative relationships between nominal level variables can be distinguished, as we shall see shortly.

Which category should be selected as the base for comparison? The decision is to some extent arbitrary, but there are several relevant considerations. Since the base category will be used in every comparison, it is desirable that there should be a substantial number of cases in it; we do not want comparisons to be made with an unreliable figure. For the same reason, it should be a category that is of substantive interest. Moreover, if there is one category that is markedly different from others, this is a good one to choose as the base, since it will focus attention on the difference. Finally, when picking the base categories for several variables whose interrelationships are to be examined, an attempt should be made to keep negative relationships between variables to a minimum: double negatives are as confusing in data analysis as they are in prose.

Which categories, then, should be selected as bases for comparison among father's class and school type? Since the working class is the largest group and the group which concerned the educational reformers of 1944, it is the natural choice of a base for the class variable. If we then pick non-selective education as the base for comparison in the school type variable, we will almost certainly avoid negative relationships. In summary, the service and intermediate classes will be compared with the working class in their attendance at selective as opposed to non-selective schools.

In order to represent one three-category variable like school type in a causal path model, we have to present it as two dichotomous variables. Instead of coding the class background of respondents as 1, 2 or 3 to denote service, intermediate or working class, for example, the information is effectively presented as two dichotomous variables – whether someone is in the service class or not, and in the intermediate class or not. Someone who was neither service class nor intermediate class would, by elimination, be working class.

Class as a three-category variable		Class as two dichotomies	
		Service or not	Intermediate or not
Service class	1	1	0
Intermediate class	2	0	1
Working class	3	0	0

Choosing one category as a base effectively turns any polytomous variable into a series of dichotomous variables known as **dummy variables**.

Figure 8.2 shows how the effect of a three-category explanatory variable on a dichotomous response variable can be portrayed in a causal path model. Social class is represented by two dummy variables; the effect of the first is denoted b_1 and the effect of the second b_2. A line is drawn under which the base category of the explanatory variable is noted; the fact that some working class children attend selective secondary schools (path a) reminds us that there are some factors influencing attendance at such schools that this particular model does not set out to explain.

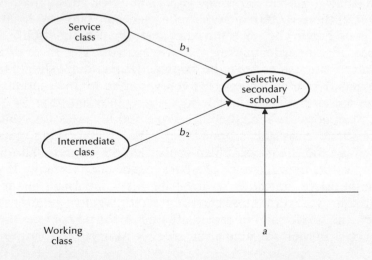

Figure 8.2 Causal path model of class background and schooling

8.3 Summarizing effects by subtracting proportions

In figure 8.2, the effect of being in the service class on the chances of attending selective secondary school is denoted b_1, and the effect of being in the intermediate class is denoted b_2. How are these to be quantified?

There is no answer to this question that commands universal acceptance. In this section we shall consider d, the difference in proportions (Davis 1976). This measure of effect has two virtues: it is simple and intuitively appealing. In later sections we shall look at alternatives.

As long as we keep cool when deciding which proportion to subtract from which, the procedure is simple. Attention is restricted to the non-base category of the response variable; in this example, it is the proportion of people who attend selective school that is at issue, and the shadow proportion who do not attend is ignored.

> The effect, d, is calculated by subtracting this proportion in the base category of the explanatory variable from this proportion in the non-base category of the explanatory variable.

In this particular example, path b_1 represents the effect of being in the service class as opposed to being in the working class on the chances of attending a selective secondary school. It is found by subtracting the proportion of the working class attending selective secondary schools from the proportion of the service class who do the same; in this case, $d = 0.719 - 0.237$, or $+0.482$. The result is positive, as we expected: service class children are more likely to attend selective secondary schooling than working class children are. Now we can quantify this: 0.482 more service class than working class children attend these schools.

If we had selected different base categories, we could have ended up with negative values of d. If, for example, we were trying to explain attendance at non-selective schools, the d for the service class would have been $0.281 - 0.763$, or -0.482; the magnitude of effect would not have altered but the sign would have been reversed.

Path b_2 represents the effect of being in the intermediate class on the chances of attending a selective secondary school. We might expect this to be lower than the effect of being in the service class. It is. In fact, $d = 0.397 - 0.237$, or $+0.160$, but it is still positive; 0.160 more intermediate than working class children go to selective secondary schools.

While the paths b_1 and b_2 are the focus of our attention, it is also important to remember the other causes which lead to people attending selective secondary schools: class membership is not a complete determinant of who goes to these schools, since some working class children do attend. Path a reminds us that some people from working class backgrounds attended selective secondary schools.

> The value of path a is given by the proportion of cases in the base category of the explanatory variable who fall in the non-base category of the response variable.

In fact, nearly a quarter of working class children went to selective secondary schools; the value of this path is therefore 0.237. It represents the starting point, the fitted value to which the other path values should be added; for this reason it does not have a sign attached.

The quantified model is shown in figure 8.3. The model allows us to recast the DFR equation for cells in a table, rather than for individual values. We decompose the proportion of service class children who attended selective secondary school (0.719) into a fitted component (0.237) and an effect (+0.482).

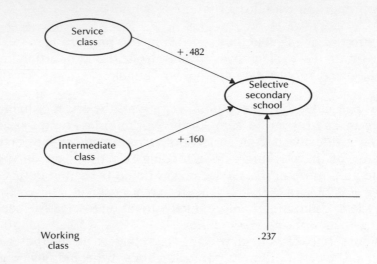

Figure 8.3 Quantifying model in figure 8.2

Some readers will have come across the idea of expressing a simple relationship between an explanatory variable X and a response variable Y as $Y = a + bX$. If the idea is familiar to you, you may like to note here that proportions can also be expressed in this way. The overall proportion Y attending selective secondary school is 2811/8014, or 0.351 (figure 8.1). This can be decomposed as:

$$Y = a + b_1X_1 + b_2X_2$$

where X_1 and X_2 are the proportion in the service class and intermediate class (0.134 and 0.308) respectively:

$$0.237 + (0.134 \times 0.482) + (0.308 \times 0.160) = 0.351$$

We shall consider equations like this for interval level variables later in the book; you may find it useful to come back to this paragraph after you have read chapter 10.

8.4 Properties of *d* as a measure of effect

The difference in proportions, *d*, has been used to summarize the effect
of being in a category of one variable upon the chances of being in a
category of another. This measure has several advantages. People
understand it intuitively (Hunter 1973). It retains the same numerical
value (while changing its sign) if the other category in a dichotomy is
chosen as the base for comparison. Furthermore, it can be used to
decompose overall proportions, as shown in the previous section, and it
can be decomposed itself when other variables are brought into the
picture. It does, however, have some properties which are less well
understood, and which, in the view of some data analysts, can make it
unsuitable for analysing some contingency tables.

If the proportions were run in the opposite direction, the value of *d*
would change; exercise 8.2 asks you to confirm this. Some statisticians
dislike this property: they prefer **symmetric** measures of association
which take the same value whichever way round the causal effect is
presumed to run. Quantitative summaries of causal effect such as *d*,
however, are nearly all **asymmetric**, taking different values depending on
which variable is presumed to be the cause of the other. Those of us who
believe that causality is central to the philosophy of data analysis prefer
measures of effect, which force us to be explicit about causal order, to
symmetric measures of association.

Secondly, because proportions are bounded numbers, we may wish to
distinguish differences between proportions in the middle of the range
from those between extreme proportions. In the above example, the
proportions attending selective schools were all in the middle range,
varying from 0.24 in the working class to 0.72 in the service class. But
imagine a society in which only 0.01 of the working class attended such
schools, while 0.10 of the service class did. The *d* between service and
working class would be much smaller, +0.09, but we might not want to
conclude that the second society displayed smaller class differentials;
after all, ten times as many service as working class children attend
selective schools in the latter case, while only three times as many do in
the former.

There are other strategies we might adopt to solve this problem. We
could look at ratios between proportions rather than differences. Or we
could apply some kind of transformation which would stretch out the tails
of the distribution, which would let us stick with arithmetic procedures
and avoid multiplicative models. Both ideas will be discussed in the next
section.

Just as a simple proportion is a bounded number, so *d* is also. The
bottom boundary, the 'floor', is easy to understand: if, for example, class
has no effect on school type, then all classes will have approximately the
same proportion of children at selective schools, and the lowest possible
magnitude of *d* will be zero.

But the top is bounded in a different place in every different table, depending on the marginal distribution of the two variables. It is, in theory, possible to get a d of 1.00; this would happen if all the service class children went to selective schools and nobody else did. But this could only occur if the number of selective secondary school places was exactly the same as the number of service class children.

The marginal distributions of both explanatory and response variables set limits to the size of effect that is possible; to put this formally, we say that d is a **marginal dependent** measure. Changes in the marginal distribution of the response variable will always produce changes in differences in proportions, even if the cells are still distributed in the same proportion; if, for example, the supply of selective school places doubled but the class composition of the schools remained the same, d would change.

However, not everyone believes that the boundedness of proportions and of ds is undesirable. The popular appeal of proportions and percentages is probably precisely because people understand that they cannot go below 0 or above 1; the boundaries set a frame of reference in which people can interpret a particular result. The marginal dependence of d can also be seen as a virtue once it is fully understood. One could take the view, for example, that important constraints on social equality are imposed by the opportunities available in society, regardless of who avails themselves of them, and that we do not want a measure that is insensitive to such constraints. As usual, we need to have a clear view of precisely what we are trying to summarize before deciding which measure does the job best.

8.5   Alternatives: ratios of proportions and odds

Proportions, as we have said, can be interpreted in terms of chances: the probability of an individual attending a selective school can be quantified as the proportion of children attending such a school. Since probabilities can be multiplied as well as added, one way of making effects among small probabilities comparable with effects when the probabilities are nearer 0.5 might be to look at ratios rather than differences.

In figure 8.1, we could have expressed the differentials between service and working class as a ratio rather than a difference; service class children had 0.719/0.237 or 3.03 times the chance of attending a selective school of some kind than working class children did. Some people find it much more appealing to express probabilities in this multiplicative way.

Ratios between two proportions are not, however, regularly used in analysing contingency tables. Adding and subtracting are easier operations than multiplying and dividing. Furthermore, ratios do not retain the same decimal value when the base for comparison is altered: if the ratio of A to B is 7/1 or 7.0, then the ratio of B to A is 1/7 or 0.143. It also turns out that the ratio of proportions is rather cumbersome to handle when dealing with many variables at once, and no-one has yet proposed a way of decomposing it into component effects as they have with ds and with measures based on odds.

If the sound of hooves on the turf makes your heart flutter, you may prefer to think of chance in terms of **odds**. The odds of an outcome are given by dividing the number of times the outcome occurred by the number of times it did not occur. Proportions can always be translated into odds. The first two columns of figure 8.4 show the results for a sample of proportions. The probability of one in ten is the same as odds of one to nine or 0.1111, a 50 per cent probability corresponds to odds of one to one, or 'evens', and so on.

Figure 8.4 Expressing probabilities as odds

Probability	Odds	Log odds
0.01	0.0101	−2.00
0.05	0.0526	−1.28
0.10	0.1111	0.95
0.20	0.2500	−0.60
0.30	0.4286	−0.37
0.40	0.6667	−0.18
0.50	1.0000	0.00
0.60	1.5000	0.18
0.70	2.3333	0.37
0.80	4.0000	0.60
0.90	9.0000	0.95
0.95	19.0000	1.28
0.99	99.0000	2.00

The second column of figure 8.4 shows that the upper ceiling has been removed once the proportions are expressed as odds; odds can become infinitely large. They do however still have a lower boundary at zero, and the whole distribution is very lop-sided; outcomes with probabilities less than evens are squashed into the number range 0 to 1, whereas probabilities above evens can range from 1 to infinity.

Logarithms effect a miraculous change on the odds. The third column of figure 8.4 shows the result of taking logs of the second column. The floor of zero has been removed: miniscule odds translate into large negative log odds. Moreover, symmetry has been restored to the concept of chance. Probabilities of 0.99 and 0.01, symmetrical in that they sum to 1.0, translate into log odds of +2.00 and −2.00. This transformation of a probability, $\log [p/(1-p)]$, is known as the **logistic** transformation. It has a characteristic shape when plotted against the raw probabilities, as

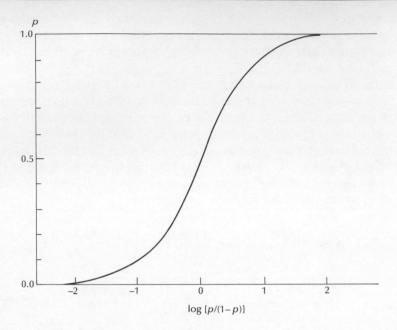

Figure 8.5 Characteristic shape of the logistic curve

Source: plot of column 1 of figure 8.4 against column 3

shown in figure 8.5; it is S-shaped and is approximately linear in the middle part of the distribution.

There are often substantive reasons for expecting proportions to respond to an explanatory variable in something resembling this flat S shape. We might argue, for example, that promoting a father from the most menial labouring job to a semi-skilled factory job is still unlikely to lead to his son going to a selective school, since so few working class children go. At the other end of the scale, promoting a father from being manager of a middle-ranking enterprise to a top-ranking enterprise is also unlikely to alter the son's chances much, because in all probability he already attends a selective school. The greatest effect of social mobility might be expected to be in the middle of the range, perhaps when fathers move from manual to non-manual jobs, for example.

An increasingly popular measure of effect is the difference not in proportions but in log odds between two categories. This turns out to be much the same as looking at ratios of odds, but avoids cumbersome multiplicative arithmetic.

8.6 Class effects on schooling

In order to illustrate the construction of these different measures, consider again the original cross-tabulation of school type by class background (figure 7.5). If we wanted to summarize the extent to which any type of school selected disproportionately from the children of particular class backgrounds, we might use the difference between the service and the working class in the proportion attending that school. Thus, since 0.266 of service class children attended secondary modern schools, while 0.747 working class children did, the *d* for secondary modern schools would be −0.481; similarly, the *d* for HMC schools would be 0.118 − 0.003, or +0.115, and so on. This is shown in the first three columns of figure 8.6.

Figure 8.6 Probabilities of attending various types of school

	Service class prop.	Working class prop.	*d*	Ratio of proportions
Secondary modern	0.266	0.747	−0.481	0.36
Comprehensive	0.015	0.016	−0.001	0.94
Technical	0.102	0.114	−0.012	0.89
Grammar	0.351	0.111	+0.240	3.16
Direct grant	0.062	0.005	+0.057	12.40
Private: non-HMC	0.088	0.005	+0.083	17.60
Private: HMC	0.118	0.003	+0.115	39.33

Source: Halsey et al. (1980: table 4.4)

However, since so few children attended some of these types of school, *d* is often calculated from proportions at the extremes of the scale; if we rank the class exclusivity of schools on the basis of the magnitude of the *d*s, we seem to be told that the secondary moderns were the most selective, followed by the grammar schools. The ratios of proportions in the fourth column of figure 8.6, calculated by dividing the first column of proportions by the second, tell a rather more convincing story. The private schools are the most select in class terms: almost forty times as many service as working class children attend HMC schools. The grammar schools and secondary moderns are similar in terms of class exclusivity. In each case, the proportion attending in one class is approximately three times the proportion attending in the other; the similarity between the two numbers (0.36 and 3.16), however, requires careful inspection to spot.

What about measures based on odds rather than probabilities? Figure 8.7 shows the worksheet for calculating the log odds and difference in log odds for the same data; the odds of a service class child attending secondary modern school are obtained by dividing 0.266 by 0.734, or 0.362, and so on. The difference in log odds gives exactly the same rank order as the ratio of proportions did: the private schools (HMC then

Figure 8.7 Odds of attending various types of school

| | Service class | | Working class | | |
	Odds	Log odds	Odds	Log odds	Difference in log odds
Secondary modern	0.362	−0.441	2.953	0.470	−0.911
Comprehensive	0.015	−1.817	0.163	−1.789	−0.028
Technical	0.114	−0.945	0.129	−0.891	−0.054
Grammar	0.541	−0.267	0.125	−0.904	0.637
Direct grant	0.066	−1.180	0.005	−2.299	1.119
Private: non-HMC	0.096	−1.016	0.005	−2.299	1.283
Private: HMC	0.134	−0.874	0.003	−2.522	1.648

Source: Halsey et al. (1980: table 4.4)

non-HMC) are the most exclusive in terms of selecting service class as opposed to working class children, followed by direct grant schools, then grammar schools, comprehensive schools, and technical schools, with secondary moderns bringing up the rear.

When the probabilities get very small, as they do with some of the school types, d is not a very suitable measure of effect. Any measure based on ratios (or, what amounts to the same thing, differences in logs) is to be preferred.

8.7 Conclusion

There has been some controversy in recent years about how best to analyse contingency data. Percentages and proportions are popular because they are easy to calculate and their magnitude is simple to interpret. However, models based on subtracting one proportion from another are only acceptable for proportions in the middle of the range. Odds ratios or differences in log odds can work better when the proportions are very small or large; they are, however, more complex to interpret for all except seasoned punters who are used to comparing the likely returns on different bets (Seaver et al. 1978).

We have also learned an important lesson about the philosophy of data analysis in this chapter. It is possible to use different techniques and arrive at different answers. The ignorant response to this is to give up in despair, and to slump back agnostically into the comfortable armchair. The wicked response is to select the technique that gives the desired answer. The response of the good data analyst is to welcome the discrepancy, and to examine the data even more closely to understand why the techniques differ; new insights could be on the horizon.

Exercises

8.1 The responses (see table) to an interview on public expenditure cuts were collected from a sample of residents of two wards in Greater Manchester in the winter of 1980–81. The researchers compared the attitudes of loyal Conservative or Labour Party voters in 1979 with Conservative defectors in their views on public spending on the welfare state (education, social services and health) and on law and order (police and armed forces).

Do you think that more should be spent on   (1) the welfare state?
(2) law and order?

	(1)		(2)	
	Yes	No	Yes	No
Loyal Conservatives	47	201	107	141
Conservative defectors	80	62	36	106
Loyal Labour	196	110	49	257

Source: Edgell and Duke (1982)

Present the results as two separate tables of proportions and causal path diagrams and discuss the findings.

8.2 The desire to isolate the factors associated with child abuse is understandable; social workers and other professionals could be given a list of tell-tale signs, and they could then keep a particularly close eye on families at risk. One way in which such factors are isolated is by comparing parents known to batter their children with a control group of parents who have no history of child abuse (Lynch and Roberts 1977, for example). On the basis of data such as the following, younger mothers are thought to be particularly at risk.

	Age of mother at birth of first child		
	Below 20	20 or above	Total
Parents with history of child abuse	25	25	50
Parents with no such history	8	42	50
Total	33	67	100

Source: hypothetical data modelled on Lynch and Roberts (1977)

Calculate both row and column proportions, and calculate the two ds; confirm that d is an asymmetric measure of effect. Decide which d summarizes the causal relationship better. Adjust the second row of the table to reflect a true incidence of child abuse of 20 in every 10,000. What happens to d?

8.3 Brown and Harris (1978) argue that the factors which lead to depression in women are of two types: some actually provoke the onset of depression (provoking agents) while others make women more vulnerable to the operation of provoking agents (vulnerability factors). In a random sample of women in Camberwell, the researchers found the following relationships between provoking agents and depression, first among a sample of women who were vulnerable and secondly among a sample of women who were not.

	Vulnerable		Not vulnerable	
	Depressed	Not depressed	Depressed	Not depressed
Provoking agent absent	2	60	2	191
Provoking agent present	24	52	9	79

Source: Brown and Harris (1978: 168)

Calculate two different measures of effect in both tables.

8.4 Using the HEIGHT dataset, construct two tables to show the cross-tabulation of a husband's social class by whether he smokes or not, first placing class in the rows and smoking in the columns, and then vice versa. Indicate your views about the likely causal relationship between these two variables by selecting the appropriate percentages in each case.

9 Smoothing Time Series

9.1 Time series

Economists are held to treat one month's figures as a freak, two months' as a fact and three months' as a trend. In this chapter we shall look at ways of smoothing the edges off the jagged initial appearance of data plotted over time; we shall look at the observations three at a time, taking seriously the spirit of this somewhat sarcastic remark, to get indications of the trend. This chapter is relatively free-standing, and could be read at any point after chapter 2.

The number of people receiving supplementary benefit for each year from 1948 to 1978, as shown in figure 9.1, is an example of a **time series**. Other examples might be the monthly Retail Price Index over a period of ten years, or the quarterly balance of payment figures during the last Labour government. The examples all have the same structure: **a well-defined quantity is recorded at successive equally-spaced time points over a specific period.** Problems occur when any one of these features is not met – for example if the recording interval is not equally spaced.

For exposition, a convenient special notation is used: $y_1, y_2, \ldots, y_N$, or y_t in general; y_t refers to the value of the quantity, y, recorded at time t. It is conventional to code t from 1 to N, the total period of observation; for example, the years 1948 to 1978 would be coded from 1 to 31.

9.2 Smoothing

Time series such as that shown in the second column of figure 9.1 are displayed by plotting them against time, as shown in figure 9.2. When such trend lines are smoothed, the jagged edges are sawn off. Two smoothed versions of the numbers of unemployed supplementary benefit claimants are displayed in figure 9.3 and figure 9.4. The version in figure

Figure 9.1 Unemployed supplementary benefit claimants: 1948–1978

November Year	Registered unemployed receiving supplementary benefit (thousands)*	Percentage of all registered unemployed
1948	53	16
1949	66	20
1950	77	25
1951	66	23
1952	102	25
1953	94	29
1954	80	30
1955	61	27
1956	73	28
1957	96	30
1958	151	29
1959	129	30
1960	107	30
1961	103	27
1962	150	28
1963	155	32
1964	111	32
1965	91	28
1966	199	25
1967	192	34
1968	190	34
1969	196	35
1970	200	34
1971	332	39
1972	358	45
1973	228	45
1974	266	43
1975	479	44
1976 (May)†	554	46
1977	659	49
1978	605	47

* National assistance to 1966; figures to 1958 from count at National Assistance Board Offices. Figures from 1959 from count of unemployed persons at Unemployment Benefit Offices.
† No count in November 1976 owing to industrial action.

Source: House of Lords *Hansard*, 22 March 1979, col. 1403

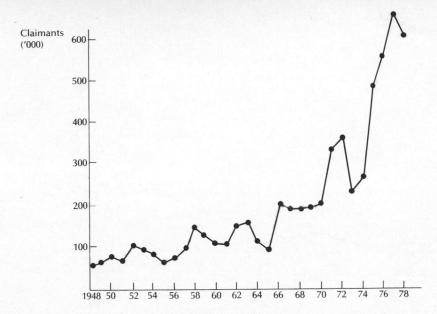

Figure 9.2 Unemployed supplementary benefit claimants: unsmoothed
Source: column 2 of figure 9.1

9.4 is smoother than the version in figure 9.3, and each is smoother than
the raw data plotted in figure 9.2.

Most people, if asked to smooth the data by eye, would probably
produce a curve similar to those in figures 9.3 or 9.4, each of which has

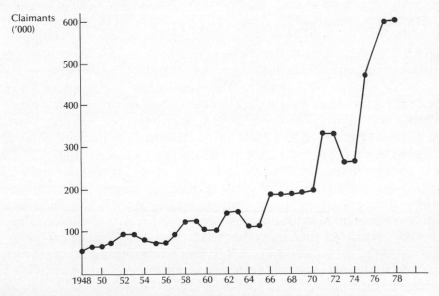

Figure 9.3 Unemployed supplementary benefit claimants: first smooth
Source: raw data in figure 9.1: calculations not shown

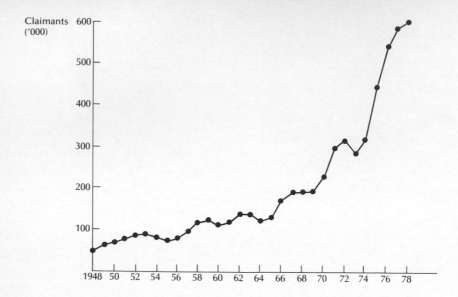

Figure 9.4 Unemployed supplementary benefits claimants: second smooth
Source: data in figure 9.1: calculations not shown

been derived using a well-defined arithmetic procedure described later in the chapter. Smoothing by an arithmetic procedure can sometimes, however, reveal patterns not immediately obvious to the naked eye.

9.3 The aim of smoothing

Figure 9.2 was constructed by joining points together with straight lines. Only the points contain real information of course; the lines merely help the reader to see the points. The result has a somewhat jagged appearance. The sharp edges do not occur because very sudden changes really occur in numbers of unemployed receiving supplementary benefit; they are an artefact of the method of constructing the plot, and it is justifiable to want to remove them. According to Tukey (1977:205), the value of smoothing 'is the clearer view of the general, once it is unencumbered by detail'. Smoothing aims to remove any upward or downward movement in the series that is not part of a sustained trend.

Sharp variations in a time series can occur for many reasons. Part of the variation across time may be error. It may be grouping error as discussed in the previous paragraph. It could be sampling error; the main data used in this chapter was collected in monthly sample surveys, each of which aimed to interview a cross-section of the general public but each of which will have deviated from the parent population to some extent. Similarly, repeated measures may each contain a degree of measurement error. In such situations, smoothing aims to remove the error component and leave the underlying true trend.

But the variable of interest may of course genuinely swing around abruptly; the monthly count of unemployed people rises very sharply when school-leavers come on to the register, for example. In these cases, we may want to smooth to remove the effect of events which are unique or which are simply not the main trend in which we are interested; it is good practice to plot the rough as well as the smooth values, to inspect exactly what has been discarded.

In engineering terms we want to recover the signal from a message by filtering out the noise. The idea is not new to us. We should by now be familiar with the general formula for decomposing data:

$$Data = Fit + Residual$$

The process of smoothing time series also produces such a decomposition of the data except that we mainly use the alternative, more suggestive form of words.

$$Data = Smooth + Rough$$

This choice of words helps to emphasize that we impose no *a priori* structure on the form of the fit. The smoothing procedure may be determined in advance but this is not the case for the shape and form of the final result: the data is allowed to speak for itself. Put in another way, the same smoothing recipe applied to different time series will produce different resulting shapes for the smooth, which, as we shall see in the next chapter, is not the case when fitting straight lines.

As so often, this greater freedom brings with it increased responsibility; the choice of how much to smooth will depend on judgement and needs. If we smooth too much, the resulting rough will itself exhibit a trend. Of course, more work is required to obtain smoother results, and this is an important consideration when doing calculations by hand. The smoothing recipe described below generally gives satisfactory results and involves only a limited amount of computational effort.

Most time series have a past, a present and a future. The upward trend in the numbers of unemployed getting supplementary benefit, for example, continued in the 1980s; the numbers trebled until two-thirds of all the unemployed received this benefit, despite the fact that it was never designed for them. The goal of the smoothing recipes to be explained in this chapter, however, is not the extrapolation of a given series into the future.

9.4 Consumer confidence

In complex market economies, where the decision to produce and the decision to consume are taken by different people at different points in time, it is important for manufacturers to have some idea of the likely demand for products. Individual manufacturers can monitor their own stock and sales to look for trends. Some market research companies specialize in providing audits of the trends in sales of particular product types across all manufacturers. But increasingly attempts are made to monitor a more general concept: the degree of confidence consumers have in the economy and in their own purchasing power.

George Katona was one of the pioneers of this sort of work. He criticized neo-classical economics for assuming that the actors in a market-place had perfect information and acted with supreme rationality to further their financial best interests. He suggested instead that economists and psychologists should link forces to study how producers and consumers actually make decisions, how they plan, what they believe, why they purchase commodities when they do, and so forth (Katona 1951).

Since the early 1970s, the Commission of the European Economic Community has sponsored a regular monthly survey into consumer confidence in all its member countries. Individuals are regularly asked about their perceptions of the economy as a whole, about inflation and unemployment levels; then they are asked about their household finances in particular, their expectations of buying consumer durables and their attitudes towards saving. This survey provides a particularly rich source of data because of the long time span covered.

Gallup does the fieldwork for the British wing of the survey. The fieldwork is conducted monthly on a quota sample of two thousand individuals selected to be representative of the adult population of Great Britain; more details about opinion polling companies and their methods are given in the appendix to this chapter. The results of each survey are published in the *Gallup Political Index* every month, except during election periods, when the European Commission takes the view that member countries should not publish opinion data for fear of influencing the outcome of the election.

In this chapter, data is presented from four of the questions, which elicit general perceptions of the economy and household finances. Respondents are asked: 'How do you think the general economic situation in this country has changed over the last 12 months?'. They select a response from a card:

- got a lot better
- got a little better
- stayed the same
- got a little worse
- got a lot worse

There is a parallel question on how they think the situation will develop in the next twelve months. Then they are asked: 'How does the financial situation of your household compare with what it was 12 months ago?' This is followed by a question on how it will change over the next twelve months. These questions have similar response categories.

There are several ways in which the five responses might be summarized into a single score for each month which could then be traced over time. The method used in figure 9.5 is to cut the distribution in two and to display the percentage in one or other group; here the percentages endorsing the two pessimistic response categories have been amalgamated (it is slightly inaccurate to describe those who think the economy deteriorated in the past as 'pessimists', but it is a convenient shorthand). An alternative would be to subtract the proportion of optimists from the proportion of pessimists. Another more comprehensive scoring system for the same questions is used in the dataset ECONOMY.

Figure 9.5 Consumer confidence items – percentage of pessimistic responses

	General economy		Household finances	
	1 Past (%)	2 Future (%)	3 Past (%)	4 Future (%)
January 1984	40	27	38	23
February	47	33	37	24
March	49	36	42	26
April	46	33	39	25
May	42	31	39	25
June	50	35	41	25
July	56	44	43	25
August	57	41	43	26
September	58	40	39	25
October	60	44	40	24
November	54	38	38	24
December	59	37	37	21
January 1985	66	42	41	24
February	72	47	45	28
March	67	41	43	28
April	57	39	44	30
May	57	41	43	31
June	63	42	43	27
July	59	41	41	26
August	60	43	44	28
September	58	38	38	26
October	55	37	36	24

Source: Gallup Political Index, nos 280 – 302; for the exact wording see the text

9.5 Techniques

Figure 9.6 shows pessimistic perceptions of the economy in the past plotted over time without being smoothed. The curve is jagged because the values of raw time series data at adjacent points can be very different. On a smooth curve, both the values and the slopes at neighbouring time points are close together. The general remarks on effective display made in the appendix to chapter 7 are important to recall when plotting, and some further remarks on this subject will be made in the next chapter. When plotting monthly or quarterly data, graph paper ruled into twelve divisions instead of ten is invaluable.

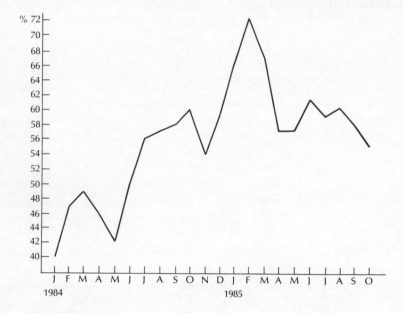

Figure 9.6 Pessimistic perceptions of the economy over the past year: unsmoothed
Source: column 1 of figure 9.5

To smooth a time series we replace each data value by a smoothed value that is determined by the value itself and its neighbours. The smoothed value should be close to each of the values which determine it except those which seem atypical; we therefore want some form of resistant numerical summary – some local typical value.

This involves two decisions: which neighbouring points are to be considered local and which changes are atypical? The answers to these questions must depend in part on the particular problem but this chapter presents some multipurpose procedures which give generally satisfactory results. These procedures answer the two questions as follows: take one point either side as local and treat as real an upward or downward change of direction which is sustained for at least two successive points.

Summaries of three

The simplest such resistant average is to replace each data value by the median of three values: the value itself, and the two values immediately adjacent in time. Consider, again, the percentage of respondents who believe that the economy got worse over the previous twelve months (column 1 in figure 9.5). To smooth this column, we take the monthly figures in groups of three, and replace the value of the middle month by the median of all three months:

$$
\left.
\begin{array}{ll}
\text{January} & 40 \\
\text{February} & 47 \\
\text{March} & 49
\end{array}
\right\} 47
$$

$$
\left.
\begin{array}{ll}
\text{February} & 47 \\
\text{March} & 49 \\
\text{April} & 46
\end{array}
\right\} \mathbf{47}
$$

In January, February and March, the median is 47 per cent so February's value is unchanged. In February, March and April, the median is also 47 per cent, so the value for March is altered to 47. The process is repeated down the entire column of figures.

Since, for the purpose of this exercise, we are supposing that the December 1983 and November 1985 rates are unknown, we simply **copy on** the first and last values, 40 and 55, for January 1984 and October 1985. More sophisticated rules for smoothing these **end values** are available, but discussion of them is postponed for the present.

The data, the smoothed values and the residuals are shown in the first three columns of figure 9.7. (In this chapter, we shall adopt the convention that all numbers that change when they are smoothed are shown in bold print.) Notice the large residuals for the somewhat atypical results in May and November 1984 and February and June 1985. The effect of median smoothing is usually to exchange the jagged peaks for flat lines.

One other possible method of smoothing would be to use means rather than medians. The result of using the mean of each triple instead of the median is shown in columns 4 and 5 of figure 9.7. As with the median smoothing, the residuals in the seemingly atypical months are large, but the sharp contrast between the typical and atypical months has been lost. Close inspection reveals that mean smoothing creates relatively large residuals in months adjacent to the strikingly atypical months, where perhaps common sense would suggest otherwise; if the percentage in February 1985 represents some kind of error, for example, then the less resistant mean has spread this error over into the adjacent months.

However, as we might expect, the median smooth is more jagged than the mean smooth (shown in figure 9.8). A sensible compromise would be

Figure 9.7 Worksheet: running medians and means of three

	1 Data	2 Medians of 3	3 Residuals	4 Means of 3	5 Residuals
January 1984	40	(40)	0	(40.0)	0.0
February	47	47	0	45.3	1.7
March	49	**47**	2	47.3	1.7
April	46	46	0	45.7	0.3
May	42	**46**	−4	46.0	−4.0
June	50	50	0	49.3	0.7
July	56	56	0	54.3	1.7
August	57	57	0	57.0	0.0
September	58	58	0	58.3	−0.3
October	60	**58**	2	57.3	2.7
November	54	**59**	−5	57.7	−3.7
December	59	59	0	59.7	−0.7
January 1985	66	66	0	65.7	0.3
February	72	**67**	5	68.3	3.7
March	67	67	0	65.3	1.7
April	57	57	0	60.3	−3.3
May	57	57	0	59.0	−2.0
June	63	**59**	4	59.7	3.3
July	59	**60**	−1	60.7	−1.7
August	60	**59**	1	59.0	1.0
September	58	58	0	57.7	0.3
October	55	(55)	0	(55.0)	0.0

Source: figure 9.5, column 1: from *Gallup Political Index*

first to use medians to set aside atypical behaviour, and then to apply some form of mean analysis to the median smooth to round off the corners. We will return to the details of how to do this later.

We could stop after one pass through the data, but we can also repeat the running three-median procedure on the values just smoothed to produce a smoother result. If we do this, most values will not change; in this case, only the value for July 1985 changes on the second pass through. This procedure is repeated until it produces no change; usually two or three passes through the data (**iterations**) are sufficient. The worksheet for repeated median smoothing is shown in figure 9.9; column 3 is headed '3R', a shorthand to denote repeated medians of three. When working by hand, it is only necessary to record those values that change upon iteration; in this text the values that change are denoted by bold print, but the other numbers are copied over for clarity.

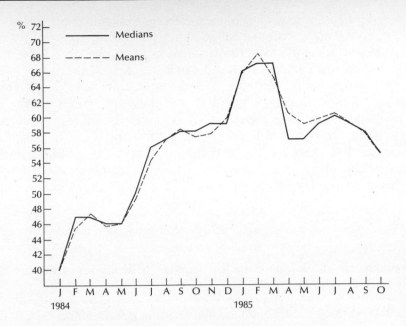

Figure 9.8 Pessimistic perceptions of the economy over the past year:
comparison of median and mean smoothing

Source: columns 2 and 4 of figure 9.7

To sum up, the recommended procedure so far is:

1 Plot the data first, as arithmetic smoothing may not be required.
2 List the times and data in two adjacent columns, rescaling and
relocating to minimize writing and computational effort. Judicious
cutting or rounding can reduce work considerably.
3 Record the median of three consecutive data values alongside the
middle value; with a little practice, this can be done quickly and with
very little effort.
4 Pass through the data, recording medians of three as many times as
required.
5 Copy on the two endpoint values.

Hanning

Although smoothing by repeated medians of three is adequate for most
purposes and successfully dealt with seemingly atypical values, the results
still have a somewhat jagged appearance. One way to smooth off the corners would be to use running means of three on the 3R smooth. We can do
better than taking simple means of three, however. This would give equal
weight, one-third, to each value; as the data has already been smoothed
it would seem sensible to give more weight to the middle value.

A procedure called **hanning**, named after its protagonist, a nineteenth century Austrian meteorologist called Julius von Hann, goes some way to meeting these criticisms. Given any three consecutive data values, the adjacent values are each given weight one quarter, whereas the middle value, the value being smoothed, is given weight one half. This is achieved in the following way: first calculate the mean of the two adjacent values – the **skip mean** – thus skipping the middle value; then calculate the mean of the value to be smoothed and the skip mean. It is easy to show that these two steps combine to give the required result.

In practice, we first form a column of skip means alongside the values to be smoothed and then form a column of the required smoothed values.

$$40$$
$$47 \quad 43.5 \quad \mathbf{45.2}$$
$$47$$

This procedure is depicted above for the first three values of the repeated median smooth, shown in full in figure 9.9:

Figure 9.9 Worksheet for repeated median smoothing and hanning (3RH)

	1 Data	2 Medians of 3	3 3R	4 Skip mean	5 Hanned (H)	6 Residuals
January 1984	40	(40)	(40)	(40)	(40)	(0.0)
February	47	47	47	43.5	**45.2**	1.8
March	49	**47**	47	46.5	**46.7**	2.3
April	46	46	46	46.5	**46.2**	−0.2
May	42	**46**	46	48.0	· **47.0**	−5.0
June	50	50	50	51.0	**50.5**	−0.5
July	56	56	56	53.5	**54.7**	1.3
August	57	57	57	57.0	57.0	0.0
September	58	58	58	57.5	**57.7**	0.3
October	60	**58**	58	58.5	**58.2**	1.8
November	54	**59**	59	58.5	**58.7**	−4.7
December	59	59	59	62.5	**60.7**	−1.7
January 1985	66	66	66	63.0	**64.5**	1.5
February	72	**67**	67	66.5	**66.7**	5.3
March	67	67	67	62.0	**64.5**	2.5
April	57	57	57	62.0	**59.5**	−2.5
May	57	57	57	58.0	**57.5**	−0.5
June	63	**59**	59	58.0	**58.5**	4.5
July	59	**60**	**59**	59.0	59.0	0.0
August	60	**59**	59	58.5	**58.7**	1.3
September	58	58	58	57.0	**57.5**	0.5
October	55	(55)	(55)	(55)	(55)	(0.0)

Source: figure 9.5, column 1: from *Gallup Political Index*

Thus 47 is the value to be smoothed, the skip mean 43.5 is the mean of 40 and 47 and the smoothed value 45.2 is the rounded mean of 47 and 43.5.

A new element of notation has been introduced into figure 9.9: the column of hanned data values is labelled 'H'. We can now summarize the smoothing recipe used in this figure as '3RH'.

The results are plotted in figure 9.10. Hanning has produced a smoother result than repeated medians alone. Whether the extra computational effort is worthwhile depends on the final purpose of the analysis. Repeated medians are usually sufficient for exploratory purposes but, if the results are to be presented to a wider audience, the more pleasing appearance that can be achieved by hanning may well repay the extra effort.

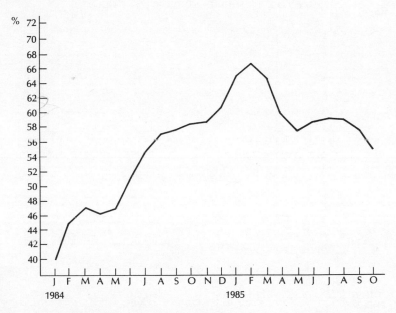

Figure 9.10 Pessimistic perceptions of the economy over the past year: median smoothed and hanned
Source: Column 5 of figure 9.9

Figure 9.10 now tells a pretty clear story; the proportion of people who believed that the economy had deteriorated in the previous year climbed from around 40 per cent at the beginning of 1984 to a peak of 67 per cent in February 1985, but declined thereafter. We shall not make any comments about this until we have had a chance to inspect a longer time span.

9.6 Residuals

As we have learned elsewhere, much can be gained by examining residuals, here called the rough. Residuals can tell us about the general level of variability of data over and above that accounted for by the fit; we can judge atypical behaviour against this variability, as measured, for example, by the midspread of the residuals.

We noted in chapter 1 that we want residuals to be small, centred around zero and patternless, and, if possible, symmetrical in shape with a smooth and bell-shaped appearance. Displaying them as a stem and leaf will reveal their typical magnitude and the shape of their distribution. Figure 9.11 shows the stem and leaf display of the residuals from the repeat median and hanning smooth (the 3RH for short); it shows that the residuals are small in relation to the original data, fairly symmetrical, centred around zero and devoid of outliers.

Figure 9.11　Residuals from the 3RH smooth

1	−5	0
2	−4	7
	−3	
3	−2	5
4	−1	7
7	−0	552
11	√	0000
11	0	35
9	1	33588
4	2	35
	3	
2	4	5
1	5	3

Source:　column 6 of figure 9.9

Zero-modifying the residuals

Note that a space on the stem in figure 9.11 has been devoted to residuals of precisely zero. Resistant numerical summaries have many desirable properties, as was discussed in chapter 2, but they can generate an excessive number of zero residuals, and thus give an unrealistically small measure of variability. This is particularly true when only median summaries have been applied to a fit; inspection of column 3 of figure 9.7, for example, reveals that the residuals from the 3R smooth alone contain a large number of zeros.

When this occurs, Tukey suggests removing half the number of exact zeros and then basing all subsequent calculations on the modified set of residuals, a process known as **zero-modifying** (Tukey 1977:223). Figure 9.12 shows the zero-modified residuals from the 3R smooth. Before zero-modification, the middle line of the figure would have been twice as long, with 14 zeros. Since 7 of the 14 zeros have been removed from the 22 residuals, the modified number of residuals is 15.

Figure 9.12 Zero-modified residuals from 3R smooth

leaf unit = percentage points
0 5 denotes 5%

1	*	5
3	−0.	41
(7)	√	0000000
5	0.	1224
1	*	5

Source: column 3 of figure 9.7

Blurring the smooth

As the rough represents the variability around the smoothed line, it is sometimes appropriate to use it to indicate the typical degree of variation around the smoothed curve. This is achieved by a process known as **blurring**. Instead of plotting each smoothed value as a point, a vertical bar of constant height centred upon the smoothed value is drawn.

Blurring has a double function. First, the vertical bars can give a somewhat smoother appearance to an otherwise jagged result; blurring can thus be viewed as an alternative to hanning. The second advantage is that the length of the vertical bar can be used to indicate the typical variability of the rough. It is conventional to use twice the median of the absolute values of the modified residuals as the length of the vertical bar used to blur the smooth.

Of course we are not restricted to blurring the repeated median smooth. In fact for many presentation purposes a blurred version of the repeated median/hanned smooth, including outliers, would represent a good summary of the data.

Pattern in the residuals

There are two generally useful ways to examine residuals for pattern. They can be plotted against the explanatory variable (here time) once more, to see if all the trend has indeed been extracted; this is discussed in the next section, under the heading 'reroughing'. Or they can be plotted against the fitted (here smoothed) values, to look for indications of non-constant variability; if the residuals get bigger as the smoothed values get bigger, this usually means that the the analysis would be better carried out on another scale. As we shall see in chapter 11, such non-constant variability is usually dealt with by a power transformation of the scale of measurement. Exercise 11.4 has been set to demonstrate this point with time series.

If we are smoothing with repeated medians, the appropriate transformation can simply be applied to the smoothed values and new residuals calculated. However, this cannot be done after hanning; it is necessary to repeat the hanning on the transformed repeated median smooth.

9.7 Refinements

There are a number of refinements designed to produce even better smooths. We can only give cursory attention to these here but more details are given in books by Tukey (1977) and Velleman and Hoaglin (1981).

Endpoint smoothing

So far we have been content to copy on the initial and final values for January 1984 and October 1985 (y_1 and y_N), but we can do better. Instead of copying on y_1, we first create a *new* value to represent y at time 0, December 1983; this will give us a value on either side of y_1 so that it can be smoothed. This value is found by extrapolating the smoothed values for times 2 and 3, which we shall call z_2 and z_3; this is shown graphically in figure 9.13.

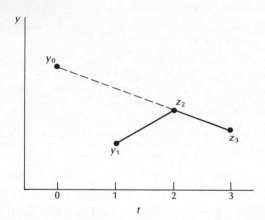

Figure 9.13 Creating a value for t_0

   To compute this new value without recourse to graph paper, the following formula can be used:

$$y_0 = 3z_2 - 2z_3$$

For example, a hypothetical value for December 1983 is given by (3×45.2) − (2×46.7) or 42.2 (data derived from figure 9.9). To provide a smooth endpoint value, we replace y_1 by z_1, the median of y_0, y_1 and z_2; in this case, the median of 42.2, 40 and 45.2 is 42.2, so this becomes the new, smoothed endpoint value. A similar rule is used to smooth y_N, by creating a new value, y_{N+1}. The letter E is added to the recipe formula to indicate that the endpoints have been smoothed; the total smooth is now '3RHE'.

Breaking the smooth

Sometimes time series exhibit an obvious change in level and it may be sensible to analyse the two halves separately, producing two roughs and two smooths. In such cases, the two sections often exhibit markedly different levels of variability. This seems to be the case in figure 9.1, for example, at the point where national assistance changes over to supplementary benefit.

Reroughing

Smoothing by taking repeated medians is very powerful, and can sometimes produce a result that departs more from the pattern of the original data sequence than we would like. Reroughing is a procedure designed to recover pattern from the discarded rough values. The residuals are smoothed using the same recipe as before, and the results are added back to the results of the first smooth; this is illustrated in exercise 9.1. This procedure, called **reroughing** (or sometimes **twicing**), takes further the idea of iterating that we met earlier in this chapter. You will find that many exploratory techniques require repeated steps before a final fit is found.

9.8 Trends in economic pessimism

Having learned the mechanisms, let us now return to perceptions of the economy. In figure 9.14, negative perceptions about the performance of the economy in the previous twelve months and pessimism about the economy in the following twelve months are plotted on the same scales over a six year period. The story line in the smoothed version of panel (b) is a lot clearer than in the rather jangled panel (a).

  If people's perception of the past performance of the economy and their prediction of future trends was accurate, one would find two identical curves which faithfully followed economic performance, with one lagging twelve months behind the other. There are several ways in which the curves in figure 9.14 depart from these idealized perceptions and forecasting abilities of rational economic man.

Figure 9.14 Pessimistic perceptions of the economy 1979–85: (a) unsmoothed (b) smoothed by 3RHE

Panel (a) Unsmoothed

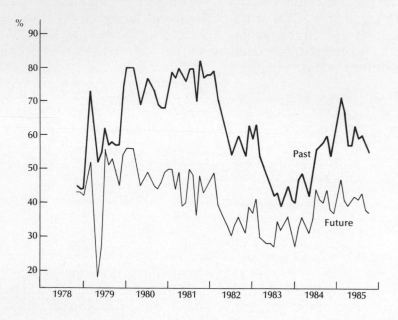

Panel (b) Smoothed by 3RHE

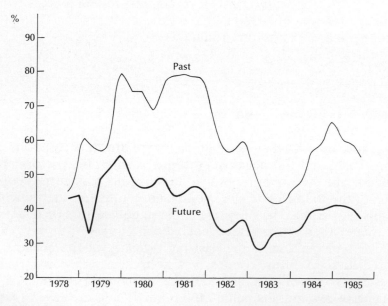

Source: *Gallup Political Index*: data for the last two years is shown in figure 9.5

First, the proportion of pessimists about the future is clearly and consistently lower than the proportion who perceived deterioration in the economy in the past; there must be a significant number of people who think things got worse in the last twelve months, but who are perpetually hopeful that the rot has stopped. Secondly, the two lines do track very closely together, but not with a twelve month **lag** as one might expect; the two curves are almost superimposed. People may be projecting the present into the past, re-evaluating the past on the basis of the present, or being influenced by some broader underlying general forces of optimism and pessimism. (One might subtract the perception of the past from the percetion of the future and smooth that once more as an index of optimism over time.) Thirdly, the shape of the curve does not match objective indicators of economic performance: on whatever measure one chooses, the economy performed disastrously in 1981, and picked up slightly in 1983, but perceptions during 1982 and 1984, perversely, move in the opposite direction.

The effect of political events is more clearly visible in the picture. Pessimism declined sharply during the Falklands War (April–June 1982), for example, and before the two elections (May 1979; June 1983). The interesting exception comes in the lead up to the 1979 election, when people were very harsh about the past period (during a Labour administration) but hopeful for the future (which was to be under Conservative administration); however, gloomy expectations about the future soon followed that 1979 election.

9.9 Summary

In this chapter, techniques have been presented for smoothing time series data. They can be performed relatively easily and effectively by hand. More powerful elaborations of the simple ideas presented here are also available in computer algorithms; readers should consult the Minitab manual to see what is done there.

In most of the examples discussed in this chapter, the finished product is a smooth curve which resembles what we might have drawn if we had smoothed the raw data by eye; looking from the smooth back to the rough we could usually see the trend in the raw data. Why bother smoothing? Well, it can sometimes reveal patterns not immediately obvious to the naked eye; an example of this is shown in exercise 9.3. It can make a story line clearer, which is always an advantage. It can sometimes, for example, help reveal that two time curves are tracking together, as with the unemployment data in figure 6.1 for example (where two curves with different scales were superimposed), or with past and future perceptions of the economy in panel (b) of figure 9.14.

All powerful tools can be misused, of course. It is always worth having a look at the roughs plotted over time, and thinking hard about what has been discarded in the smoothing operation. Moreover, there is a danger than data that presented very little pattern originally can be smoothed into an artefactually interesting story; exercise 9.4 has been designed to enable you to explore this point. But, for the data analyst who is prepared to use judgement as well as arithmetic, smoothing can clarify many otherwise ragged situations.

Exercises

9.1 Smooth the data on negative perceptions of household finances in the past (column 3 of figure 9.5). Try to plot the result on approximately the same scale as figure 9.10 so that you can compare the result with the economy in general. Discuss your results. (A very similar series over a longer time span can be found in the dataset ECONOMY.)

9.2 Most of the evidence about whether industrialism raised or diminished the living standards of the working class has centred on the wages and prices prevalent at different periods, data which is patchy and hard to interpret. In an inspired contribution to this debate, Floud and Wachter (1982) ask what happened to the heights of working class people in this period.

A complete set of records has survived which shows the heights of recruits to the Marine Society, a charity which trained young boys for the navy. The authors wanted to estimate the mean height of the population from which recruits were drawn. Unfortunately, the Society would not accept boys below a certain minimum height, and this minimum varied over time. They therefore estimated the missing lower end of the distribution of heights on the assumption that the whole distribution was Gaussian in shape (see Wachter 1981). The values for fifteen year olds are given in the accompanying table.

Year of birth of recruits	Number of cases	Estimated mean height (inches)
1756–60	216	56.0
1761–63	338	55.1
1764–66	339	55.9
1767–69	253	55.8
1770–76	860	56.9
1777–78	386	57.7
1779–81	309	56.3
1782–85	382	56.6
1786–88	350	56.3
1789–94	848	54.9
1795–99	731	55.0
1800–03	341	54.3
1804–09	766	58.5
1810–14	809	57.3
1815–16	216	57.6
1817–18	227	58.9
1819–20	439	58.8
1821–22	486	57.9
1823–24	579	57.1
1825–26	363	58.1
1827–29	473	58.1
1830–31	388	57.7
1832–35	623	57.0
1836–37	385	57.0
1838–39	547	58.8
1840–42	584	59.0
1843–44	414	56.9
1845–47	458	56.9
1848–49	325	57.0
1850–51	298	57.0
1852–53	296	57.3
1854–55	407	57.6
1856–57	403	57.5
1858–59	151	59.1

Source: data kindly supplied by Floud to the author

Ignoring the problem that the time intervals are not equal, smooth and plot the series. What can you say from the result about the effects of early industrialism on the physical health of the working class?

9.3 The dataset SCOTLAND shows the rate of stillbirths in Scotland in the period 1944 to 1983, broken down by social class. Using Minitab, plot the rates in classes I and V, then smooth them and plot them once more. The Minitab resistant smoothing command is RSMOOTH; the default smoothing recipe is not identical to the one explained in this chapter. Plots can be drawn on the same picture using the instruction MPLOT. Then calculate a measure of the differential between these two classes, smooth it and plot it once more.

9.4 In the previous exercise you may have discovered that social class V had between 150 and 250 per cent as many stillbirths as social class I. Using Minitab instruction IRAN, create a column of random data in the range 150 to 250. What should happen if you smooth this? Try it out several times, and compare results with your friends. What do you find?

Appendix: opinion polling in Great Britain

Opinion polls represent only a small fraction of all the social research which is conducted in Britain, but they have become the public face of social research because they are so heavily reported: on average there is at least one poll story in each copy of every national or local newspaper in Britain.

Predicting who is going to win an election makes good newspaper copy. The newspaper industry was therefore among the first to make use of the development of scientific surveys for measuring opinion. In all general elections in Britain since the Second World War, polls have been conducted to estimate the state of the parties at the time, and the number of such polls continues to grow. By-elections and local elections are now also the subject of such investigations.

For most companies, political opinion polling is a way to get their name known, but the bread and butter of their business comes from market research. Opinion polling is closely linked to the newspaper industry; National Opinion Polls Ltd (NOP) is owned by Associated Newspapers, for example, and Gallup earns an important part of its income through a contracted column for the *Daily Telegraph*. The political loyalties of the different companies are also well known: Harris works for the Conservative Party, while Market & Opinion Research International (MORI) is usually chosen by the Labour Party.

The interviewers who work for market research companies are usually women who wish to work part-time. They are trained on short training sessions run by the individual companies. Many interviewers, however, work for more than one company, which makes it hard for any individual company to implement standards different from the rest.

Opinion polls in Britain are almost always conducted on **quota samples**. In such a sample, the researcher specifies what type of people he or she wants in the sample, within broad categories (quotas), and it is left up to the interviewer to find such people to interview. In a national quota sample, fifty constituencies might be selected at random, and then quotas set within each constituency on age, sex and employment status: interviewers would then have to find so many women, so many unemployed and so many young people. In the better quota samples, such quotas are **interlocked**: the interviewer is told how many young housewives, how many male unemployed and so on to interview. The idea is that when all these quotas are added together, the researcher will be sure that the national profile on age, sex and employment status will have been faithfully reproduced.

Many people have doubts about such sampling methods. Interviewers are bound to seek out co-operative people, those who are not very busy and so on, thus inevitably leading to biases. It is not always easy to get up to date information on which to set the quotas, especially in a small area sample. The result is only representative on those variables selected for the quota, and may be quite unrepresentative on other factors. Little research has been done into the problems generated by quota sampling since studies over thirty years ago pointed up some major problems (Moser and Stuart 1953; Stephan and McCarthy 1958). The major defence pollsters give is that quota samples generally predict the outcome of elections pretty well.

There are three important compendiums of opinion polling results. Gallup's findings can be obtained from the *Gallup Political Index*. NOP also publish a monthly digest of their findings: *NOP Political and Economic Bulletin*. And MORI produce a monthly summary of the results of their own surveys and those of others, called *British Public Opinion*. All of these are obtainable from the company upon payment of a fairly hefty subscription. The latter two are formally published periodicals, and should therefore be obtainable through libraries. All three deposit their surveys at the ESRC Data Archive at the University of Essex, but the data arrives in a form that can be quite hard to read, and it can take several months for the Archive to be able to supply even small amounts of the raw data in a form usable on most college computers.

10 Scatterplots and Resistant Lines

10.1 Introduction

The British National Health Service set out to provide health services to everyone free of 'limitations based on financial means, age, sex, employment or vocation, area of residence or insurance qualification' (NHS Bill 1946). Before the NHS was established, critics had noted that the 'inverse care law' seemed to apply: those regions in which the need for health care was the greatest had the fewest resources. After the first thirty years of operation of the NHS, however, there had been disappointingly little change; in 1976, the Court Report noted that the variations in regional provision of service were still much the same as they had been in 1948 when the NHS began.

A new initiative was launched to address the problem, to try to reverse the inverse care law. The Resources Allocation Working Party (RAWP) was set up with a brief (RAWP 1975: 5):

> To review the arrangement for distributing NHS capital and revenue. . . with a view to establishing a method of securing, as soon as practicable, a pattern of distribution responsible objectively, equitably and efficiently, to relative need.

The recommendations of the Working Party have been used as the basis for financial allocations to the Health Service regions since 1977. They were implemented, however, at a time of general recession and reduction of public expenditure; critics accused the report of hiding cuts behind egalitarian language. The idea of determining resources according to need was only applied to the division of resources between regions, never to the total amount of resources to be allocated. Money was redistributed from London and Oxford to the North; the report was welcomed in the North and criticized in London and Oxford (Radical Statistics Health

Group 1977). In this chapter, some of RAWP's calculations and assumptions will be investigated.

The methodological focus of this chapter is to learn techniques for dealing with the relationship between two interval level variables; such data is often called paired, X–Y data, since for each case we have a pair of values which we want to display together. We shall learn how to construct a suitable display and how to interpret it and summarize it effectively. Chapters 1 and 2 are essential reading for understanding this chapter, and chapters 3 and 6 are also useful background.

10.2 Scatterplots

To depict the information about the value of two interval level variables at once, each case is plotted on a graph known as a **scatterplot**, such as figure 10.1. Visual inspection of well-drawn scatterplots of paired data can be one of the most effective ways of spotting important features of a relationship.

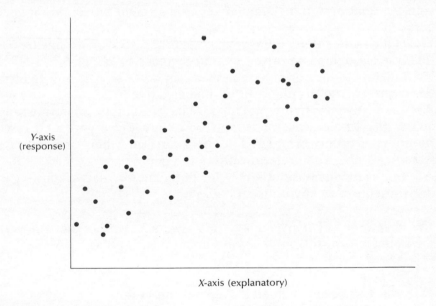

Figure 10.1 A scatterplot showing a moderately strong relationship

A scatterplot has two **axes** – a vertical axis, conventionally labelled Y and a horizontal axis, labelled X. The variable that is thought of as a cause (the explanatory variable) is placed on the X-axis and the variable that is thought of as an effect (the response variable) is placed on the Y-axis. Each case is entered on the plot at the point representing its X and Y values. Effective plotting requires practice, and achieving a good result can take time; the appendix to this chapter describes some of the ways in which plots can be improved.

Scatterplots depict bivariate relationships. To show a third variable would require a three-dimensional space, and to show four would be impossible. However, the value of a third nominal variable can often usefully be shown by using a different symbol for each value of a third variable. (Minitab achieves this by means of a **letter plot**.)

Scatterplots are inspected to see if there is any sort of pattern visible, to see if the value of Y could be predicted from the value of X, or if the relationship is patternless. If there does appear to be something interesting going on, there are several useful questions that can be asked next:

1 Is the relationship **monotonic**? In other words, does Y rise or fall consistently as X rises? The relationship in figure 10.1 is monotonic. A U-shaped relationship would not be.
2 Are the variables positively or negatively related? Do the points slope from bottom left to top right (positive) or from top left to bottom right (negative)?
3 Can the relationship be summarized as a straight line or will it need a curve?
4 How much effect does X have on Y? In other words, how much does Y increase (or decrease) for every unit increase of X?
5 How highly do the variables **correlate**? In other words, how tightly do the points cluster around a fitted line or curve?
6 Are there any gaps in the plot? Do we have examples smoothly ranged across the whole scale of X and Y, or are there gaps and discontinuities? Caution may need to be exercised when one is making statements about the relationship in the gap.
7 Are there any obvious outliers? One of the major goals of plotting is to draw attention to any unusual data points.

In this chapter we shall investigate the answers to some of these questions in an example drawn from a debate about health policy.

10.3 Indicators of health need in England and Wales

Two different types of indicator are customarily used by health policy-makers when planning and evaluating health services: input and output measures. On the one hand, attention can be focused on **inputs**: resources, both financial and human, that are devoted to health. The indicators that are traditionally used are the money spent on health care or the number of health workers per head of population. On the other hand, one can look at indicators of the success of these resources, at **output** measures of the health of citizens. The latter measures are much more difficult to obtain, and relationships between them are the subject of this chapter.

In order to allocate funding for the different categories of health care, RAWP had to produce indicators of relative need in the different regions of England and Wales. We shall examine how they arrived at an indicator of relative need for non-psychiatric hospital in-patient services (which accounts for over half of the total NHS budget).

The most important single indicator of need is crude population size; the Registrar-General's mid-year estimates of the population of each region were used. Regions also differ, however, in the structure of their population. Some have more old people (who make relatively heavy use of health services) and women of child-bearing age (who require maternity services) and so on. RAWP therefore weighted the crude population size in each region to take account of its demographic structure. The weights were derived from hospital bed utilization rates in each age-sex category; if, for example, elderly women accounted for three times as many bed-days as middle-aged men, they counted three times as heavily in calculating the weighted population total.

However, need for hospital services is not just a function of demography. Regions differ in social, industrial and cultural ways which give rise to different patterns of specific disease. A sensitive indicator of health need should reflect these disease patterns. There are, however, formidable obstacles to collecting reliable information on **morbidity** (disease). RAWP first used the treatment rates in various categories of disease, but later dropped this since they were strongly related to the availability of the treatment in the region, and thus risked confusing supply factors with need.

The authors considered several alternative indicators of health need, and opted in the end for standardized mortality rates (SMRs). Essentially, these express the number of deaths occurring as a proportion of the number of people at risk in each region in such a way that they take into account the fact that regions have different age and sex distributions; their construction will be explained fully in chapter 14. They calculated these standardized mortality rates for each cause of death, and then used them as weights in the allocation formula: areas with higher death rates from a particular disease got more money to treat that disease.

It is disease, however, not death, which is expensive. It is therefore important to know how well death rates indicate disease rates; if the link is weak, this would be very significant to resource managers. Data from the Third World suggests that it may be dubious: mortality is only a good indicator of the overall health of a population when infectious diseases are a major problem (US National Center for Health Statistics 1973).

Data on morbidity and mortality

The main conceptual tools of epidemiology are the incidence rate and the prevalence rate of disease. The **incidence** rate measures how many *new* cases of a disease appear in a given period, whereas the **prevalence** rate measures how many cases *in total* exist, either at one point of time (the **point prevalence** rate), or in a fixed period (the **period prevalence** rate). The distinction is analogous to that made in chapter 6 with respect to the unemployed – the number of new people who join the claimant count (the flow) versus the number unemployed at any one time (the stock) – and in chapter 5 with respect to income versus wealth. The incidence rate is necessary for studying the causal factors associated with illness, but the prevalence rate is better at reflecting the cost of disease to a community. With chronic diseases, in particular, it is important to have a good prevalence measure.

Respondents to the General Household Survey are regularly asked to report on their subjective state of health. From these reports, we may identify a general category of the **chronically sick**: people who replied 'yes' when asked if they had a long-standing illness, disability or infirmity which limited their activities in any way. The chronic sickness rate is a point prevalence rate, telling us how many people report long-standing health problems at one point in time.

This morbidity measure can be used to provide a limited test of the RAWP assumption. Figure 10.2 contains some paired data for all the regions of England and Wales, showing their morbidity and mortality rates. The morbidity rates were originally drawn from the General Household Survey and the mortality rates from the Registrar-General. Since the mortality rates are standardized by the age and sex structure of the region, the illness measures in figure 10.2 have been similarly standardized.

The data relates to overall death and sickness rates, whereas disease-specific SMRs were used in the RAWP formula. However,

Figure 10.2 Standardized mortality and morbidity rates 1972–3

Registrar-General's Standard region	Standardized mortality per 10,000	Standardized chronic sickness per 1,000
North	132.7	228.2
Yorkshire	126.8	232.5
North West	132.8	218.6
East Midlands	119.2	222.0
West Midlands	124.8	210.5
East Anglia	108.2	205.0
Greater London	116.3	202.6
Other South East	109.5	189.6
South West	112.2	186.8
Wales	128.6	249.9

Source: Forster (1977: 998)

RAWP themselves used similar data to validate their claim that death rates were good predictors of sickness. This particular dataset covers two years where RAWP used only one in their validation exercise, and was compiled for an article in the *Lancet* which was critical of the RAWP formula (Forster 1977).

10.4 Linear relationships

The scatterplot of the chronic sickness rate by the death rate is shown in figure 10.3; the pattern is not terribly tight, but inspection of the plot suggests a monotonic, positive relationship.

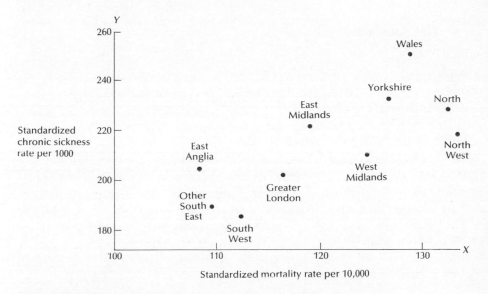

Figure 10.3 Regional sickness rate by mortality rate: scatterplot
Source: Figure 10.2

In order to summarize the relationship between two interval-level variables, we will try to fit a line if we possibly can. When describing the apparent relationship, instead of making the somewhat vague generalization 'the higher the X, the higher the Y', the linear summary permits a more precise generalization 'every time X goes up a certain amount, Y seems to go up a specified multiple of that amount'.

Straight lines are easy to visualize geometrically, but they can also be expressed algebraically. Equations of the form:

$$Y = a + bX$$

always describe lines. In this equation, Y and X are the variables, and a and b are coefficients that quantify any particular line; figure 10.4 shows this diagramatically.

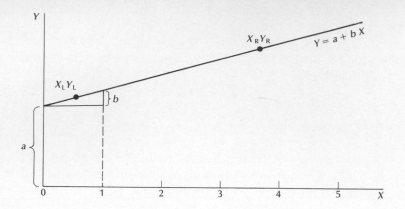

Figure 10.4 Anatomy of a straight line

The degree of tilt or **slope** of the line is given by the coefficient b; the steeper the slope, the bigger the value of b. The slope is usually the item of scientific interest, showing how much change in Y is associated with a given change in X. The **intercept** a is the value of Y when X is zero, or where the line starts. Frequently, the intercept makes little substantive sense – a mortality rate of zero is an impossibility, for example. If it is important to avoid a meaningless intercept for any reason, one could add or subtract an appropriate constant from all the Xs; interested readers can follow the idea up in Mosteller and Tukey's text (1977: 58–61).

The slope of a line can be derived from any two points on it. If we choose two points on the line, one on the left-hand side with a low X value (called X_L, Y_L), and one on the right with a high X value (called X_R, Y_R), then the slope is

$$\frac{Y_R - Y_L}{X_R - X_L}$$

If the line slopes from top left to bottom right, $Y_R - Y_L$ will be negative and thus the slope will be negative.

We only want to try to run a straight line through a cloud of data points if the relationship looks linear. *Never* try to fit a line before you have plotted the data to see if it is a sensible thing to do.

10.5 Where to draw the line?

Let us turn now to the relationship between the chronic sickness and mortality rates. Inspection of the scatterplot suggested that it would be worth trying to fit a line; the task is to find one which will come as near as

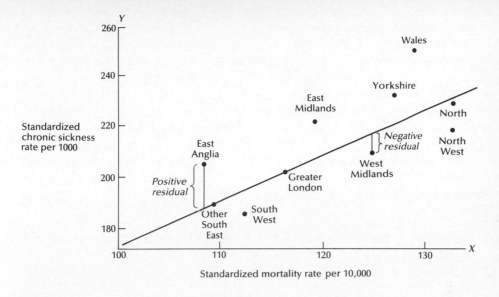

Figure 10.5 Running a line by eye through points in figure 10.3

Source: as figure 10.3

possible to the data points. A technique such as smoothing will not do because it does not ordinarily produce a linear outcome.

Before considering how we might do the job mathematically, let us just draw in a line by eye, to go through the centre of the data points. One possible line is shown in figure 10.5. This line goes through two data points, the values for the Greater London area and for the rest of the South East. This means that calculation of the slope is straightforward, according to the formula in section 10.4: it is given by finding out how much Y changes for a unit change in X, namely

$$\frac{202.6 - 189.6}{116.3 - 109.5} = 1.91$$

We can now make a fairly precise summary statement: on average, 19 more people per 1000 are chronically ill for each death; (mortality was measured per 10,000, while illness only per 1000).

The slope can be thought of as a numerical expression of the strength of causal effect of one variable on another. It can be modelled on a causal path diagram as shown, in exactly the same way as differences in percentages were in contingency data. The slope of a line is directly analogous to a difference between two proportions: both tell us how much one variable changes for a given change in the other.

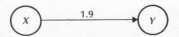

Now that the line has been fitted, the residuals tell us how actual chronic sickness rates differ from expectations formed on the basis of death rates; the West Midlands region, for example, has less chronic sickness than you would expect from its death rate, but East Anglia has more. We are naturally led to ask why this should be; if we were happy with this line, the next step might be to examine the pattern of occupational or environmentally related diseases within each region to try to understand the pattern in the residuals.

However, drawing a line so roughly has its limitations: the eye can deceive and the heart may secretly desire a particular outcome. It would be better to fit a line which met some predetermined criterion. There are many different rules one could try to follow:

1 Make half the points lie above the line and half below along the full length of the line.
2 Make each point as near to the line as possible (minimizing distances perpendicular to the line).
3 Make each point as near to the line in the Y direction as possible (minimizing vertical distances).
4 Make the squared distance between each point and the line in the Y direction as small as possible (minimizing squared vertical distances).

The choice of criterion is a matter of judgement. When drawing a line by eye, many people seem to try to follow rule 1 or rule 2. The technique explained in this chapter, resistant line fitting, produces a line which makes the absolute value of the deviations in the Y direction as small as possible (rule 3). Another very popular criterion for line-fitting is minimizing squared deviations from the line in the Y direction (rule 4); this technique is known as **linear regression**. It is less resistant than the technique shown in this chapter.

10.6 Fitting a resistant line

The method of line fitting adopted in this chapter involves joining two typical points: the X-axis is roughly divided into three parts, conditional summary points for X and Y are found in each of the end thirds, and then a line is drawn connecting the right-hand and left-hand summary points. We choose to use the outer thirds because we want the line to be drawn between two points as far away as possible without being so far out that they risk being unreliable. Some data analysts prefer to use the outer quarters (Open University 1983); the larger the number of cases the less the decision matters. In either case, the line thus calculated is only a first approximation, and will be tuned up, as we shall see in the next section.

Ordering and grouping

In dividing the X-axis, the aim is to get one-third of the cases into each of the three parts. To do this, the cases are reordered so that the X values are in order, as shown in the first two columns of figure 10.6. Notice that the corresponding Y value has been kept with each X, and the Y values are therefore not in order. (Ignore the third and fourth columns for now.)

Dividing the X-axis into three is in principle straightforward, but in practice there are snags, especially where there are not many data points. Here are guidelines which are usually helpful:

1 The X-axis should be divided into three approximately equal lengths.
2 There should be an equal number of data points in each third.
3 The left and the right batch should be balanced, with an equal number of data points in each.
4 Any points which have the same X value must go into the same third.
5 No subdivision of the X-axis should account for more than half the range of the X-values found in the data.

Since these rules are not always compatible, compromises will be needed. In this example, the number of data points is not an exact multiple of three, so the second guideline could not be met; balance in the two outer batches has been preserved by putting three points into each of them them and four into the middle.

Obtaining the summary value

A summary X and Y value must now be found within each third. The summary X value is the median X in each third; in the first third of the data, the summary X value is 109.5, the value for the other South East. Similarly, the median Y in each third becomes the summary Y value, here 189.6. **This does not have to be the value paired with the summary value for X**, although in this instance it happens also to be the value for the other South East.

The summary X and Y values for each of our batches can be read off figure 10.6:

$$X_L = 109.5 \qquad Y_L = 189.6$$
$$X_M = 122.0 \qquad Y_M = 216.2$$
$$X_R = 132.7 \qquad Y_R = 228.2$$

It is left to the reader to plot these points on figure 10.3, and to connect the first and third.

The middle summary point is not used to draw a straight line, but it should not lie too far from the line if the underlying relationship really is linear. It can be used to provide a more systematic evaluation of

Figure 10.6 Worksheet for calculating a resistant line

	1 X	2 Data Y	3 Fit $\hat{Y}$*	4 Residual Y
East Anglia	108.2	205.0	189.4	15.6
Other South East	109.5	189.6	191.6	−2.0
South West	112.2	186.8	196.1	−9.3
Greater London	116.3	202.6	202.9	−0.3
East Midlands	119.2	222.0	207.7	14.3
West Midlands	124.8	210.5	217.0	−6.5
Yorkshire	126.8	232.5	220.3	12.2
Wales	128.6	249.9	223.3	26.6
North	132.7	228.2	230.1	−1.9
North West	132.8	218.6	230.3	−11.7

* Y has been fitted by the equation $Y = 9.83 + 1.66X$; this is explained in section 10.6.

Source: X and Y data from figure 10.2: as in Forster (1977: 998)

linearity. The method involves calculating two **half-slopes**: the left-hand half-slope is calculated between the first and the middle summary point, and the right-hand half-slope between the middle and the third point. If the half-slopes are nearly equal, the relationship is fairly linear. If one is more than double the other, we should not fit a straight line.

Deriving the coefficients of the line

The slope and the intercept could be read off a graph. It is, however, quicker and more accurate to calculate them arithmetically from the summary points. The slope is given by

$$\frac{Y_R - Y_L}{X_R - X_L} = \frac{228.2 - 189.6}{132.7 - 109.5} = 1.66$$

This is not very different from the slope of the eyeballed line.

The intercept is the value of Y when X is zero, a pretty meaningless value when X is a mortality rate, as we noted above; we just treat it as a scaling factor, needed to predict a given Y value from a given X value. It is obtained by inverting the equation for a line; if $Y = a + bX$, then $a = Y - bX$. Either the upper or lower summary X values could be used to find the intercept: $a = Y_R - bX_R$, for example. But we shall get a more accurate estimate of the intercept if the mean of all three summary values is used:

$$a_R = Y_R - bX_R = 228.2 - (1.66 \times 132.7) = 7.9$$
$$a_M = Y_M - bX_M = 216.2 - (1.66 \times 122.0) = 13.7$$
$$a_L = Y_L - bX_L = 189.6 - (1.66 \times 109.5) = 7.9$$

Because we used the upper and lower summary points in finding the slope, the a_L and a_R estimates will always be the same. The intercept is given by the average of 7.9, 13.7 and 7.9, i.e. 9.83.

The full prediction equation is therefore:

Chronic sickness = 9.83 + (1.66 × Death rate)

We would predict, for instance, that East Anglia, with a standardized death rate of 108.2, would have a chronic sickness rate of 9.83 + (1.66 × 108.2) or 189.4. We can find such a predicted, or fitted, value for each case. The method is similar to that used in chapter 6, where we predicted the regional mcdian unemployment rate for each local area within that region; the difference is that the prediction from a linear equation will only be the same for two cases if they have identical mortality rates. The full set of predicted values is shown in column 3 of figure 10.6; the column is headed $\hat{Y}$ (pronounced 'Y-hat'), a common notation for fitted values.

In fact, East Anglia's sickness prevalence rate is 15.6 higher than the predicted 189.4, namely 205. Residuals from the fitted values can also be calculated for each region, and these are shown in column 4 of figure 10.6. Now all the data values can be recast in the traditional DFR form:

Data (205) = Fit (189.4) + Residual (15.6)

10.7 Inspection of residuals and polishing the fit

The residuals from the fitted values are obtained by subtraction, as shown in column four of figure 10.6. They are displayed in figure 10.7. We would always like residuals from a fit to be small and patternless. Their size can be assessed by comparing them with the original spread in the chronic sickness rates; this will be discussed at length in the next section. But can any more pattern be extracted?

As we saw in section 10.5, we are looking for a line which will make the residual Ys as small as possible. Joining two crudely calculated summary points is unlikely to produce a line with precisely that property, especially

Figure 10.7 Residuals from line in figure 10.6

leaf unit = one chronic sickness per thousand
−1 1 denotes −11

1	−1.	1					
3	−0*	96					
(3)	−0.	210					
	0.						
	0*		M 5.5		−0.5		
4	1.	24	Q 3.0	−6		14	dQ 20
2	1*	5	X 1.0	−11		26	
	2.						
1	2*	6					

Source: column 4 of figure 10.6

when, as here, N is very small. The procedure is therefore iterated, and the final fit is converged upon slowly by repeating the process until the residuals are patternless – a procedure known as **polishing the fit**.

To do this, the residuals are next treated as new Y data, and the procedure of line fitting is repeated; the fourth column of figure 10.6 becomes the new column of Ys, the Xs remain as they were, and the calculations are performed as before. The new slope might be positive, in which case the new fit would be added to the old, or it might be negative, in which case it would be subtracted from the old. The fit is polished as many times as it takes for the residuals to show no more evidence of a relationship with the X values – for the slope to be zero; the slope usually changes by gradually smaller and smaller amounts, and **converges** on a stable result. The slope in figure 10.6 is not much changed after polishing, so the technique is illustrated in exercise 10.1.

Polishing the fit in this way is analogous to reroughing in the last chapter. Many of the techniques of exploratory data analysis require the repetition of procedures to converge on a fit that minimizes the residuals; this can make the techniques rather laborious, but it is one side of the trade-off required to get methods of analysis which are resistant to outliers. The procedure can, of course, easily be handed over to a computer.

The residuals can also be used to indicate whether we have fitted the correct functional form or not. For this purpose, they are best plotted against predicted Y values. If the relationship is mildly curvy, or if the spread of the Y values is not constant for all X values, this may stand out more clearly in the plot of residual Y versus fitted Y than in the original scatterplot. What to do if the relationship is curved is discussed fully in the next chapter.

10.8 Predicting morbidity from mortality

Let us return now to the policy question: how *well* do death rates predict sickness, the condition that requires the cash? Forster is right that the correlation between the variables is far from perfect; the data points are spread quite widely to either side of the line.

We want residuals to be small. They represent the failures of prediction; the larger they are, the worse the fit. But how are we to evaluate their size in any particular instance? The general answer that we first came across in section 6.7 is: the residual spread should be small in comparison with the original spread. In this case the residual dQ is 20 (figure 10.7), compared with an original dQ of 26 (derived from column 2 of figure 10.2); the spread has been reduced to around three-quarters its original size.

Is this a big reduction? First consider two extreme cases which delineate the boundaries. If the association was perfect, all the points would lie on the line, and there would be no spread in the residuals; 100 per cent of the original spread would be accounted for, and we would describe the two variables as being perfectly correlated. If there was no relationship at all, the spread of the residuals would be the same as originally, and there would thus be no reduction; we would say that there was no correlation between the two variables. Reducing the spread by 25 per cent is not a very dramatic reduction; it is nearer zero than 100 per cent.

So regional death rates do not predict regional self-reported sickness rates very well. Critics of the decision to include death rates in the RAWP formula have implicitly argued that they should correlate nearly perfectly with sickness rates; in the light of such evidence, they have advocated dropping them (Forster 1977; Barr and Logan 1977). However, an inadequate indicator may be preferable to no indicator; failure to include death rates in the formula would mean that funds were even less related to need than at present.

Perhaps self-reports of sickness should be substituted for death rates in the RAWP formula. However, we have no guarantee that the sickness indicators themselves are reliable. Moreover, attempts to classify self-reported data into disease categories are notoriously unreliable, and a disease-specific measure of need is required since the costs of treatment differ so widely.

Every currently available indicator of health need is inadequate in one way or another. Treatment rates for different diseases reflect availability of the treatment rather than prevalence of the disease. Self-reported sickness is of unknown validity and unobtainable within reliable disease categories. Death rates seem not to be a very good indicator of disease rates either. Is the attempt to distribute resources according to need therefore impossible? Perhaps death rates will have to suffice until a more serious attempt is made by health care professionals to ascertain the regional variations in disease independently of treatment.

10.9 Conclusion

In this chapter we have looked at the extent to which chronic sickness rates as reported on the GHS are predictable from death rates. The full relationship was first examined by means of a useful pictorial device: the scatterplot. This relationship was next summarized by fitting a straight line. The strength of the association between the mortality and morbidity was given by the slope of this line, indicating how much sickness goes up for each point increase in the death rate. The spread in overall sickness rates was compared with the spread in residual sickness rates to obtain a measure of the degree of correlation around the line.

Those who have been exposed to the confirmatory techniques of linear regression may recognize the analogous measures. In regression, the criterion for line fitting is to minimize squared residuals, the 'least-squares' rule 4 of section 10.5. It is the variance, not the midspread, which is broken down into a fitted ('explained') and residual ('unexplained') component. The correlation is given by the Pearson's correlation coefficient r. Regression techniques have their advantages: the lines can be derived in one fell swoop from a formula, and do not require iterating. Moreover, if the residuals are well behaved (Gaussian, without freak values) then the calculation of the likely error associated with the coefficients is fairly straightforward.

However, error terms are often highly non-Gaussian, and outliers from the line are the rule rather than the exception. Regression techniques, because they set out to make the *squared* distances of the residuals from the line as small as possible, can be unduly influenced by a few exceptional data points. They are therefore much less resistant than the techniques introduced in this chapter.

The slope, b, is mathematically very close to the proportion difference, d. It is an asymmetric measure, just like d: the slope depends on which variable is treated as the response variable, just as d depends on which way the percentages have been run; exercise 10.2 has been set to illustrate this. Symmetric methods of line fitting exist, such as principal components analysis and factor analysis, which summarize the extent to which two variables cluster together (rule 2 of section 10.5), but they are not covered here.

In the third part of this book we shall introduce various data analytic techniques to control for the effect of a third variable. There will not be the space, unfortunately, to extend the methods introduced in this chapter, and to show how to summarize linear relationships between three variables. However, the principle is straightforward. The residuals from the fitted line can be thought of as values for a variable which have been adjusted to take the explanatory variable into account. If we want to assess the relationship between X and Y but are worried that both are associated with a third variable, Z, whose effect we therefore wish to control, we adopt a two-stage procedure. First we fit a line to Y-by-Z and X-by-Z, and calculate the residuals from each line. These residuals are then the new X and Y values controlling for Z, and we can fit a line to the relationship between residual Y versus residual X. Exercise 11.5 is designed to give you an idea of how this might work.

Exercises

10.1 A key assumption in economics is that money can be used to buy things that satisfy people's wants and make them happy ('utilities'). Surveys *within* different countries seem to confirm this; the wealthier people in those countries are actually happier than the poorer. The following data, assembled by Easterlin (1974:105), however, examined the relationship *across* various countries from surveys conducted around 1960; the personal happiness rating was the average reply to a scale where 0 indicated that respondents were very unhappy and 10 that they were very happy.

	Rating of personal happiness	Real GNP per head ($US)
United States	6.6	2790
Cuba	6.4	516
Egypt	5.5	225
Israel	5.3	1027
West Germany	5.3	1860
Japan	5.2	613
Yugoslavia	5.0	489
Philippines	4.9	282
Panama	4.8	371
Nigeria	4.8	134
Brazil	4.6	375
Poland	4.4	702
India	3.7	140
Dominican Republic	1.6	313

If money can buy happiness, what would you expect the relationship between the two variables to look like? Plot the data points and discuss the apparent relationship. Then calculate a resistant line and find the slope and intercept. How well does the line summarize the scatterplot? Polish the fit and adjust your estimate of the slope.

10.2   Plot the two variables in figure 10.2 the other way round from the plot in figure 10.3, as if one wanted to predict the mortality rate from the chronic sickness rate. Draw in a line by eye, read off the slope and intercept, and confirm that the line is different from the line fitted in the chapter.

10.3   It is hard to assess the IQ of young children. Rather than set formal tests, some researchers prefer to base their inferences on the child's performance on less formal tasks; the Goodenough draw-a-man test, for example, scores how sophisticated children's pictures are. Other researchers have criticized this test for being insufficiently rigorous. The dataset EDUCATE contains the results of the Goodenough test at age 7 and standard tests of verbal and non-verbal ability at age 11. Plot non-verbal ability at age 11 against the Goodenough test scores, fit a resistant line, sketch the line on the plot and decide how well you think the Goodenough test at 7 predicts non-verbal ability at 11. You will need to use Minitab instructions PLOT and RLINE for this exercise.

Appendix: guide to effective plotting

Some general suggestions about how to present numerical material clearly, about labelling, definitions and so on, were given in the appendix to chapter 7. In this appendix, some further consideration is given to how to draw clear and informative pictures of data (scatterplots and bar charts in particular).

The tool-kit

A pencil is the first prerequisite, so that the inevitable errors can be rubbed out; softer leads need sharpening more often but stand out better. You will find different coloured pens useful. Rulers should be perspex so you can see underneath them as you rule; check the edges are smooth.

Graph paper is essential. It is of very varied quality; look for paper ruled into divisions of ten, and with every tenth line ruled heavy and every fifth medium. If the grid lines are printed in blue they will not show up so clearly when the plot is photocopied (which is usually an advantage). In an emergency, tear a sheet from a pad of lined paper, turn it on its side and slide it under the next sheet.

Special types of graph paper can be useful in different circumstances. Divisions into twelve are invaluable when plotting monthly data (and a nuisance otherwise). If you are plotting something which requires a log transformation, graph paper exists which enables you to plot directly on to a log scale (as shown in figure 11.6). A variable that has three categories (such as three parties' share of the total vote) can be represented on triangular graph paper. Probability graph paper exists to show the extent to which a distribution deviates from the Gaussian shape. It takes a bit of time to learn to use these more specialized sorts of graph paper but it is worth the effort.

There are many aids to make plots look more professional: devices for lettering, for drawing smooth curves, for stippling and cross-hatching areas with different patterns. There are also different kinds of drawing boards which will hold the paper firmly down and provide moving X and Y axes. You should browse in your local art shop.

Drawing the axes

Ensure that the axes are long enough to cover the whole range, or be prepared to omit points from the graph. You do not have to draw each axis to the zero point, but you must label each axis clearly to show what you have done. Altering the scale of the axis can quite dramatically affect the appearance of a plot. When constructing scatterplots, make the Y-axis one-half to two-thirds the length of the X-axis; as a guide, think of exercise paper, which is usually of these dimensions, turned on its side.

Don't use awkward subdivisions of the scale; stick to units, twos and fives; computers can calculate accurately how to plot on scales rising by sevens but you will make mistakes. Label the axes and their units of measurement. When you are doing the first draft, label as many points on the axes as possible.

Plotting the points on a scatterplot

Plot each point carefully, using a symbol such as a cross; if more than one point lands on the same spot, you could plot the number of points represented (i.e. the numeral 2 if two points are superimposed). Inspect the result and decide if it would look better if you stretched or shrunk the scale.

Drawing a bar chart

Arrange the bars in some sensible order, such as in order of their lengths. There is no special significance to the width of bars, but it should be uniform. A good rule of thumb is to make the spacing between the bars one half of the width of the bars. The bars should be solid, not just drawn in outline.

Bar charts are sometimes drawn vertically in columns. In general, however, labelling the categories is easier if they are arranged horizontally. Back to back bar charts can be used as back to back stem and leaf displays were to compare two distributions. The bars may be subdivided to show the components of a second variable within categories of the first.

Displaying the results

Smart presentation of results should always be done on plain paper. If it is thin enough you will be able to trace the outlines of a plot originally drawn on graph paper. Trace the axes, but only mark sufficient points on the scale to enable the magnitudes to be assessed. A small number of faint grid lines (or lines of white space on solid bar charts) may sometimes be added if it is important that the reader should be able to gauge precisely the level of particular points.

Hand or computer?

The plotting routines available in most statistical packages are still rather crude, especially those which rely on the line-printer as their printing device; plots on machines designed for text mean that the resolution (i.e. number of subdivisions possible on either the horizontal or vertical axis) is usually poor; many values that are in fact different can end up being plotted on the same point. Specialized software and hardware for plotting is improving all the time; there are several acceptable purpose-built packages now available, especially for drawing bar charts and circular pie charts.

However, it is important to learn how to plot by hand. Many decisions about how to display the data have to be standardized within a package, and they do not always lead to sensible or pretty results. Consult Velleman and Hoaglin (1977) for a useful discussion of the problems of computer plotting, especially of EDA techniques.

Further reading

The classic work on plotting and graphs used to be a textbook by Carl Schmid (1954), which is still worth consulting. It began life as an appendix to a pre-war American survey textbook, and then ran into several editions in its own right. There are also some useful and amusing guidelines in Darrell Huff's perennial best-seller *How to Lie with Statistics* (1973).

More recently, Edward Tufte has published a masterly compendium on graphics (1983). It is on the one hand full of practical hints about all aspects of plotting, with many clear examples. But it also provides something of the history of graphics, and the visual principles which have gradually evolved to which the technical artist should adhere. Tufte divides the ink marks made to present a graphical display into two: data ink and chartjunk. His entire book is devoted to ways of improving the proportion of the ink that is devoted to conveying aspects of the data, and of erasing chartjunk; this leads him to suggest some simplification of boxplots, for example.

11 Transformations

We now shall take up an issue that has been touched on several times before: power transformation of the scale of a variable in order to make its analysis easier. This chapter has been placed after chapter 10 since one of the most appealing uses of such transformations is to unbend curvy lines. However, it follows on very naturally from the issues raised in chapter 3, and some may want to read it directly after that. Some of the illustrations require understanding of boxplots, introduced in chapter 6, and line fitting, introduced in the previous chapter.

11.1 The wealth of nations

The stated goal both of leaders of poor nations and of agencies and banks in the richer countries is the 'development' of the poorer countries. The nature of that development, however, has been a matter of some dispute. National income, or its rate of growth, has most often been used in the West to indicate success. To many poorer countries, however, the idea of turning into a replica of one of the industrialized countries, pursuing high money incomes and high growth rates as goals in their own right, appears neither feasible nor desirable.

In this chapter we shall first take a look at how the most commonly used measure of national wealth – gross national product (GNP) – is constructed, and consider the distribution of GNP across several countries. We shall return to the question of whether GNP is in fact a good indicator of well-being later, and consider a newer approach which examines the extent to which the basic human needs of citizens are being met.

Most countries in the world attempt to monitor the total value of their output, or **gross national product**. This can be defined abstractly as the sum of values of both final goods and services and investment goods in a country. Final goods are things that are consumed directly and not used to produce something else; if all goods were included in the estimate of GNP, then the cost of flour would be double-counted when the final cost of bread was included. However, a final good is not easy to operationalize. Logically, even consumption activities such as eating could be viewed as an investment required to sustain the producer; this is perhaps clearer in the case of the agricultural labourer's meal which is essential to production, than the executive's expense-account lunch which may actually impede it. However, rules have been developed to standardize what is to be included in the definition of final product; meals, for example, are always included as final goods.

Goods and services which in some countries are circulated by being exchanged on the market are circulated by the state in others; health care and medicines are a good example. It is clearly desirable that the amount that a nation spends on health be included in the estimate of GNP, so the total expenditures of the state as well as private individuals are included. Moreover, part of a nation's wealth is spent on investment goods, and not on consumption goods; these are therefore also included in the calculation.

Two methods can be used to estimate GNP. One can either directly estimate the value of all the final goods and services (a variant would be to estimate what every branch of production adds to the the value of the goods it uses as raw materials). Or one can assess the earnings which are received by those involved in production, both wages and profits, interests and the like. The job of the statisticians employed by government to produce national accounts is to piece together the picture as best they can, using both methods, and as much of the available data as possible. Standard economics textbooks detail the accounting methods typically used (e.g. Samuelson and Nordhaus 1985) and the Blue Book *Sources and Methods* volume details the methods used in Britain (Central Statistical Office 1985).

A distinction is made between domestic and national product. If one focuses on all the production that takes place within national boundaries, the measure is termed the **gross domestic product** (GDP). If, on the other hand, one focuses on the production that is undertaken by the residents of that country, the income earned by nationals from abroad has to be added to the gross domestic product, to arrive at the gross national product.

In a country where most of the goods and services exchange for money, GNP can be defined and estimated fairly reliably, given sufficient care. In countries where large proportions of goods and services are produced by those who consume them or are exchanged on a very small scale without coming to the market, estimates have to be made, and these are of varying accuracy. 'We should ask national income estimators conceptual questions such as: which of the activities a farm family does for itself without payment, such as haircutting for example, have you included in the national income?', says a leading development economist (Seers 1979: 15).

GNP is commonly used as a measure of well-being of individuals in a country. For this purpose, it is often expressed per head of population, which also brings problems of estimation. Most countries organize censuses of their population on something like ten-yearly intervals, but not all do, and they certainly do not do them at the same point in time. The quality of many of these censuses is low, and error rates of 20 per cent are not unusual. Moreover, population size changes and thus the errors are not constant.

In order to compare the GNP of different nations, the income has to be expressed in a common currency unit. US dollars are conventionally used, but the method of conversion to that scale is problematic. The World Bank method, used in the data in this chapter, is based on official exchange rates. This leads to biases in estimation of GNP when the official exchange rate over- or under-values that country's currency. In some cases where the discrepancy between the official and black market rates is very marked, the World Bank declines to publish GNP statistics.

There are therefore many problems in measuring GNP. The value of the statistics from poor countries which have neither a large statistical staff nor routine data collection activities is often especially questionable. The World Bank does its best to adjust the estimates made by the individual countries for comparability, but the process is inevitably inexact.

11.2 The distribution of GNP per capita

Let us now consider the distribution of GNP in a sample of countries in the world, as shown in figure 11.1. The boxplot of the distribution of GNP per capita is shown in figure 11.2. The distribution of incomes across countries looks similar to the distribution of incomes one finds within a country: it straggles upwards, the midspread is above the median, the midextreme is above the midspread, the lower whisker is very short and there are upper outliers. There are relatively few countries at the top of the spectrum: uncomfortably many have per capita incomes that are very low indeed.

If we consider the boxplots of GNP per capita for all the countries in the world, broken down into different country groups (figure 11.3), they also straggle upwards, in data batches at different levels, with different midspreads and shapes. One reason for the upward straggle is the existence of a floor of zero dollars below which no country can fall (in theory), whereas there is no ceiling. Moreover, the batches form a characteristic wedge shape: batches with lower medians have lower midspreads, and those with higher medians have higher midspreads; this is always a tell-tale sign that a transformation might be in order.

Figure 11.1 GNP per capital in 1984 in 15 sampled countries

Country	GNP per capita in 1984 ($US)
Zaire	140
Uganda	230
China	310
Pakistan	380
Mauritania	480
Yemen PDR	550
Nigeria	730
Mauritius	1,090
Tunisia	1,270
Chile	1,700
Korea Republic	2,110
Hong Kong	6,330
Austria	9,140
Sweden	11,860
Kuwait	16,720

Source: column 4 of WORLD dataset; every eighth country selected

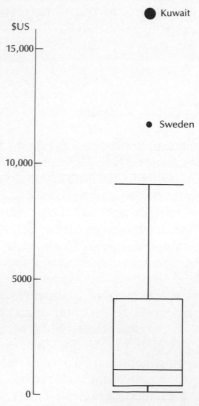

Figure 11.2 The distribution of GNP per capita in 1984: boxplot
Source: data in figure 1.1

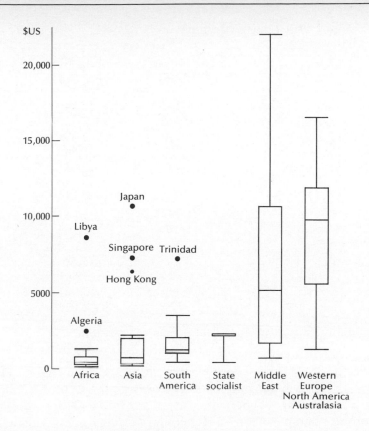

Figure 11.3: Distribution of GNP per capita in 1984 within country groups
Source: columns 1 and 4 of WORLD dataset

The upward straggle of income distributions is, in one sense, a truth about the world that we must not obscure. It does pose difficulties for the data analyst, however. Differences at the lower end of the scale are obscured by the massive differences at the top end. Multiple boxplots such as those in figure 11.3 are hard to summarize succinctly: not only do typical income levels in each group vary, but the spread and shape also vary. Finally, if income were plotted against another interval level variable, the relationship would almost certainly be curved rather than straight. In this chapter, we shall consider a family of transformations of the scale of measurement which help make the variables easier to handle in data analysis.

11.3 The log transformation

We have met one of these transformations – the log transformation – already. Taking logs of a dataset has the effect of counteracting upward straggle. Figure 11.4 shows what happens if we take a logarithm of every

Figure 11.4 Logging the numbers in figure 11.1

Country	GNP per capita in 1980 ($US)	Log GNP per capita
Zaire	140	2.146
Uganda	230	2.362
China	310	2.491
Pakistan	380	2.580
Mauritania	480	2.681
Yemen PDR	550	2.740
Nigeria	730	2.863
Mauritius	1,090	3.037
Tunisia	1,270	3.104
Chile	1,700	3.230
Korea Republic	2,110	3.324
Hong Kong	6,330	3.801
Austria	9,140	3.961
Sweden	11,860	4.074
Kuwait	16,720	4.223

number in figure 11.1; the resulting shape is shown in figure 11.5. The higher values have been pulled down towards the centre of the batch, bringing Kuwait and Sweden into the main body of the data, and the bottom of the scale has been stretched out correspondingly. The shape is now more symmetrical.

It was not necessary to transform every single data value in order to draw the boxplot in figure 11.5; it was sufficient to transform the median, the quartiles and the extremes, and to recalculate the midspread and adjacent values. Only order-based summaries such as medians can be transformed in this way; it is *not* the case that mean ($\log X$) is the same as log (mean X), for example.

There is an even easier way to see if the log transformation would help promote symmetry. Graph paper exists which has equal divisions along one axis and logarithmic divisions along the other. Raw data can be plotted straight on to such paper, as shown in figure 11.6. Care has to be taken with the adjacent values, which cannot be obtained by reading off distances on the graph paper; they must be obtained arithmetically. Log paper comes in several numbers of **cycles**; the specimen in figure 11.6 contains three cycles, allowing the highest number to be as much as 10^3 or 1000 times as high as the smallest; four cycle paper would allow it to be as much as 10^4 or 10,000 times as high.

The principles of logarithms were discovered in the seventeenth century; they gave a tremendous technical spur to navigation, astronomy and to the growing commercial sector, facilitating tedious calculations, like nineteen months' interest at an annual rate of 2.79 per cent. In the

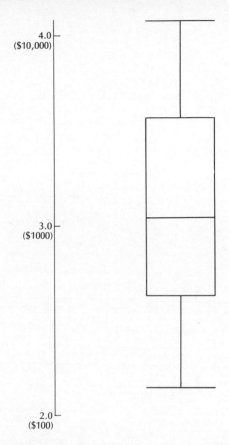

Figure 11.5 Logging GNP per capita in 1984 in 15 selected countries
Source: column 2 of figure 11.4

days of calculators and computers, we no longer use log tables to speed up hand calculations. But logs have a vital role to play in data analysis, providing one of the most useful ways of re-expressing data that straggles upwards. As we saw in chapter 3, logs convert multiplicative processes into additive ones, since $\log(ab) = \log(a) + \log(b)$. Whenever we work with data values that have been generated by a growth process, we will have a better chance of revealing regularities in their behaviour if we convert them first to logs.

11.4 The ladder of powers

Not all variables straggle upwards, however. Consider life expectancy, a measure indicating the number of years a newborn infant could typically be expected to live if patterns of mortality prevailing for all people in the year of its birth were to stay the same throughout its life. The distribution

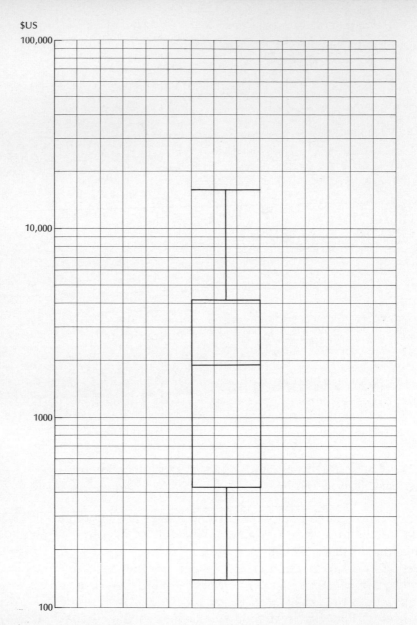

Figure 11.6 Distribution of GNP per capita: plotted on three-cycle log graph
        paper

Source: figure 11.1

of life expectancy across countries is not symmetrical: the lower half of
the distribution is more spread out than the upper half (figure 11.7);
many countries are pushing up against what looks like some kind of a
ceiling of around seventy-seven years, while some poorer countries trail
down in the forties and two countries (Sierra Leone and Guinea) even

Figure 11.7 Life expectancy in the world in 1984: stem
and leaf display of raw data

leaf unit = 1 year
3 8 represents 38 years

2	3.	88
7	4*	33444
23	4.	5555666667778899
42	5*	00011112222223334444
52	5.	5567788999
(17)	6*	00000112233344444
56	6.	555566678899999
41	7*	00000011111122233333444
19	7.	5555555666677777777

Source: WORLD dataset column 7

register a staggering thirty-eight years. A log transformation of the life
expectancy distribution would make the downward straggle even more
pronounced, since logs have the effect of stretching the bottom end of
any scale.

There is a general family of power transformations that can help
promote symmetry and sometimes Gaussian shape in many different data
batches. Look what happens, for example, when the life expectancy in
each country is raised to powers greater than one (figure 11.8). Squaring
the values makes the batch slightly more symmetrical, and cubing them

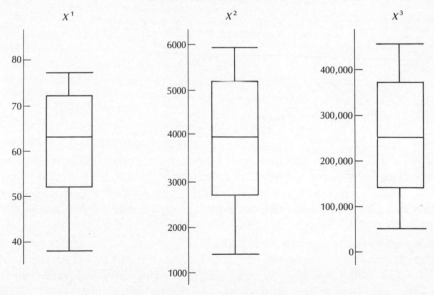

Figure 11.8 Life expectancy in the world in 1984: boxplots of raw and
transformed data
Source: as figure 11.7

even more; the effects are not dramatic, but the improvement is visible. The effect is the opposite to taking logs: squaring stretches out the upper values and compresses the lower ones, and cubing does so even more powerfully. Both transformations keep the data points in the same order, just as logging did.

There are an infinite number of possible powers to which data can be raised. The commonest values are shown in figure 11.9, placed, as Tukey suggests, on a 'ladder' in terms of their effect on distributions. There are many other points besides the ones on this **ladder of powers**, both in between the values shown and above and beneath them, but we shall rarely have any need to go beyond those shown.

Power	Expression	Name
•		
•		
3	X^3	cube
2	X^2	square
1	X^1	raw data
0.5	$\sqrt{X}$	square root
0	X^0	? (log)
−0.5	$1/\sqrt{X}$	reciprocal root
−1	$1/X$	reciprocal
−2	$1/X^2$	reciprocal square
•		
•		

Figure 11.9 The ladder of powers

Since these transformations must preserve the order of the data points, all the transformations which are powers of less than zero are multiplied by −1. The transformation is then strictly the negative reciprocal and not the reciprocal; otherwise, the order of 2 and 3 would be reversed, as the reciprocal of 2 (0.5) is larger than the reciprocal of 3 (0.33).

If we start from the raw data values X^1 we can either proceed up the ladder of powers by squaring or cubing each number or down the ladder by taking square roots or reciprocals. **Going up the ladder of powers corrects downward straggle, whereas going down corrects upward straggle.** We went up the ladder of powers when we squared the data. It was not far enough, as there was still downward straggle, so we moved further up the ladder to cubes.

What about the mystery exponent, X^0? Any number raised to the power of exactly zero is unity; clearly, it would be no help to make all the numbers identical. But we can treat the zero exponent on the ladder of powers as the log, since its effect on the shape of data batches fits exactly at this point; it corrects upward straggle more powerfully than taking roots, but it is not as strong a transformation as the reciprocal root, or reciprocals.

There are two refinements to notice about power transformations. In general, exact zeros cannot be transformed in this way (the log of zero is undefined), so it is conventional to add a very small amount (usually one-sixth or one-half) to all the values in a batch containing zeros before transforming. The second problem comes with negative numbers. If all the numbers are negative, the simplest thing is to multiply them all by -1. If some are negative and some positive, it may be possible to add a constant to make them all positive, or it may be necessary to consider treating the positive and negative numbers separately.

11.5 The goals of transformation

The number systems we use as yardsticks should be thought of as being made not of wood but of elastic which can be stretched or shrunk to our convenience. Transforming the original numbers by taking logs (or by one of the other transformations considered below) is an essentially trivial operation: the order of the numbers is preserved, and they can easily be recast in their original form by taking antilogs. There is nothing God-given about any particular system of measurement; intelligent life on another planet might easily have evolved a method of assessing people's incomes which involved multiplying by a fixed amount for each increment. Ideally, we should feel as comfortable working with logged GNP per capita or life expectancy cubed as we feel about working with the raw numbers.

However, it is reasonable to demand a more positive rationale for transforming data, especially as the resulting numbers seem so unfamiliar. There are five principal advantages to be gained, listed below in rising order of importance.

1 Data batches can be made more symmetrical.
2 The shape of data batches can be made more Gaussian.
3 Outliers that arise simply from the skewness of the distribution can be removed, and previously hidden outliers may be forced into view.
4 Multiple batches can be made to have more similar spreads.
5 Linear, additive models may be fitted to the data.

Symmetry on its own is not very important, but the advantages of the Gaussian shape were discussed in chapter 3. The third goal attempts to focus the data analyst's attention on data points that are unusual for a substantive reason, not just because of the shape of the distribution. Equality of spread in multiple batches promotes comparability between them; it is hard to summarize differences in level when spreads also vary. Linear, additive models are easier to work with than more complex mathematical models. The last two goals are the most important, and we shall consider them further in the following sections. But it is often the case that, by finding a transformation that will promote equality of spread or linearity, it is possible to achieve the first three at the same time.

If these goals can be achieved, a loss of the intuitive appeal of the simple number scale will have been worthwhile. For those who find it hard to work with or explain coherently to others a set of numbers which have been raised to a power or logged, Mosteller and Tukey (1977: 194) suggest a technique which they call 'matched re-expression' to rescale the transformed values to fall within the main range of the original number scale.

11.6 Promoting equality of spread

It is important for the spread to be independent of level in data analysis, whether fitting lines, smoothing, or dealing with multiple boxplots. No simple statement can be made summarizing typical differences in GNP between the country groups in figure 11.3, for example, because they differ systematically in spread as well as in level. A tell-tale wedge-shaped pattern appears in the multiple boxplots: batches with higher medians tend also to have higher midspreads, a sign that usually indicates the need for transformation.

Figure 11.10 shows the effect of taking logs on the distribution of GNP in the different country groups. Logging GNP per capita goes a long way towards holding the midspreads constant by making them similar in size. This means that statements can be made describing typical differences in wealth between the country groups without needing to mention the differences in spread in the same breath. But, by transforming, progress has also been made towards the first three goals: the batches are more symmetrical and bell-shaped, and some of the outliers in the original batch were not really unusual values, but merely a product of the upward straggle of the raw numbers.

There are no far outliers in the logged distribution, and the outliers that remain do seem to differ substantively from the body of the data. It was always debatable whether Turkey should have been included as a European country; its GNP suggests that it fits more comfortably with other Asian countries. Libya's unusual wealth for an African country stems from the fact that it is an oil-producing country with a relatively small population. This picture also says forcibly some other pieces of

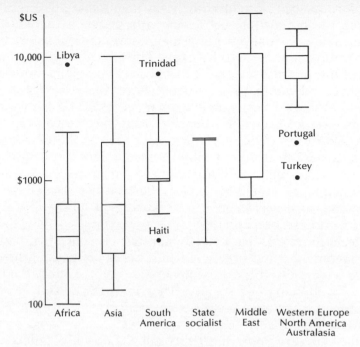

Figure 11.10 Logged GNP per capita in 1984 by country group
Source: column 4 of WORLD dataset

information which we might perhaps not have guessed: that Portugal and Haiti are very poor countries, and that Trinidad is a very wealthy country, in relative terms.

It is not always easy to spot the fact that the spread increases as the level increases. The fact may stand out in higher relief if the residuals are plotted against the fitted values. We should be concerned whenever there appears to be a positive association between the level and spread (or between residuals and fitted values), whatever data analytic technique is being used. Exercise 11.4 has been set to illustrate that the problem can occur with time series data and how transformations can help there also.

11.7 Alternatives to GNP as a measure of welfare

Before we look at the last goal of transformation, unbending curved relationships, it will be helpful to return briefly to the debate about the goals of development. There are formidable problems in estimating GNP reliably in many countries of the world. Even if these were surmounted, two fundamental questions would remain about using the average wealth of a country as an index of the well-being of its citizens. First, as you discovered in exercise 10.1, while the wealthier members of any society claim to be more happy than poorer members of that society, the cross-cultural association between the average amount of wealth in a country and the proportion who claim to be happy is extremely weak. Moreover, the measure says nothing about how the wealth is distributed; a country could raise its GNP by expanding capital intensive industries which leave the poorest sectors of that society completely untouched.

Alternative indicators of well-being have therefore been sought. Summary measures of inequality, such as quantile shares or Gini coefficients, are not available in enough countries, as you can verify in the WORLD dataset. Moreover, measures such as the Gini coefficient treat inequalities at different points in the income distribution as equivalent, whereas many development economists have argued that the goal of economic aid should be to meet the basic needs of all the citizens in any country; this usually involves focusing on how well a society is doing by its poorest members.

While the logic of this 'basic needs' approach is appealing, there is still room for argument about precisely which needs are basic. Many writers on welfare have viewed life expectancy rates as the most fundamental indicator of well-being in a society. They have the advantage that they can be calculated for most countries in the world. However, a country could have a moderately high average level, while some sections of society still had very short life expectancy. Long life expectancy also indicates the success of development rather than the potential for it.

A case has also been made for using educational variables as an alternative. Suggestions have included the proportion of adults who can read, or the proportion of females attending primary school; one can be sure that the higher either of these indicators go, the more the basic educational needs of *all* members of a given society are being met. Moreover, an educated workforce is argued to be one of the important prerequisites for economic expansion and advance. You can explore the relationships between some of the basic indicators published by the World Bank in the dataset WORLD.

11.8 Unbending curvy lines

In this section, we shall consider the relationship between life expectancy and national wealth in 1984. (It is arguable that life expectancy in 1984 would respond to the prevailing GNP sometime in the past, but we shall ignore that refinement here.) The scatterplot in figure 11.11 reveals a clear relationship between the two variables. However, the relationship is curved; fitting a straight line will not provide a sensible summary. Either a curve must be fitted, a job which is difficult to do well, or the data must be manipulated so that a straight line becomes a good summary.

Logging GNP per capita and cubing life expectancy did the best job of promoting symmetry and Gaussian shape in these two variables taken

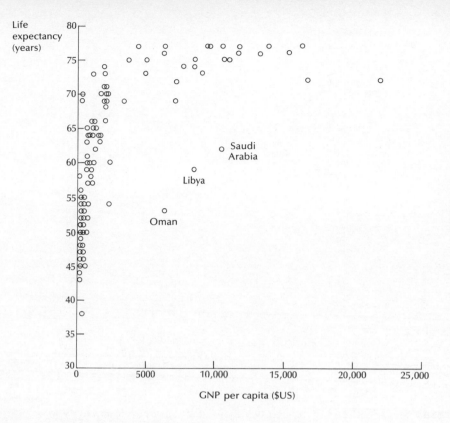

Figure 11.11 Life expectancy by GNP per capita in 1984

Source: columns 4 and 7 of WORLD dataset

individually. The same transformations also help clarify the bivariate relationship (figure 11.12): the scatterplot is more nearly linear, the relationship is capable of easy summary, and previously hidden unusual values are revealed.

We fit lines whenever possible because they are simple, not only for our computers but also for our own brains. If you prefer, however, you can think of fitting a line to transformed data as equivalent to fitting a curve to the raw data; in effect one is saying that the relationship between the two variables takes the form of a particular curve.

The curvy pattern in figure 11.11 was very clear, but sometimes, when the relationship is not so strong, it is hard for the eye to tell if a transformation is required. A useful diagnostic guide is given by the half-slope ratio, introduced in section 10.6. As a rule of thumb, we should explore the possible improvement of fit that a transformation would bring whenever the half-slope ratio is greater than 2.

The overall picture in figure 11.12 suggests that life expectancy can be predicted pretty accurately from a country's GNP: wealthy countries

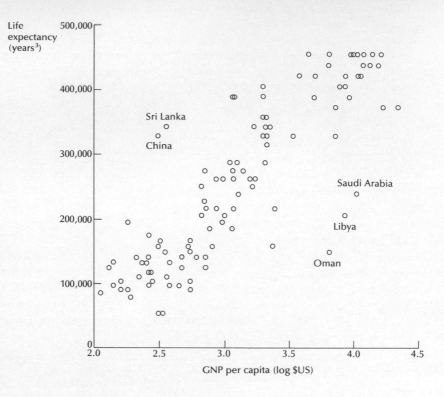

Figure 11.12 Cubed life expectancy by logged GNP per capita in 1984
Source: columns 4 and 7 of WORLD dataset

have healthier populations. GNP could be vindicated as a measure of welfare by this finding. Its defenders have certainly been reluctant to give it up in the face of criticisms, for fear that 'without it, the macro-economists would be adrift in a sea of unorganized data' (Samuelson and Nordhaus 1985).

Life expectancy is still an average measure, however, and might conceal problems for some groups within wealthy countries. And there are deviant countries. It is clear from both the untransformed and the transformed plot that the oil-producing countries tend to have low life expectancies for their level of wealth. Figure 11.12, also reveals that China and Sri Lanka have unusually high life expectancy rates for their low level of economic development, a fact that was not apparent before the transformation.

As we shall discuss in the next chapter, there is a lot more work to be done before the causal process underlying this relationship is laid bare: we do not know whether it is through buying a better diet or better medical care, for example, that richer countries improve their life expectancy. (Exercise 11.5 casts some light on this.)

11.9 Determining the best power for transformation

There are many clues in the course of data analysis that suggest that it might be better to work on a transformed scale. We have concentrated on the three most important diagnostic signs: upward or downward straggle in individual batches (figure 11.2), wedge-shaped data where batches with higher medians have greater spread (figure 11.3), and curvy lines in a scatterplot (figure 11.11).

Identifying the need for a transformation, however, does not tell us which one will do the best job of achieving the five goals mentioned above: so far we have guides to diagnosis but not to cure. There are three different ways we can get such guidance: from our substantive knowledge of the world, by experimenting with the ladder of powers, and by constructing special diagnostic plots.

We may have a theoretical reason for believing that the variable we are studying will require a particular transformation. We have already noted that a log transformation often helps when the data is the result of some process of growth. The square root transformation will often work well in cases where the data is a rare occurrence, like suicide or infant mortality. There are situations where the reciprocal of a rate would make more sense than the original rate: ergonomists, for example, might find it more natural to look at the time it takes a person to produce a fixed number of items rather than at the output a person produces from a machine in a fixed period of time.

In the absence of a rationale for a particular transformation (or in the face of competing rationales) the ladder of powers provides a useful guide. When investigating a transformation to promote symmetry in a single batch, we first examine the midpoint summaries – the median, the midquartile, and the midextreme – to see if they tend to increase or decrease. If they systematically increase in value, a transformation lower down the ladder should be tried. If the midpoint summaries then trend downwards, the transformation was too powerful, and we must move back up the ladder somewhat. We continue experimenting with different transformations from the summary values until we have done the best we can to promote symmetry and Gaussian shape.

In trying to unbend curvy lines, there is another way of deciding how to proceed on the ladder of powers. Curves which are monotonic and contain only one bend can be thought of as one of the four quadrants of a circle. To straighten out any such curves, first draw a tangent to see what you are trying to achieve. Then imagine pulling the curve towards the tangent (as shown in figure 11.13). Notice the direction in which you are having to pull the curve on each axis, and move on the ladder of powers accordingly: down in the Y direction? go down on the ladder of powers with Y, and so on. To straighten the data in figure 11.13, for example, the curve has to be pulled down in the Y-direction and up in the X-direction;

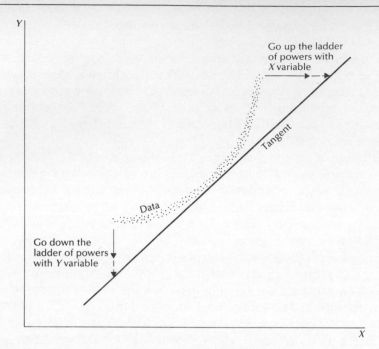

Figure 11.13 Guide to linearizing transformations for curves

linearity will therefore probably be improved by raising the Y variable to a power lower down on the ladder and/or by raising the X variable to a power higher up on the ladder.

If the curve is not a single bend, monotonic curve, power transformations will probably not straighten it out, though they may help. As we saw in chapter 8, a logistic transformation can help straighten out a flat S-shaped curve (figure 8.5). Transformations for more complex curves are rarely needed.

When there is a systematic relationship between the level of the batch and the spread of that batch, plotting the log of the dQ against the log of the median for each batch produces a useful diagnostic picture. Tukey suggests that, if a line is sketched to fit the points, (1 – slope) will yield the power which should help promote equality of spread. Thus, for instance, if the line had a slope of 1, a log transformation would be indicated; if the line had a negative slope, it would be necessary to raise the data values by a power of more than 1; if there is no relationship and the line has zero slope, power transformations are not likely to help. (A similar way of finding the best power for transformation will be explained for median polishing in chapter 15.)

11.10 Conclusion

We have looked at the distribution of two variables in this chapter: an indicator of the monetary wealth of a nation, GNP per capita, and an indicator of the material standard of living of a nation, the average age to which people can expect to live. Neither variable was symmetrical in its raw form. Altering the scale of measurement of each of these variables altered the shape of the distribution of each. A general family of transformations – involving raising the data values to different powers – was introduced as a guide to correcting straggle: if the straggle is downward, go up on the ladder of powers, and vice versa. The log transformation was found to fit nicely at the zero position on the ladder of powers.

The main goal of transformation is not aesthetic, however. The aim is to express numbers on a scale of measurement which makes data analysis easier, often by allowing simple models to be fitted, and thus enhancing our ability to understand the data. In particular, we saw how such transformations can help make the dQ of different batches more similar, and help unbend curvy lines; the result in both cases is to enable the data analyst to re-express the data simply in the conventional form: data = fit + residual.

Power transformations are a very important part of the researcher's armoury; while the exponents of exploratory data analysis stress them (Tukey 1977; Mosteller and Tukey 1977), their use is applauded by many statisticians (e.g. Kruskal 1978). Although it may take some practice to get used to the idea of changing the seemingly natural number scale, you will soon find that you automatically consider whether a transformation would aid analysis when you first look at a batch of data.

The most difficult problem comes with conveying the effect of transformation to lay audiences, who may be suspicious of statisticians 'fiddling with the numbers'; someone might fear, for example, that by taking logs in figure 11.10 the real upward straggle in national wealth has been hidden. Data analysts must not be put off using the best techniques available in case they are misunderstood, but they have an important responsibility to explain what they have done to try to ensure that misunderstandings do not arise. For presentation purposes, this usually involves converting key elements of the analysis back to the original scale. It may be possible to explain line fitting with transformed data in terms of fitting curves. However we achieve it, great care must be taken to make the exposition clear to a non-technical audience.

Exercises

11.1 Using logs to the base 10 (see the appendix to this chapter), what is:

(a) log (1)
(b) log (0)
(c) log(pqr)
(d) log (p/q)
(e) log (p^n)?

Write down the value of:

(f) $\log_{10}(2)$
(g) $\log_e(2)$

11.2 The validity of official statistics on suicide has often been questioned; some critics have claimed that different national suicide rates reflect the extent to which coroners in those countries are prepared to categorize deaths as suicide, rather than real national differences in propensity to suicide. If the more extreme versions of the criticism were true, immigrants to a country should exhibit suicide rates similar to that country, rather than to the country they came from (Sainsbury and Jenkins 1982). The following data shows the suicide rates per 100,000 of male Australian immigrants from various countries and the comparable native suicide rates.

Country	Immigrants	Country of birth
Hungary	57.7	40.3
Poland	56.6	14.3
Yugoslavia	38.6	17.8
Czechoslovakia	38.5	30.4
New Zealand	33.1	11.4
Austria	33.0	32.4
Germany	32.8	26.7
Ireland	30.5	5.3
Scotland	30.3	10.0
USA	29.5	16.3
England and Wales	25.3	13.7
Spain	15.9	7.6
Netherlands	12.7	8.2
Malta	10.7	1.4
Italy	10.4	7.6
Greece	6.8	4.7

Summarize the distribution in both batches. Is a power transformation required? How well do the immigrant and native suicide rates correspond to the native Australian suicide rate of 16.1?

11.3 Using the dataset TOWNS, identify a transformation that will pull in as many of the upper outliers in the town sizes in 1981 as possible without creating new lower outliers. (You may wish to exclude sparsely populated local areas on the grounds that they do not qualify as towns.)

11.4 Plot the legitimate and illegitimate fertility rates in the SCOT-LAND dataset on the same scale. Describe the trends in both curves. Then take logs of both variables and plot them again. Does your description stay the same?

11.5 Using Minitab, read the WORLD dataset into the worksheet.

(a) Find a transformation suitable for the number of people per doctor.
(b) Plot life expectancy cubed versus number of people per doctor as transformed in (a). Can you predict life expectancy from such an input health indicator?
(c) Plot the number of people per doctor as transformed in (a) versus log GNP, fit a line to the relationship, and calculate residuals.
(d) Repeat exercise (c) for life expectancy cubed versus log GNP.
(e) Plot residual life expectancy versus residual number of people per doctor, as in (b). Re-evaluate the extent to which life expectancy can be predicted by number of people per doctor when GNP has been controlled.

Appendix: powers and logarithms

Exponents

A number y can be raised to any **power**, say n. This is written as y^n. It means that we multiply y by itself n times. The power n is called the **exponent** of y.

The most common exponents are two and three: squaring and cubing a number. The principle is general, however, and any number, positive or negative, whole or fractional, may be used as an exponent. Two other common exponents are 0.5 (taking square roots) and -1 (the reciprocal or $1/y$).

The rules about manipulating exponents are as follows:

$$y^n y^m = y^{n+m}$$
$$(y^n)^m = y^{nm}$$
$$y^1 = y$$
$$y^0 = 1$$

Logarithms

What is a log? The idea of logarithms is based on exponents. Any positive number X can be re-expressed as 10^y where y is the power that 10 must be raised to to obtain X. When a number is re-expressed in this way, y is called the logarithm of X. The $\log_{10}$ of 3, for example, is the exponent of 10 needed to get 3. It is therefore smaller than 1, because $\log_{10}(10)$ is 1, and larger than 0, because $\log_{10}(1)$ is 0.

Any positive number can be used as the **base** for logarithms; you can have logs based on 10, or 2, or 7, or 2.71828 (called e) and so on. The two most common are $\log_{10}$ and $\log_e$. The latter are known as natural logs; the functional abbreviation is 'LN' in computerese. Any two differ only by a multiplicative constant, so for data analysis, each is as good as any other.

How do logs undo a multiplicative process?   The log of a product is the sum of the logs of the factors:

$$\log(abc) = \log(a) + \log(b) + \log(c)$$

Conversely, the log of a ratio is the difference of the logs of the numerator and denominator:

$$\log(a/b) = \log(a) - \log(b)$$

What are some anchor points in the $\log_{10}$ scale?

$$\log 1000 = 3$$
$$\log 100 \;= 2$$
$$\log 10 \;\;= 1$$
$$\log 1 \;\;\; = 0$$
$$\log 0 \text{ is not defined}$$
$$\log 0.1 \;\; = -1$$
$$\log 0.01 = -2$$

(Logs cannot be taken of negative numbers.)

How do you work out a log?   The easiest way to find the log of a number is on a calculator: enter the number and press the LOG button. If you haven't yet bought a calculator, you will have to look it up in either the old-fashioned log tables used for arithmetic calculations or in simplified 'break tables' of logarithms (see Tukey 1977).

Part III   Introducing a Third Variable

In the third part of this book, we consider ways of holding a third variable constant while assessing the relationship between two others. In chapter 13 we discuss how this is done with contingency tables; in chapter 14 the technique of standardization is presented, and you learn how to construct a standardized mortality ratio; in chapter 15 the techniques of chapter 6, of decomposing variation into a fitted and a residual component, are extended to situations with two explanatory variables.

However, before proceeding to the techniques of controlling extraneous variables, we must devote a chapter to discussing the logic of the procedure. Chapter 12 is devoted entirely to thinking about the causal issues at stake.

12 Causal Explanations

You will by now have developed some facility with handling batches of data, summarizing features of their distributions, and investigating relationships between variables. We must now change gear somewhat, and ask what it would take for such relationships to be treated as satisfactory *explanations*.

12.1 Why did the chicken cross the road?

An **explanation** is a human construction. It is an answer to the question 'why?' In everyday terms, a successful explanation is simply one that satisfies the person who asked the question. Since people who ask questions about the world vary in their interests, curiosity and knowledge, what counts as a successful explanation is also likely to vary greatly.

The question 'why?' is notoriously ambiguous. It can have many different kinds of answers. Some are motivational: 'in order to . . .'; some are causal: 'because . . . happened first'; some are typological: 'because it is an instance of . . .'; some invoke the existence of a social rule: 'because it is the custom'. The type of answer required will be given by the answerer's perception of what it is that is making the questioner curious. For this reason it is impossible to come up with universal rules dictating how explanations are to be provided.

However, scientific explanations are a very particular subset of answers to the question 'why?'. When scientists ask why something happens, they are asking for a general causal account. If they were to try to give an answer to the question at the head of this section, they would probably try to give a general account of factors which encourage or discourage chickens from crossing roads.

Causes exist in the real world; they are not just human constructions to help us understand it. They have been called 'the cement of the universe'

(Mackie 1974). They are processes which, once started, end up producing a particular outcome at a later point in time. To say that X causes Y is to say that, if X changes, it will produce a change in Y.

Some philosophers have tried to define cause in terms of statistical association, but such attempts have been unsuccessful; they are radically different concepts. The time recorded on two different watches, for example, can be perfectly associated: the time on one of them can be correctly predicted from the time on the other, but not because the time on one of them *causes* the time on the other; altering the time on one of them would have absolutely no impact on the other.

Many different component causes can add together to produce a particular outcome, a process known as **multiple causality**. Given this, we should not expect that the relationship between one cause among many and an effect to be perfect. Much everyday reasoning about causes, however, seems to demand perfect relationships: 'Smoking doesn't cause lung cancer; the man next door to us got lung cancer and he had never smoked a cigarette in his life', implying that the only cast-iron proof would be for all smokers to get lung cancer and for no non-smokers to get it.

Some people get very upset about the idea that there might be any causes operating in the social world; they fear that causal influences on human action rob people of their freedom of choice and dignity of action. This is a mistaken fear: if causes are the cement of both the natural and social universe, refusal to consider their existence will not stop them operating; it will merely mean that such causes are not uncovered, and, ironically, therefore will not be harnessed to give people greater control over and choice in their environment.

In fact, there is nothing to prevent us thinking of choice, intentions and motives in causal terms. The stock in trade of the psychologist is to understand some of the causal determinants of motivations and to show when conscious intentions really do cause behaviour and when they do not. Many different social sciences – economics, geography and sociology in particular – show how individually intended actions combine to produce social outcomes which may not have been the intentions of the actors.

12.2 Direct and indirect effects

Multiple causality means that two or more causes tend to work together to produce an effect. Moreover, the variables contributing to the effect may themselves be causally related. For this reason, we have to keep a clear idea in our heads of the relationships between the variables in the whole causal process.

In investigating the causes of absenteeism from work, for example, researchers have found different contributory factors. We shall consider two possible causal factors: being female and being in a low status job. Let us construct a causal path diagram depicting one possible set of relationships between these variables.

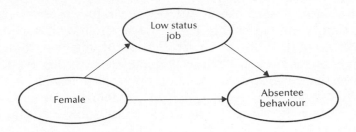

Figure 12.1 Causes of absenteeism

The diagram in figure 12.1 represents a simple system of multiple causal paths. There is an arrow showing that those in low status jobs are more likely to go absent. Being female has a causal effect in two ways. There is an arrow straight to absentee behaviour; this says that women are more likely to be absent from work than men, regardless of the kind of job they are in. This is termed a **direct effect** of sex on absenteeism. There is also another way in which being female has an effect; women are more likely to be in the kind of low status, perhaps unpleasant, jobs where absenteeism is more likely irrespective of sex. We can say that being female therefore also has an **indirect effect** on absenteeism, through the type of work performed.

You can think of figure 12.1 as a real causal process, at the moment known only to God.

12.3 Controlling the world to learn about causes

It is one thing to declare confidently that causal chains exist in the world out there. It is quite another thing, however, to find out what they are. Causal processes are not obvious. They hide in situations of complexity, in which effects may have been produced by several different causes acting together. When investigated, they will reluctantly shed one layer of explanation at a time, but only to reveal another deeper level of complexity beneath.

For this reason, something that is accepted as a satisfactory causal explanation at one point in time can become problematic at another. Researchers investigating the causes of psychological depression spent a long time carefully documenting how severe, traumatizing events that happen to people, such as bereavement or job loss, can induce it. Now that the causal effect of such life events has been established, the research effort is turning to ask how an event such as unemployment has its effect: is it through the loss of social esteem, through the decline of self-evaluation and self-esteem, through lack of cash or through the sheer effect of inactivity (Eales 1986)?

In order to answer such causal questions, careful observation of what goes on is simply not sufficient. There was a celebrated individual who devoted a large part of his life to carefully recording everything that he observed; upon his death, this complete set of observations was presented to the Royal Society in the hope that it would be of use to scientists. It was, of course, utterly useless. Deliberate learning situations have to be constructed if we want to pin causes down and further our grasp on the world.

Central to the creation of such learning situations is the idea of **control**. There are two ways in which scientists attempt to impose controls on the wayward world in order to learn. The first involves controlling the setting of the research to prevent certain variables operating. This is the method of the hard sciences like physics. Unlike physicists, however, social scientists cannot easily construct social circuits from which the effect of sexual magnetism is just banished, for example. The second type of control is therefore also necessary; it involves drawing inferences by comparing like with like. Let us consider both types of control a little more fully.

Sometimes social researchers are not able to achieve any control at all over the research setting, and are forced to observe the world as it occurs naturally. At the other extreme, they may decide they must contrive an artificial research setting in order to exclude the operation of unwanted variables. There are a continuous set of possibilities in between, and the particular design chosen is a matter of judgement. In a study investigating the effect of a particular teaching method on speed of learning, many factors could be held constant if a laboratory experiment were conducted – the identity of the teacher, the way the material was introduced and so on; a trial in real schools would be more realistic, but also more susceptible to the slings and arrows of fortune in the classroom. Researchers who were interested in people's views on blood sports could either hang around waiting for respondents spontaneously to bring the subject up, or they could ask directed questions about this on a structured questionnaire, taking care to ask everybody exactly the same question.

A balance has to be struck, since too much control of the research setting can lead to situations that lack naturalism and to indicators that lack validity; for example, the results to structured questions on a topic may not reflect the views respondents would express in any other situation. It is obviously desirable to obtain as much of this type of control as is consistent with naturalism.

Many people believe that it is the careful controlled setting of a laboratory that makes experiments very powerful situations in which to draw causal inferences. They are wrong; highly controlled settings can be achieved without any experimental manipulation. What differentiates true experiments from non-experimental enquiries is the attempt, either in the laboratory or field, to produce an effect among groups which have been randomly formed; in the simplest experiment, the researcher deliberately alters the X values of an experimental group, and sees what effect this has on their Y values by comparing them with a control group.

Unlike the first type of control, which was a spectrum, the second type – the making of controlled comparisons – forms a natural dichotomy: controlled experiments and non-experimental enquiries. In the former, the researcher can draw very strong inferences from comparisons between randomized groups. The importance of their being formed at random cannot be overemphasized; control groups start life the same as experimental groups in all respects simply by virtue of having been formed at random. When such preformed randomized control groups do not exist, inferences have to be drawn *post hoc* from comparisons between unrandomized groups.

The causal inferences that can be drawn from experiments are direct and unproblematic, at least in comparison with the inferences that can be drawn from non-experimental enquiries. If randomized control and experimental groups end up substantially different, something that happened to them in the experiment almost certainly caused this. If two uncontrolled groups prove to be different in some respect, we can only treat this as evidence of a causal relationship if we are convinced that they are not also different in some other important respect, as we shall see.

12.4 Do opinion polls influence people?

Let us take an example to illustrate the different inferences which can be drawn from experiments and non-experiments.

Some people believe that hearing the results of opinion polls before an election sways individuals towards the winning candidate. Imagine two ways in which empirical evidence could be collected for this proposition. An experiment could be conducted by taking a largish group of electors, splitting them into two at random, telling half that the polls indicated one candidate would win and telling the other half that they showed a rival would win. As long as there was a substantial number of people in each group, the groups would start the experiment having the same political preferences on average, since the groups were formed at random. If they differed substantially in their subsequent support for the candidates, then we could be almost certain that the phoney poll information they were fed contributed to which candidate they supported.

Alternatively, the proposition could be researched in a non-experimental way. A survey could be done to discover what individuals believed recent opinion polls showed, and to find out which candidates the individuals themselves supported. The preferences of those who believed that one candidate was going to win would be compared with those who believed that the rival was going to win; the hypothesis would be that the former would be more sympathetic to the candidate than the latter.

If the second survey did reveal a strong relationship between individuals' perception of the state of public opinion and their own belief, should this be taken as evidence that opinion polls have a causal effect on people's voting decisions? Should policy-makers consider banning polls in pre-election periods as a result? Anyone who tried this line of argument would be taken to task by the pollsters, who have a commercial interest in resisting such reasoning. They would deny that the effect in any way proves that polls influence opinion; it could, for instance, be that supporters of a right-wing candidate are of a generally conservative predisposition, and purchase newspapers which only report polls sympathetic to their candidate.

In short, comparing individuals in a survey who thought that candidate A would win with those who believed that candidate B would win would not be comparing two groups similar in all possible other respects, unlike the experiment discussed above.

An experiment would have a better chance of persuading people that the publication of opinion polls affected individual views. It is, however, possible that the experimental data would not be thought conclusive either; most of the experiments that have been done of this type have been rather artificial (Marsh 1985a). The famous social scientist, D. T. Campbell, once proposed a more naturalistic experiment, in which scores of towns would be selected and formed into two groups at random, the newspapers in each town would be persuaded to take part in the experiment by publishing phoney articles about the state of candidates, and comparisons would be made at the end between the two groups of towns (Campbell 1951). It will come as no surprise to learn, however, that this experiment has never been conducted.

Experiments are strong on causal logic, which accounts for the enthusiasm some social scientists have had for them. But the situations in which they can be carried out are few. Some have tried to get round this problem by constructing small scale models of the world that they really want to study, simulating wars, prison situations and so on. But only social psychologists who research aspects of small group behaviour have managed to achieve any kind of realism with such models. For practical and ethical reasons, many interesting and important issues cannot be researched by experiments: the effect of low dosage radiation on human beings, of young maternal age on child abuse, or the effects of authoritarian upbringing on fascist political views, to name but three examples.

By and large, therefore, most social science data is non-experimental, and this leads to some challenging difficulties with the process of drawing causal inferences. We cannot directly infer a causal effect from a statistical effect.

12.5 Assumptions required to infer causes

Does this mean that non-experimental data is useless for addressing causal issues? Not at all. It does mean, however, that the process of drawing inferences is more tentative than in experiments, based on if-then reasoning: if it is the case that the true causal story about the variables is as we imagine (playing God in the way that we did just now with absenteeism), then we would expect to find a statistical effect of X on Y. Any effect discovered is merely consistent with these assumptions; it does not prove that they are true. If it is not discovered, however, it is highly likely that there is something wrong with the assumptions; the data can certainly dampen over-enthusiastic imagination.

Researchers rarely conduct research with a finished model of the causal process they want to test in mind. They usually build up to a God's eye view of the causal processes slowly, starting from a simple relationship, imagining how it might be more complex, testing to see if that is in fact the case, and so on. This process is known as **elaboration**, and involves a fruitful interaction between theory and data.

Imagine a common situation. A survey is conducted and an interesting statistical effect of X on Y is discovered. There are two basic assumptions that have to be made if we wish to infer from this that X causes Y. These involve the relationship between X and Y and other variables which might be operating; they are designed to ensure that when we compare groups which differ on X, we are comparing like with like. Before giving an exposition of these assumptions, we need a bit more terminology: other variables can be causally **prior** to both X and Y, **intervene** between X and Y, or **ensue** from X and Y, as shown in figure 12.2. These terms are only relative to the particular causal model in hand: in a different model we might want to explain what gave rise to the prior variable.

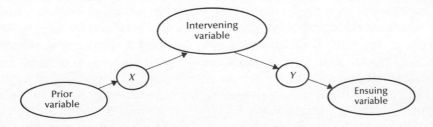

Figure 12.2 Different causal relationships between variables

Let us discuss each of the two core assumptions in turn.

Assumption 1

X is causally prior to Y.

There is nothing in the data to tell us whether X causes Y or Y causes X, so we have to make the most plausible assumption we can, based on our knowledge of the subject matter and our theoretical framework.

There are some rules which can guide us. Things which are not open to change, such as a person's age, are treated as causes; indeed, some researchers like to reserve the term 'cause' for such factors. The time ordering can sometimes help out; since causes occur before effects, knowing which variable occurred first can help. However, this is not watertight; human beings can anticipate and respond to future events before they occur. Sometimes a theoretical framework prescribes that particular factors are considered causally prior to others; Marxists, for example, assume that in the last instance economic variables take precedence over cultural, political variables. And sometimes careful measurement can indicate whether the occurrence of a variable is independent of a possible cause.

One particular problem comes from situations in which we suspect that X and Y influence each other in a reciprocating process. There is no way that non-experimental data can be made to yield two independent estimates of the effect of X on Y and of Y on X; we have to plump for one or the other. In such reciprocating systems, the magnitude of causal effect of X on Y or Y on X depends strictly on the exact time at which we conduct the survey. However, such systems tend to settle down after a time; as long as the feedback process is not in full swing, we can often assume that the net effect has balanced out in one direction or the other.

Assumption 2

Related prior variables have been controlled.

All other variables which affect both X and Y must be held constant. In an experiment, we can be sure that there are no third variables which give rise to both X and Y because the only way in which the randomized control groups are allowed to vary is in terms of X. No such assumption can be made with non-experimental data; if we compare non-experimental groups which vary on X, we cannot automatically assume that they are alike in other respects. We have to control for the other ways in which they might vary.

To illustrate this point, imagine a survey of all the fires occurring in a particular neighbourhood. If the number of fire engines which turned up was correlated with the amount of damage done at those fires, a positive relationship would probably be discovered. Beware of letting simple-minded politicians bent on public expenditure cuts get their hands on such bivariate statistics, however. Should fewer fire engines therefore be sent to fires? No; control for a prior variable (size of the fire) and the relationship will be shown to be negative.

There are different ways to control for a third factor when investigating a relationship between two variables. Precisely how third variables are brought under control will be discussed in the rest of the book. For the moment, just imagine holding variables constant; to control for the size of the fire, for example, one might only consider cases where an isolated car had caught fire.

If we want to infer that the relationship between X and Y is a direct causal effect, rather than an indirect causal effect, a third assumption must be made:

Assumption 3

All variables intervening between X and Y have been controlled.

This assumption is not required before you can assume that X causes Y, but it is required if you want to know *how* X is causing Y. The distinction between controlling for a prior variable and for an intervening variable is drawn more sharply in the next section.

In general, variables that are brought into the picture and controlled are called **test factors**. Controlling for them tests the original relationship between X and Y, and checks that it holds up. In order to infer that the effect of X on Y is a direct causal effect, any variable which is related to both X and Y and causally prior to at least one of them must be controlled.

Never forget that these assumptions are just that; we can never *prove* that a variable is prior rather than intervening or ensuing. To order the variables and decide which should be brought under control, we have to use all the theoretical and rational resources available to us; we cannot appeal to the data for help. (An excellent and eminently readable discussion of the whole logic of control in causal models can be found in Davis 1985.)

12.6 Controlling for prior variables

In the next two sections we shall pay special attention to situations in which an original effect disappears when a third variable is brought under control. The importance of such an outcome is very different depending on where in the causal chain the third variable comes. Obviously, if it ensues from the two variables originally considered, it does not need to be controlled. But there is a big difference between controlling for a prior variable and finding that the original relationship disappears and controlling for an intervening one with a similar result.

Let us first consider a hypothetical example drawn from the earlier discussion of the causes of absenteeism. Suppose previous research had shown a positive bivariate relationship between low social status jobs and absenteeism. The question arises: is there something about such jobs that directly causes the people who do them to go off sick more than others? Before we can draw such a conclusion, two assumptions have to be made.

The first decision is whether the status of the job influences the absentee rate or the absentee rate influences the type of job people get. As we argued earlier, we cannot usually allow a model which depicts reciprocal causation; while absence-prone individuals may have difficulty getting good jobs, the former effect is probably the stronger.

The second assumption is that there are no uncontrolled prior variables influencing both the type of job and the absentee rate. In fact, we already thought that sex might fit into this category: it is likely to be associated with status (women tend to do lower status jobs) and absenteeism (domestic commitments might make women more absence-prone than men). It is also the case that people's sex cannot be held to be an *effect* of their job or their work record; sex must be assumed to be causally prior to both of these variables.

Sex must therefore be held constant while the relationship between job type and absenteeism is 'tested'. While we are at it, we will check whether we were right to believe that being female is a causal influence upon job type and absenteeism.

There are many possible outcomes once the relationship between all three variables is considered at once, four of which are shown in figure 12.3. We shall systematically ask about each outcome: would it change our original interpretation of the bivariate effect?

In the first outcome, we discover that being female does affect likelihood of absence, but being female does not increase the chances of being in a low status job. The strength of the effect of type of job on absenteeism would not change by controlling for sex in this case.

In the second outcome, we discover that females are more likely to be in low status jobs, and that people in such jobs are more likely to go absent, but that being female, once type of job is controlled, does not affect absentee behaviour directly. Once again, the strength of the relationship between job and absenteeism would remain the same as in the bivariate case. The first part of the definition of a test factor should now be clear: test factors need to be introduced only when they are related to both the variables under consideration.

However, the third situation is radically different. Being female dictates the type of job, and being female affects absentee behaviour, but once sex is controlled there is no link at all between the type of job and absenteeism. The direct effect of job on absenteeism is shown to be zero.

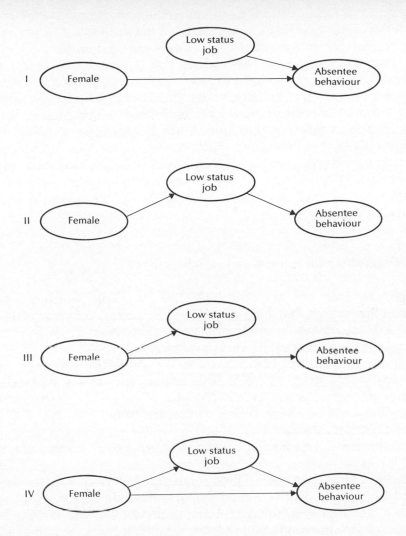

Figure 12.3 The effect of job status on absenteeism: controlling a prior variable

A causal interpretation of the bivariate effect would have been entirely faulty: it was purely a product of women being both more likely to be in low status jobs and more likely to be absent. Or, to put it another way, changing the status of a job would not have any impact on the behaviour of its incumbents.

If the relationship between two variables entirely disappears when a causally prior variable is brought under control, we say that the original relationship was **spurious**; by this we do not mean that the bivariate effect did not really exist, but rather that causal conclusions drawn from it would be incorrect. We can now introduce another meaning for that verb 'to explain': in this situation, many researchers say that the proportion of females in a job 'explains' the relationship between the status of the job and absenteeism, in the sense that it accounts for it entirely.

But what of the fourth situation which is actually the most likely outcome? It was the situation portrayed in figure 12.1. We discover that there is a direct effect of both being female and job type on absentee behaviour, and an indirect effect of being female on absenteeism through the type of job women tend to hold. Since the direction of the direct and the indirect effect is the same (which need not always be so), the size of the effect of job type on absenteeism would not be as large once sex was controlled as it had seemed in the bivariate relationship. We now know that the strength of that original relationship contained a **spurious component**.

12.7 Controlling for intervening variables

Superficially, the act of controlling for a variable which intervenes between the two original variables of interest is much the same. The third factor is held constant while the original relationship is reassessed. But the logic of the procedure is very different.

Imagine now that we introduce, as a test factor, a variable which represents the extent to which the respondent suffers from chronic nervous disorders, such as sleeplessness, anxiety and so on. Such conditions would be likely to lead to absence from work. It is also quite conceivable that they could be caused in part by stressful, low status jobs. Let us therefore assume that nervous disorders act as an intervening variable.

What will happen to the original relationship if we control for this test factor? Figure 12.4 shows similar possible outcomes. As before, in the first two situations controlling for the third variable will not affect the estimate of the causal effect of the type of job on absentee behaviour. In the first, nervous disorders are just an additional cause of absenteeism, but are unrelated to the type of job. In the second, nervous disorders have no effect on absenteeism, despite the fact that they are caused by poor jobs.

But in the third, the relationship between job type and absenteeism disappears when the existence of nervous disorders is brought under control. This test factor is said to **interpret** the relationship between the two variables; it opens up the black box to show how the effect occurs. This is radically different from showing that the original effect was spurious. It is still the case that the type of job affects the absentee behaviour. We now know *how* the causal effect works: poor jobs lead to more stress-related disorders, and these in turn lead to absence from work.

In the fourth situation, nervous disorders partially interpret the

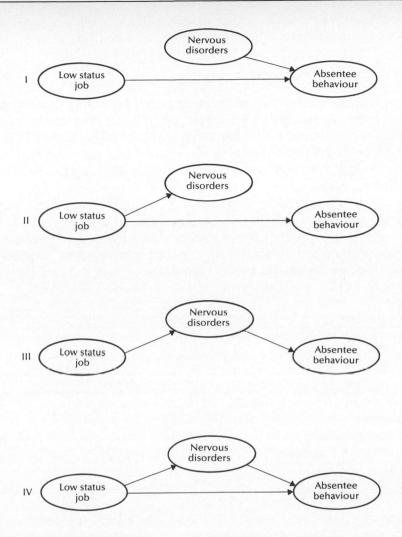

Figure 12.4 The effect of job status on absenteeism: controlling an intervening variable

relationship between the two variables, but there is still a direct effect remaining after that variable has been brought under control.

The process of drawing inferences from non-experimental data is usually one of slowly elaborating a relationship between two variables, testing that it contains no spurious component due to the operation of a prior variable, and testing to see if one can pin down whether the cause influences the effect directly or through an intervening variable.

Ultimately, of course, whether a cause is held to be direct or indirect is a statement about the state of scientific knowledge at the time; while one variable may provide an illuminating explanation for a puzzle at one point in time, it is likely to provoke further questions about how it operates at a later date.

12.8 Positive and negative relationships

There is a further important refinement to the preceding discussion that must now be addressed. The effect on the original relationship of controlling a test factor is affected by whether the third variable is positively or negatively related to the other variables. Test factors can sometimes suppress and sometimes enhance the size of the original effect, as we shall see.

Look back to figure 12.3, at outcome IV. We noted that controlling for sex would have reduced the size of the original effect, because there would have been a spurious component stemming purely from the fact that more women are in low status jobs and more women go absent. In this case, the test factor was positively related to both the variables. Now consider two other possible outcomes, as shown in figure 12.5.

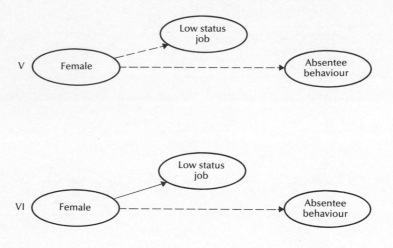

Figure 12.5 Other outcomes for figure 12.3

In situation V, the test factor, sex, is related negatively to both the other two variables. Being female makes you less likely to be in a low status job, and less likely to go absent. The original bivariate effect would have been larger than the effect once sex is controlled in this case, because once more it will contain a spurious component. Test factors which are either positively related to both the other variables or negatively related to both of them are called **enhancer variables**.

However, in case VI, sex is negatively related to one of the variables (absenteeism) and positively to the other (job type). What will happen to the original effect when sex is controlled? The size of the effect will *increase*, because the original effect was being artificially suppressed by failing to control for sex. The fact that women were less likely to go absent but more likely to be in unfavourable jobs meant that we were misled about the effect of low status jobs on absence before we controlled for sex. Test factors which are positively associated with one variable and negatively with the other are called **suppressor variables** for this reason.

Sometimes the action of a suppressor variable can be so strong that controlling for it can actually reverse the sign of the effect. If women were much more likely than men to be in low status jobs, and if female employees almost never went absent from work, it might seem that people doing low status jobs were no more likely or even *less* likely than others to absence. Suppressor variables such as this which are strong enough to reverse the sign of the relationship are called **distorter variables**.

(If you have been stimulated by all this consideration of hypothetical possibilities to find out what relationships actually hold between sex, job type and absenteeism, you might like to read Chadwick-Jones et al. 1982.)

12.9 Conclusion

Only when we are sure that all possible test factors have been controlled can we feel confident that we understand the causal process at work. Since no survey ever measures all variables, this requirement is never met in full. But in the better, more carefully planned investigations, the variables which are the most important test factors are measured, and brought under control in the analysis.

The same point is made another way when we demand that our residuals should be patternless. If there are important test factors which have been excluded from the model, the residuals from the model will contain an important degree of pattern: they will be systematically related to the omitted variable. We may or may not be aware of this.

Causal inferences are constructions built upon foundations of assumptions, and cannot be more valid than the assumptions. If this induces a feeling of unease in you such that you start routinely checking the concrete around the foundations of inferences drawn from social science data, so much the better. Your job, however, is to mend any plausible cracks you observe – to do a better survey, measuring and controlling important new variables – not to walk away from the edifice declaring it to be a hazard. Be sure to remember how poor lay reasoning about causation is: not to even try to collect the data required to test a hypothesis about the relationship between smoking and lung cancer would be to leave the doors open only to those who jump to conclusions on the basis of a sample of one.

Those of you who have been fingering your calculator buttons anxiously can now relax: the excursion into philosophy is over, and we return to the nuts and bolts of describing patterns in batches of numbers.

But take with you the lessons of this chapter. In the absence of an experiment, a statistical effect of one variable on another cannot just be accepted as causal at face value. If we want to show that it is not spurious, we have to demonstrate that there are no plausible prior variables affecting both the variables of interest. If we want to argue that the causal mechanism is fairly direct, we have to control for similar intervening variables.

The act of controlling for a third variable can have many possible results. It can both suggest that an effect previously believed to exist does not exist and that one thought not to exist does exist. It can enhance or suppress its magnitude. It can even reverse the sign of the original effect.

The first-order task is to think logically about which variables need to be included in any model, and what form their causal relations are. While it is important to know that your sample size is big enough for safe conclusions to be drawn (that effects are 'statistically significant'), this is secondary in comparison with the issue of whether a relationship can be given a causal interpetation or is merely the spurious result of the operation of third factors; the relationship between the number of fire engines and the amount of damage caused could be derived from a sample size of ten thousand and still utterly mislead if taken at face value.

This chapter was therefore important in linking the second and third parts of the book. It should have convinced you of the importance of proceeding beyond bivariate relationships to considering systems in which three or more variables are operating together.

Exercises

12.1 Decide on balance which variable you think would be the cause and which the effect in the following pairs:

(a) party supported in an election and the type of newspaper read
(b) wage rises and inflation (both measured over time)
(c) unemployment and ill health
(d) attitude towards abortion and religion
(e) the rise of capitalism in a country and the religion which predominates in that country.

12.2 Consider three variables: age last birthday, number of years of full-time education and favourableness towards nuclear defence. Draw a causal path diagram indicating the relationships you would assume to exist between these variables. Suppose the bivariate effect of age on favourableness towards nuclear defence was strongly positive. What would you expect to happen to the magnitude of the effect once you had controlled for number of years of full-time education?

13 Three-variable contingency tables

13.1 The civic culture

After the Second World War, intellectuals in both Europe and America set about trying to explain why two relatively advanced countries, Italy and Germany, had been unable to defend their liberal democracies against the rise of fascism. Many different contributory factors were suggested, from national differences in personality structure and child-rearing practices to political institutions.

In the early 1960s, Almond and Verba published an influential contribution to the debate entitled *The Civic Culture*. The thesis of the book was that democracy could not be safeguarded by attending to political institutions alone; a culture had also to exist among the population which combined tradition and modernity, encouraging attitudes of loyalty and respect for the institutions of government while at the same time fostering a degree of political activism. Such cultures would encourage citizens to participate in the political process, but only occasionally and within the limited rules of the democratic game.

A survey was conducted in five countries which were critical cases for the hypothesis: Britain and the United States of America as countries which had the most successful democratic states, Germany and Italy as countries that had experienced fascist regimes within twenty years, and Mexico as a less well-developed country struggling to establish its democratic process (Almond and Verba 1963). In each country, a random sample of the electorate were questioned about their attitudes towards the political process – their perceived ability to affect political change, their participation in various political activities, their attitude towards parties they did not support and so on.

One of the major conclusions of the study was that the stability of democracy in the USA and Britain was indeed due to the achievement of a finely balanced civic culture. Citizens in those countries retained allegiance to the political process, content most of the time to leave politics to elites, while believing that they could influence the outcome of both local and national decision-making if necessary. This belief, regardless of whether it was justified or not, both stopped leaders acting contrary to public opinion and persuaded citizens to accept the legitimacy of laws they did not themselves agree with. The belief was in some senses a 'democratic myth', but citizens participated in just enough well-behaved political activism to be able to believe in it.

Almond and Verba conducted their fieldwork in 1959, in an era of unprecedented growth and low unemployment, conditions which were perhaps conducive to consensual party politics and lack of impassioned political activism. It is interesting to ask whether the fine balance of acquiescence and participation has survived into a very different era. In the 1984 Social Attitudes Survey (see the appendix to this chapter), one of Almond and Verba's key questions was replicated. Respondents were asked:

Suppose a law was now being considered by Parliament which you thought was really unjust and harmful; which, if any, of the things on this card do you think you would do?

1 Contact my MP
2 Speak to an influential person
3 Contact a government department
4 Contact radio, TV or newspaper
5 Sign a petition
6 Raise the issue in an organization I already belong to
7 Go on a protest or demonstration
8 Form a group of like minded people

The first four are considered personal actions and the last four collective actions.

Comparison can be made with the responses in Almond and Verba's survey, as shown in figure 13.1. The question in the 1959 survey was open-ended, and it is possible that the great increase in preparedness to

Figure 13.1 Forecast of action taken in prospect of unjust and harmful law

	1959 (%)	1984 (%)
Take personal action	47	77
Take collective action	22	77
Do nothing	32	14
Don't know	6	1
	(N=963)	(N=1645)

Source: 1959: Almond and Verba (1963): 203; 1984: Social Attitudes Survey data

act is an artefact of the changed method of question administration. But the shift in the relative emphasis given to collective action in recent years is probably not explicable in this way. The shift is so striking that it has led one commentator (Young 1984: 22) to talk of an explosion of 'civic assertiveness'. It makes one ask whether the delicate balance that Almond and Verba pointed to has shifted. Is civic assertiveness now so strong that citizens would actually be prepared to break laws which they considered to be unjust? If so, what gives rise to such attitudes? These are the questions that will be addressed below.

The techniques to be presented in this chapter are designed to examine the relationship between three variables in a contingency table. They are an extension of the techniques considered in chapters 7 and 8 (the first four sections of chapter 8 in particular) and they also build on the arguments about the need for controls presented in chapter 12. We shall use differences in proportions as the summary measure for the effect of one variable on another, rather than any of the alternatives discussed in chapter 8. For the sake of simplicity, we shall stick to analysing dichotomies, but the principles established in this chapter are easily extended to situations where the explanatory variables have three or more categories.

13.2 Controlling for a prior variable

Respondents to the Social Attitudes Survey in 1984 were asked:

> In general would you say that people should obey the law without exception, or are there exceptional occasions on which people should follow their consciences even if it means breaking the law?

Overall, somewhat more than half (57 per cent) thought the law should be obeyed without exception, and slightly less than half (43 per cent) believed that it was occasionally right to follow conscience and break the law.

However, believing something is the right thing to do in principle is very different from actually doing it oneself. Respondents were therefore also asked:

> Are there any circumstances in which *you* might break a law to which you were very strongly opposed?

This question resulted in almost one-third saying that they themselves might break the law. While still a minority, the group would be large enough to create widespread disruption if they could be mobilized collectively. It is thus both interesting and important to discover what factors lead this third of the population to defy the civic culture of assent.

One plausible area for explanation might lie in the experience of material security or insecurity. Although incomes in the 1980s were substantially higher in real terms than they were at the end of the 1950s, there has been no sustained decrease in inequality; in fact, as we saw in chapter 5 (figure 5.5), income inequality in Britain increased sharply after 1976. Perhaps it is those on low incomes, watching others getting richer, who are prepared to break the law; if we look at the statistics of actual law-breaking, after all, criminal prosecutions are most often brought against people from the poorer sections of society (Baldwin and Bottoms 1976).

This hypothesis can be investigated by consulting figure 13.2, in which the sample has been subdivided according to whether respondents lived in households with a gross annual income from all sources of less or more than £6000 in 1984 (termed somewhat inaccurately 'the rich' and 'the poor' in the discussion which follows). As we learned in chapter 8, these

Figure 13.2 Preparedness to break the law by household
income: row proportions

	Might break	Never break	N
£6000 or more (rich)	0.382	0.618	767
£5999 or less (poor)	0.238	0.762	559
d	+0.144		

Missing cases = 319

results could be depicted in a causal path diagram as shown below. The model tells us that 0.238 of poor respondents say they would be prepared to break the law (the baseline). To establish the total proportion who would break the law, we must add to this a factor which reminds us how many rich people were in the sample (767/1326, or 0.578) times their increased propensity to break the law (+0.144).

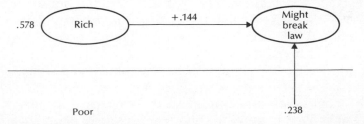

The result is quite striking: the richer respondents claim to be more prepared to break the law than the poorer ones, despite their apparent lesser chances of actually breaking it from the conviction statistics. Many questions are raised. Does the greater risk of brushing with the law among the poorer sections of society bring with it greater fear of the consequences? Are the rich more prepared to break the law because they are more likely to view laws as unjust? Are the rich and poor perhaps thinking of different laws when answering this question? Or are poorer respondents simply less prepared to admit to an interviewer that they would be prepared to break the law?

Before we embark on a major explanatory exercise, however, we must be sure that the effect is truly causal, and not just the spurious result of joint association with a prior explanatory variable, as explained in chapter 12. We have to think of possible test factors which are related to both income and preparedness to break the law. We control for them, and see if the relationship between income and reported willingness to break the law remains.

One variable which is a candidate for such a test factor is age. Age and income are strongly related in almost all samples, and the Social Attitudes Survey is no exception, as figure 13.3 shows; the exact age of the earnings high point varies, but for almost everyone old age brings with it a diminution of income.

Figure 13.3 Age by household income: row proportions

	£6000 or more (rich)	£5999 or less (poor)	N
45 years or less (young)	0.760	0.240	703
46 years or more (old)	0.374	0.626	623
d	+0.386		
Missing cases = 319			

Similarly, the literature repeatedly suggests that age is a factor associated with a preparedness to break the law; both in rebellious attitudes and in actual brushes with the law, the young preponderate (Marsh 1977: 69–70; Walker 1987). This finding is replicated in figure 13.4; overall, 0.215 more young people than old people say they would be prepared to break the law.

In short, age is associated with both income and willingness to break the law. There is thus *prima facie* evidence to suggest that we should control for age when assessing the causal impact of income.

The method of control we shall use involves literally holding one variable constant while assessing the relationship between two others. To hold age constant, we consider the relationship between income and law-breaking among people of identical ages. (In fact we will use only a dichotomy of age by crudely grouping people above and below 45, but we

Figure 13.4 Preparedness to break the law by age: row
proportions

	Might break	Never break	N
45 years or less (young)	0.422	0.578	703
46 years or more (old)	0.207	0.793	623
d		+0.215	

Missing cases = 319

shall ignore that complication for the time being.) We therefore need a
new table which shows the three-way table of age by income by attitudes
to the law (figure 13.5); the relationships cannot be inferred from
inspection of figures 13.2, 13.3 and 13.4 alone.

In chapter 8, rules were formulated which dictated which way to run
the proportions when dealing with the hypothesized effect of one
variable upon another: proportions were calculated so that they summed
to 1 within the categories of the explanatory variable. In a three-variable
table with one response variable and two explanatory variables, the
proportions are calculated to sum to 1 within each of the cells formed by
the categories of the explanatory variables. In other words, we look
separately at old poor people, old rich people, young poor people and
young rich people, and calculate in each of the four groups what
proportion would be prepared to break the law.

Figure 13.5 Preparedness to break the law by age by household income:
frequencies

	£6000 or more (rich)		£5999 or less (poor)	
	Would break	Never break	Would break	Never break
45 or less (young)	231	303	66	103
46 or more (old)	62	171	67	323

Missing cases = 315

This is shown in figure 13.6. The columns showing the proportion who
would not break the law are, strictly, redundant, since the information
can always be derived by subtracting the proportion who would from 1.0;
in future tables such as this, these shadow proportions will be omitted.

Figure 13.6 Preparedness to break the law by age by household income: row proportions

	£6000 or more (rich) Would Never break break	£5999 or less (poor) Would Never break break	d
45 or less (young)	0.433 0.567 ($N=534$)	0.391 0.609 ($N=169$)	+0.042
46 or more (old)	0.266 0.734 ($N=233$)	0.172 0.828 ($N=390$)	+0.094
d	+0.167	+0.219	

Missing cases = 315

In contingency tables, to control for a variable we look within its categories. To control for age when assessing the effect of being rich on preparedness to break the law, for example, we look separately at the young and the old. To control for wealth when assessing the effect of age on preparedness to break the law, we look separately at the rich and poor. However, complex tables soon get quite hard to read systematically. We now turn to causal path models to guide us as we summarize the various causal effects.

13.3 Causal path models for three variables

The full set of paths of causal influence, both direct and indirect, that we would want to consider, are represented in figure 13.7. Care must be taken over the signs of relationships, specifying which category has been selected as the base for comparison (see section 8.2). In the causal model in figure 13.7, we are trying to explain propensity to break the law; the

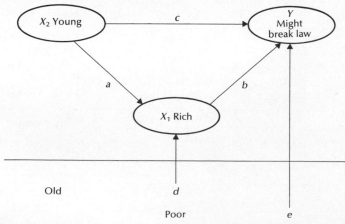

Figure 13.7 Preparedness to break the law by age by household income: causal path diagram

base is therefore 'not breaking the law'. The base categories selected for the explanatory variables are old and poor, to try to avoid negative paths; if we had used the young as the baseline, we would have certainly produced a negative effect of old age on preparedness to break the law, for example.

Each arrow linking two variables in a causal path diagram represents the *direct* effect of one variable upon the other, controlling all other relevant variables. The rule for identifying the relevant variables was given in chapter 12: when we are assessing the direct effect of one variable upon another, any third variable which is causally connected to both variables and prior to one of them should be controlled.

Coefficient b shows the direct effect of being one of the richer respondents on preparedness to break the law. To find its value, attention is focused on the proportions who say they would break the law, ignoring proportions who say they would never break it (figure 13.6). The effect of being rich is obtained by subtracting the proportion of poor people who would break the law from the proportion of rich people who would. But age (X_2) must be controlled since it is connected to both X_1 and Y and prior to both of them. So two different calculations are made; the effect of being rich among the young is $0.433 - 0.391$, or $+0.042$, and that among the old is $0.266 - 0.172$, or $+0.094$. Two ds result, one for the young and one for the old.

In general, in three-variable contingency tables, to find the direct effect of X_1 on Y controlling for X_2 we consider each category of X_2 in turn, and subtract the proportion who are Y in the base category of X_1 from the proportion who are Y in the non-base category of X_1. This is a bit of a mouthful, but it provides a systematic way of describing relationships as positive or negative; it reminds us, for example, whether young people are more or less likely to contemplate breaking the law.

How is a single number summary of the ds to be found? For the purposes of this chapter, we shall simply take the arithmetic mean; the d among the young is $+0.042$, among the old is $+0.094$, so the average effect (coefficient b) is $+0.068$. Like all summaries, this average d only makes sense if the coefficients being averaged are broadly similar; we shall discuss what to do if they are not in section 13.6. There are, of course, more sophisticated and sensitive ways of combining the two ds. One fairly obvious procedure would be to weight each d by the number of cases it was based on. One could go further and give more weight to differences with lower sampling variability, but that takes us into confirmatory statistics and beyond the scope of this book.

The effect of being rich ($+0.068$) is seen to be pretty small. Confirmatory techniques exist to assess how likely a difference of proportions of a given magnitude is to arise in sample data when it has been drawn from a population in which no such difference exists. As a rule of thumb, when ds get down much below 0.05, we can regard them as so small that they might just be a sampling fluke; we will conclude that for all practical purposes there is no effect of one variable upon another, and erase arrows with very small path coefficients from our model.

The original effect of being rich in figure 13.2 (+0.144) was spuriously high; it was a product of the fact that young people are more likely to be rich and young people are also more likely to contemplate breaking the law. The operation of these two age effects is not, however, strong enough to actually reverse the sign of the relationship between income and law-breaking. The general conclusion still holds: the poorer groups in society seem somewhat less willing than the rich to challenge society's rules if they feel a law is unjust.

We can assess the direct effect of age (X_2) on preparedness to break the law controlling for income in the same way. Among the poor, 0.391 of the young and 0.172 of the old are prepared to break the law – a difference of +0.219. Among the rich, the difference is +0.167. The average (coefficient c) is therefore +0.193. So the direct effect of being young (+0.193) is seen to be much stronger than the direct effect of being rich (+0.068).

Being young also has an indirect effect upon preparedness to break the law because young people are more likely to be rich, and, as we have seen, rich people are somewhat more prepared to break the law. It is not necessary to control for anything, since there are no other variables connected to both age and income and prior to one of them. We therefore consider the effect of age on income as shown in the original bivariate table in figure 13.3. (This effect could have been calculated from the marginals of figure 13.5, and can be called a **marginal relationship**.) While 0.760 of the younger respondents were rich, only 0.374 of the older group were, a difference of +0.386. So coefficient a is +0.386. Causal path models are excellent devices for forcing the data analyst to look at the appropriate marginal relationships in tables.

There are also two paths, d and e, in figure 13.7 which represent the other unspecified causes; all variables in a model which have causal paths leading to them must also have arrows reminding us of the proportion unpredicted by the model. The values are obtained from the proportion of the base groups who are in the non-base categories of the response variables. Path d is given by the proportion of the old who are rich (0.374 to be precise, from figure 13.3). And path e reminds us that some old and poor respondents said they would be prepared to break an unjust law; the value of coefficient e is therefore 0.172 (figure 13.6). These paths are the final coefficients to be entered on the quantified model (figure 13.8).

We can be sure that the model in figure 13.8 is better than that derived from figure 13.2. However, we cannot even be sure that it has got the causal effects absolutely right. Their accuracy still depends upon the correctness of our assumptions about causal order and the operation of other variables; if we had either specified the causal order incorrectly, or failed to control for other important variables, the coefficients would be meaningless. Worse, nothing in the data itself would alert us to this fact.

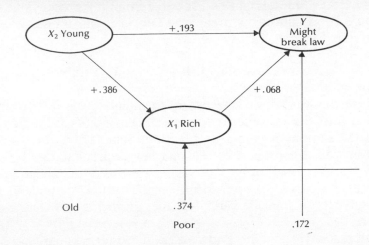

Figure 13.8 Assigning coefficients to figure 13.7

Science is a collective enterprise; over time, researchers build up a body of wisdom which tells them which are the important variables to include when modelling a particular process, and which must be controlled.

13.4 Summarizing causal effects: direct and indirect

Causal models can be manipulated in two different ways. First, they allow direct and indirect causal effects to be calculated and compared. This model in figure 13.8 suggests that being young affects attitudes towards breaking the law in two distinct ways. There is a direct effect of +0.193. But there is also an indirect effect, because the young are more likely to be rich (+0.386) and the rich are more likely to be prepared to break the law (+0.068). To calculate the effect of an indirect causal path, the values of adjacent paths are multiplied. Thus the indirect effect of age via income in this model is (+0.386 × +0.068), which is +0.026. The multiplication of paths means that indirect effects are nearly always small.

To calculate the total effect of one variable upon another, the values of all the paths, direct and indirect, between the variables are summed. Thus the total effect of being young on preparedness to break the law is 0.193 + 0.026, or +0.219. This is pretty near the 0.215 difference in figure 13.4. (It is not exactly the right answer because of the rough averaging procedure we used to arrive at the direct effects.) In short, causal path models can show us how a bivariate relationship decomposes into direct and indirect effects, an essential part of a scientific understanding.

Secondly, such models can be used to predict the proportions who say they would be prepared to break the law. We can predict the overall proportion as follows:

$$Y = 0.172 + (X_1 \times 0.193) + (X_2 \times 0.068)$$

To see how this works, it is necessary to calculate the total proportions who come into the non-base category of X_1 and X_2 from figure 13.5; 0.530 of the sample is young and 0.578 is rich. Therefore, the overall proportion who are prepared to break law is predicted to be 0.172 + (0.530 × +0.193) + (0.578 × +0.068) = 0.314. We can check that this is pretty near the correct proportion (426/1326 = 0.321); once again, it is not exactly the same because of the crudeness of the averaging procedure.

Equations such as this are known as **reduced form equations**. They are used principally in forecasting, where the aim is not so much understanding the nature of the effects but predicting the net change that will occur in Y if X goes up a unit.

13.5 Controlling for an intervening variable

Most people acknowledge that there will be some political consequences of rising levels of unemployment, but there is no unanimity about what the effect will be. Some fear that it will lead to a breakdown of the civic culture that Almond and Verba so admired in Britain. Others believe that it will lead primarily to apathy and despair rather than rebellion and protest.

The Social Attitudes Survey can shine some light on this relationship, since it collected information on respondents' experience of unemployment in the past five years, as well as the respondent's current economic status. The data seems to support the first belief: of those who had had some experience of unemployment in the previous five years, 0.480 said they would be prepared to break the law, whereas only 0.300 of those who had no such experience were (a difference of +0.180).

As we saw in chapter 12, there is another quite different intellectual reason for wanting to control for a third factor when assessing the relationship between two variables. We may have discovered a statistical effect but do not understand how it operates; the brute fact that people who have experienced unemployment are more rebellious in spirit does not itself explain why this occurs (see diagram). If we can find a mystery

variable which completely captures the causal mechanism, the effect of unemployment experience on law-breaking will disappear when the mystery variable is brought under control.

One explanation for the mechanism might be that the experience of unemployment leads to a generalized lack of trust in the institutions of authority and the state, which in turn makes people prepared to contemplate breaking the law. There is, in the survey, a set of questions which can help us investigate this; respondents were asked:

> Listed below are a number of organizations or services. From what you know or have heard about each one, can you say whether you are generally satisfied or not satisfied with the service that each one provides?

Preliminary analysis of these questions suggested that dissatisfaction with six of the organizations was importantly related to preparedness to break the law: the press, local government, the civil service, banks, the police and the local doctor. A scale was formed by simply scoring the number of times the respondent said that he or she was satisfied; the resulting scale started with a minimum of 0 and a maximum of 6, but it was dichotomized at the median value into a scale of political alienation with two values (high and low).

Figure 13.9 shows the cross-tabulation of preparedness to break the law by alienation by experience of unemployment. Those who are alienated from the institutions of authority and the state are certainly more prepared to break the law than those who are not; among those who have been unemployed, the effect is +0.140, and among those who have not it is +0.171, an average effect of +0.155. However, when we control for such views, the relationship between unemployment experience and preparedness to break the law does not disappear; in fact, it is almost as strong as it was in the bivariate table: +0.175 among the unalienated and +0.144 among the alienated, or +0.159 on average.

Figure 13.9 Proportion prepared to break the law by alienation by experience of unemployment in last five years

	Unalienated	Alienated	d
Experienced unemployment	0.389 (N=91)	0.529 (N=153)	+0.140
No unemployment experience	0.214 (N=565)	0.385 (N=563)	+0.171
d	+0.175	+0.144	

Missing cases = 273

For definition of alienation, see text.

If, once the intervening test factor had been controlled for, the relationship was reduced to zero, we would say that the original effect had been fully **interpreted**. This did not occur here; the experience of unemployment cannot be interpreted as causing preparedness to break the law by altering respondent's general level of trust in the institutions of authority and the state. It is left as an exercise for the reader to think of other mechanisms which might be at work.

13.6 Interactions

Generalizations are at the heart of social scientific activity; we aim to discover causal processes which could potentially affect everyone in society. When we find that the experience of unemployment makes people more likely to contemplate breaking an unjust law, we assume that the reasons for this are general; we suppose that the increased likelihood would operate for anyone who happened to undergo the experience of unemployment. In this example, the assumption held good in the test we submitted it to: the experience of unemployment was broadly similar for those who were unalienated as it was for those who were alienated; we could feel confident about averaging the two ds.

When no generalization can be made about the causal process at work, we say that there is an **interaction** in the relationships. An interaction can be formally defined as a situation in which the effect of one variable upon another depends upon the value of a third variable; when asked how much effect X has on Y, we are forced to answer: 'it depends.' Interactions are sometimes also called 'conditional relationships'; in other words, the relationship varies under different conditions.

To illustrate this point, let us examine a further set of findings about preparedness to break the law in the Social Attitudes Survey. In their study of civic culture in 1959, Almond and Verba repeatedly noted that the better educated in all five countries that they studied were more likely to participate in the political process, and to believe that they could do something to change laws which they felt were unjust through the conventional channels of political participation. We can examine whether the Social Attitudes Survey in 1984 finds the same pattern; we might expect, on the basis of this reasoning, that the more educated people would be less likely to say that they would break an unjust law.

Educational level is a hard variable to measure in most cultures: are we interested in formal qualifications, the number of years spent in full-time education, the content of what was learned during the educational process or what? A simple indicator of qualifications is not very practicable in Britain because so many people left school in the past without any formal qualification to show for it. However, the number of people who return to education once they have left school or college is so low that the age of finishing full-time education is often used as a simple indicator.

The bivariate relationship between terminal education age and preparedness to break the law suggests a different conclusion about the relationship between education and respect for the law in Britain in 1984: more of those who left school at 16 or above say they are prepared to break the law (0.364) than do those who left at 15 or younger (0.274), a difference of +0.090.

However, we would expect the effect of terminal education age to differ among people of different generations: 16 was the minimum school-leaving age for sample members aged 28 or less, whereas any respondents aged 80 or older did not even have to stay at school till they were 14. It therefore makes good sense for us to control for date of birth when looking at the effects of terminal education age. The cross-tabulation is shown in figure 13.10.

Figure 13.10 Proportion prepared to break the law by age by terminal education age

	45 or less (young)	46 or more (old)	d
Left school at 15 or earlier	0.445 (*N*=254)	0.195 (*N*=544)	+0.250
Left school at 16 or later	0.398 (*N*=532)	0.255 (*N*=165)	+0.143
d	+0.047	−0.060	

Missing cases = 150

Once age is controlled, the effect of education upon attitudes towards breaking unjust laws changes. Among those aged 46 or more (approximately those born before the Second World War), the relationship is as it seemed from the bivariate table: the more highly educated are more prepared to break the law. But among the post-war generations, the relationship has the opposite sign: the less educated are the ones who say they are more prepared to break the law. Neither effect is large, but the result is sufficiently different for us to feel uncomfortable about averaging the two effects; it would not do justice to the situation to say that on average there was no effect of education once age was controlled. There is, in short, an interaction present; the effect of education on law-breaking depends upon when one was born.

Once an interaction has been found in one of the effects in a table such as figure 13.10, it will also be found in the other. Sure enough, the effect of age on preparedness to break the law is larger (+0.250) among those with low education than among those who stayed on at school or college beyond 15 (0.143).

Age is always an ambiguous variable in survey research. Unless one has data from repeated surveys across time, there is no way of telling whether one is dealing with pure age effects, pure period effects or an interaction between the two, termed generation or cohort effects. If we had several surveys at our disposal, and those aged 45 or less were always more prepared to break an unjust law, regardless of when the survey was undertaken, this would be an example of a pure age effect. If we found that responses in later surveys were more favourable towards breaking the law among respondents of all ages, this would be interpreted as a pure period effect. When age and period interact, we may assume we are dealing with the unique experiences of a generation growing up under particular conditions.

Because there are interactions by age in figure 13.10, it is likely that we are dealing with a generation effect. Because the data comes from a survey conducted at one point in time, we cannot tell if the relationship is conditional upon age or period, however. If, for example, we were to find the same results in the Social Attitudes Survey in the year 2006, we could assume that these results are conditional upon age. However, we might find the same relationship among all sections of society by 2006; breaking unjust laws might become the hallmark of the less educated of all ages. It is to be hoped that repeated surveys such as the Social Attitudes Survey will be conducted for many years to come in order to allow these important distinctions to be made.

The method outlined in this section for detecting interactions involves looking for differences in the magnitude of the ds. It is not the only way to decide if the relationship between two variables depends upon the value of a third. You might find it useful to look back at exercise 8.3. The authors' argument may be put more technically now: they suggested that there was an interaction in the effect that certain provoking agents had upon the risk of clinical depression; these agents operated much more strongly on women who were in a vulnerable condition than on those who were not. In the suggested answer, we noted that if they had fitted a multiplicative model, the effect would be very similar. Differences in ds only measure the amount of interaction in an additive model.

There are formal procedures for deciding how large a difference in the ds needs to be before we decide to take the interaction seriously, but these are beyond the scope of this book. As a rule of thumb, with samples of around 1000 individuals we may say that, if the difference in proportions is greater than 0.1, then an interaction is present, and it is unwise to average the effects. General causal models cannot be drawn up when interactions exist between the variables; the only solution is to draw up a separate causal model for each of the groups for whom the effects of the variables are different.

13.7 Conclusion

In this chapter, techniques for building up systems of the joint influence of variables have been outlined, using differences in proportions as the measure of strength of effect. Causal path diagrams have been extended to three variables to show how the factors are hypothesized to interrelate; these diagrams are useful because they force explicit decisions to be made about the causal order of the variables, and lessen the risk that the analyst will control for the wrong variables. They force consideration of the marginal relationship between the variables where this might be important.

The techniques of control used in contingency tables involved literally holding a variable constant by considering its categories one at a time. When the variable to be controlled was ordered (as age and income were), we simply split it around the median. This can, however, introduce what is called **category error**; people in the category 'below median income' do not all have identical incomes. The danger is that the younger people with below median incomes actually have lower incomes than older people with below median incomes. The more categories that are used, of course, the less room there is for category error.

The techniques themselves are identical whether the variable being controlled is a prior or an intervening variable in the relationship being investigated. The interpretation of the result is however very dependent on which is the test variable. If the relationship between two variables disappears when a prior variable is controlled, the original effect has been explained away. If it disappears when an intervening variable is controlled, the mechanism linking the two variables has been interpreted.

When four or more variables are under consideration at once, the importance of modelling the relationships visually before doing any data analysis is even greater. Four variables are not considered in this text, but they do not require any new principles beyond those outlined in this chapter. The rule enunciated earlier about which variables to control for is quite general and extends to any number of variables. Exercise 13.3 has been set to give you an opportunity to try reading a table with four variables in it.

You may have heard of a technique called 'path analysis' and have wondered if it referred to the methods discussed in this chapter. Path analysis usually refers to a technique of modelling relationships between variables using **regression coefficients** as the measure of the strength of effect. (These are analogous to slopes calculated from a resistant line.) However, the logic of causal modelling is exactly the same as that discussed here. The points made in chapter 12 about test factors, suppressor and enhancer variables, about intervening and prior variables, about the importance of detecting interactions and dealing with them separately, all apply equally to path analysis. If you understand how such models work using proportions, you should find their use with other measures reasonably straightforward.

Learning exactly which proportions to calculate in a contingency table, which variables to control for by looking within their categories, and which to ignore by collapsing over their categories, takes some practice. There is no quick substitute.

Exercises

13.1 We saw in this chapter that the rich are more inclined to say that they would break an unjust law than the poor. Draw up a path diagram depicting the relationships you would expect to hold if party support were introduced as a test factor. Then inspect the table below.

| | Conservative | | Not Conservative | |
	Poor	Rich	Poor	Rich
Might break law	25	105	89	157
Would not break law	149	219	236	205

Are the relationships as you predicted?

13.2 The following table shows where a sample of school-leavers who had either been on a government Youth Opportunities Scheme (YOPS) or been unemployed for six weeks by the beginning of October 1978 had ended up by April 1979. The sample was obtained by selecting one in five of the 42 per cent of people who left school in Scotland in 1977–8 with few or no qualifications (i.e. without at least a grade O in the Scottish Certificate of Education). The table shows whether the respondent had tried to obtain an O grade pass or not.

| | October 1978 | April 1979 | | | |
		Job	Unemp.	YOPS	Other
Sat O grade but failed	YOPS	89	35	56	2
	Unemployed	71	41	48	2
Did not sit O grade	YOPS	159	92	93	4
	Unemployed	145	235	129	7

Source: Raffe (1981: 483)

The purpose of the Youth Opportunities Scheme was to prepare the less qualified for employment. On this evidence, did it succeed? In order to answer the question, dichotomize the response variable and present the table in proportional terms. Is it possible to summarize the relationships you find in a linear causal model?

13.3 Much important social research results from war. During the Second World War, many aspects of life in the US army were investigated, including the degree of social mobility in the army and attitudes towards promotion policies and opportunities. In a study conducted during the Second World War (Stouffer et al. 1949), soldiers in two different sections of the army, the Military Police and the Air Corps, were asked: 'Do you think a soldier with ability has a good chance for promotion within the army?' The following table shows the proportion who answered 'a very good chance' by section, by educational level and by rank.

	Military Police			
	Not high school graduate		High school graduate	
Officers	0.58	(N=165)	0.27	(N=241)
Privates	0.33	(N=707)	0.21	(N=470)

	Air Corps			
	Not high school graduate		High school graduate	
Officers	0.30	(N=70)	0.19	(N=152)
Privates	0.20	(N=79)	0.07	(N=123)

This is a complex table, because it contains four variables; work through the effect of each explanatory variable systematically, looking at the relevant marginal relationships as well. What do these findings tell you about attitudes towards promotion in the US army? How do attitudes to promotion relate to differences in the proportion of officers in each section?

13.4 What can you discover from the dataset CLASS about the chances of being in a job which offers an occupational pension scheme (column 16)? What are the independent effects of income (column 15) and social class (column 5)? To answer this question you will a need to give the Minitab command TABLE a third **argument**.

Appendix: the British Social Attitudes Survey

Introduction

The early Victorians who pioneered the collection of social statistics were interested in knowing what people thought as well as what they did. In the nineteenth century, however, those who conducted the research did not really believe that their subjects would tell them the truth reliably if they asked them for information directly, and so they drew inferences about people's ideas, religious beliefs, political commitments and so on from the type of literature they had on their shelf or the pictures they had on their walls. It was the poverty researcher, B. S. Rowntree, who, around the turn of the twentieth century, pioneered the revolutionary idea of asking the subjects of research to be **respondents** to surveys.

After the Second World War, interest in the attitudes and beliefs of the public grew, and several important one-off surveys were conducted. But the main features of social reality monitored on official continuous surveys such as the General Household Survey, Family Expenditure Survey, Labour Force Survey and National Food Survey were objective social conditions and demographic characteristics. Although the GHS did include some attitudinal questions, its emphasis was not primarily subjective.

In order to remedy this deficiency in our knowledge of modern British society, the British Social Attitudes Survey was established in 1983. Social and Community Planning Research, an independent, non-profit institute specializing in social surveys and social research, began conducting an annual survey to investigate public attitudes to a wide range of social and political issues. The aim was to provide important benchmark data on trends in social attitudes, a sort of continuous subjective social accounting to supplement the objective accounting of the Blue Books. The survey is now also part of an international comparative project in which many key questions are repeated in several industrialized countries.

This survey has been unusually successful in attracting financial support from a very wide range of sources. Seedcorn money for the first round of fieldwork (in 1983) was provided by the Economic and Social Research Council and by the Nuffield Foundation. Since 1984, core funding has been provided by the Monument Trust, a Sainsbury foundation, and other funds have been obtained from various government departments and quangos, for their specific areas of concern, and from industry. At the time of writing, funding has been secured for the first five years; it is to be hoped that the data will prove so useful that it will become indispensable to British social science.

The data is explicitly destined for public use. Each year, a summary volume is published, describing in broad outline the main findings of the fieldwork the previous year (Jowell and Airey 1984; Jowell and Witherspoon 1985; Jowell et al. 1986; Jowell et al. 1987). The data is then made public; the full dataset and the commands to set it up for processing by the statistical package SPSS-X can be obtained from the Economic and Social Research Council Data Archive at the University of Essex for the cost of processing.

The sample size for the first three years of the Social Attitudes Survey was between 1700 and 1800. In 1986, the sample size was increased to 3100; core questions were asked of all the sample, while other questions were asked of a random half of the respondents. The following description of sampling methods relates to the 1984 survey, but the sample design is similar every year.

The sample

The universe sampled was adults aged 18 or over living in Great Britain (i.e. excluding Northern Ireland) at the time of the survey. The sample was selected in four stages. First, 114 parliamentary constituencies were sampled from a list of all the constituencies arranged in order of region and in order of broad demographic profile of the constituency within region. The probability of a constituency being selected was proportional to its size. Within each constituency, a polling district was selected, again with probability proportional to size.

The third stage involved selecting 22 addresses in each polling district. The electoral register was used as a sampling frame of addresses (institutional inmates were excluded for practical reasons – so few of them are willing or able to answer survey questions). A random point was selected in the list of names, and then every Nth elector was noted, where N was the required fraction for the particular polling district to yield 22 addresses.

The fourth stage was the selection of the individual for interview at that address. The procedure was designed to compensate for the fact that the electoral register is not a very complete list of individuals; it therefore depended on whether the adults resident had changed since the register was compiled. If the household was identical to the register entry, the elector on whose account the address had been selected had effectively been selected at random, and was therefore nominated for interview. If not, a new selection process was required: all the adults in the household were listed and one was selected at random; this happened in 30 per cent of households.

The probability of selecting the original address had been proportional to the number of electors originally on the register; this was a sensible procedure if the number of electors had not changed. However, at addresses where the number of electors had changed, the probability of any individual being selected had also changed. In subsequent analysis, therefore, all responses from individuals at addresses which had changed electors were weighted by the number of adults at the address divided by the number of electors originally on the register for that address.

Fieldwork

The survey was conducted by Social and Community Planning Research in spring and early summer of 1984, and the response achieved was as shown.

	Number	*Per cent*
Addresses issued	2508	
of which – vacant, derelict, out of scope	101	
– in scope	2407	100
Interviews achieved	1675	70
Interviews not achieved	732	30
of which – refused	567	24
– non-contact	89	4
– other non-response	76	3

The questionnaire

The contents of the Social Attitudes Survey questionnaire are decided through a process of consultation involving many different outside bodies – researchers in government and quangos, academics and others involved in social policy formulation, and colleagues mounting equivalent surveys in the USA, Germany and Australia.

The questionnaire in 1984 took an average of 61 minutes to complete. Respondents were also left a self-completion questionnaire and asked to fill it in and either give it to the interviewer when he or she called back or return it by post; the response rate to this was 93 per cent.

The subject matter of the questionnaire was wide ranging. The survey probed attitudes towards the political process and the respondent's view of his or her own role in it, towards the monarchy, House of Lords, EEC, NATO and Northern Ireland, nuclear weapons, Britain's economic problems, taxation, pensions, the respondent's own job and job security, the welfare state and system of social security, health, housing, education, crime and the criminal process, poverty, social class, race and moral questions of various kinds. Full demographic information was obtained about each respondent, and further information was obtained about other household members. The questionnaire is included as an appendix to the report (Jowell and Witherspoon 1985).

14   Standardization

14.1 Introduction

In this chapter, we learn a rather different way of dealing with the problem outlined in chapter 12: we want to assess the effect of one variable on another, but a third variable is known to affect both. If we want to assess different risks of death, say in different occupations, we have a problem because age can be so strongly related to both the variables of interest; some occupations appear to have lower risk of death simply because they are performed by young people.

The technique to be presented for dealing with this problem, **standardization**, has become an essential part of the tool-kit of the medical statistician and epidemiologist, but is also widely used in other fields. Standardized mortality ratios were used for the example in chapter 10; now, belatedly perhaps, we learn how to construct them. The method simply involves a weighted average of the kind used in chapter 4.

14.2 Rigor mortis

Although it was during the reign of Henry VIII that parsons were first required to keep a record of the number of christenings, weddings and burials occurring in their parish, it was the prevalence of plague that frightened the London Company of Parish Clerks into publishing their accumulated Bills of Mortality on a regular basis from about the beginning of the seventeenth century. Once statistical series were published on the number of deaths of people of varying ages and places of residence, a boost was given not just to epidemiology but also to the insurance industry; the risk that a company took if it offered life insurance to an individual at a particular age could be calculated in a much more precise manner. These earliest forms of social data provided the raw material for social scientific enquiry, or 'political arithmetic', to develop.

However, as the Church of England's monopoly of effecting decorous entry and exit to the world lessened, such bills became less complete records of death, and pressure for compulsory Civil Registration began to build up. The Asiatic cholera bacillus provided the final spur in the first decades of the nineteenth century; this highly contagious bacterium found a natural home in the insanitary conditions of the early industrial slums, and produced three savage epidemics which killed rich as well as poor before the authorities learned how to control it.

In 1836 the Births and Deaths Registration Act was passed, a team of local registrars was entrusted with the job of recording deaths and causes of death, and a new General Register Office (GRO) was formed to collate the reports; this office was the precursor of the Office of Population Censuses and Surveys. The guiding spirit in the organization of the office was William Farr, an upwardly mobile Shropshire lad whose humble origins meant that he could never aspire to being the Registrar-General himself, but who served as 'compiler of abstracts', and who penned the annual reports which rank among some of the finest works of nineteenth century social science (Cullen 1975; Alderson 1983).

The existence of documented death rates helped establish the aetiology of many of the nineteenth century problems of public health. John Snow's discovery of the cause of a vicious cholera epidemic in a London borough in 1854 is well known. Snow was an advocate of an outlandish theory, 'almost too revolting and disgusting to write or read' according to Farr (Lewes 1983:10), that human excrement in the water supply was responsible. He calculated the detailed death rates from cholera in streets in the borough, mapped them, and showed they concentrated around a particular pump in Broad Street. The medical authorities at the time were mostly wedded to the theory that the disease spread because of poisonous 'miasma' in the air, and would not take action, so Snow was forced to remove the pump handle himself. Sure enough, the death rate from cholera in that particular area of Soho quickly declined.

Perhaps less well known is the detailed use made by Florence Nightingale of death rates in her battle to improve the standards in hospitals both in Scutari during the Crimean War and in Britain. The image of Nightingale immortalized by Longfellow is of a kindly Victorian lady with her lamp in one hand, the other on the brow of a fevered soldier. Nightingale's less well appreciated role was as a hard-headed and scientific statistician, carefully distilling the facts from the best data available, reasoning about cause and effect, and then throwing herself into political struggles to achieve the necessary reforms (see Kopf 1977; Cohen 1984).

By compilation and comparison of death rates within age groups, she was able to show that seven times as many soldiers died in hospital while being treated for illnesses that should not have been fatal than were killed by the Russians on the battlefield. The death rate at Scutari, calculated by Nightingale on an annual basis as a fraction of the patient population, reached 415 per cent in February 1855. The majority died from 'zymotic' (preventable, contagious) diseases. Nightingale invented an effective graphical device, the polar-area diagram, to dramatize the extent of needless deaths during the Crimean war, and to highlight the effectiveness of the basic sanitation policies she instituted in March 1855 that the military establishment resisted so strongly.

14.3 The registration and classification of death

From his earliest days at the General Register Office, Farr strove for uniformity in the system of death registration. He designed a death certificate which would encourage doctors to record information in a standard way. He and Nightingale tried to get a particular system for classifying treatment and diseases adopted as standard in all hospitals, to replace the patchy and idiosyncratic systems prevailing. Perhaps most importantly, he devised a system for classifying causes of death for the *First Report of the Registrar-General* (1837:92–100), which, with regular modification, was the system in use in Britain until the beginning of the twentieth century, when international statistical classification schemes were adopted.

When anyone dies in England or Wales today, a standard procedure is followed to register the death (the procedure in Scotland is somewhat different, but not in essential respects). The doctor in attendance certifies the death, supplying information about the cause if he or she can; in the one-third of cases where this is not possible, the case is referred to the coroner. An informant, usually a relative, supplies other essential background data to the local Registrar, who records it on the form shown in figure 14.1.

The informant gives the Registrar information about the dead person's last full-time job, and that of her husband if she is a married woman, or of his or her father if a child. This data is so important in establishing links between particular jobs and particular types of death that the Registrar-General publishes a decennial report summarizing it. It is not without error, however (Alderson 1972). It can take a skilled interviewer three or more questions of a respondent to get codable occupational data; such training is not given to clerks in registraries recording from distressed relatives. Furthermore, the deceased's last job may not be the job in which a particular disease was contracted; there is pressure to collect information on the industry and occupation in which people have spent most years of their life (Royal College of Physicians 1982).

The person who supplies the cause of death is likely to be either a junior hospital doctor, who works very long hours, or a general

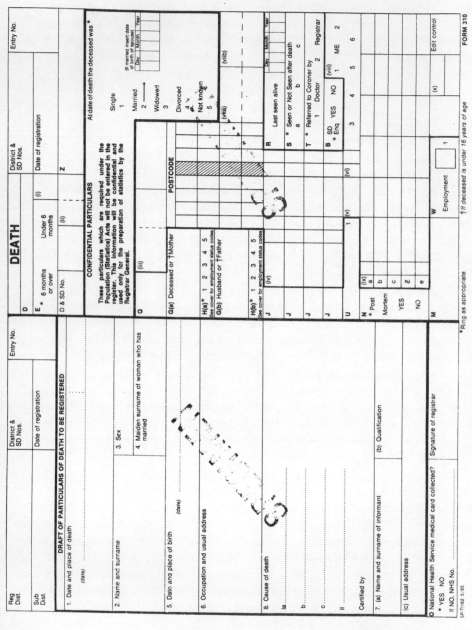

Figure 14.1: Particulars of a death registered

practitioner, who only certifies an average of twelve deaths per year. Two different causes are allowed for on the certificate. Under the first cause there is room for up to three steps in the causal narrative. An example entry might be: (a) bronchopneumonia (b) cerebrovascular accident (c) arteriosclerosis; in other words, the patient had bad arteries which caused a stroke which led to pneumonia. The first step in the causal chain (here arteriosclerosis) will be considered the primary cause. There is then space for a second, contributory condition like diabetes or alcoholism to be recorded; it is likely, however, that such conditions are significantly underreported; the mention of alcohol-related conditions is thought to be especially avoided, because it means that the coroner will immediately become involved, and burial will be delayed. The reliability of the data on cause of death is distressingly low, and there is pressure to train doctors more fully (Royal College of Physicians 1982).

The information is then coded according to the International Classification of Diseases (ICD: World Health Organization 1977). This is a scheme intended to make statistics on diseases, injuries and causes of death comparable across countries. The classification groups diseases caused by well-defined infective agents, diseases affecting particular physiological systems, particular anatomical sites or special classification such as diseases relating to pregnancy. The basic categories have three digits, although most have a further digit for subdivisions, and these categories can also be grouped into aggregate summaries.

Farr, in his first report (Benjamin 1968:82), complained bitterly of current practice in assigning a cause of death:

> Each disease has in many instances been denoted by three or four terms, and each term has been applied to as many different diseases: vague, inconvenient names have been employed, or complications have been registered instead of primary diseases. The nomenclature is of as much importance in this department of inquiry as weights and measures in the physical sciences, and should be settled without delay.

Victorian confidence that such issues could be definitively settled has given way to more humble twentieth century goals that the system should stay abreast of best medical theory, and should at least attempt to retain comparability over the years, so that the time course of diseases could be monitored. The ICD is revised by an international committee about every ten years. It cannot, however, counter fashions in diagnosis which vary over time and place, and which make inferences from trends or cross-cultural comparisons extremely difficult. We do not know, for example, how much of the meteoric rise of recorded cases of lung cancer is due to better diagnostic facilities and how much reflects a genuine increase in incidence.

The local Community Physicians send a tally of deaths in their area to the Office of Population Censuses and Surveys each Friday, and the

Registrar-General then publishes weekly returns, showing deaths in various age groups and under various causes. These are tallied into quarterly returns, and are eventually published in the OPCS series DH1, *Mortality Statistics*. Around census years, when reliable information is available on the size of particular detailed populations such as occupational groups, the death rates are calculated in more detailed categories and published in the *Decennial Supplement* (see section 14.7).

14.4 Crude death rates

We are usually interested in knowing not how many but what proportion of people died in a given period. If the number of deaths (the numerator) is divided by the population at risk (the denominator), the **crude death rate** can be calculated. But it is hard to ensure that the population at risk is exactly the one from which the deaths are drawn; **numerator-denominator biases** become more acute as the population whose mortality is under study is more finely drawn, and have to be guarded against.

Information on place of usual residence, as well as place of death, is collected on the death certificate. Deaths in Britain and in most countries now are classified and tabulated on the basis of where people usually live. This more or less solves the problem which would otherwise occur of areas containing large hospitals appearing to have a high number of deaths. Difficulties come with the 'non-transferable deaths' of those sad individuals who have been in institutions so long that they have given up claim to any residence outside, and special procedures are used to spread those deaths around different local areas; fortunately the size of the problem is diminishing with the years.

The census of population (see the appendix to this chapter) is the major source of population data, and special attention is given to collecting information about people's usual place of residence as well as their location on census day. But population censuses are conducted only every ten years. The annual changes in the population at risk of death are estimated by updating projections from the census with information on the number of registered births and deaths in each locality and some estimate of migration; the mid-year projection is used as the denominator for all deaths occurring in that year. Such estimates are not totally reliable; if an area has grown faster than projected, the denominator will not be the same as the population at risk of death from which the deaths in the numerator are drawn.

Death rates are conventionally expressed per thousand, ten thousand or million population, to get a few varying digits before the decimal point.

14.5 Direct standardization

Comparisons of crude death rates are often uninformative, however; they are dominated by differences in the age structure of the populations to be compared, age being the single most powerful predictor of death. It is therefore preferable to construct death rates in such a way that the age structure (and usually the sex structure too) of the population at risk is taken into account.

Imagine two hypothetical towns with the same population size but with age structures very different from each other and the national average. Town A is a genteel seaside resort to which the moderately affluent retire, and town B a new manufacturing town with a young population. Some hypothetical data about these two towns is shown in figure 14.2. The crude death rate can be obtained simply by dividing the total number of deaths by the total population; in town A it is 60.4 per thousand (3021/50,000), and in town B 54.0 per thousand (2700/50,000). Is town B therefore healthier than town A?

Figure 14.2 Imaginary data on deaths in two hypothetical towns

Age group	Town A (seaside resort)		Town B (manufacturing new town)	
	Deaths	Population	Deaths	Population
0–15	5	5,000	200	20,000
16–64	16	30,000	500	25,000
65+	3000	15,000	2000	5,000
Total	3021	50,000	2700	50,000

Calculation of **age-specific death rates** suggests not. The death rate within each age group is higher in town B than in town A; among the under 16s, for example, town A's death rate is 5/5000 or 1 per thousand, whereas in town B it is 200/20,000 or 10 per thousand. Rather than calculating the overall crude death rate, therefore, it might be preferable to ensure that death rates are presented within different age categories.

But there are still many good reasons for wanting to arrive at a single numerical summary of risk of death in each town. As was argued in chapter 2, such summaries focus the attention, and facilitate comparison. There are two common ways of arriving at a summary of age-specific death rates. As we shall see, the first, direct standardization, applies age-specific death rates for separate populations to a standard population, whereas the second, indirect standardization, applies a standard set of age-specific death rates to each separate population.

An overall death rate that has been **directly standardized** for age is constructed by weighting the age-specific rates by the proportion of each age group in some standard population, usually the population as a whole. Effectively, we are asking: what would the death rate in a standard population be if it were to experience the age-specific death rates observed in this particular place? The approach is exactly that used in chapter 4 in monitoring price increases in a standard basket of goods.

From now on, we shall refer to population sizes by the letter N, population proportions in each category by the letter P, deaths by the letter D and mortality rates (death rates) by the letter M. Small letters will be used to denote properties of particular populations, capitals for properties of a standard population, and the subscript a to denote age-specific rates. Thus, any particular town's age-specific mortality rate is m_a, the proportion in each age group in the standard population is P_a, and so on. The directly standardized death rate is then $\Sigma(P_a m_a)$. The calculations for town A are shown in figure 14.3.

Figure 14.3 Constructing directly age-standardized death ratios for town A

Age group	1 Town pop. size	2 Town age structure	3 Town deaths	4 Town age-specific death rate per 1000	5 Standard pop. age structure	6 Town age-specific death rates weighted by standard	7 by town
	n_a	p_a	d_a	m_a	P_a	$P_a m_a$	$p_a m_a$
0–15	5,000	0.10	5	1.0	0.20	0.2	0.1
16–64	30,000	0.60	16	0.5	0.60	0.3	0.3
65+	15,000	0.30	3000	200.0	0.20	40.0	60.0
Total	50,000	1.00	3021		1.00	40.5	60.4

Columns 1, 3 and 5 of figure 14.3 show the raw data required for the calculation. Column 2 shows the town's age structure in proportional terms, column 4 shows the derived age-specific death rates, and column 6 shows these death rates weighted by the age structure of a standard national population; these weighted age-specific death rates are finally summed. Town A thus has an age-standardized death rate of 40.5 per thousand.

Column 7 of figure 14.3 is included to show that the crude death rate, written as $\Sigma d_a / \Sigma n_a$, can also be calculated as a weighted average of the town's age-specific death rates, and written $\Sigma(p_a m_a)$. In this case, the weights are the proportions of the age group in that town. The reason why the crude death rate is unsatisfactory is that the weights vary from area to area, instead of being fixed with reference to a standard population.

Similar calculations for town B (not shown here) reveal that it has an age-standardized death rate of 94 per thousand, summarizing the fact that the risk of death is much higher than in town A within each age category.

While standardizing in these broad groups certainly helps clarify the picture, it may in certain instances be necessary to work with finer groups; two towns may contain the same proportion of people over 60, for example, but the typical age of people over 60 in one town may still be different from that in the other. Furthermore, directly-standardized death rates are dependent on the structure of the population chosen as the standard; to track mortality over time, one has to decide whether to work with a constant but increasingly dated standard population or to recalculate rates using later standard populations. They also make large demands for data, requiring:

- the age distribution of the population in each town
- the age-specific death rates for each town
- the age structure of a convenient standard population to provide weights

In practice, the first two may be difficult to obtain. Moreover, if the numbers in the age groups are small, the number of deaths may fluctuate unstably from year to year in that age group.

14.6 Indirect standardization

Another method is therefore often used, which does not involve knowing the age structure of a standard population, but rather a set of age-specific mortality rates in a standard population. The strategy is called **indirect standardization**, and entails comparing the total number of deaths in a town whose age structure is known with what one might expect if the age-specific death rates in the standard population prevailed in that town. The age-specific death rates in the national population are usually treated as standards; these are not only easier to obtain but less prone to fluctuation, being based on much larger numbers.

To see how this works, imagine that the age-specific death rates nationally are 1 per thousand among the young, 3 per thousand among those of working age and 500 per thousand among the old. Figure 14.4 applies this framework to the data for town A. The total number of deaths expected, 7595, is greater than the number actually found, 3021, expressing yet again that town A has a lower mortality rate once its age structure has been taken into account. The breakdown of the number of deaths into age groups has been bracketed to remind us that it is not needed for this calculation. Indeed, it is precisely because such information is likely to be either missing or weak that the indirect method of standardization is often required.

Figure 14.4 Constructing indirectly age-standardized death ratios for town A

Age group	1 Town size	2 Standard age-specific death rate per 1000	3 Expected deaths	4 Actual deaths
	n_a	M_a	$n_a M_a$	d_a
0–15	5,000	1	5	(5)
16–64	30,000	3	90	(16)
65+	15,000	500	7500	(3000)
Total	50,000		7595	3021

The relationship between actual and expected death rate is usually multiplied by 100 and called a **standardized mortality ratio**:

$$\text{SMR} = \frac{\text{Observed number of deaths } \Sigma d_a}{\text{Expected number of deaths } \Sigma n_a M_a} \times 100$$

In the hypothetical data, the SMR for town A is 39.8, and for town B (calculations not shown here) is 116.4. SMRs of less than 100 indicate that a particular population has a lower death rate than a standard population, and those above 100 indicate a higher rate.

Standardized mortality ratios are less demanding of local data. To sum up, they require:

- age-specific death rates for a standard population
- the age distribution of the local population
- the total deaths in the local population

Their use may therefore be extended into the study of other sub-populations, social classes, industrial or occupational groups and so on, for which age-specific death rates may not be available. However, you should note that they are highly dependent on the age structure of the specific population for which they are constructed.

Conventionally, the method of direct standardization is used to arrive at a rate, whereas indirect standardization provides a ratio. However, it is possible to express the observed number of deaths as a ratio of the number of deaths one would expect from the directly standardized death rates, in a measure known as the **comparative mortality figure** (CMF). It is given by

$$\text{CMF} = \frac{\text{Direct age-standardized death rate for particular population}}{\text{Direct age-standardized death rate for standard population}} \times 100$$

The directly age-standardized death rate for town A was calculated in figure 14.3 to be 40.5 per thousand. The denominator of the CMF for town A is $P_a M_a$, which can be calculated from the data in figures 14.3 and 14.4 to be 102.0 per thousand. Thus the CMF for town A is 39.7, virtually the same as the SMR.

However, the CMF and the SMR will only be similar if one of two conditions holds: (1) the age distribution of the standard population is similar to the age distribution of the specific population, or (2) the death rates in each age group in the specific population differ from the death rates in the standard population in the same ratio. In general, no single summary of mortality will adequately represent what is happening in a specific population if the risk of death relative to the standard population varies significantly within age groups. To express this idea in technical terms, we say that control can only satisfactorily be effected over a third variable if we can assume that there are no interactions; this point will be explained fully in chapter 15.

14.7 Class differentials in mortality

The effect of class on likelihood of death was most vividly illustrated in the queue for the lifeboats as the Titanic sank; 81 of the 179 women travelling third class drowned, 15 of the 93 women travelling second class drowned, while only 4 of the 143 first-class female passengers drowned, three of whom voluntarily chose to stay on the ship (Lord 1955).

More generally, the unequal placement of broad groups in society in the queues for a healthy life has been illustrated from the earliest tabulation of risk of death by occupation and social class. The interpretation of and policy implications which stem from such data, however, have long the been subject of fierce controversy: occupational groups such as the manual working class cannot just be removed like a contaminated water supply or a battlefield hospital.

The controversy was fanned in the 1980s by the findings of a review of inequalities in health conducted by the Department of Health and Social Security Research Working Group under the chairmanship of Sir Douglas Black. Commissioned by the 1974–9 Labour administration, it reported in 1980, during the first year of office of a Conservative administration committed to cutting back on public expenditure. The Secretary of State dismissed the report and only 260 copies were made for circulation. It was then published commercially by one of the academic members of the committee (Townsend and Davidson 1982) and received the rapt attention that press and public devote to any banned book.

Central to the evidence marshalled in the Black Report was the continuing existence of social class differentials in mortality as published in the *Decennial Supplement* of the Registrar-General. The authors of the report argued that, although mortality rates had fallen over the past 40 years, differentials in the SMRs for different classes had widened. If the calculations are made in a similar fashion for 1979–83, (figure 14.5), it seems that the trend to inequality has continued at an accelerated pace; the figures for 1979–82, however, are only available for a more restricted age group, which may have affected the differentials found.

Figure 14.5 Mortality of men aged 15–64 by social class 1930s to 1980s: SMRs

Class	1930–32	1949–53	1959–63	1970–72	1979–83*
I	90	86	76	77	66
II	94	92	81	81	76
III	97	101	100	104	103
IV	102	104	103	114	116
V	111	118	143	137	165

* Figures for 1979–83 are for men aged 20–64

Sources: Townsend and Davidson (1982: 67) and OPCS (1986: tables GD2 and GP2)

Several criticisms, however, can be made of using class differentials as numerical summaries of inequality in life chances. The Registrar-General's class scheme has low reliability and has never been demonstrated to identify social groups with distinct lifestyles (Marsh 1985b) or with similar social standing (as you discovered in exercise 6.2). The scheme was constructed at the beginning of the century on the basis of the professional judgement of workers at the GRO, and many fear that the mortality experienced by particular occupations may have determined which class they were placed in, thus rendering circular any 'explanation' of mortality by social class. Moreover, the classifications have been modified quite substantially over the decades, and the size of individual classes has changed quite dramatically, which makes trends over time very hard to interpret.

The *Decennial Supplement* for 1979–83 (OPCS 1986) therefore broke with the tradition established by the Registrar-General from the early decades of the century of doing detailed analysis of risk of death by social class. As well as echoing some of the criticisms in the previous paragraph, the *Supplement* adds a further argument against class-specific SMRs, namely the numerator-denominator biases discussed earlier; exercises 14.1 and 14.2 have been set to illustrate this point further.

Some researchers, principally health economists, have opted to study inequalities in health by a different method altogether, using Gini coefficients to summarize the differences in life expectancy of all individuals; the cumulative population total is plotted on the X-axis against the cumulative years lived on the Y-axis, and the distribution summarized. The result of this exercise suggests that individual differences have been decreasing over time, the opposite conclusion from the Black Report. However, some have argued that this is because the Gini coefficient responds to changes in the mean value of life expectancy as well as to its distribution; interested readers are invited to read a summary of a debate that took place about these issues in the Royal Statistical Society's *News and Notes* for July 1986.

The comparative life chances of groups of people as well as of individuals will almost certainly continue to be of interest, since they suggest the effects of social structures and processes as well as chance individual variation. Better validated social groupings are needed for this purpose, and attempts must be made to improve the reliability of coding fine occupational detail, especially at death registration. In the meantime, the best we can do is to collapse the existing class groupings into rather bigger categories to avoid some of the worst problems.

14.8 Conclusion

In this chapter, we have seen how a batch of numbers may be standardized to remove the effects of a contaminating variable before being summarized into a single score. The instance chosen was mortality, where standardization of death rates of subgroups to remove the confounding effects of age is routine. For simplicity, the calculations were shown for men only; to allow for different sex structures in the populations as well would have required doubling the number of categories.

Two methods of standardization were proposed, direct and indirect, and their advantages summarized. In practice, the indirect method of calculating SMRs is the more common, even when the data required by the direct method is available, principally because it is less prone to sampling error. An important conclusion about indirect standardization was drawn, which applies beyond the particular example of mortality used here: standardization is not reliable when the death rates of different subgroups differ markedly, when – to use the technical term – interactions exist in the data.

The techniques were applied to interpret the risk of death in different social classes. People have debated the trends in such risks over time, arguing over the interpretation of data whose quality is far from perfect. When the results of research fail to confirm our treasured hypotheses, or when they are politically uncomfortable, it is nearly always possible to find flaws that allow doubt to be cast on them. The task of the responsible data analyst is to use as many different methods and sources as possible, and to go as far as the data will permit in answering the big questions. One alternative source of data on death rates is the longitudinal study which allows investigation of some of the problems discussed above. We turn to this in the next chapter.

Exercises

14.1 (a) Occupations recorded at registration of death are often insufficiently detailed to allow coding to a precise category, and have to be put in a residual category, such as 'other labourers and unskilled workers not elsewhere classified'; this happens more often at death registration than at the census. What resulting numerator-denominator biases would you expect in death rates calculated for this residual category of workers?

(b) In 1979–83, the residual category of 'other labourers' etc. accounted for 44 per cent of deaths to men aged 20–64 in class V. How would you expect the class V SMR including this group to compare with the class V SMR excluding them?

(c) In 1980, the occupational classification scheme was made much more detailed; from 224 unit groups in the 1970 scheme, there are over 500 in the 1980 scheme. Would you expect this to make the problem of numerator-denominator bias more or less severe in the residual categories?

14.2 The following data is drawn from the 1979–83 *Decennial Supplement*. The occupations of only 10 per cent of individuals at the census were coded; for the purposes of calculating populations at risk they should be multiplied by ten. The deaths relate to a four year period, 1979–80 and 1982–3, since deaths were not counted in 1981. In this table, class V is grouped with class IV, semi-skilled manual workers, in an attempt to get round some of the numerator-denominator biases just identified. Calculate the crude death rate, the directly standardized death rate and the SMR over the period for men aged 20–64 in these combined classes. Compare the SMR with that shown for the classes separately in figure 14.5.

Age group	Number of men in 1981	Deaths to all men 1979–83	Classes IV and V in 1981	Deaths in classes IV and V 1979–83
20–24	204,425	7,284	44,782	2,143
25–34	385,397	14,240	70,782	3,912
35–44	324,643	25,375	59,181	6,907
45–54	300,468	76,714	66,737	22,913
55–64	287,743	213,486	75,713	70,114

Source: OPCS (1986: tables GP2 and GD2)

14.3 In the 1930s, before the widespread introduction of antibiotics which occurred after the War, a significant number of women still died in childbirth ('puerperal deaths'). The standardized death rate per thousand live births from all puerperal causes in the 1930–2 *Decennial Supplement* for wives of men in classes I and II was 4.44, for wives of class III workers was 4.11, class IV was 4.16 and class V was 3.89 (Macfarlane and Mugford 1984: 205). What do you think could account for this reversal of the usual class gradients in mortality?

Appendix: the Census of Population

Introduction

The ancient empires of China, Egypt and Rome, critically dependent on slave labour for their viability, all made periodic attempts to review their resources by conducting the earliest forms of population census. The modern census has a somewhat different complexion, but was also born of anxiety over population size, in some countries (e.g. Norway) because they feared population decline, and in others (e.g. Britain) out of fear of population explosion. Most countries in the world now make a special effort at tallying their population in greater or lesser detail every now and then.

In Britain, Parliament is required to approve each proposal by government to hold a census. One has been conducted decennially in Britain since 1801, with the exception of 1941, during the Second World War; since 1921, they have been carried out under the regulation of the 1920 Census Act.

The data collected has many administrative functions, such as making annual estimates of population in various demographic categories, which are then used to allocate large sums of money to Health Service regions and to local authorities. The data has also been used successfully by businesses for marketing their products and locating shops, and by academics, especially geographers, for research purposes. There have been repeated calls for a quinquennial census; only once however, in 1966, was there a mid-term census, and that was on a 10 per cent sample.

Strengths and weaknesses of complete coverage

In Britain, all householders are required by law to complete a census return. This makes the census the most complete source of social data available. Insistence on completeness of coverage for its own sake might seem rather outmoded given modern developments in sampling techniques; many of the functions of earlier censuses have been taken over effectively by the continuous surveys described in other chapters of this book. But there are other considerations. The census is the longest running source of data on social conditions, and is therefore a unique source documenting social change. It permits fine and comparable detail on small geographical populations and groups. And the economies of scale are great; at a little over £1 per head at 1980 prices (Thatcher 1984), it is extremely cheap.

However, many other countries have introduced some form of sampling on their census of population, to allow a wider range of questions to be asked. In the USA, for example, a longer version of the schedule is given to one in six households, and in Canada to one in five, in an attempt to minimize the average burden to respondents. Only a limited amount of sampling has been tried on the British census, and on each occasion doubts have been expressed about the validity of the field operation. In more recent British censuses, sampling has been limited to coding the detailed occupational and educational information for 10 per cent of households only.

The completeness of coverage comes principally through compulsion, accompanied by a guarantee of confidentiality. The right of government to require information of private citizens does not go unchallenged in any modern state. In Northern Ireland, where the legitimacy of the British state is disputed, the census has suffered problems of acceptability, and in 1981 a census enumerator was shot dead. There has, however, never been major public concern that confidentiality has been breached in Britain, and only a tiny proportion of people refuse to cooperate; there were, for example, only 700 prosecutions for failure to complete a return for the 1981 census. (For a general discussion of the issues of privacy and confidentiality in censuses, see Bulmer 1979.)

The experience of other countries is not so comfortable. The US small area census data probably assisted the American government to round up Japanese nationals at the beginning of World War II. And the ghastly use that the Nazis made of population lists in the Netherlands for identifying those of Jewish origin has never been forgotten. Similar fears played their part in stirring up opposition to a question on ethnicity in the British 1981 census, and the German census has had difficulties ever since: the 1983 German census, in which it was planned to enter names and addresses on a computer, was vociferously opposed and has been repeatedly postponed.

Methods

The first three British censuses were very unsystematic affairs by modern standards. The first truly modern census was conducted in 1841; a common schedule was devised and addressed to all householders, and enumerators were only used to deliver and collect the schedules, and to help the illiterate complete them. The same principles of data collection have remained ever since.

For the purpose of the 1981 census, the country was divided into around 130,000 enumeration districts each comprising around 400 people in 150 households. One enumerator was allocated to each, to complete some information on the type of housing and the way it was shared with others, to deliver a schedule to each household, to collect it and give any assistance required at the completion stage.

There are two common ways of counting a population. The way historically used in Britain is to count people where they are at a given time, regardless of whether they usually live there or not; in 1981, householders were asked to list the people at their address at midnight on Sunday 5 April. This has the advantage of accuracy, but planners are often more interested in getting estimates of where people normally live, the form of question historically asked in censuses in France and North America. In 1981, householders were asked to list both others absent that night who normally lived there, and the addresses of anyone present who normally lived elsewhere. Census tables could therefore be presented either on the basis of people present or on the basis of normal residents.

The 1981 Census was advertised on TV and in the press as the shortest since the 1930s. It contained only 21 questions, and was indeed not only shorter than the other post-war censuses but also shorter than in many other comparable countries (Redfern 1981). Sixteen questions were asked about each household member – five demographic, four on geographic mobility, six on employment and one on education; a further five questions about the housing were asked in respect of each household. There was a question about language in Wales and Scotland, and a voluntary question on religion in Northern Ireland.

Several questions are not asked in British censuses but are asked elsewhere, such as income and fertility. However, the topic about which there has been most recent discussion is that of ethnicity and race. The advocates of such a question argue that the data is vital for allocating educational and health resources, for pinpointing disadvantage and so on. The antagonists question whether information on ethnicity alone (as opposed to language, for example) is ever a basis for planning, and point to the hostility which a question on ethnicity aroused during a mock census in 1978. A question on ethnicity was finally dropped from the 1981 census after a debate in Parliament for fear of damaging the public consensus which is so vital to successful completion.

The sheer volume of the census has often forced it into methodological innovation. Hollerith, whose famous punched card is not totally obsolete even today, won a competition to provide a mechanical means of analysing the 1880 US census; without this, the data analysis would not have been finished before the 1890 census. Post-war censuses in all industrial countries have, at varying degrees of speed, transferred operations to large computers; the 1961 census was the first in Britain to be analysed on an electronic computer. Methods of automatic data entry, which involve respondents marking a form which is then scanned by a machine, are improving, and their eventual use in censuses seems inevitable.

Data quality

To look at the published tables from the 1981 census you would think that census respondents are paragons compared with usual survey respondents, as there appears to be no missing data. However, this is because an elaborate process of **editing** – correcting the data to improve its quality – takes place during processing: the enumerators do a limited check of each schedule as it is collected and the key operators are alerted if they attempt to enter a number which is not valid for that particular question.

But, most importantly, automatic procedures are used to **impute** values where these are missing or discovered to be in error through computer checks for such combinations as married three year olds. The methods, known as **hot-deck** imputation, involve creating a value on the basis of the values typically associated with an individual or household of the same type (Brant and Chalk 1985); if the number of cars in the household is missing, for example, a value will be randomly allocated by sampling from the distribution of cars in other households of the same tenure type and number of adults. (Variables which can take a very wide range of possible values, such as occupation, are not imputed, however.) While imputation makes the published data easier to handle, it is a fudge, and objections have been voiced to the whole philosophy of handling missing data in this way (Bateson 1984).

Out of nearly 18 million households to which a form was addressed in 1981, fewer than 6000 failed to complete a return. There could of course still have been underenumeration. To estimate the completeness with which the Census covered the population, its results can be compared with other estimates that exist of the population size; the number of children can be compared with school roll sizes, the number of infants with birth registrations, the number of elderly with pensioner numbers and so on. On the basis of such checks, the only substantial net underrecording in 1981 was for infants between 0 and 1, where 2 per cent were missed, and for the inhabitants of inner London, where 2.5 per cent were missed (Thatcher 1984).

However, to get more detailed information on the reliability (but not necessarily the validity) of census information, gross errors can be estimated. To obtain these, some form of repeat of the whole procedure at a slower pace by more experienced staff in a restricted set of areas has been conducted since 1961. The 1981 Census Post-Enumeration Survey (PES) broadly confirmed the demographic checks, but also permitted investigation of response errors and thus gross misclassification rates (Britton and Birch 1985). The agreement rate between the census return and the PES results was over 95 per cent for fourteen out of the twenty-one questions. However, some questions were particularly unreliable – the number of rooms, where 29 per cent of answers in the PES failed to correspond with census returns, social class, where the disagreement rate was 13 per cent, socio-economic groups, where it was 16 per cent, and detailed occupational groups at 25 per cent.

Dissemination of results

The records of the first four censuses have not been kept, but from 1841 onwards, the individual schedules have been preserved (with the exception of the sample census of 1966 whose schedules have tragically been burnt). However, they cannot be released by the Public Record Office until 100 years after they were collected. The reprocessing of the original data using modern analytic techniques is an exciting prospect for social historians.

From 1801 to 1951, the census results were published as tables in reports with commentaries, describing methods, and also identifying important changes that have taken place in the living conditions and character of the population. They form a fine and under-utilized historical source (Hakim 1982). Since 1961, the traditional commentaries have disappeared from the reports, but much more analysis is presented, and new types of commentaries have appeared (monitors, guides, maps, wall charts, articles in other journals, and so on).

The 1981 Census was published in several forms. The main results were published in a report for each county in England and Wales and each region in Scotland. Summaries are also available for regions, parliamentary constituencies, new towns, and wards and civil parishes, both using the boundaries which applied at the time of the census and using the new boundaries introduced in 1983.

There are national summaries of demographic information, country of birth, communal establishments, usual residence, housing, Welsh and Gaelic speaking, the elderly, national and regional migration, economic activity, household composition, qualified manpower, and work and transport, as well as a volume of historical trends. There is a volume of definitions. Popular summary guides have been written on the elderly, the young, the workforce and housing, and briefing packs are available for teachers.

Detail on enumeration districts is not available in printed form, but on a computer file of Small Area Statistics (which can of course be listed). The main users of such statistics are local authorities; county halls and local libraries are often very generous in supplying information on their locality in fine detail. The ESRC has purchased a complete set of Small Area Statistics, and these are distributed through the Data Archive at the University of Essex. Six other universities maintain the data on-line, together with the SASPAC retrieval software.

The boundaries of enumeration districts are shown on maps produced by OPCS. These were compiled on large scale Ordnance Survey maps and then microfilmed; the results are often far from clear. In addition, however, the National Grid coordinates of the centroids of each enumeration district, ward and so on are given in the appropriate computer record, and much mapping and analysis has been carried out using them.

Despite attempts to change policy, access to anonymous census data at the individual level has not been allowed in Britain. In North America, tapes of data for public use are prepared on random samples of the census data; care is taken to disguise individual identities by introducing some deliberate error into combinations of categories which might otherwise allow individual identification, and the system works very acceptably. It may be that the policy can be changed for the 1991 census, and other, more radical changes, have been proposed for the 200th anniversary census after that (Rhind 1985).

The Census Offices issue a guide to the census (OPCS 1985). Two other excellent guides to census material exist. The first (Rhind 1983) is more technical and concentrates somewhat on the census as a source of data for geographers, on area classification and so on. The second (Hakim 1982) describes the census as a source of social and historical data.

15 Median Polishing

15.1 Introduction

Median polishing is another technique which controls variables by holding them constant; (we used this type of control for contingency tables in chapter 13). It is used when the response variable is measured on an interval scale and we wish to separate out the direct effects of two (or more) explanatory variables which may only have been measured on a nominal scale. It is the last technique we shall deal with for controlling for the effect of a third variable.

Before we get our teeth into this final chapter, however, there is some unfinished business to attend to on the topic of statistical control. You should be aware that an alternative and somewhat weaker form of control can also be exercised over the operation of a variable: the values of the two variables whose relationship one wants to assess can be **mathematically adjusted** to take into account the effect of a third variable. Control by adjustment is weaker in the sense that it relies on the approximate correctness of assuming a particular form of relationship (usually linear) between the variable under control and the other variables. However, if all the variables are measured on interval scales, it has the advantage of being able to make more effective use of finer gradations in the variables. There is not space in this book to cover line-fitting with three variables, but exercise 11.5 should have given you a flavour of how it operates.

Holding variables more or less constant does not require such strong assumptions, but it requires a lot of cases, even when we use broad categories. If we had wanted to control for race and region as well as age in considering the relationship between income and preparedness to break the law in chapter 13, for example, we would have needed sufficient young wealthy black people living in the North to compare with young wealthy black people living in the South. It can require a very large, or exceptionally well-planned, survey to obtain sufficient cases to make all the comparisons required. What control by adjustment lacks in logical rigour it makes up for in efficient use of cases.

15.2 Class differentials in mortality

There has, over the years, been a long-running debate about the explanation for the differential risk of mortality experienced by different occupational groups and social classes. Three broad types of explanation have been put forward:

1 Work-related effects: First, differentials might reflect the direct influences of occupation; high rates of accidental death among construction workers, for example, are hard to interpret any other way.

2 Lifestyle effects: Differentials might also reflect other lifestyle patterns or socio-cultural backgrounds which tend to cluster in occupational or class groups (such as a tendency for unskilled manual workers to smoke more than average). The classic evidence that such lifestyle effects exist is that the wives of men who work in some occupational groups suffer very similar mortality rates to their husbands.

3 Selection effects: Alternatively, the causal direction might be precisely the opposite. It might be that healthy people tend to get better jobs, or that once people are not very fit, they can only get lower grade jobs. This would mean that people are selected into jobs on the basis of their pre-existing qualities in a Darwinian struggle of survival of the fittest.

The political implications of these three hypothesized processes are very different; if it is human capital that determines occupational (or marriage) outcome, then social institutions are let off the hook.

The traditional source of data on class differentials in mortality is the *Decennial Supplement*, which classifies deaths by classes according to the occupation recorded on the death certificate. The data in this chapter is drawn from a different source, however. A large and ongoing national longitudinal survey of the population of England and Wales was started in the early 1970s; a 1 per cent random sample of the population was drawn originally from the 1971 census, and new sample members have been added as they are born or immigrate. Subsequently, information from a range of official sources has been linked to this database. For our purposes, the most important of these is information on the death certificate for those who subsequently die (Fox and Goldblatt 1982). The survey overcomes most of the most important numerator/denominator biases in calculating SMRs which were identified in the last chapter. This uniquely valuable resource, known as the OPCS Longitudinal Study, is described more fully in the appendix.

In this chapter, we shall look in particular at the risk of death among married women in this survey between the years 1971 and 1981. Information is available about their own and their husband's job at the time of the 1971 census. Linking this information to details from the death certificate of those who subsequently die provides an unparalled source of data on how social class affects women's life chances. We shall look for class differentials in the standardized mortality ratios both by the wife's own job and that of her husband.

In the 1920s, Stevenson, the architect of the Registrar-General's social class scheme, compared the differential risk of death of husbands doing different jobs with the risks experienced by their wives. This became an accepted way of investigating how mortality differentials arise; if differentials were as strong for wives as for husbands, they were presumed to reflect the effects of lifestyle or socio-cultural background rather than occupation. In the 1920s, however, a historically low proportion of married women worked; Stevenson did not need to worry that the differentials among wives might reflect aspects of their own occupation. Since then, the rate of female participation in the economy has increased strongly once more, to the point where wives' mortality experience cannot be assumed to reflect husbands' occupation alone.

In this chapter we shall restrict our attention to broad social classes, rather than occupational groups. You discovered in exercise 7.1 that there was an association between husband's and wife's class; it was not so strong that husband's class could be used as a failsafe indicator of the wife's position, but it was strong enough to mean that the wife's own class should be controlled when estimating the effect of her husband's class on her own mortality experience, and her husband's class should be controlled when estimating the direct effect of her own class.

The age-standardized mortality ratios for married women in England and Wales are shown in figure 15.1, cross-classified by the class of both the woman herself and her husband as recorded at the 1971 census. The data summarizes the mortality experience of these women in the ten years after the census; illustrative jobs in each class were given in exercise 6.2.

The 'other' category is composed of two groups; the economically inactive (housewives, permanently sick and students), and those who were economically active but could not be allocated to a class because their occupation was inadequately described. If either husband or wife was unemployed at the time of the census, they should have been placed in a class category on the basis of their last job; nearly a quarter of unemployed husbands, however, were allocated to the 'other' category because their last job was inadequately described. The majority of women in the 'other' category were those who described themselves at the 1971 census as housewives, but the largest number of deaths in this group was contributed by the permanently sick.

Figure 15.1 SMRs for married women at ages 15–59 by own class and husband's class; deaths occurring between 1971 and 1981

Wife's own social class	Husband's social class			
	I+II	III	IV+V	Other
I and II	68	82	83*	124
III	64	80	89	88
IV and V	72	97	84	94
Other	77	105	127	182

Population used to standardize the death rates is all women aged 15 to 59.

* SMR is based on only 19 observed deaths.

Source: OPCS National Longitudinal Study unpublished table, Crown Copyright; reproduced by kind permission of OPCS and Peter Goldblatt

In layout, the table is superficially similar to that obtained in exercise 7.1, which showed how many couples fell into each of the joint class groups. There is, however, a critical difference: the entries in each cell of figure 15.1 are values of a third variable – risk of death – whereas the values in the simple bivariate cross-classification were frequencies (or percentages). The information about how many cases fall in each cell is not presented in figure 15.1.

Make sure you understand clearly which type of table you are dealing with, as methods of analysis suitable for tables whose cells contain the values of a third variable are different from the methods of analysis of contingency tables. Some people have an awkward habit of referring to both simple contingency tables and tables such as that in figure 15.1 as 'two-way tables'. This terminology is not ideal; it focuses on a less important aspect of a table, its physical dimensions (rows and columns), instead of a more important aspect, the number of variables presented (here three).

The effects of the woman's own class on her risk of death controlling for her husband's class can be obtained by reading down the columns of the table; the effects of husband's class controlling for her own class are found by reading across the rows of the table. However, there are so many numbers involved, and so many possible comparisons to be made, that some way of summarizing these effects is needed. That is what median polishing sets out to achieve.

15.3 Extracting medians from rows and columns

Casting an eye over figure 15.1, it is clear that there are some effects on mortality of both the wife's own class and her husband's. This observation can as usual be cast in the DFR form:

$$\text{Data} = \text{Fit} + \text{Residual}$$

As we saw in chapter 6, this can be further decomposed into fits and effects. There are two separate effects now:

$$\text{Wife's SMR} = \text{Overall fit} + \text{Husband's class effect} + \text{Own class effect} + \text{Residual}$$

Median polishing arrives at resistant quantitative summaries of these direct effects. We might therefore expect that the technique would involve first working within rows and then working within columns.

To get an estimate of the effect of the husband's class controlling for the wife's own class, we start by finding a fitted value within each category of wife's own class, and then look at the residuals from this fitted value. Since we want resistant summaries, the median of each row in the table suggests itself. A typical SMR for women whose job in 1971 was classified as being in class I or II is 82.5 (the median of the first row). The deviations of each particular SMR in the first row from this typical SMR are obtained by subtraction; 68 is 14.5 less than 82.5, and so on. This is repeated for each row:

DATA				=	FIT	+	RESIDUAL			
68	82	83	124		82.5		−14.5	−0.5	+0.5	+41.5
64	80	89	88		84.0		−20.0	−4.0	+5.0	+4.0
72	97	84	94		89.0		−17.0	+8.0	−5.0	+5.0
77	105	127	182		116.0		−39.0	−11.0	+11.0	+66.0

Reading down the column of fits, we can see that SMRs are less than 100 in the main class groupings of wife's own occupation, but over 100 in the 'other' category. The residuals contain the information about the variation associated with husband's job; they show that those whose husbands are in higher social classes tend to have lower SMRs than others. Let us complete the process before we discuss it further.

Each column is now treated in exactly the same manner: the median is extracted and residuals calculated. In the column representing women whose husbands were in the highest social classes, a typical residual is −18.5. This value is then subtracted from each of the values in that column. Be careful about signs when you are subtracting negative numbers. The process is repeated for each column, including the column of fits:

First cycle

68	82	83	124	82.5	−14.5	−0.5	+0.5	+41.5
64	80	89	88	84.0	−20.0	−4.0	+5.0	+4.0
72	97	84	94	89.0	−17.0	+8.0	−5.0	+5.0
77	105	127	182	116.0	−39.0	−11.0	+11.0	+66.0
				86.5	−18.5	−2.0	+3.0	+23.0
				−4.0	+4.0	+1.5	−2.5	+18.5
				−2.5	−1.5	−2.0	+2.0	−19.0
				+2.5	+1.5	+10.0	−8.0	−18.0
				+29.5	−20.5	−9.0	+8.0	+43.0

It is helpful to put the labels back now and inspect the results of the first cycle of this median extraction procedure.

Figure 15.2 Effect of own class and husband's class on SMR of married women aged 15–59: deaths occurring between 1971 and 1981; one cycle of analysis only

		Husband's social class			
Wife's own social class		I+II	III	IV+V	Other
	86.5	−18.5	−2.0	+3.0	+23.0
I and II	−4.0	+4.0	+1.5	−2.5	+18.5
III	−2.5	−1.5	−2.0	+2.0	−19.0
IV and V	+2.5	+1.5	+10.0	−8.0	−18.0
Other	+29.5	−20.5	−9.0	+8.0	+43.0

Source: as figure 15.1: OPCS National Longitudinal Study

Figure 15.2 shows the original data values decomposed into four components:

1 An overall fit of 86.5.

2 The effects of husband's class on wife's mortality; those whose husbands are in classes I or II, for example, typically have an SMR 18.5 points lower than the overall fit, those whose husbands are in the 'other' category have SMRs 23 points higher, and so on.

3 The effect of the woman's own class on mortality; those who are themselves in class I or II occupations have SMRs typically 4 points lower, whereas those who are in the 'other' category have SMRs 29.5 points higher, and so on.

4 A table of residuals; these indicate the extent to which any particular combination of husband's and wife's class has a higher or lower risk of mortality than one would expect from the summaries obtained in the overall fit and the row and column effects.

The value of every single entry in the original table (figure 15.1) has effectively been decomposed into four elements as the DFR equation specified. The original value of any particular cell can be obtained by adding the four components together. The SMR for women who were in class III at the 1971 census and whose husbands were in class IV or V, for example, is:

$$\text{Wife's SMR} = \text{Overall fit} + \text{Husband's class effect} +$$
$$\text{Own class effect} + \text{Residual}$$
$$= 86.5 + 3 + (-2.5) + 2$$
$$= 89$$

Before we interpret these results, however, we must go one stage further in improving the analysis.

15.4 Polishing the table

The technique, like other resistant techniques, requires iteration, or **polishing**, to make the residuals as small as possible; you must expect polishing tables to require a bit of elbow grease. We therefore start again with the final four by four table of residuals, and repeat the whole procedure. Working to the nearest 0.5, the median of 4, 1.5, −2.5 and 18.5 is 3.0, so this is subtracted from every entry in the first row, and so on. Rather than copy the table of residuals out again, we work from right to left in the second cycle of the analysis. Exact zeros are denoted by ticks; median polishing can generate a large number of zero residuals, especially when the number of rows and columns are odd, so it is best to identify them separately.

Second cycle

+1.0	−1.5	−5.5	+15.5	3.0	4.0	1.5	−2.5	18.5
+0.5	√	+4.0	−17.0	−2.0	−1.5	−2.0	2.0	−19.0
+4.5	+13.0	−5.0	−15.0	−3.0	1.5	10.0	−8.0	−18.0
−20.0	−8.5	+8.5	+43.5	−0.5	−20.5	−9.0	8.0	43.0

+1.0	−1.0	−0.5	√	−1.0

√	0.5	−5.0	+15.5	+4.0
−0.5	+1.0	+4.5	−17.0	−1.0
+3.5	+14.0	−4.5	−15.0	−2.0
−21.0	−7.5	+9.0	+43.5	+0.5

No very large changes are produced by this second cycle. The overall fit is now one point lower, and most of the row and column effects have changed fractionally (producing consequential changes in the residuals). To view the whole picture, we add the fit and effects obtained in the first cycle of the procedure to those obtained in the second, and use the residuals derived from the second cycle, as shown in figure 15.3.

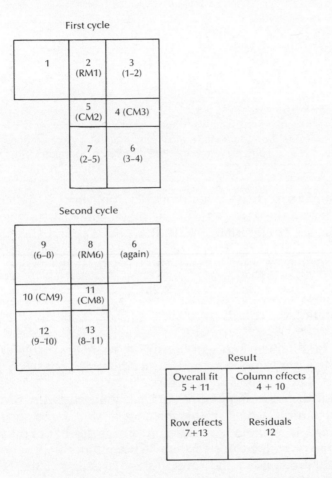

Figure 15.3 Anatomy of two cycles of median polishing. Numbers refer to the order in which the elements are calculated. CM column medians, RM row medians

In principle, the table is polished as many times as it takes for all the row and column effects to be within 0.5 of zero. In practice, more than two cycles of polishing are rarely required. The procedure could be performed by first extracting column medians and then row medians; small differences in the results will sometimes occur if it is done in this way.

Figure 15.4 Two cycles of median polishing. Effect of own class and husband's class on SMR of married women aged 15–59 in 1971: deaths occurring between 1971 and 1981

		Husband's social class			
Wife's own social class	85.5	I+II −17.5	III −3.0	IV+V +2.5	Other +23.0
I and II	√	√	−0.5	−5.0*	+15.5
III	−3.5	−0.5	+1.0	+4.5	−17.0
IV and V	+0.5	+3.5	+14.0	−4.5	−15.0
Other	+30.0	−21.0	−7.5	+9.0	+43.5

* cell only based on 19 deaths

Source: OPCS National Longitudinal Study unpublished table, Crown Copyright; reproduced by kind permission of OPCS and Peter Goldblatt

The result of these two cycles of median polishing is shown in figure 15.4. The effect of the wife being in the 'other' category, for example, has changed from the preliminary result; it is now 30 points higher than the overall fit of 85.5. This figure was obtained by adding the effect of +29.5 from the first cycle of analysis with the +0.5 from the second.

15.5 Interpreting the results

What does it all mean? A good way to read any table is to work systematically from the outside in. Let us therefore consider the overall fit, the effects and the residuals in turn.

The overall fit is an SMR of 85.5. One hundred is the SMR for the standard population, which in this instance is all women aged 15 to 59; married women as a whole have a slightly lower risk of death: an SMR of 95. Why is the overall fit not 95 then? The number 85.5 represents the median of the medians of the rows in this particular table. Nine of the sixteen cells in this table relate to women who in 1971 were in work and whose husbands also worked. Although they form a majority of cells in the table, they do not contribute a majority of the deaths. This value of 85.5 is not inherently interesting in its own right; it is the baseline we have chosen around which to see how the effects vary.

Of more interest are the row and column effects. The row effects show the effect of wife's own class on her risk of death controlling for the effect of having a husband in a particular social class. The most striking finding is that the effect of being in the 'other' category (predominantly the economically inactive) is to increase the SMR by 30 points, a very large effect. But, since the inactive include the permanently sick, this probably represents an ill-health selection effect: the sick being selected into this category, not membership of this category making people sick. Rather than conclude that a routine of unalleviated housework kills, it is more likely that people who are very ill are unlikely to be able to hold down a job outside the home at all.

The class effects for women who were working at the time of the 1971 census are small and are not arranged in the usual order; married women in the middle class (classes III non-manual and III manual combined) have a slightly lower risk of death than others. The class scheme was not constructed with women's jobs in view, and the small size and counter-intuitive ordering of these mortality effects once the husband's class has been controlled suggest one of two conclusions: either that women's mortality is not so much influenced by their own job, or that we have yet to find a good occupational classification scheme to reveal inequalities in life chances among women.

The effects of husband's class are larger than those of the wife's own class, and they are ordered in the traditional manner. This indicates that in general the cultural corollaries of occupation may be more important factors in mortality than the effects of the work itself. It also moderates some of the criticisms that have been voiced against classing women according to the jobs of their husbands: for understanding mortality at least, information about husbands' jobs is important. It does not vindicate the approach of ignoring women's own jobs, however, since the wife's own class appears to have a (weak) effect of its own.

The effect of having a husband in the 'other' category is greater than the class effects. This could represent the stressful effect on the wife of having to care for a sick husband, but it is hard to argue that this effect alone would be so strong. It could represent an effect of marriage selection, however; sick women are perhaps more likely to marry sick men. It might also be picking up an indirect effect of husband's unemployment, since a substantial minority of the inadequately described men were seeking work at the 1971 census (see Moser et al. 1984). To be sure of the interpretation of these 'other' effects, we really need to have these categories further subdivided into sick, unemployed with inadequately described last occupation, housewife and so on.

Summarizing and comparing the size of the row and column effects, we can say that the wife's own class has a smaller effect on her risk of death than her husband's class. The effects of husband's class are arranged in the traditional order of the Registrar-General's classes, and must reflect indirect, cultural effects on the wife's life chances, probably operating through income or other lifestyle indicators. Ill-health selection effects probably explain the raised SMRs of unoccupied women, and either marriage selection effects or the indirect effects of the husband's sickness or unemployment probably explain the raised SMRs of women married to men in the 'other' category.

The residuals are quite large (when compared with the effects).

Moreover, there are some particularly striking residuals which don't fit the overall pattern. If both husband and wife were in the 'other' category at the time of the 1971 census, the effects on female mortality are quite staggering, adding 43.5 to the SMR, for example. In fact, all the residuals for the row representing wives in the 'other' category are large and in the same direction as the main effects of husband's class: for wives not employed outside the home, the effect of the husband's job is at least twice the strength as for those who can be categorised into a class of their own. However, the number of deaths in some of the categories is not large, and we should not place too much confidence in any one individual cell residual.

The fact that the residuals in both the row and column representing the 'other' category are so large suggests that this category needs some more attention. We have already seen that it contains very different kinds of people – the sick, housewives, people whose current or last job was not sufficiently well described for them to be allocated to a class, and so on. One solution might be to conduct the analysis omitting this category; it is left as an exercise for the reader to try this out.

15.6 Changes in mortality over time

The high mortality rate of unoccupied women could easily be explained by ill-health selection: those who were too ill to work at the time of the census did not have a social class assigned to them on the basis of their own job, and some of them would subsequently have died. However, critics have argued that the class differentials themselves may be the result of selection effects: those who are healthy rise up the ladder, while the ill slip down.

The existence of a large longitudinal survey allows this idea of class selection to be tested; it would take us beyond the scope of this textbook to perform the necessary analysis, but the principles can be explained. The critical idea is to split the analysis up so that deaths occurring at different points in time after the census are considered separately. To the extent that any of the effects in earlier periods represent the operation of selection, it has been argued, the further away from the 1971 census one goes, the smaller the effects will be (Fox et al. 1985).

The explanation runs like this. Think of the unoccupied category. Imagine it were true that being economically inactive did not harm your health but that doing a heavy unskilled class V job did. Now suppose that some of the women who were unoccupied in 1971 previously held harmful class V jobs which they left when they became too ill to work. Such ill-health selection into the unoccupied category would make the risk of death in that category seem high, and would hide the risk of death associated with being in class V. But as we move on through the decade, similar people who were still in class V at the time of the census would fall ill, leave work and die; this would make the risk of death among the unoccupied category lower in the later years, and among class V higher.

The critical question for the interpretation of class differentials is whether they decline over the decade, as human capital theorists, arguing that they mostly represent selection effects, would predict. In fact, the social class gradients got wider as the 1970s progressed, rather than smaller (Fox et al. 1985). It is therefore most implausible that social class differentials in mortality can be explained away as selection effects. If people are so sick they are at risk of dying, they tend to fall off the occupational ladder altogether, it appears, rather than slip down the rungs.

The debate about the time course of these effects has been described in qualitative terms in this section. If we wished to get a better understanding of the processes which produce differential risks of death in different categories, the mechanism would almost certainly be clarified if formal, quantitative models of the processes of selection were elaborated, which specified a time period and a size of effect.

Because the Longitudinal Study data reported here only follows up ten years' worth of deaths, it does not permit comprehensive description of the fate of all the individuals whose economic status was monitored at the 1971 census. As time goes by and the number of deaths recorded on the Longitudinal Study increases, more definitive answers to some of these questions will become possible, and reliable data on long-term trends in class differentials will become available.

15.7 Inspecting the residuals

As usual, there is more to be said about the residuals. If they are patternless, the residual in each individual cell can be treated as indicative of the special effect of two categories in combination. Each of these residuals represents an interaction in the sense used in chapter 13 – the extent to which the particular cell combinations do not fit with the additive model of the rows and columns. Such interactions are interesting in their own right, and one of the strengths of median polishing as a technique, as opposed to extraction of arithmetic means, for example, is that the uniqueness of an individual cell shows up as a large residual rather than being smeared, in the process of averaging, all over the table.

However, we must always check that the residuals really are patternless. In particular, we should use them to check that an additive model (data = fit + residual) was not mistaken, and that the analysis would not therefore be better conducted on a transformed scale. The best way to understand this link between non-additivity, transformation and patterned residuals is to perform a mental experiment, in which a dataset is deliberately mis-analysed.

Imagine a society with three social classes, for example, in which the risk of death between the classes was a constant ratio, rather than a constant difference. Suppose women married to men in the upper class had half the risk of death of those with husbands in the middle class, and women married to men in the middle class had half the risk of those with husbands in the lower class. Furthermore, imagine that women's own occupation also had an effect, but a smaller one; women in the upper class had two-thirds the risk of death of those in the middle class, who in turn had two-thirds the risk of those in the lower class. Raw data consistent with these suppositions is shown in panel (a) of figure 15.5.

Figure 15.5 Hypothetical SMR data: generated by a multiplicative model

(a) *raw data*   (b) *median polish*

Wife's class	Husband's class		
	upper	middle	lower
upper	33	67	134
middle	50	100	200
lower	75	150	300

Wife's class		Husband's class		
	100	upper	middle	lower
		−50	√	+100
upper	−33	16	√	−33
middle	√	√	√	√
lower	+50	−25	√	50

To get a good fit to this data, we would need a multiplicative, not additive, model, which predicted: 'The SMR in the middle class will be 50 per cent lower than the working class', and so on. Because the hypothetical table of SMRs was generated without error, the residuals from such a model would be zero. But if we analyse the data in panel (a) of figure 15.5 by an inadequate additive model, we get the results as shown in panel (b). Close inspection of the residuals reveals that they are far from patternless. If data was as conveniently clean as this, we might be able to work out from eyeball inspection alone that this data should be analysed with a multiplicative model.

Since data is usually dirty stuff, however, we need some guidelines to help us spot less obvious cases. One useful method is to calculate a set of **comparison values** with which the residuals from an additive median analysis can be compared. Comparison values are given by:

$$\frac{(\text{Row effect}) \times (\text{Column effect})}{(\text{Overall fit})}$$

If we calculate the comparison value for upper class women with upper class husbands, we get $(-33) \times (-50)/100$, which is 16.5. It is left for the reader to confirm that the comparison values are identical to the residuals in this table (to within rounding error).

The residuals can then be plotted on the Y-axis against the comparison values on the X-axis, a line fitted to the points, and the slope of the line found. Once again, it turns out that subtracting the slope of the line from 1.0 gives a guide to the transformation of the data that will best promote linearity in the model. In this instance, the slope of the line will be 1.0, indicating that zero is the best exponent for transformation; this tells us that if we log the data we will improve the fit. Exercise 15.2 asks you to confirm this.

One important diagnostic for investigating the comparison values is when a characteristic saddle shape appears in the residuals from an additive fit. In panel (b) of figure 15.5, for example, the residuals in the top right and bottom left of the table are negative, while those in the opposite diagonals are positive. The rows and columns of the table have to be ordered in ascending order of effects to investigate this; if they are not presented in that manner, reorder them yourself. It can be helpful to construct a stem and leaf plot of the residuals to identify outliers, which can then be coded in some way on the residual table. By reordering the table, and coding especially striking residuals, evidence of the tell-tale saddle pattern can be sought and remedial action taken. In fact, there is a suggestion in figure 15.4, that the analysis of the SMR data should be tried on a transformed scale.

15.8 Conclusion

Median polishing is a simple but effective technique for arriving at resistant summaries of the effects of two explanatory variables. It can help simplify complicated comparisons, enabling attention to be focused in turn on different aspects of a complex social process.

In this final chapter, ideas have been brought together from previous parts of the book. The response variable, risk of death, was standardized to remove the unwanted effects of age, as explained in chapter 14. The data was drawn from a longitudinal survey, with the potential to avoid some of the problems of causal inference mentioned in chapter 12. The technique illustrated, median polishing, extended the discussion of fits and effects in chapter 6 to three variables, using the same method of control as that used in chapter 13. Because it required a thorough understanding of so many previous chapters, you may have found the arguments quite hard to follow, even if the application of the technique was relatively straightforward.

That is as it should be; there is much more to the analysis of data than number-crunching. This book will have succeeded if at least from now on you stop to think about what a set of numbers means. You will be surprised how often authors, when writing up numerical material, have failed to consider alternative interpretations of their data, or are even oblivious to glaring features contained in it. As has often been remarked,

many people use data as the drunk uses the lamp-post: more for support
than illumination. I would like to think that readers, on completing this
book, would all swear a solemn oath: never to skip over the numerical
evidence for an argument nor to take somebody else's word for what the
data has to say. The book should have equipped you with a set of critical
skills to help you arrive at independent judgements: now use them!

Exercises

15.1 The following table shows how long it took on average for a worker
in different capital cities in Europe to earn enough money to buy
various commodities in October 1975; the times are in minutes.
Median polish the table and comment on the results.

	Paris	Bonn	Rome	Amsterdam	Brussels	London	Copenhagen
Bread (1 kg)	14	16	17	10	9	10	13
Urban bus trip	7	6	2	6	4	6	5
Milk (1 litre)	6	5	7	4	4	5	3
Wine (1 litre)	14	23	14	19	15	64	30
Eggs (1 dozen)	27	17	32	16	20	19	13
Coffee (250 g)	26	31	40	16	18	27	16
A light bulb	13	11	20	9	8	8	8

Source: Fourastie and Bazil (1980: 331)

15.2 Log the hypothetical data in figure 15.5 before median polishing it,
and observe what happens to the residuals.

Appendix: the OPCS Longitudinal Study

Most studies collect information from people **retrospectively** by asking them to
recall and date events that occurred in the past. This method has the great
advantage of being available without years of forethought and of being relatively
cheap. However, it has two severe limitations. First, people's ability to recall
events in the past (Moss and Goldstein 1979) and date them accurately (Cherry
and Rodgers 1979) can be poor. Secondly, retrospective studies are plagued with
problems of biased sample design, for it is often extremely hard to establish
appropriate control groups; if one selects a sample of people with long-term
psychiatric disturbance, for example, with whom should they be compared in the
search for causal factors associated with mental disorder?

Britain is probably unique in having established a large official longitudinal
survey in which information from various official sources are linked and traced
over time. In 1973 a major continuous longitudinal study was established by the

Office of Population Censuses and Surveys, designed to collect information **prospectively** about a sample of half a million individuals, about 1 per cent of the population of England and Wales. Most of these were drawn by random selection of four birth dates from the 1971 census records. Subsequent additions to the population (either by new births or by immigration) are sampled on a similar basis and added to the database; these are balanced by those who die or emigrate, so the sample should remain a fairly stable 1 per cent of the population.

Information from a variety of official sources is then linked for the study members. The principal means of making the links is via the National Health Service Central Register (NHSCR), which records people's National Health Service number and address. For each person in the sample, information from the 1971 and 1981 censuses have been linked, subsequent deaths and immigration or emigration added, and vital events occurring in the period 1971–81 have been incorporated into the dataset:

1 live and still births to men and women in the sample
2 deaths under one year of age to their children
3 death of a spouse
4 cancer registration

Marriage records at present do not include date of birth, and so the only means of studying change of marital status is by looking at inter-censal changes, but consideration is being given to the possibility of adding marriage and divorce data to the events covered for the period 1971–81 (Brown and Fox 1984).

The study has not been running for long enough to have many complete life records; additional vital information is only added slowly. Eventually, however, the sample will be fully representative of the population in all details, and a typical record will look like those shown in figure 15.6.

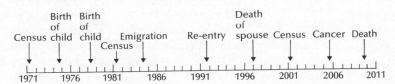

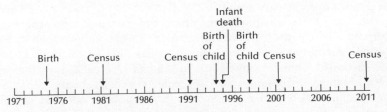

Figure 15.6 Examples of spacing of longitudinal survey records
Source: Fox and Goldblatt 1982: figure 2.1

The survey is already considered to be one of the most important databases for the study of mortality, fertility and mobility available to researchers, and its value increases as the years go by. The study size ensures that there are sufficient numbers in particular demographic subgroups for quite detailed analysis; there are, for example, 5000 members who in 1971 were lone parents with dependent children. The Economic and Social Research Council, the Medical Research Council and the Cancer Research Campaign all recognize the value of the study, and have collaborated in establishing a Social Statistics Research Unit at City University to promote analysis of the data.

Tracing and linking information from all these sources is a massively complex job. Ninety-seven per cent of all individuals originally sampled from the 1971 census have been traced in the NHSCR (Fox and Goldblatt 1982). However, tracing them through to the 1981 census has proved more difficult, and only 91 per cent success has been achieved (Brown and Fox 1984). It is especially difficult to find married women who have changed their name, people in non-private households and those born outside England and Wales, especially from New Commonwealth origins. However, people from New Commonwealth origins are not underrepresented in the Longitudinal Study sample, because a greater proportion of them than one would expect to have occurred by chance had birthdays on the four sample dates; if anything, they are slightly *over*represented in the sample.

In fact, the proportion of the population sampled in various groups (sex groups, age groups and class groups) is fairly constant. While some bias may occur in inferring characteristics of the population from characteristics of the sample, comparisons between different subgroups within the sample are robust. The only exception is comparisons between different marital status groups, because the proportion of married women who have been traced is lower; this will have the effect of slightly underestimating mortality differentials by marital status.

The way in which the mortality information is constructed is slightly more complex than that used by the Registrar-General in the *Decennial Supplement* (described in chapter 14), but it is essentially an indirect method of obtaining age-standardized SMRs. To calculate the SMR for a particular subgroup, such as people who were in class II in 1971, the first stage is to calculate the denominator for the death rate. This is not fixed, precisely because some class members die but also because others emigrate as time goes by; instead, the total number of **person-years** of people who were in class II is calculated for every age category. The deaths within this group can then expressed per million person-years at risk, again within age categories.

Such death rates get very small in detailed subcategories, so they are usually re-expressed as SMRs, comparing the actual number of deaths experienced by a subgroup to the deaths one would expect if that subgroup had the same age-specific mortality rates as a standard population. To calculate the expected number of deaths among council house tenants (for each agegroup and each year), for instance, the person-years at risk among such tenants are multiplied by the age-specific death rate for a standard group. The SMR is calculated by dividing the actual number by the expected number and multiplying by 100.

The Datasets

The datasets documented here contain much more information than was used in the text or the exercises. It is hoped that they will provide interesting material for you to explore, either by hand or on a micro or mainframe computer.

The data has been taken from many different sources, and permission to reproduce it here has been given by the appropriate government department or original collector of the data. In some cases, the values are still under revision; the longer leading cyclical indicator of economic performance in ECONOMY, for example, is updated for at least thirty months. The figures supplied here are the best that were available in September 1986.

The convention throughout is to record missing values as -1. Take care when analysing the data not to treat such values as valid. If you are using Minitab, they can be altered by means of the CODE instruction to '*'; this is a special code which Minitab recognizes as missing and will ignore in any calculations it performs.

All the datasets are available in machine-readable form for teaching purposes from the ESRC Data Archive at the University of Essex. Brief documentation about them is supplied here, but fuller details are often given in the chapters where the dataset is first used; consult the index for page references. Readers are referred to the original sources for a complete documentation of the data.

CLASS

This data is a random sample of two hundred men aged 20 to 59 drawn from the General Household Survey 1979 (see appendix to chapter 1). A subset of the survey was first extracted by Gilbert et al. (1984). This is a further subset of cases and variables taken from their data.

Column

1   Age of respondent
2   Age left full-time education; 14 means 14 or younger, and 21 means 21 or older
3   Number of children in the family
4   Chronic illness; the variable indicates whether respondents have any long-standing illness, disability or infirmity, and, if so, whether it limits their activities in any way:
   0   no chronic illness
   1   yes but not limiting
   2   yes and limits activity
5   Current social class of respondent (combined socio-economic groups):
   1   professional
   2   managers and employers
   3   intermediate and junior non-manual
   4   skilled manual
   5   semi-skilled manual
   6   unskilled manual
6   Respondent's opinion of own health in last year:
   1   good
   2   fairly good
   3   not good
7   Highest educational qualification obtained:
   0   no qualifications
   1   apprenticeship
   2   CSE, 1 to 4 O levels
   3   5 or more O levels
   4   A levels
   5   HND, teaching or nursing qualifications
   6   degree
8   Standard Industrial Classification of job:
   1   consumer goods
   2   raw materials
   3   capital goods
   4   construction
   5   utilities
   6   distributive
   7   professional and financial
   8   administration and defence
9   Satisfaction with 'the job as a whole'; the question was only asked to men who worked more than ten hours per week at their main job:
   1   very satisfied
   2   fairly satisfied
   3   not satisfied or dissatisfied

    4   rather dissatisfied
    5   very dissatisfied
10 Length of time with current employer (or length of time self-employed):
    1   less than 3 months
    2   between 3 and 12 months
    3   more than 12 months but less than 5 years
    4   5 years or more
11 Marital status (common law marriages included):
    1   married
    2   single
    3   widowed
    4   divorced
    5   separated
12 Hours of overtime worked each week
13 Tenure of accommodation:
    1   owns or is buying on a mortgage
    2   rents or lives rent free
14 Current or last social class of father for respondents aged under 50. Codes as in column 5
15 Gross weekly pay in pounds; amount last paid before deducting income tax, National Insurance, pensions etc.
16 Whether employer runs a pension scheme; only asked of employees:
    1   no pension scheme
    2   pension scheme exists but respondent not in it
    3   belongs to a pension scheme
17 Socio-economic group of respondent's job:
    1   employer with 25 or more workers
    2   manager in establishment of 25 or more workers
    3   employer with fewer than 25 workers
    4   manager in establishment with fewer than 25 workers
    5   self-employed professional
    6   employee professional
    7   ancillary occupations, artists etc.
    8   non-manual foreman or supervisor
    9   junior non-manual
  10 personal service worker
  11 manual foreman or supervisor
  12 skilled manual
  13 semi-skilled manual
  14 unskilled manual
  15 own account worker, non-professional
  16 farmers – employers and managers
  17 farmers – own account
  19 agricultural workers
18 Self-employed or employee:
    1   employee
    2   self-employed
19 Whether respondent is paid by employer when sick; only asked of those who worked more than 10 hours per week at their main job:
    1   yes
    2   no

20   Annual unearned income in pounds. It includes income from property, investments and building society accounts.

21   Age of wife, if married

22   Current social class of wife, if married. Codes as in column 5

23   Whether wife does paid work:
   0   wife not in paid work
   1   10 hours per week or less
   2   11 to 30 hours per week
   3   more than 30 hours per week

24   Highest educational qualification obtained by wife. Codes as in column 7

1	2	3	4	5	6	7	8	9	10	11	12	13	14	15	16	17	18	19	20	21	22	23	24
58	14	0	1	4	2	1	5	1	4	1	0	2	−1	58	1	12	1	1	25	54	3	3	0
55	14	0	2	3	2	0	7	2	2	2	0	2	−1	32	1	9	1	−1	71	−1	−1	−1	−1
57	16	0	2	2	2	6	7	−1	4	2	0	1	−1	135	−1	3	2	−1	1540	−1	−1	−1	−1
32	21	1	0	1	1	6	7	4	4	1	0	1	4	115	3	6	1	1	15	30	3	0	5
42	15	1	0	5	2	0	6	4	4	1	0	1	4	75	1	13	1	1	0	39	3	2	2
36	15	2	2	3	2	5	3	4	4	1	4	1	4	120	3	7	1	2	0	35	3	2	2
51	14	0	2	4	1	1	3	2	4	1	2	2	−1	93	3	11	1	1	125	50	3	3	2
45	14	0	0	4	1	1	4	1	3	2	0	2	4	89	1	12	1	2	0	−1	−1	−1	−1
46	15	0	0	4	1	0	5	1	4	1	4	1	3	94	3	12	1	1	0	51	5	0	0
27	15	1	0	4	1	4	6	4	3	1	1	1	4	75	1	12	1	1	25	26	3	0	0
50	16	0	1	4	2	−1	3	1	4	1	0	1	−1	−1	3	11	1	1	0	51	3	2	2
58	14	0	0	4	1	1	6	1	4	1	1	2	−1	85	3	12	1	1	0	57	4	0	0
55	16	0	0	4	1	3	7	1	4	1	0	1	−1	147	3	12	1	1	0	56	2	1	0
30	15	4	0	4	1	0	6	2	3	1	2	2	−1	68	1	12	1	2	0	30	5	0	−1
33	16	2	0	3	1	4	1	1	1	1	0	1	2	110	3	9	1	1	6	31	4	0	−1
26	15	1	0	4	1	3	1	4	4	1	0	2	4	105	3	12	1	2	0	22	5	0	0
37	15	0	0	4	1	0	8	1	3	1	4	2	3	100	3	12	1	1	0	35	5	3	0
23	18	0	0	3	1	4	8	2	3	2	0	2	5	69	3	7	1	1	1	−1	−1	−1	−1
30	15	0	0	3	1	0	8	2	4	2	0	2	5	55	3	7	1	1	0	−1	−1	−1	−1
48	14	0	2	5	2	0	6	2	4	4	0	−1	5	91	1	13	1	1	0	−1	−1	−1	−1
44	16	2	0	1	1	5	5	2	3	1	1	1	5	141	3	6	1	1	12	40	3	2	0
29	15	2	0	4	1	5	3	2	3	1	3	2	5	82	2	12	1	2	0	25	5	2	0
46	14	0	0	4	1	0	6	2	4	1	0	1	4	52	3	12	1	1	870	52	1	2	6
37	15	2	0	4	1	1	3	3	4	1	1	1	3	103	3	12	1	1	3	34	3	3	0
57	14	0	1	4	1	1	3	1	4	1	0	2	−1	87	1	12	1	1	0	56	6	3	0
50	19	0	0	3	2	3	3	1	4	1	0	1	−1	106	3	9	1	1	25	50	2	3	0
33	21	2	0	3	1	5	7	1	4	1	0	1	4	96	3	7	1	1	2	32	4	1	6
30	15	2	2	4	1	1	3	5	3	1	0	2	4	115	3	12	1	1	10	30	3	2	0
37	16	0	0	2	1	5	7	1	4	1	1	1	2	112	3	2	1	1	0	36	2	3	5
59	14	0	0	5	1	0	8	2	4	1	1	2	−1	65	3	13	1	1	0	−1	6	0	0
42	15	0	0	4	2	0	5	2	4	1	0	1	4	72	3	12	1	1	0	40	4	0	1
56	14	0	0	3	1	3	3	1	4	1	0	2	−1	−1	3	9	1	1	0	53	5	2	0
26	16	0	0	4	1	0	5	1	4	2	4	2	3	80	3	12	1	1	0	−1	−1	−1	−1
38	15	1	1	4	1	3	2	2	3	1	2	1	5	120	3	12	1	1	74	28	4	1	0
27	18	0	0	3	1	5	5	2	2	2	0	1	1	−1	3	9	1	−1	0	−1	−1	−1	−1
26	17	2	0	2	1	3	6	2	3	1	2	2	4	78	1	4	1	1	0	25	5	2	0
28	15	3	0	4	1	4	1	1	3	1	3	2	3	116	2	12	1	1	0	30	3	0	0
49	14	2	0	2	1	0	5	−1	4	1	0	1	5	93	−1	3	2	−1	0	47	2	2	0
41	15	2	0	5	2	−1	5	4	4	1	2	2	5	56	3	13	1	1	50	41	4	0	0
30	16	2	1	4	2	4	1	2	3	1	3	1	5	75	2	12	1	1	94	28	5	1	3

1	2	3	4	5	6	7	8	9	10	11	12	13	14	15	16	17	18	19	20	21	22	23	24
45	16	1	0	4	1	1	3	2	3	1	4	2	4	125	1	12	1	1	0	43	-1	-1	-1
51	14	0	1	5	2	0	3	2	3	4	2	2	-1	68	2	13	1	2	0	-1	-1	-1	-1
39	16	0	0	1	1	3	4	2	3	2	0	2	4	118	3	5	1	1	0	-1	-1	-1	-1
29	17	2	1	4	1	4	2	1	4	1	3	1	4	90	-1	12	1	1	0	26	5	2	2
26	16	1	0	4	1	4	1	1	3	1	2	1	4	127	3	12	1	1	40	23	3	0	6
55	15	0	0	3	1	0	8	2	4	2	0	1	-1	-1	3	9	1	1	0	-1	-1	-1	-1
45	15	2	0	4	1	1	4	1	4	1	4	1	5	198	1	12	1	1	0	33	3	2	2
53	14	0	0	3	1	4	8	1	4	1	2	1	-1	-1	3	8	1	1	0	54	3	0	0
20	16	5	0	4	1	3	6	2	3	2	2	1	4	65	2	12	1	1	10	-1	-1	-1	-1
24	15	0	1	4	2	4	3	2	4	1	2	1	4	80	3	12	1	1	0	22	3	3	4
48	14	0	2	4	3	0	5	-1	4	1	0	1	5	37	-1	15	2	-1	0	41	5	2	0
36	15	1	0	4	1	0	1	3	2	1	0	1	4	95	1	11	1	1	0	30	3	0	0
57	14	0	1	4	2	-1	5	2	3	1	4	2	-1	97	1	12	1	2	0	56	4	0	0
46	14	2	0	2	2	1	6	1	4	1	2	1	3	138	3	4	1	1	0	44	4	0	0
58	14	0	0	4	1	0	6	2	4	1	1	2	-1	75	3	12	1	1	95	54	3	2	0
55	15	2	0	6	1	0	2	1	4	1	4	1	-1	-1	3	14	1	2	0	55	3	3	0
35	15	4	0	4	2	1	4	1	2	1	0	2	4	100	1	12	1	-1	0	32	6	2	0
44	14	6	0	4	-1	0	1	1	4	1	2	1	2	100	3	12	1	1	2	28	-1	0	0
25	21	0	0	4	1	4	3	3	4	2	2	2	5	88	1	12	1	1	15	-1	-1	-1	-1
57	21	0	0	2	1	-1	6	-1	4	1	0	1	-1	-1	-1	3	2	-1	0	57	-1	-1	-1
50	14	0	1	5	1	0	5	1	4	1	4	1	-1	58	3	13	1	1	65	50	5	2	0
52	14	0	2	4	2	0	2	2	4	1	1	2	-1	95	2	12	1	1	3	48	6	2	0
26	21	0	0	3	1	6	7	2	3	1	0	1	6	81	3	7	1	1	15	25	3	2	6
33	15	2	0	2	2	0	4	-1	3	1	0	1	4	-1	-1	3	2	-1	0	31	3	0	0
26	20	2	0	4	1	1	2	2	3	1	3	2	4	130	3	12	1	1	0	26	3	0	2
26	21	0	0	3	1	6	7	2	3	1	1	1	2	84	3	7	1	-1	38	23	3	2	5
41	15	3	1	3	2	1	2	2	3	1	0	1	4	97	3	9	1	1	0	39	5	2	0
25	20	0	2	4	1	3	1	2	4	1	2	1	4	90	3	12	1	1	18	24	3	3	5
22	16	0	2	4	1	2	6	2	2	1	3	1	4	90	2	12	1	1	1	22	3	3	5
31	21	0	2	1	1	6	7	1	4	1	0	1	3	108	3	6	1	1	0	29	3	3	6
31	15	0	0	5	1	0	3	3	4	1	0	1	5	74	3	13	1	1	3	27	2	3	0
43	15	1	0	2	1	0	6	2	4	1	0	1	-1	62	3	4	1	1	3	29	3	0	0
35	15	2	0	4	1	1	4	1	4	1	0	1	4	103	3	11	1	1	0	30	6	2	0
46	14	1	0	4	1	0	4	1	2	1	3	2	2	80	1	12	1	2	0	39	2	3	3
42	14	5	0	5	1	0	4	2	2	1	1	2	4	88	1	13	1	2	0	33	5	2	0
35	20	1	0	4	1	1	2	2	4	1	1	1	4	104	3	12	1	1	6	33	3	0	0
50	16	0	0	2	2	-1	5	2	4	1	0	1	-1	123	3	4	1	1	1090	40	3	3	6
37	16	2	0	4	2	4	3	1	4	1	2	1	4	110	3	12	1	1	5	36	3	3	5
55	14	0	0	4	3	0	7	3	4	1	2	1	-1	75	3	11	1	1	20	52	-1	-1	-1
26	17	1	0	4	1	4	2	4	2	1	0	2	6	80	2	12	1	1	0	24	3	3	0
57	14	0	0	6	1	0	3	1	3	1	0	1	-1	59	3	14	1	2	9	54	5	3	0
29	16	3	0	3	1	5	7	1	3	1	0	1	2	93	3	9	1	1	0	30	3	1	2
53	14	1	0	3	1	0	3	2	4	1	0	2	-1	82	3	9	1	1	36	54	5	3	0
51	14	0	0	3	1	0	6	1	4	1	0	1	-1	71	3	9	1	1	0	48	4	0	0
31	15	0	0	3	1	3	8	2	4	2	2	1	-1	111	3	9	1	1	16	-1	-1	-1	-1
28	21	0	0	1	1	4	7	1	2	2	0	2	1	87	1	6	1	2	0	-1	-1	-1	-1
51	14	0	0	5	1	0	3	2	4	1	0	1	-1	77	3	13	1	1	68	48	2	3	2
52	14	1	0	2	1	0	4	-1	4	1	0	1	-1	77	-1	3	2	-1	0	44	3	1	0
26	15	2	0	4	1	5	4	2	3	1	3	1	5	100	3	12	1	1	0	28	4	0	0
36	15	2	1	4	1	0	4	-1	4	1	0	1	5	-1	-1	15	2	-1	0	34	5	2	-1

1	2	3	4	5	6	7	8	9	10	11	12	13	14	15	16	17	18	19	20	21	22	23	24
27	16	2	0	1	-1	-1	4	-1	2	1	0	2	2	-1	-1	5	2	-1	0	25	5	0	3
48	16	2	1	2	2	4	3	1	4	1	0	1	4	128	3	2	1	1	2	44	3	2	0
25	18	0	0	6	1	0	2	3	4	2	0	2	4	49	-1	14	1	1	0	-1	-1	-1	-1
49	-1	3	2	3	3	0	6	5	3	1	0	1	4	63	1	9	1	2	532	35	-1	0	-1
52	21	0	0	2	2	6	2	1	3	1	0	1	-1	242	3	2	1	1	32	53	3	0	3
47	14	1	0	2	1	0	6	2	3	1	0	1	4	75	3	4	1	1	43	40	6	2	0
25	21	0	0	1	1	6	7	3	3	2	0	1	2	36	2	6	1	1	0	-1	-1	-1	-1
43	21	2	0	3	1	2	5	2	3	1	0	1	1	67	1	9	1	1	0	30	3	3	-1
42	15	0	0	4	1	5	6	-1	4	1	0	1	2	144	-1	15	2	-1	0	37	-1	-1	-1
21	16	0	0	4	1	4	5	1	4	2	2	2	-1	65	3	12	1	1	0	-1	-1	-1	-1
47	14	1	0	4	1	1	3	2	3	1	3	1	4	150	1	12	1	2	0	45	2	3	0
26	16	3	1	4	1	4	6	2	4	1	0	2	4	80	3	12	1	1	0	24	5	0	0
31	15	1	0	5	1	4	8	2	1	1	0	2	1	56	-1	10	1	1	0	24	5	0	1
29	16	0	1	3	1	1	3	2	4	2	0	1	2	75	3	9	1	1	0	-1	-1	-1	-1
39	18	2	0	2	1	3	7	1	4	1	0	1	2	101	3	2	1	1	0	32	5	0	3
49	19	1	0	3	1	4	3	2	4	1	0	1	-1	116	3	8	1	1	150	50	5	-1	3
22	15	0	0	5	1	0	1	1	2	2	0	2	5	67	1	18	1	1	20	-1	-1	-1	-1
27	21	0	2	3	1	5	7	1	3	1	0	1	-1	67	3	7	1	1	0	27	3	3	4
48	17	1	0	2	1	0	2	-1	4	1	0	1	4	27	-1	3	2	-1	0	29	3	2	5
26	15	0	2	5	1	0	1	1	4	2	1	2	4	71	1	18	1	1	3	-1	-1	-1	-1
23	16	0	0	3	1	2	6	-1	1	2	0	2	2	-1	-1	7	2	-1	200	-1	-1	-1	-1
44	14	0	0	5	2	0	5	1	4	1	2	2	6	58	3	13	1	1	0	50	3	2	0
35	15	0	0	6	2	0	8	2	4	2	0	2	4	54	-1	14	1	1	0	-1	-1	-1	-1
33	15	0	2	4	2	0	8	2	4	2	0	2	4	64	-1	12	1	1	0	-1	-1	-1	-1
36	15	3	2	4	2	0	4	2	3	1	0	2	5	-1	3	12	1	1	0	30	5	0	0
25	16	0	0	4	2	3	5	2	4	2	0	2	4	76	3	12	1	1	44	-1	-1	-1	-1
38	15	2	0	4	1	3	3	2	2	1	1	1	4	76	3	12	1	1	2	35	3	3	3
42	16	1	1	2	1	6	3	1	4	1	0	1	2	143	3	2	1	1	506	41	3	2	2
38	15	0	1	4	2	0	4	2	4	2	0	2	5	60	3	11	1	1	0	-1	-1	-1	-1
33	15	3	1	4	1	0	2	1	4	1	0	1	6	78	3	11	1	1	2	33	5	3	0
33	15	3	0	4	1	0	6	2	4	1	1	2	4	83	1	12	1	2	0	38	5	0	0
46	21	3	0	2	1	6	7	1	4	1	0	1	1	-1	3	2	1	1	0	39	3	2	6
33	18	2	2	2	2	4	7	1	2	1	0	1	4	103	3	4	1	1	12	29	3	2	-1
40	14	1	0	4	2	0	2	1	3	1	1	1	5	80	-1	12	1	2	0	37	5	3	0
36	17	1	0	3	1	5	8	2	4	1	1	1	4	110	3	7	1	1	10	31	3	0	5
40	17	2	0	3	1	6	2	2	4	1	0	1	4	111	3	8	1	1	0	35	5	2	2
38	21	2	0	2	1	6	3	2	4	1	1	1	3	157	3	2	1	1	10	38	3	2	2
45	17	1	0	2	1	5	7	1	4	1	0	1	2	187	3	2	1	1	0	44	4	0	0
30	15	1	0	2	1	0	3	2	3	1	0	1	6	95	3	2	1	1	3	27	3	2	2
22	-1	1	0	1	1	4	7	1	3	2	-1	1	4	53	1	6	1	1	0	-1	-1	-1	-1
29	16	2	1	5	2	2	2	2	2	1	2	1	6	90	3	13	1	1	1	26	3	0	4
32	15	2	0	4	2	0	4	-1	4	1	0	2	4	58	-1	15	2	-1	0	29	-1	0	0
34	15	3	0	4	1	3	3	5	3	1	2	2	5	78	1	11	1	1	0	35	5	2	-1
30	15	2	1	4	1	0	3	2	3	1	2	2	4	87	3	12	1	2	0	24	6	3	0
49	21	2	0	2	1	3	3	1	3	1	0	1	3	195	2	4	1	1	20	48	3	0	0
40	15	2	2	4	1	0	6	5	2	1	4	2	5	111	1	11	1	2	0	39	6	0	0
35	-1	2	0	4	2	4	4	1	2	1	0	2	6	82	3	12	1	1	0	34	3	2	0
31	17	1	0	3	1	4	8	2	4	1	0	1	4	76	3	7	1	1	6	30	3	0	4
37	18	2	1	2	1	-1	6	2	4	1	0	1	4	125	2	2	1	1	0	35	5	0	0
53	14	0	2	6	2	0	8	3	4	1	0	2	-1	62	3	14	1	1	1	50	5	0	-1

1	2	3	4	5	6	7	8	9	10	11	12	13	14	15	16	17	18	19	20	21	22	23	24
29	19	2	2	2	1	5	6	2	4	1	0	1	2	81	3	4	1	1	3	29	3	0	2
21	16	0	0	5	1	5	3	2	2	2	0	1	5	57	-1	13	1	2	1	-1	-1	-1	-1
22	15	1	0	6	1	-1	3	2	3	1	1	1	-1	67	2	14	1	2	0	22	-1	0	0
42	15	0	0	4	1	0	1	2	2	1	2	2	5	73	1	12	1	2	300	43	5	3	-1
40	15	3	0	4	2	0	4	4	1	1	1	2	4	77	1	11	1	2	0	32	3	2	0
22	15	1	0	4	1	0	6	2	2	1	0	2	1	45	1	12	1	-1	1	20	5	0	0
54	15	2	0	2	1	0	6	-1	4	1	0	1	-1	67	-1	3	2	-1	0	49	2	3	2
36	21	2	0	2	1	5	2	3	3	1	0	1	4	98	1	4	1	1	3	33	3	2	3
30	15	0	0	4	1	0	3	1	3	2	2	2	4	90	3	12	1	1	2	-1	-1	-1	-1
34	18	0	0	3	1	5	7	1	4	2	0	2	6	90	3	9	1	1	170	-1	-1	-1	-1
25	16	1	0	4	2	3	3	2	4	1	1	2	4	70	1	12	1	2	1	26	5	2	4
38	15	1	0	4	1	0	4	2	4	1	0	1	6	168	1	12	1	1	0	35	5	0	0
32	15	3	0	3	1	3	7	1	4	1	1	1	5	70	3	7	1	1	10	32	5	1	3
20	16	2	0	4	2	5	1	5	3	2	1	2	4	57	3	12	1	1	0	-1	-1	-1	-1
49	14	1	2	4	2	0	1	2	4	1	0	2	5	127	2	12	1	2	0	43	5	2	0
37	15	2	0	4	1	3	3	2	3	1	1	1	3	93	3	12	1	1	0	33	3	0	2
39	15	0	0	4	2	0	4	2	4	5	1	2	4	105	3	12	1	1	2	-1	-1	-1	-1
20	18	1	0	3	2	4	6	-1	2	2	0	2	4	9	-1	9	1	-1	0	-1	-1	-1	-1
43	14	1	2	5	2	0	1	2	4	1	2	2	5	55	1	18	1	2	0	41	6	3	0
29	15	0	0	4	2	1	2	1	4	1	2	1	4	91	3	12	1	1	0	31	5	3	0
38	21	0	0	3	1	4	7	1	4	2	0	1	2	136	3	7	1	1	0	-1	-1	-1	-1
31	15	3	0	4	1	0	4	2	4	1	0	1	4	87	-1	12	1	1	1	33	5	0	0
40	21	2	0	1	1	6	3	2	4	1	0	1	-1	130	3	6	1	1	540	33	3	0	3
36	17	1	0	2	1	4	4	-1	3	1	0	1	5	115	-1	4	1	-1	0	33	2	2	2
47	14	3	0	3	2	0	5	1	4	1	4	2	4	77	3	9	1	1	0	45	3	2	0
46	14	0	0	2	1	0	6	-1	4	1	0	1	2	-1	-1	3	2	-1	0	42	2	3	0
43	21	2	0	1	1	6	3	2	4	1	0	1	3	170	3	6	1	1	20	42	3	2	6
51	17	1	0	2	1	4	7	1	4	1	0	1	-1	55	3	2	1	1	160	50	3	0	5
22	15	0	0	2	1	0	6	1	3	2	0	2	4	83	1	4	1	1	80	-1	-1	-1	-1
32	15	1	1	3	2	2	6	1	3	1	0	1	5	119	3	7	1	1	0	24	3	0	0
52	14	0	0	3	1	0	1	2	3	1	0	2	-1	108	1	9	1	2	0	52	6	1	0
51	14	0	0	6	1	0	7	3	1	2	0	2	-1	12	-1	14	1	-1	0	-1	-1	-1	-1
32	17	0	0	4	1	4	3	4	3	2	2	1	3	103	1	12	1	1	0	-1	-1	-1	-1
24	18	0	0	3	1	5	7	1	4	1	0	1	5	65	3	9	1	1	2	20	3	3	2
44	16	0	1	3	1	6	6	1	4	1	0	1	3	60	3	9	1	1	0	53	3	2	0
20	16	0	0	3	-1	-1	7	-1	1	2	0	1	2	-1	3	9	1	1	0	-1	-1	-1	-1
22	15	3	0	3	-1	-1	5	-1	3	1	0	2	5	-1	3	9	1	-1	0	31	3	0	0
46	14	0	2	5	3	0	2	1	4	4	3	2	4	80	3	13	1	1	0	-1	-1	-1	-1
36	15	1	0	4	1	0	3	4	4	1	4	2	4	126	1	12	1	2	0	45	5	2	0
55	14	0	0	4	-1	-1	4	-1	4	2	0	1	-1	-1	3	12	1	2	0	-1	-1	-1	-1
50	14	1	0	5	-1	-1	2	-1	4	1	2	1	-1	-1	3	13	1	2	0	47	6	2	0
20	19	0	0	3	-1	-1	7	-1	1	2	0	1	1	-1	3	9	1	1	0	-1	-1	-1	-1
45	14	2	0	5	2	0	3	2	3	1	2	1	4	71	2	13	1	1	0	45	5	0	0
21	16	2	0	4	1	2	4	3	3	2	0	1	4	41	1	12	1	1	2	-1	-1	-1	-1
25	15	1	0	3	1	2	1	2	4	1	0	2	4	90	3	9	1	1	0	22	3	0	0
39	15	2	0	5	2	0	3	2	3	1	0	2	5	71	2	13	1	1	0	38	5	2	0
42	15	2	0	3	1	0	6	2	4	1	0	1	5	43	3	9	1	1	28	25	3	0	0
41	15	1	0	4	1	0	3	2	3	1	0	2	-1	76	3	12	1	1	0	38	4	3	0
41	15	1	0	1	1	6	4	1	4	1	0	1	4	182	3	6	1	1	75	41	5	0	0
44	18	1	2	3	2	4	3	2	2	1	0	1	3	90	3	7	1	1	40	43	5	2	0

1	2	3	4	5	6	7	8	9	10	11	12	13	14	15	16	17	18	19	20	21	22	23	24
20	16	1	0	4	1	0	1	3	4	2	0	2	5	63	3	12	1	2	2	−1	−1	−1	−1
51	16	0	0	4	1	4	1	2	3	1	0	1	−1	89	3	12	1	1	0	45	3	3	2
48	14	0	0	4	2	0	6	2	4	1	1	2	5	67	1	12	1	1	0	44	3	3	2
50	21	0	0	3	1	5	1	4	4	1	0	2	−1	82	3	9	1	1	20	47	3	3	0
52	14	1	1	3	1	0	5	2	4	1	2	1	−1	82	1	9	1	2	0	47	6	2	0
23	18	0	0	3	1	4	3	1	3	2	0	2	1	102	3	9	1	1	27	−1	−1	−1	−1
59	14	0	0	5	1	0	7	1	4	3	2	2	−1	74	3	13	1	1	6	−1	−1	−1	−1
44	15	1	1	2	3	0	7	−1	4	1	0	2	6	−1	−1	3	2	−1	1	49	5	0	0
50	14	0	0	4	1	0	5	4	4	1	2	1	−1	84	3	12	1	1	0	45	2	3	0
24	18	0	0	2	1	4	7	1	4	2	0	1	3	101	2	4	1	1	32	−1	−1	−1	−1

ECONOMY

This dataset documents public confidence in the economy and in the government in Great Britain on a monthly basis between January 1977 and December 1985; objective indicators of the performance of the economy are also attached so that these can be compared with movements in the subjective measures.

The subjective indicators are drawn with the permission of Gallup from the *Gallup Political Index*; the first six (columns 2–7) come from a consumer confidence survey Gallup do on behalf of the European Commission (see chapter 9), and the political indicators (columns 12–15) come from their monthly surveys. The unemployment figures (column 10) and the Retail Prices Index (column 11) are drawn from the *Employment Gazette*. The cyclical indicator of general economic performance (column 8) is constructed by the Central Statistical Office, published in *Economic Trends* and explained in vol. 257, March 1975, although updated figures, kindly supplied by the Central Statistical Office, are shown here. The household income data (column 9) comes from the General Household Survey, and was kindly supplied by the University of Surrey.

The six confidence items are presented here as a score. They were originally asked as questions with five responses; for example, in December 1984, when asked how they thought the economic situation had changed over the past 12 months, respondents replied:

got a lot better	1
got a little better	16
stayed the same	21
got a little worse	33
got a lot worse	26
(don't know)	4

For all such questions, very optimistic responses were scored +2, optimistic ones +1, no change 0, pessimistic −1 and very pessimistic −2; thus the score in December 1984 is $(2 \times 1) + 16 - 33 - (2 \times 26)$, or −67. On eighteen occasions, when the questions were not asked, values have been linearly interpolated; in six months when two separate surveys were conducted, the arithmetic mean of replies has been used. (The scoring and interpolation was done by the author, not Gallup.) The wording of all six questions changed somewhat in December 1981, so discontinuities around that date should be treated as artefactual.

Column
1   Month; e.g. 7701 is January 1977
2   How do you think the general economic situation in this country has changed over the last 12 months?
3   How do you think the general economic situation in this country will develop over the next 12 months?
4   How does the financial situation of your household compare with what it was 12 months ago?

5   How do you think the financial situation of your household will change over the next 12 months?

6   How do you think the level of unemployment (I mean the number of people out of work) in the country as a whole, will change over the next 12 months?

7   By comparison with what is happening now, do you think that in the next 12 months: there will be a more rapid increase in prices; prices will increase at the same rate; prices will increase at a slower rate; prices will be stable; prices will fall slightly?

8   Longer leading cyclical indicator of the performance of the economy as at September 1986; index formed from movements in the *Financial Times* 500 share index, the rate of interest, the financial surplus/deficit of industrial and commercial companies (deflated), the number of new dwellings started and the Confederation of British Industry's quarterly survey of optimism in British industry

9   Median weekly gross household income from all sources; pounds

10   Total unemployed claimants in Great Britain without any adjustment; thousands

11   Retail Prices Index; all items with no seasonal adjustment; 15 January 1974 = 100

12   'Conservative' in answer to question 'If there was a General Election tomorrow, which party would you support?' (excluding don't knows who couldn't be persuaded to name a party)

13   'Labour' as column 12

14   'Alliance' as column 12

15   Do you approve or disapprove of the government's record to date? Proportion replying 'approve' minus proportion replying 'disapprove'.

1	2	3	4	5	6	7	8	9	10	11	12	13	14	15
7701	−123	−35	−49	−23	−93	−142	102.03	62.62	1330.5	172.4	47.0	34.0	14.5	−39
7702	−104	−34	−51	−25	−84	−147	102.96	65.38	1306.5	174.1	46.0	33.5	14.0	−41
7703	−123	−47	−67	−38	−89	−148	104.00	66.46	1269.6	175.8	49.5	33.0	13.0	−41
7704	−116	−46	−66	−37	−77	−145	105.22	65.65	1271.5	180.3	49.0	33.5	11.5	−39
7705	−109	−44	−66	−32	−68	−143	106.52	63.40	1224.1	181.7	53.5	33.0	8.5	−36
7706	−92	−14	−59	−21	−59	−142	107.13	64.21	1302.9	183.6	47.5	37.0	10.5	−27
7707	−86	−21	−61	−16	−69	−130	107.76	68.44	1452.2	183.6	49.0	34.5	10.5	−34
7708	−65	−4	−48	−15	−72	−105	109.23	65.96	1471.7	184.7	48.5	37.5	9.0	−20
7709	−6	45	−45	4	−52	−94	110.47	65.75	1449.9	185.7	45.5	41.0	8.5	−17
7710	−6	31	−37	12	−45	−90	111.32	68.15	1367.7	186.5	45.0	45.0	8.0	−2
7711	−2	22	−34	5	−47	−93	111.17	70.44	1353.1	187.4	45.5	42.0	8.5	−2
7712	2	23	−29	4	−47	−98	110.28	63.27	1338.8	188.4	44.0	44.5	8.0	−3
7801	6	24	−25	4	−49	−108	109.39	68.06	1404.5	189.5	43.5	43.5	8.5	3
7802	12	34	−13	17	−30	−92	108.52	72.75	1365.2	190.6	48.0	39.0	9.0	3
7803	11	16	−14	13	−47	−91	107.90	74.83	1320.0	191.8	48.0	41.0	8.0	−3
7804	6	25	−11	14	−63	−95	107.67	75.88	1308.5	194.6	45.5	43.5	7.5	5
7805	9	11	−7	16	−61	−102	108.02	73.75	1245.6	195.7	43.5	43.5	8.5	1
7806	−8	−7	−8	6	−59	−102	108.17	71.44	1281.9	197.2	45.5	45.5	6.0	−2
7807	6	−1	−1	15	−74	−97	108.76	71.58	1401.4	198.1	45.0	43.0	8.5	−4
7808	4	1	−3	18	−74	−104	109.39	77.23	1429.3	199.4	43.5	47.5	6.0	−3
7809	6	2	−1	17	−63	−103	109.10	74.94	1350.8	200.2	49.5	42.5	6.0	−8
7810	8	2	2	16	−52	−104	108.64	82.08	1274.4	201.1	42.0	47.5	7.5	2
7811	1	−13	3	15	−77	−101	107.28	78.00	1244.7	202.5	43.0	48.0	6.5	26
7812	−30	−35	−12	3	−79	−118	105.76	84.69	1222.0	204.2	48.0	42.5	6.0	−7

1	2	3	4	5	6	7	8	9	10	11	12	13	14	15
7901	−26	−29	−6	3	−57	−119	104.27	83.37	1311.5	207.2	49.0	41.5	6.0	−18
7902	−81	−62	−15	−8	−95	−139	103.54	92.81	1307.8	208.9	53.0	33.0	11.0	−40
7903	−98	−55	−19	−1	−98	−142	104.71	91.40	1260.6	210.6	51.5	37.0	8.5	−29
7904	−87	−33	−17	1	−65	−126	106.09	73.24	1203.0	214.2	50.0	40.0	8.0	−17
7905	−47	15	−15	20	−23	−90	106.08	86.13	1160.9	215.9	43.0	41.0	13.5	−7
7906	−68	−25	−12	−3	−54	−132	105.09	85.91	1175.0	219.6	42.0	43.5	12.0	−7
7907	−69	−56	−24	−7	−90	−154	104.09	86.06	1279.0	229.1	41.0	46.0	11.5	−14
7908	−59	−47	−14	−12	−94	−141	103.11	98.09	1277.0	230.9	41.0	44.0	12.5	−6
7909	−68	−55	−15	−3	−117	−141	102.41	100.97	1226.3	233.2	40.5	45.5	12.0	−10
7910	−65	−48	−13	−2	−108	−142	102.08	99.99	1206.0	235.6	40.5	45.0	12.5	−14
7911	−63	−38	−11	−4	−96	−143	101.11	98.03	1199.1	237.7	39.0	43.5	15.5	−12
7912	−100	−61	−21	−23	−117	−151	100.37	103.07	1200.7	239.4	38.0	42.0	18.0	−19
8001	−108	−77	−35	−32	−123	−153	100.00	103.05	1310.9	245.3	36.0	45.0	16.0	−20
8002	−117	−77	−40	−29	−140	−148	99.13	115.97	1325.1	248.8	37.5	42.0	18.0	−25
8003	−116	−64	−36	−26	−132	−146	98.04	114.80	1313.0	252.2	37.0	49.5	11.5	−29
8004	−87	−50	−29	−13	−123	−139	97.55	102.66	1353.4	260.8	36.5	45.0	15.0	−16
8005	−94	−36	−39	−10	−121	−128	97.52	104.63	1340.2	263.2	39.0	43.5	15.5	−15
8006	−94	−39	−43	−14	−125	−128	98.15	113.23	1444.3	265.7	40.5	45.0	11.5	−17
8007	−114	−46	−35	−15	−135	−115	98.57	106.29	1656.9	267.9	40.0	43.5	14.0	−21
8008	−107	−43	−39	−17	−133	−106	98.61	115.48	1763.1	268.5	38.5	44.0	14.5	−18
8009	−96	−38	−39	−18	−124	−95	98.95	117.36	1806.5	270.2	35.5	45.0	16.5	−28
8010	−97	−28	−39	−19	−105	−92	99.74	116.36	1831.6	271.9	40.0	43.0	13.5	−23
8011	−108	−37	−39	−19	−116	−93	100.76	109.03	1929.5	274.1	36.5	47.0	15.0	−31
8012	−117	−46	−39	−20	−127	−95	101.66	128.91	2011.2	275.6	35.0	47.5	14.5	−30
8101	−118	−46	−40	−23	−126	−97	102.09	111.47	2177.6	277.3	33.0	46.5	18.5	−37
8102	−118	−46	−39	−25	−126	−97	102.64	123.64	2218.0	279.8	36.0	35.5	20.0	−31
8103	−116	−35	−42	−21	−121	−89	103.33	125.11	2239.1	284.0	30.0	34.0	32.0	−44
8104	−123	−47	−51	−27	−119	−113	103.84	119.23	2279.3	292.2	30.0	34.5	31.0	−43
8105	−116	−27	−56	−22	−112	−98	104.37	113.99	2311.6	294.1	32.0	35.5	29.0	−31
8106	−119	−39	−53	−22	−119	−101	104.52	124.91	2299.3	295.8	29.5	37.5	30.5	−37
8107	−123	−50	−51	−24	−125	−104	104.58	119.39	2413.8	297.1	30.0	40.5	26.5	−43
8108	−123	−40	−51	−20	−109	−104	103.77	115.71	2488.4	299.3	28.0	38.5	32.0	−43
8109	−94	−15	−43	−14	−88	−97	101.86	120.19	2643.2	301.0	32.0	36.5	29.0	−37
8110	−131	−48	−59	−25	−99	−105	100.19	126.97	2667.7	303.7	29.5	28.0	40.0	−38
8111	−120	−37	−58	−23	−86	−87	100.23	108.18	2667.7	306.9	26.5	29.0	42.0	−43
8112	−125	−48	−68	−38	−75	−78	100.89	138.61	2662.9	308.8	23.0	23.5	50.5	−52
8201	−108	−33	−68	−26	−71	−75	101.12	−1	2790.4	310.6	27.5	29.5	39.5	−41
8202	−123	−50	−63	−26	−96	−76	101.05	−1	2765.5	310.7	27.5	34.0	36.0	−42
8203	−102	−25	−62	−24	−63	−64	101.35	−1	2717.5	313.4	31.5	33.0	33.0	−30
8204	−91	−20	−59	−23	−48	−63	101.13	−1	2714.2	319.7	31.5	29.0	37.0	−24
8205	−63	−6	−52	−19	−41	−58	101.07	−1	2695.2	322.0	41.5	28.0	29.0	−4
8206	−34	7	−46	−7	−39	−61	101.82	−1	2663.8	322.9	45.0	25.0	28.5	8
8207	−59	−4	−53	−10	−67	−62	102.61	−1	2744.4	323.0	46.5	27.5	24.0	6
8208	−67	−15	−42	−8	−73	−39	103.83	−1	2789.8	323.1	44.5	26.5	27.5	−2
8209	−71	−19	−45	−9	−81	−39	105.19	−1	2950.3	322.9	44.0	30.5	23.0	−8
8210	−57	−9	−40	−7	−80	−33	106.59	−1	2935.2	324.5	40.5	29.0	27.0	−9
8211	−52	−1	−40	−3	−73	−20	107.60	−1	2950.8	326.1	42.0	34.5	21.5	−9
8212	−76	−25	−37	−13	−86	−45	107.48	−1	2984.6	325.5	41.0	34.5	22.0	−13

1	2	3	4	5	6	7	8	9	10	11	12	13	14	15
8301	−66	−23	−32	−6	−94	−46	107.15	−1	3109.1	325.9	44.0	31.5	22.5	0
8302	−77	−29	−34	−6	−99	−50	107.11	−1	3084.6	327.3	43.5	32.5	22.0	−10
8303	−56	−4	−33	−1	−77	−48	107.19	−1	3058.7	327.9	39.5	28.5	30.0	−7
8304	−34	10	−33	2	−61	−41	107.25	−1	3053.5	332.5	40.5	35.0	22.5	−11
8305	−16	26	−33	4	−46	−33	107.31	−1	2934.4	333.9	49.0	31.5	17.5	2
8306	−20	14	−27	2	−50	−37	108.07	−1	2870.5	334.7	45.5	26.5	26.0	−1
8307	−24	4	−24	2	−55	−41	108.68	−1	2903.5	336.5	44.0	28.5	26.0	3
8308	−31	−10	−26	−9	−77	−66	108.30	−1	2892.8	338.0	44.5	25.0	29.0	−1
8309	−25	−5	−27	−1	−82	−56	107.56	−1	3043.8	339.5	45.5	24.5	29.0	5
8310	−34	−15	−21	−5	−73	−70	106.83	−1	2974.1	340.7	42.0	35.5	20.5	−6
8311	−36	−14	−28	−6	−59	−68	106.94	−1	2964.7	341.9	43.5	36.0	19.5	−9
8312	−28	−9	−29	−6	−41	−68	107.57	−1	2961.0	342.8	42.5	36.0	19.5	−12
8401	−24	2	−24	−1	−45	−70	108.01	−1	3077.4	342.6	41.5	38.0	19.5	−4
8402	−43	−13	−24	−5	−66	−69	108.01	−1	3063.8	344.0	43.0	33.5	21.5	−4
8403	−47	−19	−31	−5	−57	−78	108.09	−1	3021.9	345.1	41.0	38.5	19.5	−8
8404	−35	−12	−29	−5	−60	−65	107.69	−1	2987.6	349.7	41.0	36.5	20.5	−3
8405	−27	−6	−26	−4	−49	−68	106.81	−1	2963.9	351.0	38.5	36.5	23.0	−14
8406	−48	−19	−30	−6	−65	−81	105.30	−1	2910.9	351.9	37.5	38.0	23.0	−17
8407	−62	−37	−33	−5	−70	−83	104.08	−1	2978.9	351.5	37.5	38.5	22.0	−18
8408	−66	−36	−36	−9	−74	−84	104.24	−1	2995.1	354.8	36.0	39.0	22.5	−20
8409	−68	−28	−28	−4	−66	−84	104.54	−1	3156.6	355.5	37.0	36.0	25.5	−18
8410	−74	−38	−30	−4	−77	−85	104.68	−1	3103.1	357.7	44.5	32.0	21.5	0
8411	−59	−23	−25	−4	−65	−89	104.98	−1	3101.5	358.8	44.5	30.5	23.5	−5
8412	−67	−23	−20	6	−67	−79	105.24	−1	3100.0	358.5	39.5	31.0	27.5	−18
8501	−73	−27	−27	−3	−69	−84	104.80	−1	3217.9	359.8	39.0	33.0	25.5	−21
8502	−103	−48	−42	−14	−85	−92	103.97	−1	3200.7	362.7	35.0	32.0	31.5	−24
8503	−91	−29	−36	−12	−69	−107	103.36	−1	3145.9	366.1	33.0	39.5	25.5	−28
8504	−64	−26	−38	−15	−68	−88	103.28	−1	3150.3	373.9	34.0	37.5	26.5	−25
8505	−67	−30	−35	−16	−68	−87	103.44	−1	3120.0	375.6	30.5	34.0	33.5	−30
8506	−80	−36	−36	−11	−72	−93	103.00	−1	3057.2	376.4	34.5	34.5	30.0	−28
8507	−73	−32	−31	−9	−60	−79	102.65	−1	3116.1	375.7	27.5	38.0	32.5	−31
8508	−74	−38	−38	−13	−72	−78	102.68	−1	3120.4	376.7	24.0	40.0	34.0	−42
8509	−69	−30	−27	−10	−68	−71	102.54	−1	3219.7	376.5	29.0	29.5	39.0	−27
8510	−61	−23	−23	−3	−70	−71	102.45	−1	3155.0	377.1	32.0	38.0	28.0	−30
8511	−59	−24	−27	−7	−58	−70	102.19	−1	3125.3	378.4	35.0	34.0	29.5	−30
8512	−55	−23	−25	−5	−53	−70	101.09	−1	3151.6	378.9	33.0	32.5	32.5	−18

EDUCATE

This data is drawn from the National Child Development Study, a longitudinal survey of children who were born in 1958, and who have been investigated periodically since then (see appendix to chapter 3). This file relates to 238 individuals drawn at random from all NCDS respondents for whom information on school attainment at age 16 was available.

Column
1 Sex: 1 = male; 2 = female
2 Registrar-General's social class of father when child was born:
   1 class I: higher professional and managerial
   2 class II: lower professional and managerial
   3 class IIIN: routine non-manual
   4 class IIIM: skilled manual
   5 class IV: semi-skilled manual
   6 class V: unskilled manual
3 Number of children under 21 in household when respondent was aged 11; 9 = 9 or more
4 Goodenough draw-a-man IQ test administered at age 7
5 Score on test of general verbal ability at age 11
6 Score on test of general non-verbal ability at age 11
7 Number of persons per room in household at age 16:
   1 up to 1
   2 over 1 to 1.5
   3 over 1.5 to 2.0
   4 more than 2.0
8 Score on test of reading comprehension at age 16
9 Score on test of mathematics attainment at age 16
10 Social class of respondent at age 23 – current job or last job:
   1 professional
   2 intermediate
   3 skilled non-manual
   4 skilled manual
   5 semi-skilled non-manual
   6 semi-skilled manual
   7 unskilled

1	2	3	4	5	6	7	8	9	10
1	4	4	18	25	23	1	22	18	3
2	4	2	25	16	12	−1	20	4	6
2	4	3	27	38	31	2	26	18	6
2	4	3	1	8	15	−1	18	5	4
2	5	2	12	−1	−1	1	23	10	3
1	5	2	26	30	20	1	29	27	−1
2	5	4	19	19	12	3	34	14	7
2	4	−1	26	16	15	1	17	7	6
1	4	2	24	24	24	2	34	29	2
1	3	7	16	11	17	2	20	9	6

1	2	3	4	5	6	7	8	9	10
2	3	2	27	25	26	1	26	14	3
2	6	6	23	2	10	3	11	7	6
1	4	2	22	29	23	1	23	23	4
1	5	2	27	28	28	1	33	23	6
1	4	1	17	16	17	1	12	13	4
2	2	3	25	28	29	1	31	14	6
1	5	4	18	14	12	3	20	9	6
1	4	3	10	5	12	2	9	6	4
2	3	3	26	36	20	3	29	14	3
2	4	2	28	28	23	1	25	20	3
1	6	1	16	19	19	1	29	15	6
1	3	3	18	−1	−1	1	34	25	2
2	4	5	27	19	22	−1	19	11	3
1	4	3	10	13	13	2	17	6	6
2	4	1	11	20	13	1	31	9	2
1	−1	1	21	24	17	1	30	10	3
1	4	−1	32	−1	−1	2	22	11	4
1	4	4	22	20	17	−1	15	6	4
2	5	3	20	25	16	1	27	19	3
1	3	4	27	23	22	2	31	17	4
2	5	3	28	26	23	−1	23	19	3
2	4	4	32	17	25	−1	24	11	3
2	6	7	34	13	19	2	22	5	6
1	3	3	21	8	20	1	31	11	3
1	4	3	19	21	17	−1	23	22	2
2	3	1	16	17	19	−1	29	4	3
2	4	1	21	32	23	1	28	22	3
1	−1	5	21	8	19	2	17	9	4
1	−1	5	31	8	12	1	24	5	4
2	−1	5	−1	−1	−1	2	15	2	6
1	−1	4	21	40	29	−1	32	20	6
1	−1	2	31	37	33	1	29	29	1
1	−1	5	−1	8	7	2	24	10	3
2	−1	3	−1	−1	−1	1	31	13	2
1	−1	3	−1	25	24	2	26	−1	6
2	−1	2	−1	39	27	1	32	20	2
1	−1	−1	−1	−1	−1	3	15	3	6
2	−1	−1	−1	−1	−1	2	6	4	6
1	−1	−1	−1	−1	−1	2	15	7	4
1	−1	−1	−1	−1	−1	2	32	23	3
2	4	2	30	22	14	1	31	5	3
1	−1	−1	21	−1	−1	1	31	17	6
1	4	4	35	26	21	2	29	7	4
2	4	2	27	8	13	−1	23	2	3
1	4	4	23	18	25	2	23	5	6
2	4	3	−1	36	28	1	31	14	2
2	−1	3	22	7	6	2	14	9	4
2	4	2	18	−1	−1	1	31	16	2
1	4	6	−1	−1	−1	−1	15	8	7
1	5	3	23	7	10	2	22	3	6

1	2	3	4	5	6	7	8	9	10
2	4	3	35	−1	−1	1	29	20	6
2	2	2	31	27	25	1	32	21	2
1	4	3	−1	33	32	2	33	29	−1
2	4	1	29	31	23	1	33	27	2
1	4	3	32	28	20	1	32	11	3
2	5	3	24	33	25	1	31	11	2
1	4	4	15	19	20	1	20	8	4
2	4	9	23	12	22	2	9	5	6
2	4	2	40	17	16	1	16	10	3
2	4	8	12	3	14	2	23	−1	6
2	2	3	18	27	25	−1	26	5	3
1	6	5	23	26	26	2	33	14	4
2	−1	3	23	16	20	−1	29	5	−1
2	2	−1	31	27	24	1	29	14	2
1	4	−1	−1	36	28	−1	30	22	2
1	4	−1	−1	8	12	3	13	7	4
1	4	−1	−1	37	32	2	35	24	2
2	2	3	17	34	29	1	35	26	6
1	4	4	12	30	28	2	24	14	4
1	4	3	24	18	19	1	22	8	6
2	2	−1	31	−1	−1	−1	32	14	2
1	5	1	29	29	29	1	30	19	6
1	4	2	17	−1	−1	1	13	1	6
1	2	3	28	27	22	1	33	19	2
1	4	2	−1	21	27	1	33	20	4
2	2	−1	14	−1	−1	1	27	13	4
2	2	2	40	25	23	1	31	16	3
1	5	4	20	9	10	2	17	11	6
2	4	5	27	26	22	3	18	8	3
1	4	3	16	22	19	1	23	9	4
1	4	5	21	20	16	2	27	9	4
2	4	3	34	36	30	1	30	13	2
1	4	2	−1	22	22	−1	32	20	1
2	4	3	47	32	29	1	34	6	2
1	5	6	−1	14	14	3	28	13	6
1	3	3	20	31	28	1	22	14	−1
2	5	−1	17	13	22	2	24	5	6
2	6	3	26	25	15	−1	22	10	3
1	4	3	28	19	23	1	27	10	6
1	4	2	6	24	24	1	29	18	−1
1	5	3	26	25	24	1	30	13	4
2	2	−1	11	−1	−1	−1	14	5	3
1	4	3	15	37	39	−1	34	26	1
1	4	3	29	36	28	−1	32	28	1
2	3	2	−1	33	25	1	29	11	3
2	4	1	29	35	25	1	33	24	2
2	4	1	16	29	21	1	33	22	2
1	6	2	−1	16	11	−1	16	−1	7
1	3	2	24	15	18	1	28	7	2
1	2	2	30	32	31	1	35	24	1

1	2	3	4	5	6	7	8	9	10
1	4	2	21	33	25	1	32	15	2
2	4	−1	19	22	14	1	22	8	3
1	5	2	27	6	6	1	15	5	7
2	5	5	16	36	31	2	29	14	6
2	3	1	16	20	16	1	27	9	3
2	3	2	27	32	30	1	30	23	2
2	6	2	29	24	25	1	27	4	6
1	4	−1	24	27	30	1	31	11	2
2	1	2	18	36	38	1	34	30	2
2	6	4	28	24	22	2	23	2	3
1	3	−1	19	14	16	1	28	9	4
1	4	1	44	38	36	−1	33	19	4
2	1	2	24	36	29	−1	32	23	1
2	6	5	18	10	12	2	16	1	4
2	4	2	22	21	21	1	28	11	3
1	5	2	20	23	23	2	26	16	3
2	4	2	17	11	15	1	18	9	4
2	4	4	18	24	22	−1	26	9	3
2	6	2	18	19	27	1	24	7	3
1	4	1	33	18	20	1	23	10	6
2	4	2	28	22	22	1	24	12	3
1	4	5	26	15	23	−1	22	22	4
1	4	4	23	29	35	1	32	26	1
1	5	4	26	31	25	1	34	8	7
1	5	5	28	20	17	2	31	8	4
1	−1	4	21	24	12	−1	26	7	6
2	4	2	17	22	13	1	23	5	4
1	3	2	22	28	22	1	31	24	2
2	2	2	30	34	29	−1	35	29	3
2	4	4	26	21	22	2	26	8	3
2	5	7	24	29	32	1	30	19	4
1	6	5	9	9	4	3	30	4	4
2	1	−1	−1	−1	−1	1	32	12	3
1	4	3	23	20	22	1	21	13	4
1	1	3	19	33	30	1	33	28	3
2	1	3	39	27	24	−1	33	9	3
2	4	2	−1	28	28	1	32	16	−1
1	2	2	16	17	22	1	33	17	2
2	4	5	11	13	22	3	15	11	5
2	4	4	−1	27	26	2	28	17	3
2	−1	1	32	23	25	1	29	−1	3
1	2	−1	−1	−1	−1	1	33	18	1
1	3	3	31	19	19	1	32	22	2
1	4	2	27	26	28	1	27	16	2
2	6	2	−1	21	13	2	21	10	3
2	4	2	15	25	21	1	31	21	3
2	4	3	23	16	12	−1	22	1	3
2	4	3	−1	31	32	2	32	14	3
2	5	−1	−1	−1	−1	−1	23	10	3
2	4	2	24	29	25	1	29	10	3

1	2	3	4	5	6	7	8	9	10
1	1	2	-1	31	34	1	34	25	1
1	4	4	-1	13	8	1	23	4	7
2	3	2	18	26	19	1	30	10	3
2	3	1	-1	-1	-1	-1	15	8	3
1	5	2	19	15	28	1	18	5	4
2	4	2	18	-1	-1	2	27	1	3
2	4	-1	32	38	33	1	31	23	3
2	4	2	24	32	18	2	31	14	3
1	4	4	45	31	21	2	29	5	2
2	4	4	15	-1	-1	2	25	7	3
1	2	2	30	25	29	1	32	25	-1
2	1	1	24	18	21	1	27	16	2
2	4	3	16	22	19	-1	32	22	5
2	4	6	-1	-1	-1	3	17	7	4
1	4	-1	20	27	25	-1	21	1	4
1	4	2	19	28	30	1	33	17	4
1	4	5	30	23	25	1	30	11	2
1	3	5	27	36	28	1	27	19	3
2	3	2	23	-1	-1	1	32	25	2
1	4	1	24	12	23	1	25	14	4
1	2	-1	-1	-1	-1	1	29	24	1
1	4	3	36	14	15	1	26	4	4
2	4	2	32	16	14	1	22	6	3
2	2	3	31	32	30	1	21	8	3
2	4	4	25	24	22	2	34	10	2
2	4	3	21	32	28	2	35	23	3
1	2	2	19	12	11	1	19	9	2
2	5	3	26	34	28	1	32	20	3
1	4	3	17	18	19	-1	24	9	3
2	4	3	19	-1	-1	1	24	11	6
1	1	3	28	-1	-1	1	33	28	2
2	6	-1	-1	-1	-1	2	17	5	6
1	4	2	17	4	6	-1	6	1	3
2	4	2	12	12	16	-1	14	5	3
1	4	-1	31	29	29	1	33	22	4
2	6	2	26	8	9	1	24	1	6
1	2	2	37	32	32	-1	34	24	1
1	6	-1	27	-1	-1	1	5	-1	6
1	4	2	-1	25	23	1	25	23	2
2	4	2	18	31	24	1	28	10	3
1	2	3	23	35	26	1	33	29	2
1	4	1	16	13	19	1	31	5	6
2	4	4	12	12	18	3	15	3	6
1	2	4	26	33	29	1	35	26	1
2	4	2	21	31	21	1	28	12	3
1	-1	-1	33	4	14	1	15	-1	4
1	5	4	29	24	27	-1	23	8	6
2	4	1	27	34	22	1	30	10	3
2	5	3	-1	-1	-1	1	33	12	3
2	4	3	38	19	20	1	25	11	3

1	2	3	4	5	6	7	8	9	10
2	4	3	19	21	28	1	17	10	3
1	4	2	18	23	22	1	22	12	3
1	2	2	18	33	30	1	31	13	4
2	4	7	35	14	10	−1	19	4	7
2	2	1	29	30	19	1	25	13	6
1	4	3	32	28	19	1	33	9	3
2	2	4	27	38	37	2	32	22	1
2	4	3	34	18	17	1	28	10	3
2	2	3	30	20	22	−1	33	14	3
2	2	−1	26	−1	−1	1	33	25	2
2	4	4	21	5	3	2	9	4	7
1	3	2	25	29	30	1	32	29	−1
1	4	3	37	35	35	−1	24	24	2
2	4	1	32	30	32	1	32	7	3
2	4	−1	21	9	10	−1	15	6	4
1	4	−1	31	−1	−1	1	29	19	2
1	4	3	18	18	32	1	27	24	2
2	4	7	23	17	12	3	20	5	6
2	4	−1	18	17	13	1	25	2	6
1	2	1	22	24	19	1	34	15	2
2	5	5	20	20	18	3	19	−1	6
2	4	5	27	20	19	3	24	11	4
1	4	3	−1	29	28	1	29	18	3
1	2	2	−1	27	27	1	32	20	1
1	−1	−1	27	−1	−1	−1	30	10	2
2	4	4	23	7	12	−1	22	8	7
2	4	2	39	28	29	1	33	17	3
2	3	2	22	32	24	1	30	15	3

HEIGHT

This is a random sample drawn from the OPCS study of the heights and weights of the adult population of Great Britain in 1980 (Knight 1984). It represents a sample of two hundred married men and their wives. Nine pieces of information are recorded about each couple, as detailed below.

Column
1 Husband's age
2 Registrar-General's social class of the husband:
   1 class I: higher professional and managerial
   2 class II: lower professional and managerial
   3 class IIIN: routine non-manual
   4 class IIIM: skilled manual
   5 class IV: semi-skilled manual
   6 class V: unskilled manual
3 Height of the husband in millimetres
4 Wife's age
5 Registrar-General's social class of the wife (as column 2)
6 Height of wife in millimetres.
7 The type of tenancy which they have:
   1 live rent free
   2 own property on a mortgage
   3 own property outright
   4 Council house tenant
   5 private rented accommodation
8 The age of the husband at the time of this marriage
9 Whether the husband smokes or not:
   0 did not smoke today
   1 smoked today

1	2	3	4	5	6	7	8	9
49	5	1809	43	5	1590	4	25	1
25	−1	1841	28	5	1560	5	19	1
40	6	1659	30	5	1620	4	38	1
52	6	1779	57	−1	1540	5	26	1
58	−1	1616	52	−1	1420	4	30	1
32	4	1695	27	5	1660	4	23	1
43	4	1730	52	−1	1610	4	33	1
42	3	1753	−1	−1	1635	4	30	1
47	4	1740	43	5	1580	4	24	1
31	4	1685	23	−1	1610	4	26	1
26	2	1735	25	−1	1590	2	23	0
40	1	1713	39	−1	1610	2	23	1
35	2	1736	32	2	1700	2	31	0
45	1	1715	−1	−1	1522	2	41	1
35	2	1799	35	3	1680	2	19	0
35	3	1785	33	6	1680	2	24	0
47	−1	1758	43	5	1630	5	24	1
38	−1	1729	35	5	1570	4	27	1
33	3	1720	32	3	1720	2	28	0
32	3	1810	30	5	1740	2	22	1

1	2	3	4	5	6	7	8	9
38	2	1725	40	−1	1600	2	31	0
45	5	1764	−1	−1	1689	4	24	1
29	4	1683	29	−1	1600	2	25	1
59	2	1585	55	2	1550	3	23	0
26	5	1684	25	5	1540	4	18	0
50	4	1674	45	5	1640	2	25	1
49	1	1724	44	5	1640	2	27	0
42	5	1630	40	−1	1630	2	28	1
33	4	1855	31	−1	1560	2	22	1
31	5	1796	−1	−1	1652	4	25	1
27	4	1700	25	−1	1580	4	21	0
57	3	1765	51	2	1570	2	32	0
34	2	1700	31	3	1590	2	28	1
28	2	1721	25	3	1650	2	23	0
46	3	1823	−1	−1	1591	2	−1	0
37	4	1829	35	3	1670	2	22	0
56	3	1710	55	3	1600	2	44	0
27	2	1745	23	3	1610	2	25	0
36	3	1698	35	2	1610	2	22	1
31	4	1853	28	3	1670	2	20	1
57	4	1610	52	6	1510	2	25	0
55	3	1680	53	5	1520	2	21	0
47	4	1809	43	5	1620	4	25	1
64	3	1580	61	−1	1530	4	21	1
60	4	1600	−1	−1	1451	4	26	1
31	4	1585	23	−1	1570	4	28	0
35	2	1705	35	−1	1580	2	25	0
36	1	1675	35	−1	1590	2	22	0
40	2	1735	39	−1	1670	2	23	0
30	4	1686	24	5	1630	2	27	0
32	4	1768	29	6	1510	4	21	1
27	3	1721	−1	−1	1560	2	26	0
20	4	1754	21	3	1660	2	19	0
45	4	1739	39	3	1610	2	25	1
59	4	1699	52	3	1440	2	27	0
43	3	1825	52	3	1570	2	25	0
29	5	1740	26	2	1670	2	24	0
48	4	1704	−1	−1	1635	2	27	1
39	4	1719	−1	−1	1670	2	25	1
47	4	1731	48	2	1730	2	21	0
54	4	1679	53	3	1560	3	−1	1
43	1	1755	42	3	1590	2	20	1
54	4	1713	50	−1	1600	4	23	1
61	4	1723	64	−1	1490	2	26	0
27	4	1783	26	3	1660	4	20	0
51	5	1585	−1	−1	1504	5	50	0
27	4	1749	32	−1	1580	5	24	0
32	4	1710	31	−1	1500	2	31	1
54	4	1724	53	5	1640	4	20	0
37	4	1620	39	−1	1650	4	21	1

1	2	3	4	5	6	7	8	9
55	4	1764	45	6	1620	4	29	0
36	2	1791	33	−1	1550	2	30	1
32	2	1795	32	1	1640	2	25	−1
57	5	1738	55	5	1560	4	24	0
51	4	1639	−1	−1	1552	2	25	1
62	2	1734	−1	−1	1600	3	33	0
57	2	1695	−1	−1	1545	2	22	0
51	2	1666	52	2	1570	5	24	1
50	5	1745	50	2	1550	1	22	0
32	3	1775	32	2	1600	2	20	1
54	5	1669	54	6	1660	3	20	0
34	4	1700	32	3	1640	2	22	0
45	−1	1804	41	3	1670	2	27	0
64	2	1700	61	−1	1560	3	24	1
55	4	1664	43	3	1760	3	31	0
28	5	1750	41	−1	1550	4	21	1
27	5	1753	28	−1	1640	4	23	1
55	4	1788	51	5	1600	2	26	0
27	4	1765	−1	−1	1571	4	−1	1
41	6	1680	41	5	1550	4	22	1
44	2	1715	41	3	1570	3	24	0
22	5	1755	21	3	1590	2	21	0
30	3	1764	28	3	1650	5	29	1
53	2	1793	47	3	1690	2	31	0
42	3	1731	37	3	1580	2	23	1
31	4	1713	28	3	1590	2	28	1
36	4	1725	35	5	1510	4	26	1
56	3	1828	55	−1	1600	3	30	0
46	4	1735	45	2	1660	2	22	1
34	2	1760	34	3	1700	2	23	0
55	4	1685	51	3	1530	4	34	1
44	2	1685	39	5	1490	5	27	0
45	2	1559	35	−1	1580	2	34	1
48	5	1705	45	5	1500	2	28	0
44	2	1723	44	5	1600	2	41	0
59	5	1700	47	−1	1570	3	39	1
64	5	1660	57	−1	1620	4	32	0
34	5	1681	33	−1	1410	2	22	0
37	3	1803	38	5	1560	2	23	1
54	2	1866	59	3	1590	2	49	0
49	3	1884	46	2	1710	2	25	0
63	3	1705	60	2	1580	3	27	0
48	2	1780	47	−1	1690	2	22	0
64	5	1801	55	3	1610	5	37	1
33	2	1795	45	3	1660	4	17	0
52	1	1669	47	3	1610	2	23	0
27	2	1708	24	2	1590	2	26	1
33	3	1691	32	3	1530	2	21	0
46	2	1825	47	2	1690	2	23	1
54	4	1760	57	5	1600	2	23	1

1	2	3	4	5	6	7	8	9
27	2	1949	−1	−1	1693	2	25	0
50	4	1685	−1	−1	1580	4	21	1
42	2	1806	−1	−1	1636	2	22	0
54	1	1905	46	3	1670	2	32	0
49	2	1739	42	5	1600	2	28	1
62	1	1736	63	−1	1570	3	22	0
34	3	1845	32	−1	1700	2	24	0
23	4	1868	24	−1	1740	2	19	1
36	1	1765	32	−1	1540	2	27	1
53	2	1736	−1	−1	1555	2	30	0
32	5	1741	−1	−1	1614	2	22	1
59	4	1720	56	5	1530	4	24	1
53	5	1871	50	−1	1690	3	25	0
55	5	1720	55	6	1590	4	21	1
62	3	1629	58	−1	1610	5	23	0
42	4	1624	38	−1	1670	2	22	1
50	6	1653	44	5	1690	3	35	1
37	2	1786	35	2	1550	2	21	1
51	2	1620	44	5	1650	2	30	0
25	3	1695	25	5	1540	2	19	0
54	3	1674	43	−1	1660	3	35	0
34	2	1864	31	3	1620	2	23	0
43	5	1643	35	5	1630	4	29	1
43	5	1705	41	3	1610	2	22	1
58	4	1736	50	3	1540	2	32	1
28	3	1691	23	−1	1610	2	23	0
45	4	1753	43	3	1630	2	21	1
47	2	1680	49	3	1530	4	20	1
57	3	1724	59	−1	1520	3	24	0
27	5	1710	−1	−1	1544	4	20	0
34	4	1638	38	−1	1570	4	33	1
57	2	1725	42	−1	1580	-1	52	1
27	5	1725	21	−1	1550	2	24	1
54	2	1630	−1	−1	1570	2	34	0
24	4	1810	−1	−1	1521	4	16	1
48	1	1774	42	3	1580	2	30	1
37	5	1771	35	5	1630	2	28	0
25	4	1815	26	−1	1650	2	20	0
57	3	1575	57	3	1640	3	20	0
40	2	1729	34	5	1650	3	26	0
61	3	1749	63	6	1520	1	21	1
25	4	1705	23	2	1620	2	24	0
32	4	1875	−1	−1	1744	2	22	1
37	1	1784	−1	−1	1647	2	22	1
45	4	1584	−1	−1	1615	4	29	1
24	2	1774	23	4	1680	2	22	1
47	5	1658	46	6	1670	4	24	0
44	4	1790	40	3	1620	2	24	0
52	3	1798	53	5	1570	2	25	0
45	2	1824	40	2	1660	2	23	1

1	2	3	4	5	6	7	8	9
20	4	1796	22	−1	1550	4	19	0
60	2	1725	60	1	1590	2	21	1
36	1	1685	32	5	1620	2	25	0
25	4	1769	24	5	1560	5	18	1
25	3	1749	28	−1	1670	2	21	1
35	6	1716	40	2	1650	2	17	0
35	5	1664	−1	−1	1539	4	22	1
49	5	1773	48	−1	1470	3	21	1
33	5	1760	33	5	1580	2	20	0
50	2	1725	49	3	1670	3	23	0
63	−1	1645	64	−1	1520	3	28	0
57	2	1694	55	2	1620	3	24	1
41	3	1851	41	3	1710	2	23	1
38	1	1691	38	2	1530	2	20	0
30	4	1880	31	3	1630	4	22	1
52	2	1835	52	−1	1720	4	30	1
51	4	1730	43	6	1570	4	22	1
46	4	1644	51	−1	1560	4	27	0
50	3	1723	47	3	1650	4	25	0
32	2	1758	−1	−1	1635	2	24	1
52	5	1718	32	3	1590	2	25	1
30	4	1723	33	−1	1590	4	22	1
33	2	1708	−1	1	1566	3	21	0
20	4	1786	18	5	1590	4	19	1
32	4	1764	−1	−1	1662	−1	−1	1
51	5	1675	45	5	1550	4	25	1
64	5	1641	64	3	1570	4	30	1
44	5	1743	43	3	1560	4	25	1
40	2	1823	39	3	1630	2	23	0
59	4	1720	56	5	1530	4	24	1

POVERTY

This data is a random sample of fifty family units drawn from the General Household Survey 1979 (see appendix to chapter 1). A subset of the survey was first extracted by Dale et al. (1984); this is a further subset of cases and variables taken from their data.

Column

1   Gross weekly income of family unit (pounds)
2   Social class of head of household (combined socio-economic groups):
    1   professional
    2   managers and employers
    3   intermediate and junior non-manual
    4   skilled manual
    5   semi-skilled manual
    6   unskilled manual
3   Net family income relative to entitlement to supplementary benefit
4   Region:
    1   North
    2   Midlands and East Anglia
    3   London
    4   South East
    5   South West and Wales
    6   Scotland

1	2	3	4
20	3	67	2
65	3	275	4
79	4	123	5
47	3	193	3
28	5	119	1
75	4	277	6
23	4	72	2
98	5	232	5
255	1	530	4
31	2	85	5
21	−1	117	5
36	5	95	2
139	5	302	2
24	6	113	5
73	4	109	4
140	2	327	1
20	6	50	4
111	4	248	3
79	4	335	1
112	4	162	1

1	2	3	4
35	5	81	6
84	3	145	2
130	5	292	2
81	4	143	5
22	6	88	3
59	1	225	2
26	5	141	1
67	4	297	5
97	4	182	3
42	4	126	2
124	3	172	1
11	6	44	1
117	4	179	5
62	5	134	1
146	1	228	1
29	-1	110	1
27	3	106	6
26	5	125	1
57	3	201	2
26	4	122	6
95	4	233	1
79	4	233	1
112	3	230	3
27	3	114	6
80	5	328	1
34	5	182	5
156	4	369	2
25	6	105	6
61	3	165	6
76	5	303	3

SCOTLAND

This dataset shows stillbirths broken down by social class and fertility rates in Scotland, for a forty year period from 1944 to 1985.

Stillbirths are so described when the foetus has survived to twenty-eight weeks, but the baby is eventually born dead; if the baby breathes at all after birth, it is classified as an infant death. The stillbirths are expressed as rates per 10,000 total births, live and still.

The social class of the infant is coded according to the occupation of the father if legitimate, and of the mother if illegitimate. The Registrar-General's class scheme split class III into manual and non-manual from 1979; in order to preserve the time series, they have been recombined in this dataset for the years 1979 to 1983. The data was taken from the Registrar-General for Scotland's *Annual Report* of 1984, table D1.6, and similar previous publications; the data needed to combine the classes was kindly supplied by the GRO Scotland.

The fertility rates were formed by dividing the total number of legitimate and illegitimate births in the year by the size of the female population in that year.

Column
1 Year
2 Stillbirth rate in social class I – professional
3 Stillbirth rate in social class II – intermediate
4 Stillbirth rate in social class III – skilled
5 Stillbirth rate in social class IV – semi-skilled
6 Stillbirth rate in social class V – unskilled
7 Legitimate fertility rate per 1000 women
8 Illegitimate fertility rate per 1000 women

1	2	3	4	5	6	7	8
1944	253	270	326	366	338	−1	−1
1945	209	260	313	371	391	−1	−1
1946	188	260	217	356	383	37.1	2.6
1947	178	302	295	311	384	40.4	2.3
1948	198	267	260	316	389	35.6	2.1
1949	173	214	265	287	350	34.1	1.9
1950	163	226	264	291	323	32.9	1.8
1951	147	230	252	312	324	32.3	1.7
1952	200	241	254	281	301	32.3	1.6
1953	132	212	241	277	299	32.5	1.5
1954	176	221	243	285	302	33.0	1.5
1955	166	175	234	298	309	33.1	1.4
1956	176	201	230	256	299	34.1	1.5
1957	171	208	215	292	297	35.1	1.5
1958	165	207	219	247	271	35.5	1.5
1959	135	154	218	244	269	35.3	1.5

1	2	3	4	5	6	7	8
1960	128	168	208	247	264	35.9	1.6
1961	129	164	201	232	257	35.7	1.7
1962	111	166	191	217	270	36.7	1.8
1963	108	156	182	210	251	35.9	1.9
1964	93	123	176	199	237	36.4	2.0
1965	95	123	177	211	217	34.9	2.1
1966	121	119	156	167	224	33.4	2.2
1967	106	134	158	164	179	33.1	2.4
1968	80	121	150	141	197	32.4	2.5
1969	102	107	132	165	190	30.8	2.4
1970	128	104	137	158	167	29.7	2.4
1971	83	109	128	133	181	29.4	2.5
1972	77	106	129	153	178	26.5	2.4
1973	74	85	112	135	162	25.0	2.4
1974	86	93	115	135	172	23.5	2.3
1975	78	77	112	129	144	22.8	2.3
1976	71	90	91	119	95	21.7	2.2
1977	56	71	89	100	114	20.9	2.2
1978	68	63	82	88	104	21.5	2.3
1979	50	58	67	73	103	22.9	2.5
1980	51	56	66	79	66	22.9	2.8
1981	43	55	65	68	67	22.5	3.1
1982	35	39	61	74	55	21.2	3.5
1983	36	50	54	71	65	20.8	3.5
1984	35	50	56	63	66	20.4	3.9
1985	26	47	54	74	55	20.4	4.6

TOWNS

This dataset describes features of all British towns. The data was kindly supplied by the Centre for Urban and Regional Development Studies (CURDS) at the University of Newcastle upon Tyne. The geographic units in this dataset have been formed by dividing Britain up into 280 local labour market areas (LLMAs), on the basis of the 1981 census small area statistics; all are relatively self-contained in commuting terms and thus are meaningful units for studying patterns of change over time.

The Centre has developed an index which measures the overall economic success of British towns, based on five indicators: population change; past employment change; more recent employment change; unemployment rate; and percentage of households with two or more cars, used as a crude indicator of affluence. The index value for each town is included in this dataset (column 10) along with the component indicators. The centre has also developed a classification of towns based on their functional place in Britain's national and local economy, which is shown in columns 8 and 9.

Information in columns 1, 2, 6 and 7 was derived from the census (see appendix to chapter 14), columns 3–5 from Department of Employment statistics (see appendix to chapter 6) and columns 8–10 from CURDS (Champion and Green 1985).

Column

1 Population in 1971
2 Population in 1981
3 Percentage employment change 1971–8
4 Percentage employment change 1978–81
5 Unemployment rate, May 1985
6 Percentage of households with 2 or more cars, 1981
7 Registrar-General's Standard Regions:
    1 South East
    2 East Anglia
    3 South West
    4 West Midlands
    5 East Midlands
    6 Yorkshire and Humberside
    7 North West
    8 North
    9 Wales
    10 Scotland

8 Urban size classification of LLMAs:

    1 London
    2 Conurbation Dominants
    3 Provincial Dominants
    4 Cities
    5 Towns
    6 Rural Areas

9   Nineteen-fold classification of LLMAs:

1   London dominant
2   Conurbation dominants
3   Provincial dominants
4   Subregional dominants
5   London subdominant cities
6   London subdominant towns
7   Conurbation subdominant cities
8   Conurbation subdominant towns
9   Smaller northern subdominants
10   Southern freestanding cities
11   Northern freestanding towns
12   Southern service towns
13   Southern commercial towns
14   Southern manufacturing towns
15   Northern service towns
16   Northern commercial towns
17   Northern manufacturing towns
18   Southern rural areas
19   Northern rural areas

10   Index score

The Local Labour Market Area name appears at the end of each row of data.

1	2	3	4	5	6	7	8	9	10	LLMA
68899	67143	−5.85	−7.63	14.4	9.41	7	5	09	0.331673	Accrington
196219	195636	6.16	−12.42	12.5	12.85	7	4	04	0.400530	Blackburn
54508	57984	11.85	4.49	9.4	28.15	4	5	08	0.618457	Stratford
1511661	1447862	−3.05	−8.95	15.2	15.21	4	2	02	0.353921	Birmingham
229089	232653	2.32	3.72	21.0	17.14	4	4	07	0.342259	Dudley
58383	85744	25.56	2.00	16.9	19.91	4	5	08	0.573664	Redditch
46398	51893	11.10	4.95	10.6	26.92	4	6	19	0.605045	Evesham
68881	94630	24.07	−12.46	26.0	16.69	4	5	08	0.350296	Tamworth
136320	128901	−1.89	−11.71	12.9	7.55	4	5	08	0.333598	West Bromwich
280495	278634	1.04	−13.17	16.9	14.41	4	4	07	0.329028	Walsall
217545	209997	−4.79	−22.18	14.4	10.86	4	4	07	0.297983	Smethwick
422307	421789	−0.75	−16.96	17.3	15.81	4	4	07	0.317345	Wolverhampton
75299	82691	22.53	−15.75	10.9	15.91	9	5	09	0.495181	Bridgend
445001	441283	−3.52	−4.66	14.9	15.18	9	4	04	0.377454	Cardiff
74590	74728	7.16	−14.29	20.3	9.51	9	5	09	0.261620	Gelligaer
237796	233884	5.55	−10.54	17.3	9.56	9	4	09	0.309814	Pontypridd
65071	63146	−0.39	−14.84	21.2	8.48	10	5	09	0.215160	Bathgate
688194	684115	5.52	−0.57	12.0	10.59	10	3	03	0.427051	Edinburgh
48717	50826	1.62	−3.14	11.6	15.37	10	6	19	0.456411	Berwick
57565	58388	10.64	−4.74	7.9	13.54	10	6	19	0.510892	Hawick
228513	234618	4.64	−4.51	12.3	11.48	5	4	09	0.421676	Mansfield
679227	672024	6.63	−7.80	13.2	12.73	5	3	03	0.402356	Nottingham
56460	59279	5.52	18.76	16.6	18.49	5	5	09	0.476022	Newark
107268	114238	0.63	12.64	16.4	13.12	5	5	09	0.420131	Heanor
110015	110667	−12.66	−9.12	24.3	7.64	10	5	08	0.159488	Coatbridge
78979	78273	−0.77	−11.63	20.0	11.18	10	5	08	0.262780	Dumbarton
1373097	1206904	−4.71	−8.91	16.8	8.31	10	2	02	0.266318	Glasgow
286213	284966	−1.50	−10.35	19.1	9.67	10	4	07	0.270122	Motherwell
41128	40332	17.93	12.34	19.2	14.93	10	6	19	0.410333	Lanark
169933	163744	3.02	−18.12	16.5	10.09	10	4	07	0.292083	Paisley

1	2	3	4	5	6	7	8	9	10	LLMA
120962	125124	13.86	−3.70	6.8	29.23	1	5	06	0.637811	St Albans
70863	80886	7.94	−5.13	11.1	22.68	1	5	06	0.539786	Braintree
107284	134852	28.91	6.03	8.2	23.44	1	5	06	0.696863	Basingstoke
65938	84446	32.16	−1.30	7.6	27.00	1	5	06	0.718960	Bracknell
188398	220190	8.72	0.48	8.6	23.55	1	5	06	0.607061	Chelmsford
76271	86712	18.81	−1.48	4.8	22.47	1	5	06	0.668281	Crawley
274925	312412	21.92	1.28	7.2	29.35	1	4	05	0.689636	Aldershot
209180	213648	−0.32	2.51	5.2	29.35	1	5	06	0.644091	Guildford
108592	107846	−0.91	−19.33	16.3	19.43	1	5	06	0.345618	Gravesend
65968	69124	24.07	−12.44	4.7	29.00	1	5	06	0.669352	Hertford
72940	82425	22.95	1.61	6.6	23.01	1	5	06	0.662050	Haywards Heath
96029	98273	−2.75	−34.14	9.5	20.57	1	5	06	0.413013	Harlow
63162	75270	24.09	9.33	6.7	27.24	1	5	06	0.725786	Horsham
107329	114951	13.60	−2.12	7.8	25.15	1	5	06	0.610445	Hemel Hempstead
243217	259067	15.09	−2.27	6.1	34.25	1	5	06	0.692930	High Wycombe
8577139	7836858	−5.93	−3.13	10.1	15.50	1	1	01	0.432202	London
175526	191831	13.68	3.04	7.8	24.14	1	4	05	0.624706	Maidstone
84125	92124	10.70	1.67	6.1	33.63	1	5	06	0.697149	Maidenhead
226022	237180	4.24	−7.53	16.9	15.47	1	4	05	0.372464	Medway Towns
65164	74514	22.55	−3.42	8.0	25.17	1	5	06	0.641527	Newbury
295894	312168	20.26	2.72	7.9	25.52	1	4	05	0.637678	Reading
88717	87167	−0.55	−2.48	6.2	26.13	1	5	06	0.585457	Reigate
71727	79161	13.52	4.63	7.4	30.58	1	5	06	0.676560	Bishops Stortford
100894	109634	10.92	−2.30	15.5	17.20	1	5	06	0.443687	Sittingbourne
198872	194480	0.74	−3.82	7.1	25.40	1	4	05	0.565637	Slough
305907	316410	13.15	−1.86	15.9	18.43	1	4	05	0.439882	Southend
143611	168445	12.24	11.83	18.1	18.61	1	5	06	0.477857	Basildon
180588	184596	10.92	4.36	7.8	23.88	1	5	06	0.604367	Tunbridge
182856	175698	0.67	−2.05	6.8	24.67	1	4	05	0.566873	Watford
75644	75521	−4.24	−0.30	6.1	21.60	1	5	06	0.560701	Welwyn Garden City
165222	170960	1.33	6.26	6.0	30.89	1	5	06	0.659506	Woking
97670	99308	13.08	−11.86	14.8	14.04	9	5	09	0.395998	Cwmbran
196244	193225	1.00	−13.99	15.0	14.06	9	4	04	0.350785	Newport
56641	63694	5.73	1.94	17.2	23.52	9	6	19	0.465466	Monmouth
110067	110923	3.12	3.04	11.7	17.52	7	5	08	0.481703	Chester
72187	77936	−5.62	−15.55	11.2	16.17	7	5	08	0.421677	Ellesmere Port
111726	122619	25.79	−21.62	17.2	18.54	9	5	08	0.407266	Shotton
158886	156949	11.61	−10.80	17.1	11.56	7	5	08	0.339581	St Helens
1078854	944483	−9.20	−12.71	19.0	9.27	7	2	02	0.216578	Liverpool
100021	104038	8.36	−0.72	18.3	17.64	7	5	08	0.392520	Southport
112804	139419	3.82	1.93	21.1	12.26	7	5	08	0.359531	Widnes
370498	355738	−1.31	−4.09	24.0	14.59	7	4	07	0.237638	Birkenhead
216043	244701	1.12	−10.69	22.7	11.71	7	4	07	0.265110	Wigan
212605	212178	1.23	−10.96	16.0	11.56	7	4	07	0.333183	Ashton & Hyde
262535	264059	−1.76	−9.83	16.0	12.48	7	4	07	0.336770	Bolton
135653	136105	10.18	−15.38	13.5	14.90	7	5	08	0.400300	Bury
52394	53912	8.12	−9.57	10.2	17.21	5	5	08	0.481753	Buxton
119712	118822	8.30	−15.41	16.7	11.45	7	5	08	0.324510	Leigh
1313288	1167913	−2.94	−8.07	13.6	12.27	7	2	02	0.347244	Manchester
68112	72706	13.75	−2.84	8.9	24.00	7	5	08	0.584428	Macclesfield

1	2	3	4	5	6	7	8	9	10	LLMA
102417	108694	7.94	−0.69	15.3	21.18	7	5	08	0.462764	Northwich
223976	220017	−5.76	−14.46	14.3	10.39	7	4	07	0.320960	Oldham
144169	152858	−4.88	−4.48	17.9	12.30	7	5	08	0.328042	Rochdale
246541	254141	10.15	−1.37	13.7	19.04	7	4	07	0.469987	Stockport
186922	192133	1.13	−4.48	14.2	16.62	7	5	08	0.416519	Warrington
126098	126836	0.92	−0.33	14.0	10.92	8	5	08	0.391613	Ashington
51056	48472	6.17	−33.60	24.5	11.08	8	5	08	0.137106	Consett
81636	85639	26.43	−1.55	12.4	12.00	8	5	08	0.488977	Durham
953132	944714	3.51	−11.42	16.5	8.45	8	2	02	0.309332	Newcastle
36571	37347	9.00	−3.70	10.5	17.88	8	6	19	0.498977	Hexham
177088	160394	−2.53	−15.09	23.2	6.83	8	4	07	0.154688	South Shields
307994	335681	25.45	11.47	7.3	15.83	10	4	11	0.633872	Aberdeen
46880	54899	21.62	−4.96	12.3	13.18	10	6	19	0.503925	Peterhead
39760	40437	8.51	2.13	11.7	16.12	10	6	19	0.485425	Banff
150886	154003	6.09	−13.00	18.7	10.03	8	5	17	0.294235	Bishop Auckland
56594	58802	15.67	9.89	7.6	19.03	1	5	14	0.609324	Andover
49600	51920	−3.66	−7.90	17.8	11.98	10	5	17	0.317331	Alloa
153701	152645	6.05	−3.32	16.6	12.42	10	5	16	0.362331	Ayr
41693	42832	9.51	−1.23	17.8	14.81	10	6	19	0.381094	Stranraer
79090	85968	9.04	−0.30	12.4	19.91	1	5	14	0.508011	Ashford
99106	110786	16.63	−7.40	16.1	17.64	3	5	12	0.443049	St Austell
42025	47595	22.48	9.10	13.2	20.28	3	6	18	0.568357	Truro
58968	63520	2.78	−10.75	20.6	17.42	3	6	18	0.322359	Falmouth
50917	57065	7.70	−12.47	18.8	14.52	3	6	18	0.348171	Redruth
46682	49868	11.62	−5.54	22.5	12.48	3	6	18	0.298293	Penzance
92771	107725	24.56	−0.11	6.6	24.22	1	5	13	0.675256	Aylesbury
373352	358159	−0.21	−10.14	15.3	9.83	6	4	11	0.323323	Bradford
150089	168315	15.69	−0.52	9.0	20.85	1	5	13	0.587541	Bedford
117784	117417	−1.54	−1.10	10.4	12.07	8	5	16	0.442241	Barrow
441110	477751	12.59	0.05	12.6	19.80	3	4	10	0.512806	Bournemouth
66577	78550	25.13	3.24	11.9	21.49	1	5	14	0.594919	Banbury
83592	91646	7.02	−2.83	17.4	16.16	5	5	12	0.400334	Boston
70493	79564	16.07	6.09	14.5	17.48	3	5	12	0.506920	Barnstaple
36101	38731	12.82	−7.12	16.7	17.12	3	6	18	0.412445	Bideford
73522	80333	8.64	−4.96	13.6	19.51	3	5	13	0.474217	Bridgwater
96592	94078	0.32	−10.90	12.7	9.28	7	5	15	0.361208	Burnley
133649	134475	0.39	−5.06	11.6	14.67	8	5	16	0.435125	Carlisle
40024	42223	7.82	0.34	10.5	21.14	8	6	19	0.535567	Penrith
224218	245474	19.59	−0.99	6.6	19.82	2	4	10	0.618994	Cambridge
83821	98940	13.48	−2.50	8.5	21.51	2	4	18	0.601353	Newmarket
57011	71083	5.53	3.00	10.3	22.97	2	6	18	0.595746	Huntingdon
169248	170253	10.74	−8.56	13.6	11.79	5	4	11	0.401954	Chesterfield
55186	59570	10.16	−21.84	10.1	17.28	5	5	17	0.463794	Coalville
106801	123958	7.66	2.85	8.6	18.93	1	5	12	0.581617	Chichester
155471	161748	27.72	4.22	8.7	19.96	3	5	12	0.610784	Cheltenham
61892	70985	15.60	−5.24	20.3	12.84	1	5	12	0.361626	Clacton
192369	218141	15.17	−1.52	11.6	18.02	1	5	13	0.530162	Colchester
58838	61637	4.66	−1.57	9.1	20.98	3	5	14	0.540709	Chippenham
110122	117158	10.94	2.59	13.8	15.72	1	5	12	0.469415	Canterbury
126148	129711	11.56	−7.56	10.1	17.68	7	5	16	0.500034	Crewe

1	2	3	4	5	6	7	8	9	10	LLMA
60874	60810	−5.12	−29.51	16.5	11.70	5	5	14	0.256932	Corby
255135	243285	1.32	−7.35	15.9	10.10	10	4	11	0.326568	Dundee
59711	64267	9.23	−6.25	15.9	11.96	10	6	19	0.387852	Arbroath
315751	313056	4.56	−5.10	11.6	14.14	5	4	11	0.438360	Derby
44537	46196	8.43	−5.04	7.4	20.88	5	6	19	0.561875	Matlock
121832	125983	0.41	−1.61	15.2	11.24	10	5	17	0.377048	Dunfermline
97405	98446	8.17	7.09	12.2	15.70	10	5	15	0.487791	Dumfries
113517	114051	5.85	−9.76	13.8	12.89	8	5	15	0.390204	Darlington
81888	86038	20.08	−7.79	10.8	20.45	6	6	19	0.531109	Northallerton
248363	258610	9.86	−9.93	17.5	9.79	6	4	11	0.333427	Doncaster
49645	51988	1.41	−6.80	19.1	14.15	1	5	13	0.326480	Deal
49394	48963	7.21	−6.47	9.4	11.53	1	5	13	0.457602	Dover
124504	136344	15.82	3.36	9.8	14.99	1	5	12	0.545749	Eastbourne
100982	100978	−10.98	−7.47	19.0	11.27	9	5	17	0.268288	Ebbw Vale
59824	70168	17.58	1.71	8.4	22.27	2	5	13	0.627932	Bury St Edmunds
224813	238492	11.81	5.37	11.7	17.19	3	4	10	0.519302	Exeter
36925	40838	8.88	0.42	12.7	20.76	3	6	18	0.514759	Tiverton
146176	149300	−3.26	−7.30	18.1	10.71	10	5	17	0.302072	Falkirk
82015	86503	8.88	−0.79	16.2	14.99	1	5	12	0.412139	Folkestone
295624	295905	8.40	−3.08	16.3	12.87	7	4	11	0.377645	Blackpool
134889	125200	−3.64	−9.74	19.1	8.57	10	5	16	0.244810	Greenock
58798	63348	8.36	−4.03	15.9	13.70	10	6	19	0.403155	Oban
172869	184627	7.59	−2.08	11.2	19.63	3	5	13	0.511223	Gloucester
49606	55379	21.51	−2.67	12.6	17.24	5	5	14	0.518157	Grantham
213267	218608	6.51	−8.66	16.6	13.21	6	4	11	0.359729	Grimsby
209037	209775	−4.02	−15.83	12.0	12.57	6	4	11	0.373507	Huddersfield
117928	128402	14.61	4.78	9.2	19.69	6	5	15	0.583153	Harrogate
103828	110728	7.07	−3.48	12.3	21.56	4	5	16	0.500798	Hereford
143458	151220	11.33	−4.90	14.1	14.09	1	5	12	0.431625	Hastings
431976	428248	2.69	−7.74	16.6	11.27	6	4	11	0.333924	Hull
51116	56496	18.80	−1.95	16.9	13.13	6	6	19	0.422062	Bridlington
40254	43582	21.95	−18.15	16.1	14.54	6	6	19	0.397141	Goole
195190	191122	1.53	−10.72	12.2	11.75	6	5	17	0.388283	Halifax
243988	258462	10.47	−1.35	9.3	17.20	2	4	10	0.531883	Ipswich
50917	52084	7.34	−2.32	8.9	22.01	2	6	18	0.548497	Woodbridge
109480	116152	8.12	−15.87	23.0	8.73	10	5	17	0.227570	Irvine
54060	61634	30.45	3.69	13.0	14.37	10	5	15	0.540162	Inverness
42536	47301	27.95	19.59	21.1	12.82	10	6	19	0.444238	Stornoway
37505	50244	40.15	12.86	26.4	15.66	10	6	19	0.443249	Dingwall
47284	48741	13.74	−3.51	14.2	14.70	10	6	19	0.438368	Thurso
72496	80920	11.97	3.38	15.0	14.90	10	6	19	0.463177	Elgin
109515	118553	10.64	−3.73	14.4	14.57	1	5	12	0.438331	Isle of Wight
81003	82154	−9.40	−12.54	17.3	10.97	10	5	16	0.283907	Kilmarnock
98894	106703	−1.45	−8.83	14.2	24.35	4	5	16	0.456144	Kidderminster
104335	111904	4.42	−4.98	11.5	14.44	6	5	16	0.460131	Keighley
72382	79324	5.65	−7.25	11.1	16.49	5	5	14	0.480120	Kettering
99770	110247	13.84	1.14	15.2	17.92	2	5	12	0.473828	Kings Lynn
59044	64393	6.54	−0.09	6.3	18.33	8	5	15	0.585084	Kendal
160460	156903	16.73	−9.84	15.6	10.21	10	5	16	0.366535	Kirkcaldy
40269	39937	−17.99	10.04	11.8	14.78	10	6	19	0.430359	St Andrews

1	2	3	4	5	6	7	8	9	10	LLMA
130148	127822	3.59	0.31	15.3	13.52	7	5	15	0.390802	Lancaster
65326	69944	13.07	−15.08	7.8	16.62	5	5	16	0.519050	Loughborough
539196	554158	8.19	−2.48	10.9	15.73	5	4	10	0.483086	Leicester
50018	56040	6.97	5.60	12.0	20.29	5	6	18	0.536383	Melton Mowbray
137296	146670	3.98	−5.36	8.2	22.91	1	5	14	0.557799	Letchworth
76948	75406	0.94	−17.68	14.7	10.55	9	5	17	0.321866	Llanelli
40773	41916	22.17	−8.94	8.4	20.62	9	6	19	0.564429	Carmarthen
39363	43933	0.78	1.22	25.9	22.64	9	6	19	0.314265	Cardigan
91279	100304	11.81	0.12	21.2	18.46	9	6	19	0.378197	Pembroke
41195	45537	−0.95	5.20	23.1	16.20	9	6	19	0.322181	Ammanford
88987	92082	10.99	−1.87	15.3	15.54	9	5	15	0.426238	Llandudno
49837	49492	4.43	−9.28	15.8	19.62	9	6	19	0.396599	Ffestiniog
66035	68017	30.11	−6.48	18.3	17.69	9	6	19	0.425243	Bangor
47224	52189	10.97	−3.58	23.0	18.34	9	6	19	0.339058	Holyhead
197639	210664	10.70	−4.02	13.5	15.88	5	5	13	0.455253	Lincoln
293617	324412	5.24	−8.46	11.3	20.04	1	4	10	0.496203	Luton
68592	74648	4.17	−7.27	15.0	12.44	2	5	12	0.391907	Lowestoft
100340	161335	47.32	22.35	17.4	18.61	1	5	14	0.701789	Milton Keynes
63203	60708	14.65	−20.68	15.1	7.83	9	5	17	0.318682	Merthyr
36074	39417	7.98	−1.78	12.1	20.88	9	6	19	0.512798	Brecon
69733	74873	14.29	3.57	13.3	18.07	3	5	12	0.504257	Newton Abbot
85510	85744	7.73	−13.67	13.4	11.59	7	5	16	0.380764	Nelson & Colne
204998	241908	25.02	−2.33	10.9	17.71	5	4	10	0.570271	Northampton
367451	401828	12.19	−3.80	11.0	17.08	2	4	10	0.510411	Norwich
47069	53852	8.47	−6.81	14.4	19.15	2	6	18	0.465929	Dereham
54026	70446	13.38	−1.74	15.5	17.85	2	6	18	0.504589	Thetford
340844	349708	5.73	−0.27	7.8	20.98	1	4	10	0.561606	Oxford
59323	62728	−17.94	4.36	8.4	22.67	1	6	18	0.527410	Didcot
161428	199180	6.21	8.09	14.9	15.58	2	5	13	0.495783	Peterborough
56862	62040	4.79	−3.03	12.0	19.61	5	6	18	0.494937	Spalding
40268	41304	11.49	−3.54	16.8	19.52	2	6	18	0.422190	Wisbech
50598	54364	7.20	−0.22	12.8	21.45	5	6	18	0.504381	Stamford
94262	95685	6.58	−0.40	10.4	15.09	10	5	15	0.486112	Perth
329749	354502	9.20	−4.82	14.5	13.74	3	4	10	0.423468	Plymouth
40925	46534	14.74	−8.93	15.7	21.30	3	6	18	0.466626	Launceston
51470	53548	−7.52	−15.06	12.9	13.10	7	5	16	0.365618	Rossendale
79962	88836	10.53	−0.19	19.8	17.45	9	5	16	0.391781	Rhyl
74407	77101	16.41	−8.51	13.9	9.94	6	5	15	0.406758	Scarborough
178460	186540	7.97	−22.35	15.1	14.83	6	5	17	0.359696	Scunthorpe
79332	84284	3.63	6.88	9.7	20.66	4	5	16	0.555644	Stafford
75648	84274	9.90	4.10	10.4	17.70	1	5	14	0.545650	Stevenage
239663	262803	10.92	−1.23	10.6	19.61	3	4	10	0.537006	Swindon
419735	440221	9.80	1.77	10.6	18.98	1	4	10	0.528488	Southampton
118042	119779	9.86	−0.66	9.3	19.61	3	5	13	0.536962	Salisbury
300742	274210	−6.16	−11.66	21.5	6.98	8	4	11	0.183884	Sunderland
529892	530972	−1.35	−9.09	12.1	14.96	4	4	11	0.412429	Stoke
35216	35389	2.35	−4.59	9.4	19.42	4	6	19	0.502624	Leek
63355	69950	16.29	−3.43	10.6	23.16	3	5	14	0.566565	Stroud
126685	134135	15.05	−9.36	12.5	20.92	4	5	16	0.493801	Shrewsbury
38863	43639	12.56	0.91	14.1	23.65	9	6	19	0.525436	Welshpool

1	2	3	4	5	6	7	8	9	10	LLMA
42673	44267	11.94	2.40	12.9	18.54	9	6	19	0.495790	Aberystwyth
67610	70959	34.55	5.11	13.4	15.63	10	5	15	0.535163	Stirling
109694	116918	10.51	−5.88	10.4	17.81	3	5	13	0.507379	Taunton
133782	163888	18.78	−9.84	20.9	17.66	4	5	17	0.393709	Telford
114806	121715	5.00	−8.90	18.1	10.96	1	5	12	0.327347	Margate
113106	126921	12.56	1.09	9.3	20.38	3	5	13	0.577666	Trowbridge
153769	164370	7.95	−4.92	19.1	15.28	3	5	12	0.359387	Torquay
138247	152057	5.82	−5.57	11.5	17.50	4	5	16	0.486549	Burton
92848	104706	11.13	−8.73	11.2	16.36	5	5	14	0.493739	Wellingborough
61568	62797	10.60	7.41	13.4	12.17	8	5	17	0.457246	Whitehaven
103947	108480	21.68	−8.53	12.7	14.46	5	5	16	0.466320	Worksop
73113	74697	−0.21	−16.40	15.8	12.57	8	5	16	0.328228	Workington
131226	137830	1.90	−1.13	12.9	23.57	4	5	15	0.494992	Worcester
43755	46234	9.60	2.98	12.7	23.17	4	6	19	0.527449	Malvern
60687	63041	49.16	7.00	4.1	24.14	1	5	12	0.763776	Winchester
158285	166083	8.68	−7.53	16.3	16.91	9	5	17	0.400720	Wrexham
107524	113578	11.81	−4.07	10.2	16.70	3	5	12	0.509871	Weymouth
75633	80810	7.06	−6.60	16.8	12.72	2	5	12	0.371025	Yarmouth
110305	125405	10.54	7.42	8.0	21.05	3	5	13	0.618408	Yeovil
55825	61259	12.38	−4.42	10.2	18.71	3	6	18	0.531737	Chard
240549	257034	4.53	2.36	10.2	14.72	6	4	11	0.502272	York
156519	166561	11.50	−3.38	13.1	18.16	1	5	14	0.478490	Gosport
375360	369012	2.31	5.91	13.2	16.31	1	4	04	0.452849	Portsmouth
101066	117825	8.98	−11.68	13.2	17.78	7	5	09	0.467325	Leyland
220907	223511	1.35	5.43	12.4	15.89	7	4	04	0.465087	Preston
200905	201493	13.59	−6.38	16.9	9.45	6	4	09	0.350937	Barnsley
89957	86386	−17.60	−6.31	23.4	6.82	6	5	09	0.154122	Mexborough
167920	169834	7.70	−9.04	20.4	9.33	6	4	09	0.277967	Rotherham
660496	642449	−1.66	−9.14	14.8	10.64	6	3	03	0.338269	Sheffield
99450	94870	−5.85	−8.36	23.9	9.33	8	5	09	0.182342	Hartlepool
362144	362269	5.95	−16.62	21.4	12.77	8	4	04	0.254869	Middlesbrough
74854	69962	−3.54	−5.08	18.9	7.12	8	5	09	0.254432	Peterlee
177105	186433	8.32	−8.04	18.4	12.93	8	4	09	0.343560	Stockton
513313	496804	−3.45	−14.39	15.0	14.25	4	4	04	0.336352	Coventry
57601	66609	0.31	−2.85	11.1	18.91	5	5	09	0.508443	Hinckley
108441	113409	6.31	1.65	10.2	21.86	4	5	09	0.542628	Leamington
77522	80189	2.80	2.34	12.6	19.34	4	5	09	0.482535	Rugby
68396	67192	−1.28	−12.70	15.8	9.93	9	5	09	0.311615	Neath
111763	108453	−20.91	−7.95	17.8	10.41	9	5	09	0.249228	Port Talbot
251109	247461	16.96	−8.09	16.4	13.85	9	4	04	0.384157	Swansea
369404	358665	−1.50	2.76	12.8	13.29	1	4	04	0.419346	Brighton
169718	181224	17.10	3.64	9.6	15.00	1	4	12	0.546457	Worthing
160279	162180	0.58	−5.70	15.3	12.34	6	5	09	0.365522	Dewsbury
770980	743606	−0.31	−6.39	12.6	12.41	6	3	03	0.391367	Leeds
110882	109276	15.37	−3.20	13.6	9.89	6	5	09	0.412594	Pontefract
199453	212063	11.07	−5.97	13.1	12.05	6	4	09	0.432474	Wakefield
148026	152508	5.85	−2.09	10.0	16.92	3	5	12	0.499946	Bath
53027	54431	8.39	3.30	6.5	23.14	3	6	18	0.611136	Wells
734903	740245	3.09	−3.72	11.1	19.15	3	3	03	0.480446	Bristol
84979	95541	13.03	−1.96	16.2	19.57	3	5	12	0.462225	Weston

WORLD

This dataset contains indicators of economic and social performance of the 128 countries in the world; most of the data is for 1984. The reliability and validity of the data for different countries varies enormously, so not too much reliance should be placed on the figure for any one variable in any one country. The information is drawn from the World Bank reports (e.g. 1986); full explanation of the sources and methods should be sought in these volumes.

Column

1 country group
   1 Asia
   2 Africa
   3 South America
   4 Middle East
   5 Western Europe, North America, Japan and Australasia
   6 State socialist
2 Population in mid-1984 in millions
3 Area (thousands of square kilometres)
4 GNP per capita in 1984 (US dollars)
5 Average annual growth rate (per cent) 1965–84
6 Percentage share of household income of top 10 per cent of households
7 Life expectancy at birth (years) in 1984
8 Infant (0–1 years) mortality rate per thousand live births in 1984
9 Number of people per doctor in 1984
10 Number of people per nurse in 1984
11 Percentage of females enrolled in primary school in 1983; numbers may exceed 100 when pupils enrolled are above or below the country's standard primary school age
12 Percentage of adult population literate in 1980.

The country name is appended at the end of each row.

1	2	3	4	5	6	7	8	9	10	11	12	Country
2	42.2	1222	110	0.4	−1	44	172	88120	5000	34	15	Ethiopia
1	98.1	144	130	0.6	32.0	50	124	9010	19400	55	26	Bangladesh
2	7.3	1240	140	1.1	−1	46	176	25380	2320	18	10	Mali
2	29.7	2345	140	−1.6	−1	51	103	−1	−1	−1	55	Zaire
2	6.6	274	160	1.2	−1	45	146	49280	3070	20	−1	Burkina Faso
1	16.1	141	160	0.2	−1	47	135	30060	33430	43	19	Nepal
1	36.1	677	180	2.3	−1	58	67	4660	4890	−1	66	Burma
2	6.8	118	180	1.7	−1	45	158	52960	2980	52	25	Malawi
2	6.2	1267	190	−1.3	−1	43	142	−1	−1	19	10	Niger
2	21.5	945	210	0.6	−1	52	111	−1	−1	84	79	Tanzania
2	4.6	28	220	1.9	−1	48	120	−1	−1	36	25	Burundi
2	15.0	236	230	2.9	−1	51	110	22180	2000	49	52	Uganda
1	2.9	57	250	0.5	−1	51	98	18550	1640	80	18	Togo
2	2.5	623	260	−0.1	−1	49	138	23090	2120	51	33	Central Afr. Rep.
1	749.2	3288	260	1.6	33.6	56	90	2610	4670	68	36	India
2	9.9	587	260	−1.6	−1	52	110	9940	1090	−1	50	Madagascar
2	5.2	638	260	−1	−1	46	153	15630	2550	15	60	Somalia
2	3.9	113	270	1.0	−1	49	116	16980	1660	43	28	Benin
2	5.8	26	280	2.3	−1	47	128	29150	10260	60	50	Rwanda
6	1029.2	9561	310	4.5	−1	69	36	1730	1670	93	69	China
2	19.6	583	310	2.1	45.8	54	92	7540	990	97	47	Kenya
2	3.7	72	310	0.6	−1	38	176	17670	2110	−1	15	Sierra Leone
3	5.4	28	320	1.0	−1	55	124	−1	−1	64	23	Haiti
2	5.9	246	330	1.1	−1	38	176	−1	−1	23	20	Guinea
2	12.3	239	350	−1.9	−1	53	95	6760	630	70	−1	Ghana
1	15.9	66	360	2.9	28.2	70	37	7620	1260	99	85	Sri Lanka
2	21.3	2506	360	1.2	−1	48	113	9070	1440	42	32	Sudan
1	92.4	804	380	2.5	−1	51	116	3320	5870	33	24	Pakistan
2	6.4	196	380	−0.5	−1	46	138	13060	1990	42	10	Senegal
1	−1	648	−1	−1	−1	−1	−1	−1	−1	−1	20	Afghanistan
1	1.2	47	−1	−1	−1	44	135	18160	7960	17	−1	Bhutan
2	4.9	1284	−1	−1	−1	44	139	−1	−1	21	15	Chad
1	−1	181	−1	−1	−1	−1	−1	−1	−1	−1	−1	Kampuchea
1	3.5	237	−1	−1	−1	45	153	−1	−1	80	44	Laos PDR
2	13.4	802	−1	−1	−1	46	125	33340	5610	68	33	Mozambique
1	60.1	330	−1	−1	−1	65	50	4310	1040	105	87	Vietnam
2	1.7	1031	450	0.3	−1	46	133	−1	−1	29	17	Mauritania
2	2.1	111	470	0.5	−1	50	128	8550	2940	57	25	Liberia
2	6.4	753	470	−1.3	46.3	52	85	7110	1660	89	44	Zambia
2	1.5	30	530	5.9	−1	54	107	−1	−1	126	52	Lesotho
3	6.2	1099	540	0.2	−1	53	118	1950	−1	81	63	Bolivia
1	158.9	1919	540	4.9	34.0	55	97	11320	−1	112	62	Indonesia
4	7.8	195	550	5.9	−1	45	155	7070	3440	21	21	Yemen Arab Rep.
4	2.0	333	550	−1	−1	47	146	7120	820	36	40	Yemen PDR
2	9.9	322	610	0.2	−1	52	106	−1	−1	64	35	Côte dIvoire
1	53.4	300	660	2.6	38.5	63	49	2150	2590	113	75	Philippines
2	21.4	447	670	2.8	−1	59	91	17230	900	61	28	Morocco
3	4.2	112	700	0.5	−1	61	77	−1	−1	100	60	Honduras
3	5.4	21	710	−0.6	29.5	65	66	3220	−1	69	62	El Salvador
1	3.4	462	710	0.6	−1	52	69	16070	960	55	32	Papua New Guinea

1	2	3	4	5	6	7	8	9	10	11	12	Country
2	45.9	1001	720	4.3	33.2	60	94	800	790	76	44	Egypt
2	96.5	924	730	2.8	−1	50	110	10540	2420	−1	34	Nigeria
2	8.1	391	760	1.5	−1	57	77	6650	1000	127	69	Zimbabwe
2	9.9	475	800	2.9	−1	54	92	−1	−1	98	−1	Cameroon
3	3.2	130	860	−1.5	−1	60	70	2290	590	103	90	Nicaragua
1	50.0	514	860	4.2	34.1	64	44	6770	2140	97	86	Thailand
2	1.0	600	960	8.4	−1	58	72	9250	700	102	−1	Botswana
3	6.1	49	970	3.2	−1	64	71	1390	1240	115	67	Dominican Rep.
3	18.2	1285	1000	−0.1	42.9	59	95	−1	−1	112	80	Peru
1	1.0	2	1090	2.7	46.7	66	26	1730	570	112	−1	Mauritius
2	1.8	342	1140	3.7	−1	57	78	−1	−1	−1	−1	Congo
3	9.1	284	1150	3.8	−1	65	67	−1	−1	114	81	Ecuador
3	2.2	11	1150	−0.4	−1	73	20	−1	−1	107	90	Jamaica
3	7.7	109	1160	2.0	−1	60	66	−1	1360	67	−1	Guatemala
5	48.4	781	1160	2.9	40.7	64	86	1500	1240	107	60	Turkey
3	2.5	51	1190	1.6	39.5	73	19	−1	−1	100	90	Costa Rica
3	3.3	407	1240	4.4	−1	66	44	1310	650	99	84	Paraguay
2	7.0	164	1270	4.4	−1	62	79	3620	950	102	62	Tunisia
3	28.4	1139	1390	3.0	−1	65	48	−1	−1	122	81	Colombia
4	3.4	98	1570	4.8	−1	64	50	1170	1170	98	70	Jordan
4	10.1	185	1620	4.5	−1	63	55	2160	1370	96	58	Syrian Arab Rep.
2	9.9	1247	−1	−1	−1	43	144	−1	−1	−1	−1	Angola
3	9.9	115	−1	−1	−1	75	16	600	−1	105	95	Cuba
6	19.9	121	−1	−1	−1	68	28	−1	−1	−1	−1	Korea PDR
4	−1	10	−1	−1	−1	−1	−1	−1	−1	−1	−1	Lebanon
6	1.9	1565	−1	−1	−1	63	50	440	240	107	−1	Mongolia
3	11.8	757	1700	−0.1	−1	70	22	950	−1	110	−1	Chile
3	132.6	8512	1720	4.6	50.6	64	68	1200	1140	99	76	Brazil
5	10.2	92	1970	3.5	33.4	74	19	450	−1	123	78	Portugal
1	15.3	330	1980	4.5	39.8	69	28	3920	1390	98	60	Malaysia
3	2.1	77	1980	2.6	44.2	71	25	1010	−1	101	85	Panama
3	3.0	176	1980	1.8	−1	73	29	510	−1	107	94	Uruguay
3	76.8	1973	2040	2.9	40.6	66	51	1140	−1	117	83	Mexico
1	40.1	98	2110	6.6	27.5	68	28	1440	350	102	93	Korea PDR
6	23.0	256	2120	4.3	22.9	69	28	670	300	101	85	Yugoslavia
3	30.1	2767	2230	0.3	35.2	70	34	−1	−1	107	93	Argentina
2	31.6	1221	2340	1.4	−1	54	79	−1	−1	−1	−1	South Africa
2	21.2	2382	2410	3.6	−1	60	82	−1	−1	82	35	Algeria
3	16.8	912	3410	0.9	35.7	69	38	930	−1	104	82	Venezuela
5	9.9	132	3770	3.8	−1	75	16	390	370	105	−1	Greece
4	4.2	21	5060	2.7	22.6	75	14	400	130	97	−1	Israel
1	5.4	1	6330	6.2	31.3	76	10	1260	800	104	90	Hong Kong
3	1.2	5	7150	2.6	31.8	69	22	1390	390	108	95	Trinidad
1	2.5	1	7260	7.8	−1	72	10	1100	340	111	83	Singapore
4	43.8	1648	−1	−1	−1	61	112	2630	1160	88	50	Iran
4	15.1	435	−1	−1	−1	60	74	1790	2250	99	−1	Iraq
4	1.1	300	6490	6.1	−1	53	110	1680	440	72	−1	Oman
2	3.5	1760	8520	−1.1	−1	59	91	660	360	−1	−1	Libya
4	11.1	2150	10530	5.9	−1	62	61	1800	730	56	25	Saudi Arabia
4	1.7	18	16720	−0.1	−1	72	22	600	180	94	60	Kuwait

1	2	3	4	5	6	7	8	9	10	11	12	Country
4	1.3	84	21920	−1	−1	72	36	720	390	95	56	Un. Arab Emirates
5	38.7	505	4440	2.7	24.5	77	10	360	280	110	−1	Spain
5	3.5	70	4970	2.4	25.1	73	10	780	120	97	98	Ireland
5	57.0	301	6420	2.7	28.1	77	12	750	250	102	98	Italy
5	3.2	269	7730	1.4	28.7	74	12	590	110	101	99	New Zealand
5	56.4	245	8570	1.6	23.4	74	10	680	120	101	99	United Kingdom
5	9.9	31	8610	3.0	21.5	75	11	380	130	97	99	Belgium
5	7.6	84	9140	3.6	−1	73	11	580	170	98	99	Austria
5	14.4	41	9520	2.1	21.5	77	8	480	−1	97	99	Netherlands
5	54.9	547	9760	3.0	30.5	77	9	460	110	107	99	France
5	120.0	372	10630	4.7	22.4	77	6	740	210	100	99	Japan
5	4.9	337	10770	3.3	21.7	75	6	460	100	101	100	Finland
5	61.2	249	11130	2.7	24.0	75	10	420	170	100	99	German Fed. Rep.
5	5.1	43	11170	1.8	22.3	75	8	420	140	101	99	Denmark
5	15.5	7687	11740	1.7	30.5	76	9	500	100	104	100	Australia
5	8.3	450	11860	1.8	28.1	77	7	410	100	99	99	Sweden
5	25.1	9976	13280	2.4	23.8	76	9	510	120	102	99	Canada
5	4.1	324	13940	3.3	22.8	77	8	460	70	99	99	Norway
5	237.0	9363	15390	1.7	23.3	76	11	500	180	100	99	United States
5	6.4	41	16330	1.4	23.7	77	8	390	130	−1	99	Switzerland
6	10.7	93	2100	6.2	20.5	70	19	320	140	101	99	Hungary
6	36.9	313	2100	1.5	−1	71	19	550	−1	100	98	Poland
6	2.9	29	−1	−1	−1	70	43	−1	−1	97	−1	Albania
6	9.0	111	−1	−1	−1	71	17	400	190	100	−1	Bulgaria
6	15.5	128	−1	−1	−1	70	15	350	130	89	−1	Czechoslovakia
6	16.7	108	−1	−1	−1	71	11	490	−1	96	−1	German Dem. Rep.
6	22.7	238	−1	−1	−1	71	25	650	280	99	98	Romania
6	275.0	22402	−1	−1	−1	67	−1	260	−1	−1	100	USSR

Answers to Exercises

Chapter 1

1.1 Below is the stem and leaf display of the income data expressed relative to what those families would get if they claimed long-term supplementary benefit:

leaf unit = 10
0 5 represents 50–59%

```
         0*
   6     0.   567889
  (5)    1*   01112
  10     1.   69
   8     2*   34
   6     2.   77
   4     3*   023
         3.   ⟩
        HI  530
```

We might define 100 as the value of the poverty line: it is, after all, the value which the state views as the subsistence level. The centre of the distribution is above this poverty line, but not by much. Incomes range from around 50 per cent of the poverty line to five times its level. There is a clump of families between 50 and 120, and the rest of the families have incomes substantially higher than this, causing marked upward straggle in the distribution. There is one data value which seems out of line with the rest: the family whose income is five times its entitlement under supplementary benefit.

On the face of it, the state is not managing to provide a safety net of income for all its citizens: there are substantial numbers falling below the minimum. There is one way in which these figures may exaggerate the numbers living in poverty, however. The units here are families as defined for the calculation of welfare entitlement. There are a very large number of single person families (45 per cent), and such families tend to have very low recorded incomes; some of them may live with others who contribute to their upkeep (parents of teenagers, for example).

However, one could argue that setting the poverty line at 100 underestimates poverty, since the level of welfare payments is too low to allow many families to take part in the normal activities of modern British society. Using this as his definition of poverty, Townsend (1979) argues that the line should be set at 40 per cent more than the supplementary benefit entitlement.

1.2   If we subtract 100 from every point in column 3 of figure 1.1, the resulting stem and leaf plot looks like this:

```
              −1*
     1       −0. 5
     6       −0* 32110
    (5)       0* 01112
    10        0. 69
     8        1* 34
     6        1. 77
     4        2* 023


     1       HI  430
```

If you compare this stem and leaf plot with the answer to exercise 1.1, you can see that all that has happened is that the whole stem and leaf plot has been pushed 100 points down the stem scale. Otherwise the spread and shape of the distribution has remained entirely the same. This illustrates an important point which we shall come back to in chapter 3.

1.3   Any answer provided here would be outdated too fast to be worth giving. But I bet you found that people tend to underestimate typical male earnings, often very dramatically. It is always worth remembering, when criticizing the shortcomings or biases of a particular source of statistical data, that it is almost certainly better than just guessing.

1.4   These are the Minitab instructions required to run the job. (You may have to say something rather different on the first line to read the data into Minitab on different computers.) I use the convention of putting the essential parts of the program in capital letters, and the text which helps me remember what I am doing in small letters.

```
READ 'POVERTY' into C1–C4
NOTE   This data is from 1979 GHS, as derived by Dale and colleagues
SAMPLE 21 cases from C1 and put them into C5
STEM and leaf of data in C5
STEM and leaf of data in C3
STOP
```

The shape of the income distribution may differ somewhat from that shown in the chapter because it was based on a different sample; the larger the samples, the less they fluctuate. The distribution of income relative to supplementary benefit shows a sizeable minority of people living on incomes lower than they would be if the family were claiming state benefits.

Chapter 2

2.1 Consider the numbers 3, 6 and 12. The median of these numbers is 6 and the mean is 7. The calculations are laid out in the worksheet below; note the use of the two vertical lines to denote an absolute value, ignoring the sign.

		Residuals from mean		Residuals from median		
Y_i	$\overline{Y}$	$\lvert Y_i - \overline{Y} \rvert$	$(Y_i - \overline{Y})^2$	$M(Y)$	$\lvert Y_i - M(Y) \rvert$	$[Y_i - M(Y)]^2$
3	7	4	16	6	3	9
6	7	1	1	6	0	0
12	7	5	25	6	6	36
Sum 21		10	42		9	45

The sum of absolute residuals from the median is 9 and from the mean is 10, so the median has done better viewed in this way. But the mean has smaller squared residuals, 42 as opposed to 45.

2.2 The following represents a back to back stem and leaf plot of male and female weekly earnings in 1979:

leaf unit = £1
3 9 denotes £39

	Men			Women	
		3	9	1	
		4	02679	6	
3	855	5	048	9	
5	69	6	0378	(4)	
6	8	7	67	7	
9	532	8	07	5	
(2)	94	9	09	3	
9	72	10			
7	5	11	6	1	
6	320	12			
		13			
3	4	14			
2	40	15			

		Men				Women	
M 10.5		96.5				61.5	
Q 5.5	73.5	121	47.5		48	78.5	30.5
X 1.0	55	154			39	116	

The low pay of women compared with men is emphasized in this back to back plot; 8 of the 20 women earn less than any of the men earn. The male median of £96.5 per week is over one and a half times the female median of £61.5 per week. Similarly the spread of the male earnings is also about one and a half times the female spread – £47.5 compared with £30.5. Moreover, this data source underestimates the full spread of earnings because it excludes part-time workers from its published tables; this will exclude many more women than men.

2.3 The worksheet used to calculate the mean and standard deviation is shown below.

Y_i	$(Y_i - \overline{Y})$	$(Y_i - \overline{Y})^2$
150	51.95	2,698.8
55	−43.05	1,853.3
82	−16.05	257.6
107	8.95	80.1
102	3.95	15.6
78	−20.05	402.0
154	55.95	130.4
85	−13.05	170.3
123	24.95	622.5
66	−32.05	1,027.2
58	−40.05	1,604.0
122	23.95	573.6
120	21.95	481.8
83	−15.05	226.5
115	16.95	287.3
69	−29.05	843.9
99	0.95	0.9
94	−4.05	16.4
144	45.95	2,111.4
55	−43.05	1,853.3
Sum 1961		18,256.9

$$\overline{Y} = 1961/20 = 98.05$$

$$s = \quad 18{,}256.9/19 = \sqrt{960.9} = 31.0$$

The mean is higher than the median because male earnings straggle upwards slightly. The fact that the difference between them is not great indicates that the upward straggle is not very marked, which inspection of the stem and leaf display confirms. We would expect the standard deviation to be smaller than the midspread. Here it is £31 compared with a midspread of £47.5.

2.4   The median income of the family units in the 1979 GHS survey can be read off figure 1.6; it is £65 per week. Median male pay in the same survey is given as £84 per week. The estimate from the New Earnings Survey in exercise 2.2 suggested that in the same year median male earnings were £96 per week.

One source of discrepancy between these figures is differences in the population covered. The New Earnings Survey is restricted to full-time adult workers in uninterrupted employment; it excludes part-time workers, the self-employed and home workers, many of whom are very lowly paid. The General Household Survey, on the other hand, covers everyone, whether or not they do paid work, except people living in institutions. The individuals covered by the GHS but excluded from the NES must have lower than average incomes.

A second and probably more significant source of discrepancy is the unit. The difference between £65 per week and £84 per week is that in the first case we are dealing with family units and in the second individual male earners who are currently in employment. The figure of £65 represents income, from whatever source, whereas the other two both relate to earnings from a job.

2.5   Here is the Minitab program I used to calculate various numerical summaries of family income:

```
READ 'POVERTY' C1–C4
NOTE   I can refer to variables by names as well as column numbers
NAME C1 'FAMINC'
AVERAGE gives the arithmetic mean of 'FAMINC'
STDEV gives the standard deviation of 'FAMINC'
MEDIAN does the obvious to 'FAMINC'
DESCRIBE provides some useful summary statistics of 'FAMINC'
NOTE   The DESCRIBE command calculates quartiles by a slightly
#   different formula to the one given in this book
LVALS stands for letter-value display of 'FAMINC'
NOTE   The LVALS command calls Q(uartiles) H(inges)
STOP
```

2.6   The examples in this book are all based on sample data, and sometimes the samples are very small. When we calculate summary statistics such as means and medians from sample data, it is unlikely that such summaries will hit precisely on the true population value. The following program will give you a flavour of how variable you can expect them to be:

```
READ 'HEIGHT' into C1–C9
DESCRIBE C6 to obtain true values of statistics
STORE the following instructions
SAMPLE 5 cases from C6 and put them into C10
AVERAGE C10
MEDIAN C10
END of instructions to be stored
EXECUTE these stored instructions 10 times
STORE
SAMPLE 50 cases from C6 and put them into C10
AVERAGE C10
MEDIAN C10
END
EXECUTE these stored instructions 10 times
STOP
```

Sample statistics can be displayed as a stem and leaf, as with raw data; such displays are called **sampling distributions**.

(a) You probably found that the sampling distributions based on small samples had the same typical value as those based on larger samples (and pretty close to the true value), but that the spread of the former was much wider than the latter. If you went on sampling and calculating summaries an infinite number of times, the sampling distribution of the median for many distributions would have a higher and narrower peak than the mean.

(b) This extension to the program allows you to see how stable the original sample of 200 cases was:

```
STORE the following instructions
SAMPLE 180 cases from C6 and put them into C10
AVERAGE C10
MEDIAN C10
END stored instructions
EXECUTE stored instructions 10 times
```

This technique is part of what is called the **jack-knife** (Mosteller and Tukey 1977, chapter 8); the idea is to see how widely statistics such as means and medians vary when only a small portion of the data has been omitted.

Chapter 3

3.1   There are several ways to express the data to make the British and Italian distributions comparable. The average earnings in each occupational group could be expressed relative to one of the occupational categories in each country in both sexes; this would enable differentials within the sexes to be compared for each country, but would hide comparisons across sexes. The women's earnings could be expressed relative to those of men in similar occupational groups in each country; this would encourage sex comparisons and hide occupational differentials. A solution which would allow both these comparisons to be made at once would be to set all the earnings in one country relative to one sex-specific occupational category – male skilled manual workers, for example; this way of expressing the data makes the story line less clear, however. All the numbers could be expressed in either lire or pounds on the basis of the 1972 exchange rate; this would enable comparisons between the real earning power of British and Italian workers.

These are just four of the possibilities, and there is not the space to document the story that each would tell. In general, the broad ordering of occupational groups is similar; such gross similarities in reward in most industrialized countries have led some social scientists to draw strong conclusions about the functional necessity of the occupations being ordered in this way. But there are also differences in the finer grain: the male distributions are more spread out than the female, the rewards of being a non-manual as opposed to a manual worker in Italy are higher than in Britain, only among British men is there much spread among manual jobs, and so on.

Similar general points can be made about sex differences. Predictably, men earn more than women in both countries. However, rather more surprising perhaps is the fact that the differentials are greater in Britain, where equal pay legislation has been in force longer and where many more women than in Italy are in paid employment. One consideration is that the European survey, on grounds of practicality, excludes employees in establishments employing fewer than ten people. There are many more such establishments in Italy than Britain, and it may be that disproportionately more Italian women work in them, and get relatively lower rewards.

3.2 The scores 51 and 99 are both two standard deviations (2×12) either side of the mean of 75. We learned in the chapter that 95 per cent of cases lie two standard deviations either side of the mean in a Gaussian distribution.

3.3 In this small sample, the median and midspread of the three tests are 24 and 8, 19 and 9, and 17 and 8 respectively. The following worksheet demonstrates the calculation of a composite IQ score; each test score is first standardized by subtracting the median and dividing by the midspread for the test, and the results are summed.

Test scores			Standardized scores			Composite score
1	2	3	1	2	3	4
18	25	23	−0.75	0.67	0.75	0.67
25	16	12	0.12	−0.33	−0.62	−0.83
27	38	31	0.37	2.11	1.75	4.23
1	8	15	−2.87	−1.22	−0.25	−4.34
26	30	20	0.25	1.22	0.37	1.84
19	19	12	−0.62	0.00	−0.62	−1.24
26	16	15	0.25	−0.33	−0.25	−0.33
24	24	24	0.00	0.56	0.87	1.43
16	11	17	−1.00	−0.89	0.00	−1.89

The composite score is much more spread out than the individual scores; if we wish to preserve a scale with a midspread of 1, the component scores could be rescaled. Doubts have been expressed about the reliability and validity of Goodenough's draw-a-man test; by combining it with other test procedures, the aim is that the resulting IQ score will more faithfully reflect each child's underlying abilities (this will be discussed again in exercise 10.3). We now have one single scale of IQ which we might use to predict a child's performance in state examinations, for example.

3.4 The following program will create a standardized score for the two indicators of attainment in columns 8 and 9. (I used a program like this to standardize the scales on which to plot figure 6.1.)

```
READ 'EDUCATE' into C1–C10
NOTE   First examine the distribution of the raw scores
DESCRIBE C8 and C9
NOTE   Now create the standardized scores and sum
LET C11 = (C8 – AVER(C8))/(STDEV (C8))
LET C12 = (C9 – AVER(C9))/(STDEV (C9))
LET C13 = C11 + C12
DESCRIBE C11–C13
STEM and leaf plot of the composite score in C13
STOP
```

The mean of the composite score is still zero, like its component parts, but the standard deviation is almost double that of the components.

3.5 The following program first creates two hundred random numbers with a Gaussian shape and a mean of 0 and a standard deviation of 1, and then repeats the exercise of doubling values and logging them, as in exercise 3.2:

```
NOTE   The Minitab instruction Noprint stops printing of numbers
NOPRINT
NRAN 200 observations with mean 0 and stand. dev. of 1 into C1
STEM C1
NRAN 200 observations with mean 100 and s 15 into C2
LET C3 = C2 * 2
LET C4 = LOGT (C2)
LET C5 = LOGT (C3)
DESCRIBE C2–C5
STOP
```

3.6 If you had gone on and on drawing samples, the sampling distribution of the means would have become more and more Gaussian in shape. For many empirical distributions, the sampling distribution of the median has a higher, narrower peak.

Chapter 4

4.1 The data for this exercise draws attention to how different the rate of inflation in the main groups has been since January 1974; price inflation in fuel has been double that in household durables, for example. The worksheet for calculating the overall movement in the RPI for the first five months of 1986 using the simple weighted average formula is given below.

	Weight w	Price Jan.	Price May	Price relative R	Rw
Food	185	341	349	102	18,870
Alcohol	82	424	429	101	8,282
Tobacco	40	546	594	109	4,360
Housing	153	464	483	104	15,912
Fuel and light	62	507	504	99	6,138
Household durables	63	265	269	102	6,426
Clothing	75	225	228	101	7,575
Transport	157	393	384	98	15,386
Miscellaneous goods	81	403	408	101	8,181
Services	58	393	400	102	5,916
Meals out	44	427	436	102	4,488
Total	1000				101,534

Index number = 101,534/1000 = 101.5

We can therefore say that the cost of a basket of typical goods being bought in 1985 had increased by 1.5 per cent in the first five months of 1986. You might be tempted to multiply this up to an annual inflation rate of 3.7 per cent, but this is not a very safe procedure; the rate of inflation can vary considerably over a few months.

Saying that 'the' cost of living went up 1.5 per cent is more problematic. Not everyone buys goods in these average quantities; families who do not smoke, for example, will have experienced lower inflation in this period.

Furthermore, the very phrase 'cost of living' implies the cost of a standard of living of fixed quality, an even more problematic idea. The RPI is a chained Laspeyres index; thus if, as goods become more expensive, fewer people buy them, their weight in the index drops (after a year's delay). But there is no reason to assume that people substitute things that give them equal satisfaction. The cost of living of someone who has substituted lamb for beef may be constant as measured by the RPI while the subjectively perceived standard of living has dropped. The committee which has administrative responsibility for overseeing the RPI changed its name from the Cost of Living Advisory Committee to the RPI Advisory Committee precisely in order to avoid implying that the RPI makes direct claims about the cost of a fixed standard of living.

4.2 It is hard to define a unit of housing consumption; if everyone rented, then a week's rent could be the unit, but some people borrow money to buy their property, others own outright and only pay rates, while still others occupy housing rent-free through their jobs. The imputed rental value of all property was originally calculated and monitored for the RPI; the calculation was very artificial, however, especially as owning became the most popular form of tenure. Moreover, the simplicity of using rental values became complicated as various rent subsidies were introduced.

Calculating the costs of owner-occupation is particularly hard. Some argue that people who borrow on a mortgage are indulging in a form of saving, and their costs should not feature in an index which measures the costs of current consumption. While this is in part arguable, if people live in the house they are buying they are clearly *consuming* something as well. But should the costs of repaying capital be included as well as interest? Should mortgage costs be taken before or after tax relief?

There are, furthermore, two major problems with assessing the cost of house purchase. The first is the timing problem: the housing costs of a couple who bought their house on a mortgage ten years ago are not affected by price rises since then. (This is a problem with all large consumer durables, such as cars, but is at its most acute with housing.) The second is the quality problem: prices and rents sometimes go up because a property has been improved, whereas the RPI is trying to get at the price increases in goods of fixed quality. These problems both imply that current purchase costs are a poor guide to consumption standards.

At present, the three main elements included in the RPI housing costs are rental values, owner-occupiers' mortgage interest payments and rates. All are taken net of tax relief and subsidies. Readers interested in pursuing this topic should read DE RPI Advisory Committee (1986) and Fry and Pashardes (1986) for a defence and an attack respectively on the current methods of calculating housing costs.

4.3   To continue the series after 1974 on the old base, every number is just multiplied by 191.8 and divided by 100.

	16 January 1962 = 100		
1962	101.6	1974	208.1
1963	103.6	1975	258.5
1964	107.0	1976	301.3
1965	112.1	1977	349.1
1966	116.5	1978	378.0
1967	119.4	1979	428.7
1968	125.0	1980	505.8
1969	131.8	1981	565.8
1970	140.2	1982	614.5
1971	153.4	1983	642.7
1972	164.3	1984	674.8
1973	179.4	1985	715.8

The interpretation is unaffected, since no meaning is attached to the absolute value of an index. Since 1947 when the series started, the index has been rebased whenever it approached 200, in the belief that three varying digits conveyed an appropriate degree of precision. This happened in 1952, 1956, 1962 and 1974; as inflation gathered speed in the 1970s, the index was left alone for longer periods, but it was once more rebased in January 1987.

4.4   The Minitab program for the job is as follows:


```
READ 'ECONOMY' into C1–C11
CODE (−1) to '*' in C9 and replace in C9
NOTE   Reset the RPI so that the index month is December 1985
LET C11 = C11/378.9
LET C12 = C9/C11
NOTE   The incomes are now expressed in 1985 pounds
PRINT month C1, RPI C11, money incomes C9 and real incomes C12
NOTE   Plotting the result is useful; it is discussed more fully
#   in chapter 10, but you can get an idea of what this does:
GENERATE the integers from 1 to 108 in C13
PLOT C12 against these generated numbers in C13
NOTE Smooth off rough edges using techniques from chapter 9
RSMOOTH C12, discard rough in C14 put smooth in C12
PLOT C12 versus C13 once more
STOP
```


Real incomes rose at the end of the 1970s and fell back somewhat at the beginning of the 1980s.

Chapter 5

5.1   The worksheet for calculating cumulative income shares, and the resulting Lorenz curves are shown. The totals do not cumulate to exactly 100 per cent because of rounding error.

Percentage of income units	Percentage of total income	
	USSR	UK
100	99	101
90	78	73
80	64	58
60	42	34
40	24	17
20	10	6

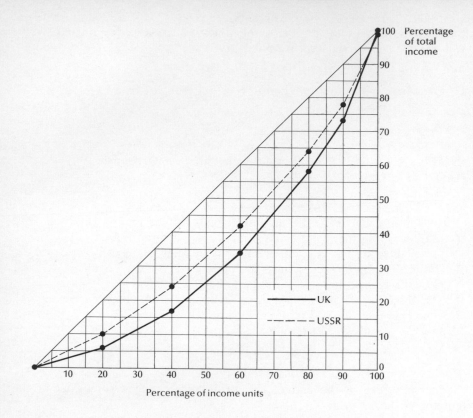

On the face of it it seems that there is less inequality in the USSR than in the UK. However, the two datasets are not completely comparable. The farm population is ignored in the USSR data, a factor that will certainly underestimate the degree of inequality. However, the unit in the USSR data is the individual; this will overestimate the amount of inequality in the USSR compared with in the UK, since individual inequality is almost certainly greater than inequality based on larger units. Both surveys stem from sources which have difficulty recording the incomes of the very lowest quantile groups, but the bias may not be so large in the UK data where the FES sample is not based on employment records.

5.2 People who are widowed or divorced for part of the tax year, new entrants to the workforce, people who die during the year, and emigrants and immigrants only have an income for part of the tax year. There were 1.8 million part-year incomes in 1978–9, comprising 6 per cent of all tax units. The effect of including them with whole-year incomes is to increase the degree of measured inequality in the distribution, so the Gini coefficient will fall if they are excluded; in fact it falls from 37.5 per cent to 35.5 per cent (*Economic Trends* February 1981: 86). The quantile group most affected is the bottom decile.

5.3 The Minitab program to display the decile shares is very simple:

```
READ 'WORLD' into C1–C6
CODE (−1) to '*' in C6 and replace in C6
STEM and leaf display of C6
STOP
```

The information is available for one-third of countries. The top 10 per cent of households get 20 per cent of the income in Hungary (the lowest) and 50 per cent in Brazil (the highest).

5.4   This program will calculate a Gini coefficient of column 1:

```
READ 'POVERTY' only read the first column C1
ORDER the values in C1 and put them back in C1
AVERAGE of C1 and put it in K1
GENERATE the first 50 integers and put them in C2
LET C3 = C2 * C1
PRINT C1–C3 to see the interim calculations
LET K2 = SUM (C3)
LET K3 = (2/(K1 * 50**2)) * K2 − 51/50
PRINT K3, the Gini coefficient
STOP
```

The answer is 0.362.

Chapter 6

6.1   If there were no difference in unemployment between the different regions, all the regional medians would be the same as one another and the overall national median, so the variation in the residuals would be as large as the variation in the original values, 5.0 per cent. If, however, the unemployment level in a particular area could be predicted accurately from its region, then all the areas within one region would have the same unemployment rate and there would be no spread around the region medians; all the variation would stem from the fact that the regional medians differed. The residuals from the regional fit would therefore all be zero.

The result of fitting a model to data based on an explanatory variable is usually somewhere between these two extremes. The proportional reduction in variation in the residual batch as compared with the original batch measures the strength of the effect of the explanatory variable on the response variable. It will be bounded by 0 at one extreme and 1 at the other.

6.2   The calculations for and display of the boxplots of the social standing of the occupations in different social classes are as shown.

	I	II	IIIN	IIIM	IV	V
Lower adjacent value	62	52	30	27	17	18
Lower quartile	70	55	36	37	32	28
Median	74	64	51.5	42	35	30
Upper quartile	76	66	61.5	49	53	40
Upper adjacent value	82	71	67	66	61	52

| Outliers | | 30 | | | | |

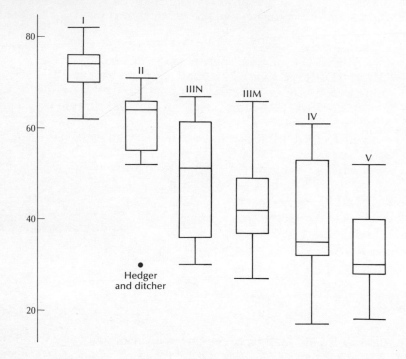

The typical social status of occupations in different classes descend in the way one would expect. However, if social class divided the occupational ladder up purely on the basis of social standing, one would expect to find little variation in status within classes, and little or no overlap between classes. While classes I, II and V cluster relatively tightly, the standing of jobs in the middle classes varies much more. The overlap between the classes is so marked that the class allocation of the occupations of one-third of the population would have to be changed in order to remove it, and social class IIIN would disappear altogether (Bland 1979).

There is one outlier, self-employed hedgers and ditch-cutters. Hedgers were allocated to class II in the 1971 classification, but those designing the 1981 classification agreed with the judgement of this analysis that they were in the wrong class; of all the jobs presented in this exercise, this one alone was reallocated in 1981.

6.3 This Minitab job will display employment change in the two periods:

```
READ 'TOWNS' C1–C10
BOXPLOT of C3 overall first
BOXPLOT of C3 within categories of C7
BOXPLOT of C4
BOXPLOT of C4 within categories of C7
STOP
```

There are more outliers and even far outliers in both of these distributions than there were in the distribution of unemployment; perhaps the labour force does indeed equalize conditions in local labour markets to some extent by moving. To find out which the overall outliers are you could SORT, LVALS and PRINT the growth rate column; having established the values of the outliers, you would have to look through the TOWNS dataset until you identified them. To find out the regional outliers you would have to COPY the column first and only USE one category of region at a time, then SORT, LVALS and PRINT – very cumbersome.

Chapter 7

7.1 The completed table looks like this:

Husband's class	Wife's class						
	I	II	IIIN	IIIM	IV	V	Total
I	0	0	5	0	2	0	7
II	0	5	16	2	4	1	28
IIIN	0	1	17	3	7	2	30
IIIM	1	4	24	6	23	6	64
IV	0	2	3	1	5	3	14
V	0	0	1	0	2	0	3
Total	1	12	66	12	43	12	146

Missing cases = 54

In only 33 out of the total 146 valid cases does the wife do a job categorized in the same social class as the husband; in 74 cases the husband's class is 'higher' than the wife's, and in 39 cases it is 'lower'. One cannot assume that wives work in the same types of jobs as their husbands.

However, the rationale for indexing the class of family members by the class of the male head of household is not based on that assumption. The argument is that consequences of the social placement of the household head may be more significant for other family members than those of their own job (Goldthorpe 1983); we shall look at some evidence in chapter 15 which suggests that this may be true of relative risk of death. The high proportion of missing values for wives' jobs certainly suggests that women's involvement in the labour market is more intermittent than men's. However, the wife's job (or lack of it) may contribute important further information about the family's likely lifestyle which should not be thrown away prematurely on the grounds of a precarious assumption. Dale et al. (1985) discuss some of these issues and propose an improved method for classifying women's social position.

7.2   Fiegehan et al. argue that policy-makers concerned with understanding and alleviating poverty should look at explanatory factors such as household size from two points of view: to what extent do they identify differential risks of poverty and to what extent do they account for the total numbers who are poor? In this case, risk is calculated from the row percentages and accountability from the column percentages:

Number in household	Risk of poverty	Accountability for poverty
1	20.7	50.8
2	6.4	29.0
3	3.3	8.8
4	1.6	4.1
5	2.7	3.1
6 or more	6.1	4.1

Policy-makers should, it is argued, concentrate resources on groups which have both high risk of and high accountability for poverty. Single person households constitute a prime example of such a group; they have more than a one in five risk of being poor, and constitute over half of the poor.

7.3   The following Minitab program calculates both inflow and outflow percentages for a collapsed three-class mobility table:

```
READ 'EDUCATE' into C1–C10
CODE (−1) to '*' in C2 and C10 and replace in C2 and C10
CODE (2) to 1 (4) to 3 and (6,7) to 5 in C2 and C10 into C2 and C10
NAME C2 'PACLASS'
NAME C10 'SONCLASS'
NOTE that subcommands must be preceded by ; and end with/.
TABLE C2 BY C10;
ROWPERCENTS;
COLPERCENTS.
STOP
```

7.4   This Minitab program constructs the table used in exercise 7.1 with a different random ten cases excluded:

```
READ 'CLASS' into C1–C22
CODE (−1) to '*' in C5 and C22 and replace in C5 and C22
SAMPLE 190 rows from C5 and C22 and replace in C23 and C24
TABLE C23 by C24
STOP
```

The principal results are not likely to be very different from the original table. Dropping a random subset of cases to see how much it affects the stability of one's results ('jack-knifing', as illustrated in exercise 2.6 (b)), is one approach to the problem of inferring how likely the patterns observed in the data are to have arisen from a fluke of the particular sample drawn (Mosteller and Tukey 1977: 133–63). Another approach is to construct a table of the frequencies one would expect if there was no relationship at all between husband's and wife's class and to compare this table with the table one actually obtained, calculating a statistic known as chi-square (Gilbert 1981).

Chapter 8

8.1   It is always hard to decide whether it is party identification which makes people take up particular political positions, or adherence to particular political positions which influences which party people vote for. Unless we believe that this is the kind of political issue which is capable of causing people to change parties, we shall usually prefer the former idea of the direction of causality, and run the proportions within categories of party identification.

	Proportion believing more should be spent on			
	(1) welfare state		(2) law and order	
Loyal Conservative	0.190	(N=248)	0.431	(N=248)
Conservative defectors	0.563	(N=142)	0.254	(N=142)
Loyal Labour	0.641	(N=306)	0.160	(N=306)

These proportions can be cast in the form of two causal path models as shown.

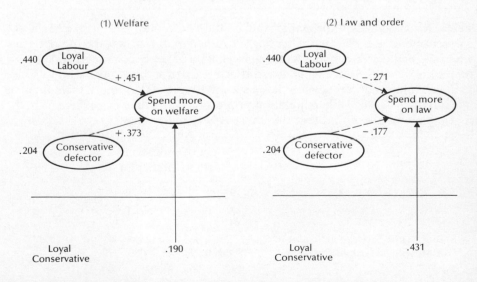

The calculations can be checked by verifying that they produce the correct proportions endorsing higher spending levels for both items:

Proportion wanting more spending on welfare
$$= (0.440 \times 0.451) + (0.204 \times 0.373) + 0.190 = 0.464$$
Proportion wanting more spending on law/order
$$= (0.440 \times -0.271) + (0.204 \times -0.177) + 0.431 = 0.277$$

In both items, the Conservative defectors are different from those loyal to the Conservative Party, but less different than Labour voters. Attitudes towards wanting more spent on welfare are more strongly differentiated by party than are attitudes towards spending on law and order (the effects are stronger).

8.2   Running the proportions in both directions yields the following tables:

	Age of mother at birth of first child		
	Below 20	20 or above	
Parents with history of child abuse	0.76	0.37	$d = +0.39$
Parents with no such history	0.24	0.63	
Total	1.00	1.00	
	(N=33)	(N=67)	

	Age of mother at birth of first child		
	Below 20	20 or above	Total
Parents with history of child abuse	0.50	0.50	1.00 (N=50)
Parents with no such history	0.16	0.84	1.00 (N=50)
$d = +0.34$			

The statistic d takes a different value in the two tables. The first table is the correct one to use when investigating a causal hypothesis that the mother's age when she has her first child affects the likelihood of her becoming a child abuser; the causal hypothesis that child abuse affects the age of the mother is impossible.

If we multiply all frequencies in the second row by 500 to return the marginals to something like feasible population proportions, and then calculate d as in the first table above, we find that the effect is very much smaller.

	Age of mother at birth of first child				
	Below 20		20 or above		
	N	Prop.	N	Prop.	
Parents with history of child abuse	25	0.006	25	0.001	$d = +0.005$
Parents with no such history	4000	0.994	21,000	0.999	
Total	4025	1.000	21,025	1.000	

It is dangerous to calculate the predictive power of an explanatory variable on data where the marginals on the response variable have been artificially constrained by the research design. If, on the basis of this data, social workers were told to watch all young mothers, they would be harbouring suspicions about a group the overwhelming majority of whom are probably loving and devoted mums.

8.3 Since we are interested in the things that cause depression, we look within the categories of provoking agents; among the vulnerable, for example, two of the 62 people (0.032) who had not experienced a provoking agent became depressed. For the same group, the odds of being depressed were 2/60, which, when logged, gives −1.48.

	Vulnerable		Not vulnerable	
	Proportion depressed	Log odds of depression	Proportion depressed	Log odds of depression
Provoking agent absent	0.032	−1.48	0.010	−1.98
Provoking agent present	0.316	−0.34	0.102	−0.94
Difference	+0.284	+1.14	+0.092	+1.04

The difference of proportions seems to bear out Brown and Harris's thesis: among vulnerable women, having a provoking agent has a much larger effect (+0.284) than among non-vulnerable women (+0.092). However, the differences in the log odds suggests that the effect in both vulnerable and non-vulnerable conditions would be seen to be approximately the same (+1.14 among vulnerable and +1.04 among non-vulnerable). There has been a fierce debate in the psychological literature about which conclusion is correct.

8.4 The following Minitab program illustrates that the explanatory variable can be placed in either rows or columns; most data analysts adopt a personal convention about which to select.

```
READ 'HEIGHT' into C1–C9
CODE (−1) to '*' in C2 and C9 and replace in C2 and C9
TABLE C2 by C9;
ROWPERCENTS.
TABLE C9 by C2;
COLPERCENTS.
STOP
```

The resulting table shows a marked class effect on smoking; manual workers, especially unskilled manual workers, are much more likely smoke than non-manual workers.

Chapter 9

9.1　The worksheet for smoothing negative perceptions of household finances in the past is shown in the accompanying table. The smooth has been reroughed by performing the calculations twice, first on the raw data and then on the roughs from the first smooth.

	First smooth						Second smooth				Result
1	2	3	4	5	6	6	7	8	9	10	5 + 10
Data	Medians	3R	Skip	3RH	Resid.	Data	Medians	3R	Skip	3RH	3RH twice
38	38	38	38.0	38.0	0.0	0.0	0.0	0.0	0.0	0.0	38.0
37	**38**	38	38.5	**38.2**	−1.2	−1.2	**0.0**	0.0	0.0	0.0	**38.2**
42	**39**	39	38.5	**38.7**	3.3	3.3	**0.0**	0.0	0.0	0.0	38.7
39	39	39	39.0	39.0	0.0	0.0	0.0	0.0	0.0	0.0	39.0
39	39	39	40.0	**39.5**	−0.5	−0.5	**0.0**	0.0	0.0	0.0	39.5
41	41	41	41.0	41.0	0.0	0.0	0.0	0.0	0.0	0.0	41.0
43	43	43	42.0	**42.5**	0.5	0.5	0.5	0.5	0.2	**0.3**	**42.8**
43	43	43	41.5	**42.2**	0.8	0.8	**0.5**	0.5	0.5	0.5	**42.7**
39	**40**	40	41.0	**40.5**	−1.5	−1.5	0.8	0.5	0.3	**0.4**	**40.9**
40	**39**	39	39.0	39.0	1.0	1.0	−0.2	−0.2	0.3	0.0	39.0
38	38	38	38.5	**38.2**	−0.2	−0.2	−0.2	−0.2	−0.2	−0.2	**38.0**
37	**38**	38	39.5	**38.7**	−1.7	−1.7	−0.2	−0.2	0.0	−0.1	**38.6**
41	41	41	40.5	**40.7**	0.3	0.3	0.3	0.3	0.0	**0.1**	**40.8**
45	**43**	43	42.0	**42.5**	2.5	2.5	**0.3**	0.3	0.3	0.3	**42.8**
43	**44**	43	43.0	43.0	0.0	0.0	**1.0**	0.3	0.1	**0.2**	**43.2**
44	**43**	43	43.0	43.0	1.0	1.0	**0.0**	0.0	0.1	0.0	43.0
43	43	43	43.0	43.0	0.0	0.0	0.0	0.0	0.1	0.0	43.0
43	43	43	43.0	43.0	0.0	0.0	0.0	0.0	0.0	0.0	43.0
41	**43**	43	42.0	**42.5**	−1.5	−1.5	**0.0**	0.0	0.0	0.0	42.5
44	**41**	41	40.5	**40.7**	3.3	3.3	−0.2	**0.0**	0.0	0.0	40.7
38	38	38	38.5	**38.2**	−0.2	−0.2	**0.0**	0.0	0.0	0.0	38.2
36	36	36	36.0	36.0	0.0	0.0	0.0	0.0	0.0	0.0	36.0

end value smoothing of column 5:

$$t_0 = 3z_2 - 2z_3 = 3(38.2) - 2(38.7) = 37.2$$
$$y_1 = \text{median}\,(37.2, 38.0, 38.2) = 38.0\ (\text{no change})$$
$$t_{N+1} = 3(38.2) - 2(40.7) = 33.2$$
$$y_N = \text{median}\,(33.2, 36.0, 38.2) = 36.0\ (\text{no change})$$

If the result is plotted on the same scale as figure 9.10 (not shown here), it is clear that people's perceptions of their household finances are more stable than are their perceptions of the economy. If the scale is magnified by running the Y-axis from 38 to 43, relative high points of pessimism stand out in the summer of 1984 and in the spring of 1985. The resulting curve does not look strikingly like the curve of perceptions of the economy in figure 9.10. However, over a longer period in the dataset ECONOMY, closer correspondence between the variables relating to the household and those relating to the economy in general can be found. Interested readers could see if changes in perceptions of household finances come before or after changes in perceptions of general economic fortunes (experiment with the Minitab LAG command).

9.2　Experience suggests that smoothing datasets with unequal time intervals as if the intervals were equal often produces satisfactory results. The plot of both

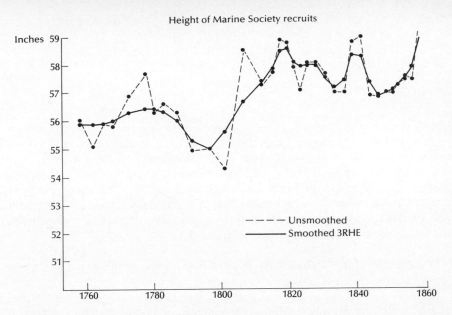

Height of Marine Society recruits

the raw data and a 3RHE smooth are shown, plotted on the midpoints of the time interval.

The years refer to when the recruits were born. Floud argues that height reflects net nutritional status (balance between inputs and outputs) throughout the whole growing period from conception to maturity. We must therefore remember that the height of recruits born in, say, 1758, reflects the standard of living between 1757 and 1773.

From a mideighteenth century level of around 56 inches, the height of Marine Society recruits declined at the end of the eighteenth century, and then climbed very steeply to almost 59 inches. However, heights (and by implication living standards) did not remain so high in these years of early industrialism; they underwent further periods of decline in the early nineteenth century, before setting off on an upward trajectory at midcentury. The sharpness of the increase around 1800 is rather suspicious, and researchers might want to investigate whether the rules of recruitment to the Society changed; if they did, the time series should be smoothed in two halves, before and after the 1800 cohort.

9.3   Here is the Minitab job I ran on this exercise:

```
READ 'SCOTLAND' into columns C1–C8
MPLOT C6 versus C1 and C2 versus C1
NOTE   The subcommand for RSMOOTH changes the default recipe;
#   it performs running medians of three, splitting and hanning.
#   Splitting is explained by Velleman and Hoaglin (1981: 177–8)
RSMOOTH C2 put the rough in C9 and replace the smooth in C2;
SMOOTH 3RSSH.
RSMOOTH C6 put the rough in C10 and replace the smooth in C6;
SMOOTH 3RSSH.
MPLOT C6 versus C1 and C2 versus C1
```

```
LET C11 = C6/C2
NOTE   C11 now shows how much greater the risk of stillbirth is
#   in class V than in class I
RSMOOTH C11 put the rough in C12 and the smooth in C13;
SMOOTH 3RSSH.
PLOT C13 versus C1
STOP
```

Stillbirth rates declined sharply over this period. When class V rates and class I rates are plotted on the same scale, they appear to be converging over time. But the relative difference between them is not declining, as the ratio of V to I shows; instead, class V stillbirths undulate between being one and half times as big as the class I number and two and a half times as big. One interpretation of this might be that improvements occur first in social class I, then class V catches up, then class I moves ahead again, and so on. However, temper any conclusions you draw from this by the results of exercise 9.4.

9.4   When smoothing completely random data, a patterned curve sometimes appears; you probably found this happened if you said:

```
STORE the following Minitab commands
IRAN 50 integers between 150 and 250 and put them in C1
RSMOOTH C1 discard the rough in C2 and replace smooths in C1
GENERATE the integers from 1 to 50 in C3
PLOT C1 versus C3
END of stored commands
EXECUTE stored commands 5 times
STOP
```

Such artefactual results do not invalidate the procedure as a way of distinguishing general from unique when there is a real pattern there. They draw attention to the fact that the technique will always produce a smooth answer; whether it is a sensible answer is still a matter of judgement. It is always best to test any hypothesis by more than one method; in the class differential example, we could try repeating the procedure with neo-natal mortality to see if we got substantially the same results.

Chapter 10

10.1   If the absolute level of wealth determines how happy individuals are, then we would expect people living in wealthier countries to be happier than those living in poorer ones. The plot of these variables suggests that the relationship is, at best, very weak. Our attention is drawn to the Dominican Republic which seems to have an exceptionally miserable population (so much so that it had to be excluded from the plot) and, to a lesser extent, Cuba, with a relatively happy population.

To calculate a resistant line, the data must be reordered and grouped. The calculations for the first attempt at a resistant line are shown in columns 1–4 of the accompanying table.

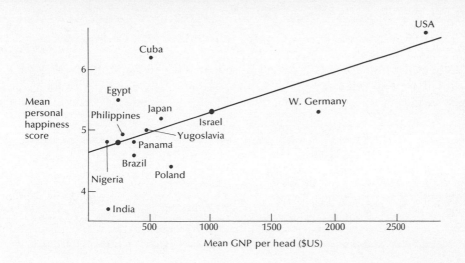

	1	2	3	4	5	6
				First residuals		Second residuals
	X	Y	$\hat{Y}$	Y′	$\hat{Y}′$	
Nigeria	134	4.8	4.73	0.07	4.72	0.08
India	140	3.7	4.74	−1.04	4.73	−1.03
Egypt	225	5.5	4.79	0.71	4.77	0.73
Philippines	282	4.9	4.82	0.08	4.80	0.10
Dominican Republic	313	1.6	4.84	−3.24	4.82	−3.22
Panama	371	4.8	4.88	−0.08	4.85	−0.05
Brazil	375	4.6	4.88	−0.28	4.85	−0.25
Yugoslavia	489	5.0	4.95	0.05	4.91	0.09
Cuba	516	6.4	4.97	1.43	4.93	1.47
Japan	613	5.2	5.03	0.17	4.98	0.22
Poland	702	4.4	5.09	−0.69	5.03	−0.63
Israel	1027	5.3	5.29	0.01	5.21	0.09
West Germany	1860	5.3	5.80	−0.50	5.66	−0.36
United States	2790	6.6	6.38	0.22	6.17	0.43

The initial value of the slope is found from the summary points in columns 1 and 2:

$$\text{Slope} = \frac{Y_R - Y_L}{X_R - X_L} = \frac{5.3 - 4.8}{1027 - 225} = 0.00062$$

and the intercept is the arithmetic mean of estimates for a_R, a_M and a_L (4.66,

4.63 and 4.66 respectively), yielding 4.65. An initial set of fitted values (column 3 of the table) is found from the equation:

Predicted happiness score = 4.65 + 0.00062 × $US GNP per head

To polish the fit, the **first residuals** in column 4 are treated as the new Y data (denoted Y') and summary points are calculated once more. The slope in the first residuals is

$$\text{Slope} = \frac{Y'_R - Y'_L}{X_R - X_L} = \frac{0.01 - 0.07}{1027 - 225} = -0.000075$$

The new estimate of the slope, b'_2, is therefore 0.00062 + (−0.000075), or 0.00054. Without adjusting the intercept, a new set of fitted values can be found for the equation:

Predicted happiness score = 4.65 + 0.00054 × $US GNP per head

These fitted values and **second residuals** are shown in columns 5 and 6 of the table. The process is repeated until the residuals show no evidence of slope. At this point, the intercept can be adjusted.

The variation in the residuals confirms the weakness of the relationship, as it is almost as large as the variation in the original Y values. Yet wealth is a good predictor of individual happiness within each country. It's the old story of social comparisons; rich people in poor countries may be poorer than poor people in rich countries, but they probably do not make that comparison, and so it does not affect their happiness.

10.2 Whatever line you drew representing the equation predicting mortality rates from sickness rates, it will have been different from that predicting sickness from mortality rates. The two variables have different scales – one is sickness per 1000 and the other is mortality per 10,000 – so the effect of a unit change in the mortality rate on sickness is bound to be a very different number from the effect of a unit change in the sickness rate on mortality. Like d, the difference in proportions, the slope of a line is an asymmetric measure of effect.

10.3 This Minitab program uses the Goodenough test as the X variable and the test of non-verbal ability as the Y variable:

```
READ 'EDUCATE' into C1–C10
CODE (−1) to '*' in C4 and C6 and put back in C4 and C6
PLOT C6 versus C4
NOTE   the BRIEF command with RLINE will display iterations of slope
BRIEF 4
RLINE with C6 as y and C4 as x, put residuals into C11
OMIT rows with '*' in C6 and C11 and put back in C6 and C11
LVALS of the original y data in C6
LVALS of the residual Ys in C11
STOP
```

The relationship between the two variables is not very strong; the dQ of the original data is 10 points, and the dQ of the points around the fitted line only reduces to 9. (Compare, for example, the strength of relationship between the test of verbal and non-verbal ability.) The weakness of the relationship supports the critics of the Goodenough draw-a-man test.

Chapter 11

11.1   (a) $\log(1) = 0$
(b) $\log(0)$ is undefined $(-\infty)$
(c) $\log(pqr) = \log(p) + \log(q) + \log(r)$
(d) $\log(p/q) = \log(p) - \log(q)$
(e) $\log(p^n) = n\log(p)$
(f) $\log_{10}(2) = 0.301$
(g) $\log_e(2) = 0.693$

11.2 Suicide is a relatively rare occurrence, so a square root transformation may help.

(a) Native suicide rates

		Raw data					Square roots		
M	8.5		12.5		dQ		3.54		dQ
Q	4.5	7.6	14.9	22.2	14.65	2.76	3.73	4.70	1.94
X	1.0	1.4	20.8	40.3		1.18	3.76	6.35	

(b) Suicide rates among Australian immigrants

		Raw data					Square roots		
M	8.5		30.4		dQ		5.51		dQ
Q	4.5	14.3	25.0	35.8	21.5	3.77	4.87	5.97	2.20
X	1.0	6.8	32.3	57.8		2.61	5.11	7.60	

The native suicide rates do straggle up before transformation; the square root counters the straggle reasonably well. The immigrant rates, perhaps because they are somewhat higher, do not consistently straggle upwards, and so it might appear that the square root transformation is not called for here. However, if we want to analyse this dataset as a whole, the same scale must be used throughout. The square root scale is preferable, since the midspreads of the two batches are more similar.

The distribution of immigrant suicide rates certainly does not cluster closely around the native Australian value or, indeed, around any other single value. In fact, the suicide rate of immigrants to Australia can be predicted fairly well from knowledge of the suicide rate prevailing in their country of origin. It would therefore seem wrong to conclude that coroners' practices explain all international differences in suicide rates.

11.3 Some geographers have suggested that the distribution of town sizes approximates to 'Zipf's law': if towns are ranked in order of size, the population of each town would be the inverse of its rank order: there would be one big metropolis, the next town would be half that size, the next one-third, the next one-quarter and so on. If this law holds in modern Britain, we would expect that taking the negative reciprocals of town sizes would produce a flat distribution.

The following Minitab program investigates several possible transformations to correct the upward straggle in the distribution of town sizes:

```
READ 'TOWNS' into C1–C2
NOTE   Exclude all areas with small populations
COPY C2 back into C2;
USE only values where C2 is in the range 50000:50000000.
STEM C2
LET C3 = SQRT (C2)
LET C4 = LOGT (C2)
LET C5 = −1/(SQRT (C2))
LET C6 = −1/(C2)
NOTE   Multiply C5 and C6 by a constant to make numbers easier to read
LET C5 = C5 * 1000
LET C6 = C6 * 1000000
STEM C6, the distribution which should be flat according to Zipf
LVALS C2
LVALS C3
LVALS C4
LVALS C5
LVALS C6
STOP
```

The distribution is not exactly as predicted by Zipf's law; there are rather more moderately large towns than would be expected.

11.4   This exercise requires a plot of two variables which are very different in magnitude: both the level and the variation in legitimate fertility rates is higher than in the illegitimate rates.

```
READ 'SCOTLAND' into C1–C8
COPY C1 C7 and C8 back into C1 C7 and C8;
OMIT rows where C7 is −1.
RSMOOTH C7 put the rough in C7 and overwrite with smooth in C7
RSMOOTH C8 put the rough in C8 and overwrite with smooth in C8
MPLOT C7 versus C1 and C8 versus C1
LET C9 = LOGT(C7)
LET C10 = LOGT (C8)
MPLOT C9 versus C1 and C10 versus C1
STOP
```

The resolution on Minitab is poor, so the resulting plots are redrawn as shown. When they are both plotted on the same scale (panel (a)), the legitimate rate dominates, and one is easily deceived into thinking that changes in the

Fertility rates in Scotland 1946–85

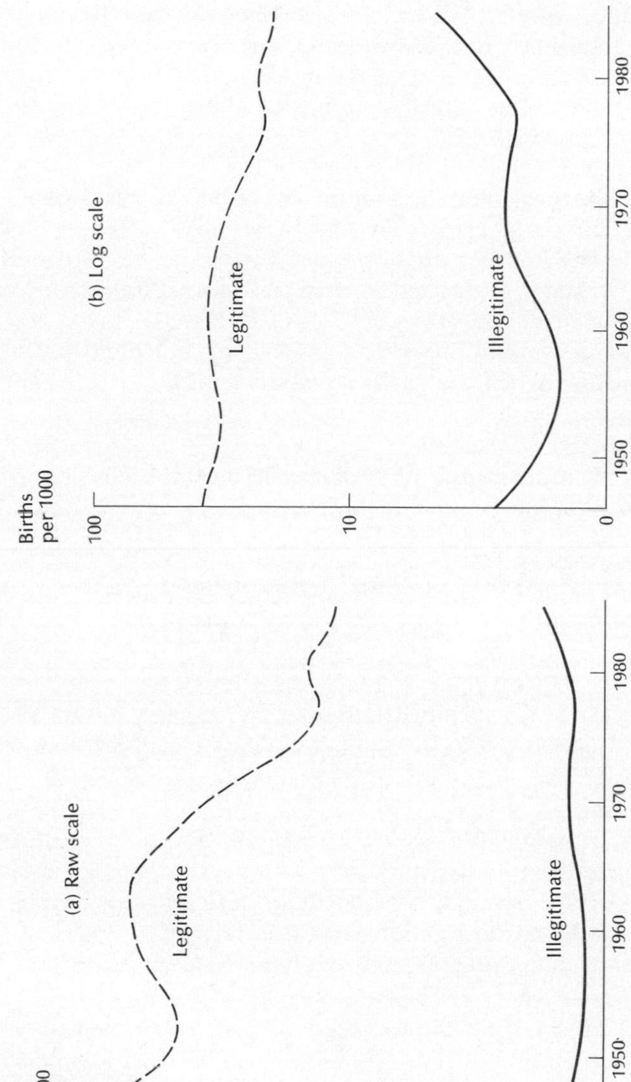

(a) Raw scale

Births
per 1000

40

30

20

10

0

1950   1960   1970   1980

Legitimate

Illegitimate

(b) Log scale

Births
per 1000

100

10

0

1950   1960   1970   1980

Legitimate

Illegitimate

illegitimate rate are much smaller. However, plotting them on a log scale (panel (b)) reveals that the relative changes in illegitimate fertility have, if anything, been somewhat greater than changes in the legitimate rate.

Over the last four hundred years in Britain, legitimate and illegitimate fertility tracked together: as one went up, the other went up (Laslett et al. 1980: 13–26), reflecting similar influences on fertility both inside and outside marriage. Since the 1960s, the pattern has not only broken down but actually become the converse: as legitimate fertility has gone down, illegitimate fertility has gone up, perhaps reflecting changes in fashions for marriage, or perhaps the effect of more readily available contraception and abortion on the rate of unwanted illegitimate pregnancies.

11.5 When there are very large numbers of people per doctor, as in Ethiopia, many people have no access to medical care; this can be highlighted by taking the inverse of the number of people per doctor, i.e. the proportion of a doctor per person. On the basis of such *a priori* reasoning, I took negative reciprocals of people per doctor.

The following Minitab program creates values for life expectancy and people per doctor adjusting for a country's overall wealth:

```
READ 'WORLD' C1–C9
CODE (−1) to '*' in C1–C9 and replace in C1–C9
LET C9 = 1/(C9)
LET C7 = C7**3
LET C4 = LOGT (C4)
PLOT C7 versus C9 life expectancy versus doctors per person
PLOT C9 versus C4 doctors per person versus GNP
RLINE C9 versus C4, put residual doctors per person in C10
PLOT C7 versus C4 life expectancy versus GNP
RLINE C7 versus C4, put residual life expectancy in C11
PLOT C11 versus C10 residual life expectancy vs residual doctors per person
CORRELATE C4 C7 C9 C10 C11
STOP
```

Both the correlation matrix and the plots suggest that the association between the numbers of doctors and life expectancy declines once GNP is controlled; the strength of the bivariate relationship (the plot of C7 versus C9) comes in part from the fact that wealthier countries have both more doctors and higher life expectancy.

Chapter 12

Don't worry if your answers to the exercises in chapter 12 in particular differ greatly from those I give; what matters is that you make a good case for your decisions.

12.1 (a) Clearly there is a possibility of reciprocal influence here, with the choice of paper being determined by political attitudes and the attitudes also being determined by the contents of the paper. In the short term, I would on balance suggest newspaper readership influences political attitudes: preferences for a morning paper probably fluctuate less than voting preferences.

(b) When both variables are measured over time, they can be plotted to see if they track together and if changes in one precede changes in the other. In general, changes in the rate of inflation seem to predate changes in wage levels.

(c) The unemployed are not very healthy as a group. This could be because of the debilitating effects of unemployment, but it could also be because people who are already ill find they cannot work. If the onset of ill-health can be carefully timed, attention can be restricted to illness which onset after the period of unemployment began. If the unemployed were still found to have higher illness rates, we could then be confident that this represented the effects of unemployment on health rather than vice versa. Information on the same people over time also helps resolve this problem, as we shall see in chapter 15.

(d) People very rarely change their religious denomination, so religion is best viewed as the cause and attitudes towards abortion as effects.

(e) There are some important theoretical ideas to turn to in deciding the causal primacy of production relations and religious ideas. Max Weber argued that the belief system of early Protestantism was a particularly fruitful breeding ground in which the ethics of the modern business enterprise might arise. Others, drawing their inspiration from a Marxist tradition in historical scholarship, have argued that it was precisely in those areas where early capitalist relations were burgeoning that Protestantism took hold. Writers within different traditions of scholarship would therefore take different views on the causal primacy of religious ideas and production relations.

12.2   Older people, who have lived through wars before, may be less worried about nuclear war than young people. The more educated are likely to be more aware of the risks and therefore more worried about nuclear war. But older people will also tend to have had less education than younger people (see diagram).If this model were accurate, once years of full-time education had been controlled, the relationship between age and favourableness towards nuclear defence would appear weaker than the simple bivariate effect.

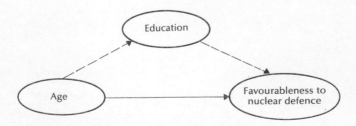

Chapter 13

13.1 I would expect those on higher incomes to be more likely to vote Conservative, and Conservative voters to be less likely to contemplate breaking a law which they considered unjust. If this is right, then higher income will have a negative indirect effect on preparedness to break the law and a positive direct effect. In a causal model where breaking the law is the final response variable, the proportions must add up to 1 within the categories of party cross-classified by income. The following shows the proportions prepared to break the law:

	Rich	Poor	Difference d
Conservative	0.324 ($N=324$)	0.144 ($N=174$)	+0.180
Not Conservative	0.434 ($N=362$)	0.274 ($N=325$)	+0.160
Difference d	−0.110	−0.130	

We can average the two ds in each case, and say that the direct effect of being a Conservative supporter is −0.120 and of being in the higher income group is +0.170.

To calculate the effect of income on party support, we have to go back to the marginals, ignoring the information about attitudes towards the law. From the collapsed table, we find, as expected, that 0.472 (324/686) of the rich support the Conservatives while only 0.349 (174/499) of the poor do, yielding a d of +0.123. This gives us a completed causal model as shown. The effect of being rich on preparedness to break the law is therefore +0.170 directly and (+0.123 × −0.120) or −0.015 indirectly. In fact, we know that the situation is more complex than this; we saw in this chapter that the effect of income is substantially attenuated once age is brought into the picture. This three-variable model is mis-specified as it stands.

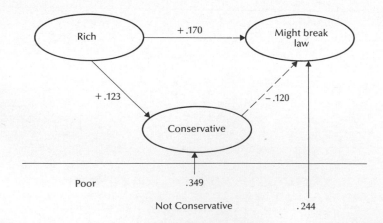

13.2 I chose to dichotomize the outcome in April 1979 into having versus not having a job; the question, after all, focussed on the effect of various experiences on the likelihood of getting a job. The following shows the proportions who had obtained jobs by April 1979 in various subgroups:

	Situation in October 1978	
	On a YOPS scheme	Unemployed
Sat O grade but failed	0.489 (N=182)	0.438 (N=162)
Did not sit O grade	0.457 (N=348)	0.281 (N=516)

An interesting result is revealed. Attendance on one of the government's youth opportunities schemes only improved the chance of getting a job among those who did not even sit the O grade examination; 0.457 of them were in work six months later, compared with only 0.281 of those who had been unemployed. Among the group who tried to get an O grade pass but failed, there was no substantial effect. This interaction stops us from concluding that YOPS experience generally helped people get jobs. Another uncontrolled variable – motivation – may explain the patterns we see. The only group which was substantially different from the other three was those who neither tried for qualifications nor went on a YOPS scheme; it may be that they as a group were less well motivated than the rest. We cannot tell from the data whether experience on a scheme really improved the chances of those without qualifications, or merely reflected a pre-existing personality variable.

The interactions in this table prevent us from drawing up a linear causal model in which the direct causal effect of each variable upon others is given a single numerical value. The d for those who sat O grade is 0.051, and for those who did not is 0.176; the difference in ds is greater than 0.1, so the rule of thumb suggests that we do not average them.

The marginals also reveal important aspects of recruitment to YOPS schemes. Less than half of these less well-qualified youngsters (530/1208) went on a YOPS programme in October 1978; this could have been because of lack of demand for or supply of places. This represented over half of the 344 youngsters who had sat O grade but only 40 per cent of the 864 who did not try for this qualification. Given the conclusion of the previous paragraph, it would seem important for youth employment schemes of this kind to recruit more heavily from school-leavers who had not even tried to obtain qualifications.

13.3   To find the direct effect of any of the three explanatory variables upon attitudes, we need to control for the other two. By extension from the three-variable situation in the chapter, we perform this controlling operation by looking within categories of all the controlled variables. Thus, to assess the direct effect of being an officer, four comparisons between officers and privates in the proportions who believe that chances of promotion are good are made – first among the less educated Military Police, then the better educated Military Police, then the less educated Air Corps, and finally among the better educated Air Corps. It should not have surprised you to discover that, in each case, officers are more satisfied that the promotion system operates well than privates are.

More surprising, perhaps, is the finding that the more educated are more cynical about promotion; high school graduates are consistently less satisfied than non-graduates.

But Sam Stouffer drew particular attention to a different feature of this rich and famous table: those in the Military Police were consistently more satisfied with promotion possibilities than those in the Air Corps, whether officers or privates, educated or uneducated. This struck him as very odd, since the marginal associations seemed to suggest that the objective chances of becoming an officer in the Air Corps (222/424 or 0.528) were much higher than the chances in the Military Police (406/1583 or 0.256). On the basis of this finding, he coined the theory of relative deprivation; people only feel deprived, he argued, if they can easily make comparisons with others more fortunate than themselves. The reason that the Air Corps felt more deprived, he suggested, was precisely because there were more officers in evidence in that section.

13.4 This Minitab program creates two tables of class by pension scheme, first for those of less than median incomes, and secondly for those with median incomes or above:

```
READ 'CLASS' into C1–C24
CODE (−1) to '*' in C1–C24 and replace in C1–C24
NOTE   Collapse class categories into manual and non-manual
CODE (1:3) to 1 and (4:6) to 2 in C5 and replace in C5
NOTE   Find out what the median income is
MEDIAN C15
NOTE   Collapse the income categories at the median
CODE (0:83) to 1 and (84:500) to 2 in C15 and replace in C15
TABLE C5 class by C16 pensions within categories of C15 income;
ROWPERCENTS.
STOP
```

The result suggests that access to an occupational pension scheme is not just a feature of a well-paid job; it is one way in which the effect of the colour of one's collar is felt on life chances, independent of income.

Chapter 14

14.1 (a) The death rate among the 'other labourers' will be inflated, because the population at risk in the denominator will not be as large as the group of workers who might have been coded into such categories by the death registration process. A compensating deflation of the risk of death in the more specific labourer categories will also result.

(b) The SMR for 'other labourers' was very high in 1979–83, at 355, almost certainly as a result of overuse of this category at death registration. If this category is excluded, the SMR for class V men aged 20–64 drops from 163 to 73. If we were satisfied that those coded in the 'other labourers' category should still have been coded elsewhere in class V, we need not worry about the bias in the class as a whole. But this is not a safe assumption; it is better to group classes IV and V as in exercise 14.2.

(c) The discrepancy between the ability of census coders to classify the detail given on the census and that of registrars to code the particulars given when a death is registered widened when the classification scheme became more detailed, and the problem of numerator-denominator biases in individual occupations increased; the SMR for the residual labouring category, for example, leapt from 201 in 1970–2 to 355 in 1979–83 (OPCS 1986: 45). However, these biases are worse for individual occupations than for classes as a whole, just as the reliability of occupational information is worse than that for classes (see appendix to chapter 14). It is therefore ironic that the 1979–82 *Decennial Supplement* continued to publish occupational SMRs, albeit with cautionary asterisks in many cases, but abandoned class SMRs.

14.2   The two arithmetic complications about the data were that occupations in the 1981 census were only coded on a 10 per cent sample, and the deaths are given over a period of four years. We therefore work with a four year death rate and multiply the mortality rates by ten. The calculations of the age-specific mortality rates for men 20–64, both as a whole and for semi- and unskilled workers, are shown in the accompanying worksheet.

Age group	Number of men in 1981	Deaths to all men: 1979–83	National mortality rates per 1000	Classes IV + V in 1981	Deaths to IV + V: 1979–83	Mortality rate to IV + V per 1000
20–24	204,425	7,284	3.5632	44,782	2,143	4.7854
25–34	385,397	14,240	3.6949	70,782	3,912	5.5268
35–44	324,643	25,375	7.8163	59,181	6,907	11.6710
45–54	300,468	76,714	25.5315	66,737	22,913	34.3333
55–64	287,743	213,486	74.1956	75,713	70,114	92.6050
Total	1,502,676	337,099		317,195	105,989	

The crude death rate is given by 105,989/317,195, or 33.4 deaths per thousand over the four year period. Direct standardization of this rate involves applying age-specific mortality rates within classes IV and V to the national age structure; those in the 20–24 age group account for 0.136 of the total, for example:

$$0.13604 \times 4.7854 = 0.651$$
$$0.25647 \times 5.5268 = 1.417$$
$$0.21604 \times 11.6710 = 2.521$$
$$0.19996 \times 34.3333 = 6.865$$
$$0.19149 \times 92.6053 = 17.733$$

Summing these, we arrive at a directly standardized rate for classes IV and V of 29.2 per thousand; it is lower than the crude death rate because workers in these classes are older than average.

The SMR is given by applying the national mortality rates to the age structure of classes IV and V to arrive at the expected number of deaths if this group behaved the same as the rest of the population:

$$0.035632 \times 44,782 = 1,595.7$$
$$0.036949 \times 70,782 = 2,615.3$$
$$0.078163 \times 59,181 = 4,625.8$$
$$0.255315 \times 66,737 = 17,039.0$$
$$0.741956 \times 75,713 = 56,175.7$$

Summing these, we get 82,051.5 expected deaths, compared with 105,989 actual deaths occurring to men whose occupations at death were classified into one or other class. This represents an SMR of 124.6. The result is nearer the class IV than the class V SMR reported in figure 14.5 because class IV is almost three times as big as class V.

14.3   Septicaemia was the commonest cause of maternal mortality before the widespread introduction of antibiotics. Middle class women were more likely to have their babies in nursing homes and hospitals, where the risk of infection was greater, which may explain this unusual finding. Certainly, the class gradients in maternal mortality in the more recent *Decennial Supplements* have reverted to the more usual pattern of greater risk among wives of manual workers.

Chapter 15

15.1   The results of two cycles of median polishing are shown below; the table has been reorganized so that the rows and columns are arranged in ascending order of effects.

		Brussels	Copen-hagen	Amster-dam	London	Paris	Bonn	Rome
	13	−2	−2	−1	√	+1	+1	+4
Milk	−8	1	√	√	√	√	−1	−2
Bus trip	−7	√	1	1	√	√	−1	−8
Light bulb	−3	√	√	√	−2	2	√	6
Bread	√	−2	2	−2	−3	√	2	√
Eggs	+6	3	−4	−2	√	7	−3	9
Wine	+7	−3	12	√	44	−7	2	−10
Coffee	+12	−5	−7	−8	2	√	5	11

The overall fit of 13 minutes just tells us the typical time it took to make these particular commodities in these particular cities. The row effects express the fact that more labour goes into producing 250 grams of coffee than 1 litre of milk. The column effects are the most interesting, since they suggest differences in the cost of living (albeit on the basis of only seven items) in these European cities: Brussels is the cheapest and Rome the most expensive. However, the residuals also have a story to tell about which commodities were particularly expensive in which cities; the high cost of wine in London stands out starkly, for example.

Less obviously, perhaps, the result shows evidence of the saddle pattern with negative diagonals in the corners of the table which have mixed sign effects. If you took the trouble to calculate the comparison values, and plot the residuals against these values, you will have found that the best fit to the data was a line with a slope of about one; this suggests that logging the times would be an improvement before conducting the median polishing; the midspread of the residuals relative to the midspread of the original cell values is smaller on the logged data than on the raw data.

15.2   The logged data and the result of median polishing are as follows:

	Husband's class					Husband's class		
Wife's class	Upper	Middle	Lower	Wife's class		Upper	Middle	Lower
Upper	1.52	1.83	2.13		2.00	−0.30	✓	+0.30
Middle	1.70	2.00	2.30					
Lower	1.88	2.18	2.48	Upper	−0.17	−0.01	✓	✓
				Middle	✓	✓	✓	✓
				Lower	+0.18	✓	✓	✓

Logging the data has revealed both the symmetry of the effects and the fact that the data fits the model by which it was generated exactly (to within rounding error).

References

Numbers in square brackets are page numbers indicating discussion in the text

Alderson, M. R. (1972) 'Some sources of error in British occupational mortality data', *British Journal of Industrial Medicine* 29, 245–54 [263]

Alderson, M. R. (1983) 'William Farr's contribution to present day vital and health statistics', *Population Trends* 31, 5–8 [262]

Almond, G. A. and Verba, S. (1963) *The Civic Culture: political attitudes and democracy in five nations*, Princeton: Princeton University Press [240–42]

Atkinson, A. B. (1983) *The Economics of Inequality*, 2nd edn., Oxford: Clarendon Press [81, 92]

Atkinson, A. B. and Micklewright, J. (1983) 'On the reliability of income data in the Family Expenditure Survey 1970–77', *Journal of the Royal Statistical Society* (A) 146(1), 33–61 [76]

Baldwin, J. and Bottoms, A. E. (1976) *The Urban Criminal: a study in Sheffield*, London: Tavistock [243]

Barr, A. and Logan, R. F. L. (1977) 'Policy alternatives for resource allocation', *The Lancet*, i, 994–6 [193]

Bateson, N. (1984) *Data Construction in Social Surveys*, London: Allen & Unwin [278]

Benjamin, B. (1968) *Health and Vital Statistics*, London: Allen & Unwin [265]

Bland, R. (1979) 'Measuring "social class"', *Sociology* 13(2), 283–92 [348]

Board of Inland Revenue (1985) *The Survey of Personal Incomes 1982–83*, London: HMSO [95]

Booth, C. (1892–) *The Life and Labour of the People of London*, London [4]

Bosanquet, N. and Townsend, P. (eds) (1980) *Labour and Equality: a Fabian study of Labour in power, 1974–79*, London: Heinemann [78]

Brant, J. D. and Chalk, S. M. (1985) 'The use of automatic editing in the 1981 Census', *Statistical News* no. 68, February, 13–15 [278]

Britton, M. and Birch, F. (1985) *1981 Census Post-Enumeration Survey*, London: HMSO [278]

Brown, A. and Fox, J. (1984) 'OPCS Longitudinal Study: ten years on', *Population Trends* no. 37, 20–2 [295, 296]

Brown, G. W. and Harris, T. (1978) *The Social Origins of Depression: a study of psychiatric disorder in women*, London: Tavistock [156, 353]

Bulmer, M., (ed.) (1979) *Censuses, Surveys and Privacy*, London: Macmillan [276]

Butler, N. R. and Bonham, D. G. (1963) *Perinatal Mortality*, London: E. & S. Livingstone [58]

Campbell, D. T. (1951) 'On the possibility of experimenting with the "bandwagon effect"', *International Journal of Opinion and Attitude Research* 5, 251–60 [228]

Central Statistical Office (1985) *United Kingdom National Accounts: sources and methods* 3rd edn, Studies in Official Statistics, no. 37, London: HMSO [84, 200]

Central Statistical Office (1986) 'The effects of taxes and benefits on household income 1984', *Economic Trends* no. 393, July, 101–16. [81]

Chadwick-Jones, J. K., Nicholson, N. and Brown, C. (1982) *Social Psychology of Absenteeism*, New York: Praeger [237]

Chamberlain, R., Chamberlain, G., Howlett, B. and Claireaux, A. (1975) *British Births 1970*, London: Heinemann Educational [58]

Champion, A. G. and Green, A. E. (1985) 'In search of Britain's booming towns: an index of local economic performance for Britain', University of Newcastle upon Tyne Centre for Urban and Regional Development Studies, Discussion Paper no. 72 [324]

Chapman, M. (1986) *Plain Figures* (in collaboration with B. Mahon), Cabinet Office and Civil Service College, London: HMSO [142]

Cherry, N. and Rodgers, B. (1979) 'Using a longitudinal study to assess the quality of retrospective data', in L. Moss and H. Goldstein *The Recall Method in Social Surveys*, University of London Institute of Education, Studies in Education 9 [294]

Cohen, I. B. (1984) 'Florence Nightingale', *Scientific American*, 250(3), 98–107 [262]

Court Report (1976) *Fit for the Future*, Report of the Committee on Child Health Services, vol. 1, London: HMSO, Cmnd 6684 [180]

Cowell, F. A. (1977) *Measuring Inequality*, London: Philip Allan [89, 90]

Cullen, M. J. (1975) *The Statistical Movement in Early Victorian Britain*, Hassocks, Sussex: Harvester [2, 262]

Dale, A., Gilbert, G. N. and Arber, S. (1985) 'Integrating women into class theory', *Sociology* 19(3), 384–409 [350]

Dale, A., Gilbert, G. N., Rajan, L. and Arber, S. (1984) *Exploring British Society*, Unit 3 'Poverty and income', Department of Sociology, University of Surrey [320]

Daniel, W. W. (1981) *The Unemployed Flow. Stage 1: an interim report*, London: Policy Studies Institute [101, 103]

Davie, R., Butler, N. and Goldstein, H. (1972) *From Birth to Seven: the second report of the National Child Development Study*, London: Longman [60]

Davis, J. A. (1976) 'Analyzing contingency tables with linear flow graphs: *d* systems', in D. Heise (ed.) *Sociological Methodology*, San Francisco: Jossey Bass, 111–145 [147]

Davis, J. A. (1985) *The Logic of Causal Order*, Beverly Hills: Sage [231]

Department of Employment (1983) 'Unemployment flows: new statistics', *Employment Gazette* August [103]

Department of Employment (1985) 'Unemployment adjusted for discontinuities and seasonality', *Employment Gazette* July [122]

Department of Employment (1986a) 'Classification of economic activity', *Employment Gazette* January [103, 119]

Department of Employment (1986b) 'Family expenditure: a plain man's guide to the Family Expenditure Survey', available from the Department of Employment, Stats A6, Caxton House, Tothill St, London SW1H 9NF [76]

Department of Employment (1986c) *Family Expenditure Survey: report for 1984 giving results for the United Kingdom*, London: HMSO [76]

Department of Employment (1986d) 'Unemployment figures: the claimant count and the Labour Force Survey', *Employment Gazette* October [103, 120]

Department of Employment Retail Prices Index Advisory Committee (1986) *Methodological Issues affecting the Retail Prices Index*, London: HMSO, Cmnd 9848 [344]

Douglas, J. W. B. (1964) *The Home and the School: a study of ability and attainment in the primary school*, London: Macgibbon and Kee [57, 58]

Eales, M. (1986) 'Unemployment and depression', PhD thesis, Bedford and Royal Holloway New College [226]

Easterlin, R. (1974) 'Does economic growth improve the human lot? Some empirical evidence', in P. A. David and M. W. Reder (eds) *Nations and Households in Economic Growth*, New York: Academic Press, 89–126 [195]

Edgell, S. and Duke, V. (1982) 'Reactions to the public expenditure cuts', *Sociology* 16(3), 431–9 [155]

Ehrenberg, A. S. C. (1975) *Data Reduction: analysing and interpreting statistical data*, London: Wiley [142]

Eurostat (1980) *Methodology of Surveys of Family Budgets* [75]

Fiegehan, G. C., Lansley, P. S. and Smith, A. D. (1977) *Poverty and Progress in Britain 1953–73*, Cambridge: Cambridge University Press [76, 138, 143, 350]

Fisher, I. (1922) *The Making of Index Numbers*, Boston and New York: Houghton Mifflin [72]

Fitzroy, A. W., (Chairman) (1904) *Report of the Interdepartmental Committee on Physical Deterioration*, London: HMSO, Cd 2175 [25]

Floud, R. and Wachter, K. W. (1982) 'Poverty and physical stature: evidence on the standard of living of London boys 1770–1870', *Social Science History* 6(3), 422–52 [176]

Fogelman, K. (ed.) (1983) *Growing up in Great Britain*, London: Macmillan [60]

Forster, J. (1977) 'Mortality, morbidity and resource allocation', *The Lancet* i, 997–8 [184–5, 190, 193]

Fourastié, J. and Bazil, B. (1980) *Le jardin du voisin: les inegalités en France*, Paris [294]

Fox, A. J. and Goldblatt, P. O. (1982) *Longitudinal Study Socio-demographic Mortality Differentials,* a first report on mortality in 1971–5 according to 1971 Census characteristics, based on data collected in the OPCS Longitudinal Study, Series LS no. 1, London: HMSO [281, 295, 296]

Fox, A. J., Goldblatt, P. O. and Jones, D. R. (1985) 'Social class mortality differentials: artefact, selection or life circumstances?', *Journal of Epidemiology and Community Health* no. 39, 1–8 [290, 291]

Fry, V. and Pashardes, P. (1986) *The Retail Prices Index and the Cost of Living*, The Institute for Fiscal Studies Report Series no. 22, 180–2 Tottenham Court Road, London W1P 9LE [71, 72, 344]

General Household Survey (1985) *The General Household Survey: 1983*, London: HMSO [21]

Gilbert, G. N. (1981) *Modelling Society*, London: Allen & Unwin [351]

Gilbert, G. N., Rajan, L., Dale, A. and Arber, S. (1984) *Exploring British Society*, Unit 1 'Class and stratification', Department of Sociology, University of Surrey [298]

Goldthorpe, J. H. (1983) 'Women and class analysis: in defence of the conventional view', *Sociology* 17(4), 465–488 [349]

Goldthorpe, J. H. and Hope, K. (1974) *The Social Grading of Occupations*, Oxford: Clarendon [117]

Goldthorpe, J. H. and Llewellyn, C. (1980) *Class Structure in Modern Britain*, Oxford: Clarendon [127]

Goodenough, F. (1926) *Measurement of Intelligence by Drawings*, World Book Company [57]

Gowers, Sir E. (1973) *The Complete Plain Words*, revised by Sir Bruce Fraser, London: HMSO [142]

Goyder, J. (1987) *The Silent Minority: non-respondents to survey interviews*, Cambridge: Polity Press [23]

Hakim, C. (1982) *Secondary Analysis in Social Research: a guide to data sources and methods with examples*, London: Allen & Unwin [279]

Halsey, A. H., Heath, A. and Ridge, J. (1980) *Origins and Destinations: family, class and education in modern Britain*, Oxford: Clarendon [125, 127, 128, 136, 137, 153]

Hartwig, F. and Dearing, B. E. (1979) *Exploratory Data Analysis*, Beverley Hills: Sage [xix]

Huff, D. (1973) *How to Lie with Statistics*, Harmondsworth: Penguin [198]

Hunter, A. A. (1973) 'On the validity of measures of association: the nominal-nominal, two by two case', *American Journal of Sociology* 79(1), 99–109 [149]

Huxley, A. (1958) *Brave New World Revisited*, New York: Harper and Row [20, 28]

Illsley, R. (1955) 'Social class selection and class differences in relation to stillbirths and infant deaths', *British Medical Journal* ii, 1520 [37]

Jowell, R., and Airey, C. (eds) (1984) *British Social Attitudes: the 1984 report*, Aldershot: Gower and Social and Community Planning Research [258]

Jowell, R. and Witherspoon, S. (eds) (1985) *British Social Attitudes: the 1985 report*, Aldershot: Gower and Social and Community Planning Research [258, 260]

Jowell, R., Witherspoon, S. and Brook, L. (eds) (1986) *British Social Attitudes: the 1986 report*, Aldershot: Gower and Social and Community Planning Research [258]

Jowell, R., Witherspoon, S. and Brook, L. (eds) (1987) *British Social Attitudes: the 1987 report*, Aldershot: Gower and Social and Community Planning Research [258]

Katona, G. (1951) *Psychological Analysis of Economic Behaviour*, New York: McGraw-Hill [162]

Kemsley, W. F. F., Redpath, R. U. and Holmes, M. (1980) *Family Expenditure Survey Handbook; sampling, fieldwork, coding procedures and related methodological experiments*, London: HMSO [75, 76]

Kendall, M. G. (1969) 'The early history of index numbers', *International Statistical Review* 37, 1–12 [61, 70]

Kendall, M. G. and Buckland, W. R. (1971) *A Dictionary of Statistical Terms*, 3rd edn, London: Longman for the International Statistical Institute [62, 63]

Knight, I. (1984) *The Heights and Weights of Adults in Great Britain*, Office of Population Censuses and Surveys, Social Survey Division, London: HMSO [25, 38, 315]

Kopf, E. W. (1977) 'Florence Nightingale as statistician' (1916), in M. Kendall and R. L. Plackett, *Studies in the History of Statistics and Probability*, vol. II, London: Charles Griffin, 310–27 [262]

Kruskal, J. B. (1978) 'Transformations of statistical data', *The International Encyclopaedia of Statistics*, eds W. H. Kruskal and J. M. Tanur, New York: Free Press, Macmillan, vol. II, 1044–56 [217]

Laslett, P., Oosterveen, K. and Smith, R. M. (eds.) (1980) *Bastardy and its Comparative History*, London: Edward Arnold [362]

Le Grand, J. (1985) 'Inequalities in health: the human capital approach', London: London School of Economics, Suntory Toyota Centre Welfare State Programme no. 1 [92]

Lewes, F. (1983) 'William Farr and cholera', *Population Trends*, 31, 8–12 [262]

Lord, W. (1955) *A Night to Remember*, New York: Henry Holt [271]

Lynch, M. A. and Roberts, J. (1977) 'Predicting child abuse: signs of bonding failure in maternity hospital', *British Medical Journal* 1, 624–26 [155]

McAuley, A. (1985) 'Income and wealth in the USSR', Unit 19 of Open University course D210, *Introduction to Economics*, Milton Keynes: Open University Press [93]

Macfarlane, A. and Mugford, M. (1984) *Birth Counts: statistics of pregnancy and childbirth*, National Perinatal Epidemiology Unit in collaboration with OPCS, London: HMSO [275]

Mackie, J. L. (1974) *The Cement of the Universe: a study of causation*, Oxford: Clarendon [224]

Marsh, A. (1977) *Protest and Political Consciousness*, London: Sage [244]

Marsh, C. (1985a) 'Do polls affect what people think?', in C. Turner and E. Martin (eds), *Surveys of Subjective Phenomena*, vol. II, New York: Russell Sage Foundation, 565–91 [228]

Marsh, C. (1985b) 'Social class and occupation', in R. G. Burgess (ed.). *Key Variables in Social Investigation*, London: Routledge & Kegan Paul [272]

Maurice, Sir Frederick (1902) 'Where to get men?', *Contemporary Review*, 78–86 [24]

Miles, I. (1983) 'Adaptation to unemployment?', Science Policy Research Unit Occasional Paper no. 20, August [104]

Moser, C. A. and Stuart, A. (1953) 'An experimental study of quota sampling', *Journal of the Royal Statistical Society* (*A*), 116, 348–405 [179]

Moser, K. A., Fox, A. J. and Jones, D. R. (1984) 'Unemployment and mortality in the OPCS longitudinal study', *The Lancet* ii, 1324–9 [289]

Moss, L. and Goldstein, H. (1979) *The Recall Method in Social Surveys*, University of London Institute of Education, Studies in Education 9 [76, 294]

Mosteller, F. and Tukey, J. W. (1977) *Data Analysis and Regression: a second course in statistics*, Reading, Mass.: Addison-Wesley [xix, 186, 210, 217, 340, 351]

Newman, K. J. (1985) *United Kingdom National Accounts: 1985 edition*, Central Statistical Office, London: HMSO [84]

NHS Bill (1946) *Summary of the Proposed New Service*, London: HMSO, Cmd 6761 [180]

Nicholson, J. L. (1974) 'The distribution and redistribution of income in the United Kingdom', in D. Wedderburn (ed.), *Poverty, Inequality and Class Structure*, Cambridge: Cambridge University Press [81]

Office of Population Censuses and Surveys (1985) *Guide to Sources of Census Statistics*, OPCS User Guide 199, GRO (Scotland) User Guide 24, London: HMSO [279]

Office of Population Censuses and Surveys (1986) *Occupational Mortality: the registrar-general's supplement for Great Britain, 1979–80, 1982–83*, Series DS no. 6, London: HMSO [272, 274–5, 367]

Open University (1983) *Statistics in Society*, Course MDST 242, 16 volumes, Milton Keynes: Open University Press [xix, 188]

Pahl, J. (1983) 'The allocation of money and the structure of inequality within marriage', *Sociological Review* 31(2), 237–62 [5]

Piachaud, D. (1978) 'Evidence submitted to the Royal Commission on the Distribution of Income and Wealth', Selected Evidence for Report no. 6: Lower Incomes, 441–57 [72]

Pringle, M., Butler, N. and Davie, R. (1966) *11,000 Seven Year Olds*, London: Longman [58]

Radical Statistics Health Group (1977) *Rawp Deals*, London: Radical Statistics, 9 Poland St, London WC2 [180–81]

Raffe, D. (1981) 'Special programmes in Scotland: the first year of YOP', *Policy and Politics*, 9(4), 471–87 [256]

Raffe, D. (1985) 'Youth unemployment in the UK 1979–84', paper commissioned by International Labour Office, Centre for Educational Sociology, University of Edinburgh [121]

Rauta, I. (1985) 'A comparison of the census characteristics of respondents and non-respondents to the 1981 GHS', *Statistical News* no. 71, 12–15 [23]

Redfern, P. (1981) 'The Census 1981 – an historical and international perspective', *Population Trends*, 23, 2–15 [277]

Redpath, B. (1986) 'Family Expenditure Survey: a second study of differential response, comparing Census characteristics of FES respondents and non-respondents', *Statistical News* no. 72, 13–16 [75]

Resources Allocation Working Party (1976) *Sharing Resources for Health in England*, Department of Health and Social Security, London: HMSO [180]

Rhind, D. W. (ed.) (1983) *A Census Users' Handbook*, London: Methuen [279]

Rhind, D. W. (1985) 'Successors to the Census of Population', *Journal of Economic and Social Measurement*, 13(1), 29–38 [279]

Robinson, R., O'Sullivan, T. and Le Grand, J. (1985) 'Inequality and housing', *Urban Studies* 22, 249–56 [92]

Rowntree, B. S. (1901) *Poverty: a study of town life* London: Macmillan [74, 258]

Royal College of Physicians (1982) 'Medical aspects of death certification: a joint report of the Royal College of Physicians and the Royal College of Pathologists', *Journal of the Royal College of Physicians*, 16(4), 206–18 [263, 265]

Royal Commission on the Distribution of Income and Wealth (1975) *Report no. 1, Initial Report on the Standing Reference* (Chairman: Lord Diamond), London: HMSO [81, 91, 94]

Royal Commission on the Distribution of Income and Wealth (1979) *Report no. 8, Fifth Report on the Standing Reference* (Chairman: Lord Diamond), London: HMSO [79, 93]

Ryan, B. F., Joiner, T. A. and Ryan, T. (1985) *Minitab Handbook*, 2nd edn, Boston: Duxbury [xx]

Sainsbury, P. and Jenkins, J. S. (1982) 'The accuracy of officially reported suicide statistics for purposes of epidemiological research', *Journal of Epidemiology and Community Health* 36, 43–8 [218]

Samuelson, P. A. and Nordhaus, W. D. (1985) *Economics*, 12th edn, New York: McGraw-Hill [200, 214]

Saunders, C. and Marsden, D. (1981) *Pay Inequalities in the European Community*, London: Butterworths [57]

Schmid, C. F. (1954) *Handbook of Graphic Presentation*, New York: Ronald Press [198]

Seaver, D. A., von Winderfeldt, D. and Edwards, W. (1978) 'Eliciting subjective probability distributions on continuous variables', *Organizational Behavior and Human Performance*, 21, 379–91 [154]

Seers, D. (1979) 'The meaning of development' in D. Lehmann (ed.), *Development Theory: four critical studies*, London: Frank Cass [201]

Shepherd, P. M. (1985) 'The National Child Development Study: an introduction to the background to the study and the methods of data collection', NCDS User Support Group Working Paper no 1, Social Statistics Research Unit, City University [59]

Sorokin, P. (1927) *Social Mobility*, New York and London: Harper & Brothers [37]

Stephan, F. F. and McCarthy, P. J. (1958) *Sampling Opinion: an analysis of survey procedures*, New York: Wiley [179]

Stouffer, S. A. et al. (1949) *The American Soldier*, Princeton: Princeton University Press [257, 366]

Tanner, J. M. (1978) *Foetus into Man: physical growth from conception to maturity*, London: Open Books [38]

Tawney, R. H. (1964) *Equality* (1931), with an introduction by Richard M. Titmuss, London: Unwin [78, 92]

Thatcher, A. R. (1984) '1981 Census of Population in England and Wales', *Statistical News* no. 66, 9–15 [276, 278]

Thomson, A. and Gregory, M. (eds) (1988) *Pay Developments since 1970*, Oxford: Oxford University Press [41]

Tipping, D. G. (1970) 'Price changes and income distribution', *Applied Statistics*, 19(1), 1–17 [72]

Todd, J. and Butcher, B. (1982) *Electoral Registration in 1981*, London HMSO [22]

Townsend, P (1979) *Poverty in the United Kingdom*, Harmondsworth: Penguin [338]

Townsend, P. and Davidson, N. (1982) *Inequalities in Health*, Harmondsworth: Pelican [272]

Tufte, E. R. (1983) *The Visual Display of Quantitative Information*, Cheshire, Conn.: Graphics Press [198]

Tukey, J. W. (1977) *Exploratory Data Analysis*, Reading, Mass.: Addison-Wesley [xix, 160, 170, 172, 217, 220]

Unemployment Unit (1986) *Unemployment Bulletin* no. 20, Unemployment Unit, 9 Poland Street, London [122]

US National Center for Health Statistics (1973) *Health Statistics Today and Tomorrow*, series 4, no. 15 [183]

Velleman, P. F. and Hoaglin, D. C. (1981) *Applications, Basics and Computing of Exploratory Data Analysis*, Boston: Duxbury [xix, xx, 172, 198, 355]

Wachter, K. W. (1981) 'Graphical estimation of military heights', *Historical Methods*, 14(1) [176]

Walker, N. (1987) *Crime and Criminology*, Oxford: Oxford University Press [244]

Wilson, P. R. and Elliot, D. J. (1987) 'An evaluation of the Postcode Address File as a sampling frame and its use within OPCS', *Journal of the Royal Statistical Society (A)* 150(3), 230–40 [22]

World Bank (1986) *World Development Report*, Oxford: Oxford University Press [331]

World Health Organization (1977) *Manual of the International Classification of Diseases, Injuries and Causes of Death*, based on the recommendations of the Ninth Revision Conference, 1975; vol. I: tables, vol. II: index, London: HMSO [265]

Young, K. (1984) 'Political attitudes', in R. Jowell and C. Airey (eds), *British Social Attitudes: the 1984 Report*, Aldershot: Gower and Social and Community Planning Research, 11–45 [242]

Index